Duanaire na Sracaire

Duanaire na Sracaire

Songbook of the Pillagers

Anthology of Scotland's Gaelic Verse to 1600

Edited by

Wilson McLeod and Meg Bateman

Translations by Meg Bateman

BIRLINN

First published in 2007 by
Birlinn Limited
West Newington House
10 Newington Road
Edinburgh EH9 1QS

www.birlinn.co.uk

ISBN13: 978 1 84158 181 1
ISBN10: 1 84158 181 X

British Library Cataloguing-in-Publication Data
A catalogue record for this book is available from the British Library

Chuidich Comhairle nan Leabhraichean am foillsichear le cosgaisean an
leabhair seo.

Typeset in Plantin by Edderston Book Design, Peebles
Printed and bound by Antony Rowe Ltd, Chippenham

Clàr-Innse / Contents

LIST OF POEMS

THE LEARNED TRADITION

RELIGION

ELEGY

INCITEMENT

SATIRE AND HUMOUR

LOVE

The Song Tradition

INTRODUCTION

Gaelic is often described as Scotland's oldest living language, and
this anthology spans almost a thousand years, beginning with the
earliest Gaelic compositions from Scotland, dated to the later
seventh century, and continuing to the end of the sixteenth. It can
be seen as the first (albeit the last to appear) of a series of anthologies
published in recent years, Colm Ó Baoill and Meg Bateman's *Gàir
nan Clàrsach* (Birlinn 1994), Ronald Black's *An Lasair* (Birlinn
2001), Donald Meek's *Caran an t-Saoghail* (Birlinn 2003) and
Ronald Black's *An Tuil* (Polygon 1999), which cover the seventeenth,
eighteenth, nineteenth and twentieth centuries respectively.

The period covered here is a long one and the poetry is
consequently very diverse in character. A number of different
kinds of poems were produced at different periods — indeed,
several distinct kinds of poems were being composed at any given
time — and much more has survived from some periods than
from others. This collection is divided into two main sections, the
Learned Tradition and the Song Tradition, with each section
arranged thematically rather than chronologically. The Learned
poems are divided into the topics of Religion, Panegyric, Elegy,
Incitement, Satire and Humour, Love, Ballads, and Occasional
Verse while the Songs move from Panegyric to Elegy, Occasional
Verse, Love, Satire and Ballads, before concluding with a Lullaby.
Three of the poems given here date to the first millennium and
perhaps thirteen to the period 1000–1400; the remainder come
from the last stage of the era covered by this collection, from the
fifteenth and especially the sixteenth century. This imbalance is
largely determined by the distribution of the sources themselves, a
significant issue discussed in detail below.[1]

We have chosen to provide only full texts, rather than pruned
and edited selections from poems, and have thereby privileged
integrity of form. Some of the chosen texts are necessarily long,
and we have not included some important poems, essentially
historical texts in verse form, because their length does not
correspond to their literary interest.

To place this poetry in its context, we begin with a discussion of
the history of Gaelic and Gaeldom in medieval Scotland, the role
and functions of poetry in Gaelic society, and the structure and
rhetoric of Gaelic poetry.

THE SHIFTING STATUS OF GAELIC IN SCOTLAND

The early history of Gaelic and Gaeldom in Scotland remains less than entirely clear, but the once-dominant vision of a straightforward migration from Ireland has been increasingly questioned in recent decades. While speakers of the Celtic language from which Gaelic developed appear to have reached Ireland well before 500 BCE, Gaelic settlement in north Britain seems to have begun some centuries later, early in the common era. As in Ireland, these Gaelic speakers referred to themselves as *Gáedil* (a term retained as the modern *Gàidheil*). The principal Gaelic settlement was associated with the kingdom of Dál Riata, a small kingdom in northeast Antrim – one of perhaps 150 petty kingdoms in Ireland at the time – that came to establish a beachhead in Argyll. According to one account, this Scottish Dál Riata was established by Fergus Mór mac Eirc, whose death was placed in 501, but it is probably more realistic to envision a steady series of movements and migrations across Sruth na Maoile (the North Channel between Ireland and Scotland) to western Scotland, movements that probably began long before the sixth century.[2]

With the coming of Colum Cille (St Columba) from Ireland in 563 and his establishment of the immensely influential monastery at Iona (*Í Choluim Chille*), the consolidation of Dál Riata in western Scotland, and the spread of Gaelic cultural influence in north Britain more generally, received an important boost. Even so, the Picts, a confederation of tribes generally dominated by the kingdom of Fortriu (now thought to have been based in Moray), remained the principal political force in northern Scotland during this period, and Dál Riata seems generally to have functioned as a vassal kingdom under Pictish control. Dál Riata itself was no unitary polity, but rather a fragmented constellation of kingships, without, it appears, any single over-king.[3]

A new stage began in the middle of the ninth century when the king of Dál Riata, Cináed mac Ailpín (†858), took control of the kingdom of the Picts in 843. The process by which this political transformation took place is by no means clear, although the disruption and instability brought about by Norse incursions, culminating in a catastrophic defeat of the Picts and their allies in 839, seem to have played a critical role; the traditional notion of a 'union of the Picts and Scots', achieved by reinforcing dynastic claims, has been jettisoned. Cinaed and his immediate successors were styled *rex Pictorum* (king of the Picts), but from the turn of the tenth century onwards the form *rí Alban* (king of *Alba*) came into use, and *Alba* emerged as a distinctive kingdom. At this stage, the term *Alba*, once used as a name for all of Britain and cognate with the English *Albion*, referred only to the territory north of Forth and Clyde (and in its narrow sense only to the inner region south of the Spey and east of Druim Alban, the range dividing Perthshire from Argyll), not, as in later Gaelic, to all of modern 'Scotland'.[4] From the time of Cináed's grandson Cusantin mac Cusantin meic Cináeda (reigned 900–43; †952), at least, this kingdom was firmly Gaelic in language and culture. The seats of royal and ecclesiastical power were established not in the Dalriadic heartland of Argyll but in the east, in Scone and Dunfermline, and later in Edinburgh and St Andrews. Gaelic culture reached its zenith in Scotland during the eleventh century, when the borders of the kingdom were extended southwards, reaching to the Tweed and Solway, and Gaelic was the language of the court and government, of the aristocracy, clergy, and intelligentsia, used throughout the royal territory. Despite its dominant role, Gaelic co-existed with other languages: Pictish in the north (until its disappearance, probably sometime in the eleventh century), Cumbric (the northern form of what was to become Welsh) in the south-west, which probably passed from use not long after Pictish, and Anglo-Saxon (or early Scots) in the south-east.[5] In the Lothians, Gaelic seems to have had a relatively limited role, probably spoken only for some 150–200 years, by a landowning Gaelic-speaking aristocracy and their followers.[6]

From the middle of the twelfth century onwards, however, Gaelic language and culture began a long decline in Scotland. Norman French and Latin came to take the place of Gaelic as the languages of authority, before yielding in turn to Scots in the fourteenth and fifteenth centuries. Feudal institutions, ultimately of Continental origin and brought to Scotland through Norman influence, came to replace Gaelic ones. The Gaelic language itself was slowly replaced by Scots as the vernacular in the south and east of the country (which became the 'Lowlands') and eventually became confined to the north and west.

This process of de-Gaelicisation in southern and eastern Scotland has received surprisingly little attention from historians, and some familiar interpretations are rather misleading. St Margaret (†1093), the Anglo-Saxon wife of king Máel Coluim III (reigned 1054–93; †1093), who instituted a range of church reforms along Continental lines while placing little value on Gaelic institutions and practices, has long been identified as a key figure in this transformation, indeed a demon figure to some. A similar role is often assigned to the Northumbrian and Anglo-Norman lords placed in positions of power throughout the country by Máel Coluim III and his successors, especially David I (reigned 1124–1153; †1153), but many of these nobles, particularly those who settled in outlying regions, outwith the core of the kingdom, adapted to Gaelic environments and became assimilated into Gaeldom.[7]

Yet institutional changes were probably more determinative in this process of language and culture shift than the actions of a few key individuals. The slow penetration of feudal structures and institutions certainly played a significant role, but most important of all, it seems, was the growth of the new trading burghs from the early twelfth century onwards. These trading centres were populated largely by speakers of Germanic speech varieties – Scots/English, Flemings, Germans – and Scots eventually became the predominant language of commerce. The burghs, concentrated on the east coast, seem to have served as crucibles of language and culture shift, and Gaelic slowly became confined to the hinterland. By the early thirteenth century, Gaelic had probably disappeared from the core of the kingdom in the Lothians and the Forth valley; by 1400, the language shift seems to have extended to the entire east coast, including Buchan and the Moray littoral.[8] At the same time, Gaelic probably remained in use in some upland areas of Fife well into the fifteenth century and in Carrick and Galloway until some point in the seventeenth century. As late as 1500, Gaelic was still spoken by about half the population of Scotland, a proportion that has dropped steadily since, especially since c. 1750.

From the late fourteenth century onwards, if not earlier, a defined division between 'Highland' and 'Lowland' Scotland, marked by a 'Highland Line', seems to have been perceived, at least by those in the newly defined Lowlands. Although the distinction may appear a natural consequence of geography and geology, no such division had previously been recognised: the concept 'had simply not entered the minds of men.'[9] Earlier polities, notably the kingdom controlled by Cináed mac Ailpín and his successors, had straddled this line; the southern borders, not the western, had been the most unstable and problematic.

Unfortunately, the traditionally overwhelming focus on 'the making of the kingdom' among late medieval Scottish historians means that the processes of language and culture shift from the twelfth century onwards remain incompletely understood. Recent research by scholars studying the residual Gaelic element in Lowland Scotland in the twelfth and thirteenth centuries from different disciplinary perspectives – history, literature, onomastics – does suggest that the process of de-Gaelicisation was considerably more gradual and diffuse than once supposed.[10]

A significant but not yet satisfactorily explained aspect of the problem is the halt of the language and culture shift away from Gaelic along this new 'Highland Line', which remained in place, to a meaningful if not absolute degree, for some four centuries, from the middle of the fourteenth to the middle of the eighteenth, when language shift began in earnest within the 'Highlands'. Some scholars have emphasised the limited reach of burgh-based trading zones in interior river basins, which meant that the hinterland remained untouched by their influence, and the impact of climate change, war and plague in the first half of the fourteenth century, which eased population pressure and led to an abandonment of upland zones, thereby widening the gap between 'highland' and 'lowland' populations.[11]

The earliest statement (*c.* 1380) of the division between Highland and Lowland is that of the historian John of Fordun:

> The customs and habits of the Scots differ according to the difference of language; for two languages are in use, the Scottish [Gaelic] and the Teutonic [Scots/English]. The latter is the language of those living by the sea coast and in the plains, while the race of Scottish speech inhabits the highlands and outlying islands. The people of the coast are home-loving, civilised, trustworthy, tolerant and polite, decently attired, affable and pacific, devout in their worship of God, yet always ready to resist an injury at the hands of their enemies. The highlanders and people of the islands, on the other hand, are a wild and untamed race, primitive and proud, given to plunder and the easy life, clever and quick to learn, handsome in appearance, though slovenly in dress, consistently hostile to the people and language of the English, and, when the speech is different, even to their own nation. They are, however, loyal and obedient to their king and country, and provided they be well governed they are obedient and ready enough to respect the law.[12]

Fordun's rhetoric is typical of medieval western European discourse on the struggle between 'civility' and 'barbarity', a discourse that echoes conventional classical descriptions of barbarian peoples; his depiction of Lowlanders and Highlanders may be understood, to some extent at least, as a stereotyped statement rather than an original ethnographic observation on cultural politics in late medieval Scotland.[13] From Fordun's time onwards, anti-Gaelic rhetoric from Lowland writers became commonplace, but until the end of the sixteenth century, when a new strain of violent antipathy came to dominate government policy under James VI (reigned 1567–1625; †1625), such views were generally tempered by an awareness of Scotland's Gaelic past and some degree of sympathy for Gaeldom as a repository of traditional virtues.[14]

Fordun continued to refer to Gaelic as the 'Scottish' language, but from the fifteenth century onwards the term 'Scots' came to be used (alongside 'Inglis') for the Germanic vernacular of the Lowlands, while 'Irish' became the dominant Lowland term for Gaelic, a usage that reflected the new, polarised Lowland interpretation of Highland society and culture. Only in the later eighteenth century did the term 'Gaelic' emerge as the norm in Scots and English in place of 'Irish'. Following the Wars of Independence (1296–1328), the identity of the kingdom of Scotland became largely de-Gaelicised, with the Irish origins of the nation significantly downplayed, and those on the margins of the kingdom and the so-called 'community of the realm' came to be deemed quasi-foreigners.[15] As discussed below, however, the Gaels themselves never accepted this ideological banishment, but always considered themselves as Scots, indeed the original and quintessential Scots.

Kingdom and lordship in the Isles

If eastern Scotland became steadily less Gaelic from the mid-twelfth century onwards, the opposite is true of the Hebrides and the western mainland from Kintyre northwards. The Hebrides had not formed part of the kingdom controlled by Cináed mac Ailpín and his successors; instead, from the ninth century onwards, the isles, together with the adjoining mainland, were controlled by Norse rulers, generally based in Dublin, Man, or, indirectly, Norway itself. Slowly, by virtue of intermarriage and political and economic interaction, a mixed Norse-Gaelic culture took root in the region, and Gaelic seems to have been the vernacular at least from the tenth century, except, perhaps, in the far north. Scottish sovereignty became complete only in 1266, when the Hebrides were ceded to Scotland by Norway. Even so, royal authority – Norwegian and, later, Scottish – was weak in the region, and local rulers enjoyed substantial autonomy.

The key institution in the west was the Kingdom of the Isles, established at the end of the tenth century. In the middle of the twelfth century the northern part of this kingdom, from Islay to Skye, evolved into a new polity, shaped by Somhairle mac Gille Brighde, or Somerled (†1164). In Gaelic tradition Somhairle is recognised as the founder of the 'Lordship of the Isles', an entity that dominated the Hebrides and West Highlands until the end of the fifteenth century, and arguably several decades beyond. The descendants of Somhairle continued to use the title *rí Innsi Gall* (king of the Hebrides) during this period; from the middle of the fourteenth century, a related Latin form, *Dominus Insularum* (Lord of the Isles), was used in legal documents. The adoption of this new Latin styling has led many historians to identify the 'Lordship' as a new creature dating from the mid-fourteenth century, but this interpretation is ultimately unhelpful, for no fundamental institutional restructuring occurred at this stage: essential continuity can be traced from Somhairle onwards, and the use of titles and honorifics seems to have been somewhat fluid.[16] Certainly, however, the power of *ríoghacht Innsi Gall* – by then consolidated in the hands of Clann Domhnaill, the descendants of Somhairle's grandson Domhnall mac Raghnaill mhic Somhairle (†1247((?)) (the subject of poem 15) – reached new heights in the fourteenth and fifteenth centuries (as reflected in poems 17–19). This era of relative peace and cultural vitality in the West Highlands and Isles is sometimes remembered in Gaelic tradition as *Linn an Àigh*, the 'age of joy' or the 'age of prosperity'.[17]

With their growing power and substantial autonomy, the Lords of the Isles came into increasing conflict with the kings of Scots over the course of the fifteenth century. Through a tactical marriage alliance, Clann Domhnaill came to claim the earldom of Ross, significantly expanding its power base, although its hold on the earldom was never secure. In 1476, the earldom was forfeited as a punishment for secret scheming with Edward IV of England and the earl of Douglas to divide up the kingdom of Scotland, and in 1493, following further unrest, the lordship itself was forfeited entirely (a setback that appears to be the basis for in poem 29). Several risings were launched over the successive decades to restore the lordship, efforts that ceased only in 1545 with the death of Domhnall Dubh MacDhomhnaill, grandson of the last 'Lord', Eòin, who had died in 1503.

The period following the demise of the Lordship of the Isles is remembered in Gaelic tradition as *Linn nan Creach*, the 'age of raids' or the 'age of forays'. While new regional powers slowly emerged in place of Clann Domhnaill, including the MacCoinnichs in the northern Highlands and, most notably, the Caimbeuls in the southwest, the relative stability of the Lordship period was replaced by an era of disruption, lawlessness and unease. In the later sixteenth century, central government became increasingly assertive in its efforts to secure control over the region, and increasingly repressive measures were adopted, usually carried out by local proxies such as the Caimbeuls, who were often licensed to use violence against the government's perceived enemies. But only at the very end of the period covered by this collection, from 1587 onwards, did the government's anti-Gaelic ideology harden significantly, a hardening manifested most dramatically by the notorious Statutes of Iona (1608), which imposed a number of strictures on the Highland clans and endeavoured to suppress various aspects of Gaelic culture.[18]

Following the Reformation, religion also became an important factor in government policy towards the Highlands, with the persistence of Catholicism an ongoing concern, but the full impact of this new controversy falls outside the scope of this book. During the later sixteenth century, tentative reforming initiatives began to take root in different parts of the Highlands, notably Argyll and the far north, but the principal impact of the Reformation was the implosion of the Catholic church, as priests fled and churches were abandoned.[19]

THE EVOLUTION OF GAELIC IDENTITIES

During the thousand years covered by this collection, the borders of 'Gaeldom' varied enormously, and often we can only speculate about how Gaelic speakers perceived the boundaries of their own community and their relationships to other communities around them, or indeed the extent to which language functioned as a badge of identity and belonging, and a boundary marker, for Gaelic speakers.

Given the dearth of pertinent historical documentation, we have almost no evidence that might shed light on the Gaelic response to the eastward spread of Gaelic and the securing of the kingdom of Alba as a Gaelic polity from the ninth century onwards. Indeed, there is unfortunately little direct or contemporary evidence that survives to show the Gaelic reaction to the slow de-Gaelicisation of southern and eastern Scotland, which brought about a newly divided society, an effectively partitioned Gaelic and de-Gaelicised Scotland.

From the sixteenth century onwards, however, a variety of sources, in Scots and English as well as Gaelic, suggest a strong resentment on the part of the Gaels, centred on a view that the nation had been stolen by outsiders or betrayed by traitors who abandoned Gaelic language and culture. It is probably reasonable to assume that such interpretations and attitudes had been taking shape slowly over the course of the earlier centuries as the de-Gaelicisation of the Lowlands proceeded.

Perhaps the most famous and powerful statement in this connection is not actually in Gaelic at all, but in Scots: the complaint of the Gaelic-speaking Carrick poet Walter Kennedy in William Dunbar's 'The Flyting of Dunbar and Kennedie' (*c.* 1500):

> Thow lufis nane Irische, elf, I understand,
> Bot it suld be all trew Scottis mennis lede;
> It was the gud language of this land,
> And Scota it causit to multiply and sprede,
> Quhill Corspatrik, that we of tresoun rede,
> Thy forefader, maid Irisch and Irisch men thin,
> Throu his tresoun broght Inglise rumplis in,
> So wald thy self, mycht thou to him succede.[20]

The rhetoric of betrayal is also expressed in eighteenth-century Gaelic poetry, as in Maighstir Seathan MacGill'Eathain's 'Air teachd on Spáin, do shliochd an Gháoidhil ghlais' ('When the descendants of Gàidheal Glas came from Spain'), composed in 1707, in which the poet (a minister from Mull) complains that:

> Reic iád san chúirt í, air cáint úir o Nde
> 's do thréig le hair [.i. tàir] budh nár leo ncán'mhain fein.

> (They sold it [Gaelic] in the court for a new speech dating from only yesterday
> and scornfully abandoned it: they were ashamed of their own language.)[21]

The early eighteenth-century commentator Edmund Burt report-
ed the Highlanders' 'tradition, that the Lowlands, in old times
were the possession of their ancestors', a view that John MacInnes
has summarised as the Gaels' self-perception as 'the dispossessed
of Scotland'.[22]

Explicit statements of this kind are only to be found from a
relatively late period, but it seems clear that the Gaels had long felt
significant alienation from 'Lowland' Scotland, even though they
always retained their formal allegiance to the kingdom and
considered themselves as Scots, indeed the original and pure
Scots.[23] Even as the northwest became steadily more integrated
into the Scottish kingdom from the late thirteenth century
onwards, following the cession of the Hebrides, the south and east
of Scotland, and with it 'Scotland' or 'Alba' as some kind of entity,
have little prominence in the Scottish Gaelic worldview during
this period: 'Lowland' Scotland is almost completely invisible in
late medieval Gaelic poetry, and Ireland serves as the touchstone
of all historical and cultural prestige. Tellingly, there is no Scottish
counterpart to the Irish concept of the 'sovereignty goddess', the
imagining and depiction of Ireland as a woman and sovereignty as
the marriage of ruler and land (illustrated in poem 23), a potent
device that is worked and reworked in different forms of Irish
poetry through the centuries.[24]

We are handicapped by our sources here, however, for the
surviving evidence, especially formal bardic poetry (discussed in
detail below), tends to reflect the distinct worldview of the literati,
many of whom received their training in Ireland and looked to
Ireland as the centre of learning and excellence. Yet at the same
time, it is obvious that chiefs and leaders throughout Gaelic
Scotland (including the poets' patrons) were deeply enmeshed in
Scottish politics, paying close attention to their relations with the
kings and magnates in the Lowlands and, in the process, often
coming into close contact with the Lowland cultural sphere. As for
the outlook of the mass of the Highland population, the lack of
sources means that it must remain entirely unknown.

Unfortunately, there are only very occasional hints in
contemporary Gaelic sources that communicate any recognition
of the new linguistic and cultural division in Scotland and/or a
dissociation from the de-Gaelicised south and east. The
distinction between *Gàidhealtachd* and *Galldachd* in modern
Gaelic is as clear and fundamental as the distinction between
Highlands and Lowlands in English, but neither these terms nor

any terms of similar meaning are attested in Gaelic sources from Scotland before the seventeenth century.[25] By the same token, it is not clear when the Gaels began to view and conceptualise the inhabitants of southern and eastern Scotland as *Goill* (singular *Gall*), that is, as 'foreigners' or 'non-Gaels'. In Irish usage, the label *Gall*, originally connected to Gaul, was associated with the Vikings and Hiberno-Norse, before coming to serve as the main term used for the English. The term *Gall* is sometimes applied to thirteenth-century Hebridean chiefs in eulogies composed by Irish poets (see poems 15 and 16), in recognition of their Norse antecedents, but only rarely is it used to mean 'Lowland Scot' in sources dating from before the seventeenth century, when this usage becomes ubiquitous in Gaelic Scotland, often communicating considerable bitterness and distaste. Contrary to a surprisingly resilient misconception, the term *Sasannach*, originally a Gaelic form of 'Saxon', was reserved for the English and was never applied to the Lowland Scots.[26]

The division between *Gàidheal* and *Gall* was never absolute and clear-cut. Dynastic marriages across the Highland Line were commonplace during the late medieval period, and the by-name *Gallda* ('Anglicised' or 'Lowlandised') was given to many Gaelic aristocrats, including Eòin Gallda MacDubhghaill (†1376/77), Ruairidh Gallda MacAoidh (†1411) and Domhnall Gallda MacDhomhnaill of Lochalsh (†1519). This appellation may indicate that they had been fostered with a Lowland family or spent time in England, or simply that they had some facility in Scots or English.[27]

The term *Gall* in the context of Lowland Scotland may have been used initially as a label for the Anglo-Norman lords and their followers, rather than the mass of the ordinary population of the south and east. The lower orders of the 'Lowland' population would probably have remained culturally similar to ordinary 'Highlanders' – in using the Gaelic language, among other things – much longer than these foreign and foreign-influenced aristocrats. Certainly by the seventeenth century, however, the entirety of the Lowland population were classified as *Goill*, with the poets frequently expressing disdain for the ordinary agricultural population of the Lowlands, denigrated as *gallbhodaich* or Lowland churls.

If Gaelic identity in Scotland underwent significant shifts and changes over the centuries, there may well also have been considerable variation and diversity at any given time; indeed, it

seems distinctly unlikely that cultural uniformity could have
prevailed across the entirety of the Gàidhealtachd. The relative
proximity to the Lowlands would seem to be an obvious
differentiating factor; economic and political contact, and thus
cultural contact, was more frequent and intense in 'border' areas
along the eastern fringe of the Gàidhealtachd than in the West
Highlands and Hebrides (the sphere of the Lordship) – a
variegation expressed by James VI, who distinguished 'two sorts of
people: the one that dwelleth in our maine land, that are
barbarous for the most parte, and yet mixed with some shewe of
civilitie: the other, that dwelleth in the Iles and are alluterlie
barbares, without any sorte or shewe of civilitie'.[28] Nevertheless, it
is difficult to find any concrete evidence of regional cultural
divisions or distinctions from the surviving Gaelic sources; indeed,
there appears to have been a striking degree of cultural common-
ality across the region in some important respects. For example,
the extent to which Fenian tales and ballads and indeed particular
popular songs, such as those arising from the struggle between the
MacGriogairs and the Caimbeuls, spread throughout the
Gàidhealtachd is remarkable (see introduction to poems 54 and
71). By the same token, relatively late evidence (*c.* 1700) concern-
ing the different grades and practitioners of poetry (an issue
discussed in detail below) from the north-eastern Gàidhealtachd
is closely concordant with evidence of Hebridean and even Irish
practice.[29]

The texts given here, both learned poems and early vernacular
songs, are overwhelmingly from the southern and western
Gàidhealtachd (Argyll, Perthshire, Lochaber and the Hebrides),
or from Ireland. This reflects the nature of the material surviving
from our period, in which the northwestern and northeastern
Gàidhealtachd (to say nothing of the 'lost Gàidhealtachd' of what
became the Lowlands) are very poorly represented.

Gael and Norse

If much of Scotland was undergoing de-Gaelicisation in the later
Middle Ages, an important part, indeed the area that was to
become the heartland of modern Gaelic Scotland, was actually
becoming re-Gaelicised (or perhaps, in some parts of the Outer
Hebrides, Gaelicised for the first time). The Hebrides (still
known in Gaelic as *Innse Gall*, literally 'islands of the *Goill*') and
the West Highland littoral moved from being a mixed Norse-

Gaelic cultural and political environment in the first centuries of the millennium, and then underwent a fundamental re-Gaelicisation.

Unfortunately, here as in other respects, our surviving sources concerning shifting perceptions and identities are relatively scanty. This process was probably slow and evolutionary, varying from district to district and from kindred to kindred, but the progress of this shift cannot be traced with any confidence, largely because there is so little surviving evidence concerning cultural attitudes and identities in the early part of the period, when perceptions of Norse connections would surely have been stronger.

Significantly, this process of re-Gaelicisation and turning away from Scandinavia was not simply a movement among the elite, but something that came to percolate through all levels of society, eventually producing a thoroughly Gaelic culture throughout all levels of society in Gaelic Scotland. Most likely, re-Gaelicisation took place through an essentially top-down process, driven by the shifting political outlooks of the aristocracy and by the intellectual culture of the learned classes. At some stages at least, these shifts must have been deliberate, with Gaelic identity being consciously promoted and Scandinavian connections consciously discarded and disregarded. The systematic nature of this development is demonstrated by 'the homogeneity of the culture of the Highlands between those districts where the Norse ruled for five hundred years and those where they never penetrated.'[30]

The intensity of this re-Gaelicisation is immensely significant for an understanding of Scottish Gaelic culture from the late medieval period onwards. Although Scottish Gaeldom continued to be referred to with ossified labels that communicated the Norse link, such as *Gall* and, later, *Fionnghall* (see introduction to poem 25), self-understanding and self-location within Scottish Gaeldom made very little of the Norse background. In recent centuries certainly, the Norse heritage has been very largely obliterated from Scottish Gaelic tradition; Norse linguistic influence on Scottish Gaelic also seems to have been relatively limited, with lexical borrowing confined for the most part to distinct domains such as ship-building.[31] According to the eminent folklore collector Donald Archie MacDonald, there has been an 'almost total loss of awareness in modern Gaelic oral tradition that there was at any time a powerfully established Norse-speaking or even bilingual Gaelic/Norse population in the Hebrides'; the dominant view instead confines 'the role of the Norse to that of a raiding and plundering enemy who were usually defeated'.[32] How early this viewpoint developed cannot now be known, but it is illuminating that the history of Clann Domhnaill, and its Clann Raghnaill branch written by the learned poet Niall MacMhuirich at the end of the seventeenth century presents the emergence of the Lordship of the Isles under Gille Brighde and his son Somhairle in the middle of the twelfth century as something of a campaign of liberation from Norse occupiers, an interpretation quite at odds with the political realities of that era.[33]

This process of re-Gaelicisation and turning away from Scandinavia does not mean that the Norse heritage is completely absent in Scottish Gaelic literature of the medieval period. The most fascinating example is the 'Castle Sween' poem (33 here), composed early in the fourteenth century. Norse heritage is occasionally noted in bardic and vernacular poetry, often by means of references to prestigious Norse ancestors, as in poems 15 and 16, most notably in MacLeòid poetry, and there are also some stray scraps in the poetry, song, and prose-tale traditions of later centuries.

THE IRISH CONNECTION

The connection between Scotland and Ireland was of immense importance throughout the period covered by this collection, but the nature of the relationship underwent significant change and evolution over the centuries. In the initial phase of settlement, the Gaelic community in Scotland, centred on Dál Riata, was to some extent at least an offshoot of Ireland, and Ireland seems to have been understood as the 'mother country'. Unsurprisingly, the nature of the perceived connection shifted over the centuries, and the distinctiveness of Gaelic Scotland became steadily more apparent. This divergence became increasingly perceptible following the emergence of the hybrid, but Gaelic-dominated, kingdom of Alba from the ninth century onwards, which developed its own distinct institutions and which Irish commentators began to conceptualise in different terms, as a discrete entity rather than a mere adjunct of Ireland.[34] The de-Gaelicisation of the Scottish monarchy over the following centuries brought about another transformation, as the Irish connection became less ideologically relevant to those in 'central' Scotland; in particular, Lowland chroniclers and other scholars writing after the Wars of Independence (1296–1328), which secured Scotland's role as an independent kingdom in the mainstream of late medieval Europe, paid much less attention to the Irish dimension and endeavoured to assert Scotland's own ancient and indigenous identity.[35]

Conversely, the residual Gaelic community of Scotland – that is to say, those living in what was coalescing as the Gàidhealtachd – came to place increasing emphasis on the Irish connection during the later medieval period. Especially during the era of the Lordship of the Isles, the political and cultural heartland of the Gàidhealtachd appears to have been in the west, including the isles, a region which had not formed part of the Scottish kingdom during the period when Gaelic culture was at its apogee; in this sense, there is not necessarily a direct lineal connection between the 'eastern Gaelic' culture associated with the kingdom of Alba and the later 'western Gaelic' culture centred on the Lordship of the Isles. Among the literati of the western Gàidhealtachd, at least, the Irish connection was valued very highly, and Ireland was viewed as the source of all prestige; the highest praise for a chief was to claim him as the destined high-king of Ireland (a claim that need not, indeed rarely did, have any relationship to political reality). Rhetoric of this kind is seen, for example, in poem 18. The imagined connection to Gaelic Ireland seems to have become more meaningful and more fundamental than the link to Lowland Scotland, and this association with Gaelic Ireland appears to have been central to Scottish Gaeldom's sense of cultural location and identity during the late medieval period.

Connections with Ireland were political as well as cultural: intermarriage between the leading families of the Isles and of Gaelic Ireland, especially Ulster, was common until the seventeenth century, and military power from the Scottish Gàidhealtachd, both the hereditary *gallóglaigh* or 'galloglasses' and the short-term mercenary 'redshanks', played a key role in sustaining Irish Gaelic resistance to English rule. Branches of several Scottish families became established in different parts of Ireland, most notably Clann Domhnaill, who gained a toehold in northeast Ulster near the end of the fourteenth century and expanded their Irish territories over the following centuries.[36]

Even so, it is unhelpful to imagine a single, unified Gàidheal-tachd during the late Middle Ages, stretching from Cape Clear to Cape Wrath; the Scottish/Irish divide seems to have been important, indeed fundamental, throughout this period. Scottish Gaeldom often functioned separately from Irish Gaeldom, especially in political and economic terms, and vice versa. Many poets and other learned men travelled from one country to the other, especially, in the case of Scottish Gaels, for training and instruction; yet even so, evidence across the range of cultural and intellectual activity suggests that Ireland was systematically dominant, and that Gaelic Scotland looked to Ireland much more than vice versa. This dominance should not be understood in terms of perceived superiority or inferiority, however, let alone of 'complexes'; this order seems to have been considered natural and normal, and thus accepted, indeed almost venerated, in this highly conservative society.[37]

The changing Gaelic language

Along with these political and sociolinguistic shifts, the Gaelic language itself underwent significant evolution and change over the thousand years covered by this volume. Distinct stages of the language can be discerned, along with different varieties in different parts of the Gaelic-speaking area.

A conventional division breaks the language into three main stages: Old, Middle and Modern Gaelic.[38] These distinctions relate to forms of the written language: Old Gaelic is the language of the earliest texts, which date from the late 500s, up to *c.* 900, Middle Gaelic the language of texts from *c.* 900 to *c.* 1200, and Modern Gaelic the language of texts from *c.* 1200 onwards. (In many cases the language of a given text is much older than the actual manuscript in which it has been preserved, as texts were copied and recopied over the centuries). A few texts in this collection are in Old or Middle Gaelic (nos. 1–4, 54) and the remainder in various forms of Modern Gaelic. The term 'Modern Gaelic' is a very broad one, however, taking in both the Early Modern Gaelic of the late Middle Ages (discussed below) and the distinct vernaculars of Scotland and Ireland, which have themselves undergone considerable change over recent centuries. The vernacular songs (poems 65–85) are for the most part readily understandable to a modern Gaelic readership or audience in a way that is by no means true of the Early Modern compositions, to say nothing of those in Middle Gaelic.

Linguists have disagreed as to how Gaelic became fragmented into different varieties and when Scottish Gaelic came to diverge from Irish and emerge as a distinct form. The once widely accepted theory of 'Common Gaelic' suggested that significant differentiation did not begin until *c.* 1300, roughly a thousand years after Gaelic was brought to Scotland. More recently, some scholars have challenged this view, arguing that divergence probably began to set in as soon as Gaelic speakers began to settle in Scotland.[39] This view is inherently plausible given that significant physical barriers would have limited opportunities for language contact between Scottish and Irish Gaels; it is axiomatic that linguistic divergence develops in the absence of regular contact between particular groups of speakers. Conversely, contact between Scottish Gaeldom and speakers of the 'P-Celtic' languages used in early Scotland, Pictish and Cumbric, may also have played a role in shaping a distinctly Scottish Gaelic vernacular.[40]

By the late sixteenth century, the end of the period covered in this collection, Irish speakers certainly perceived Scottish Gaelic as a distinct (though perhaps still intelligible) variety. For example, an account of a group of MacDhomhnaill and MacLeòid warriors from Skye serving in Ulster in 1595, in Aodh Ruadh Ó Domhnaill's army, describes them as being distinguishable from the Irish troops by virtue not only of their attire and equipment but also of their speech, while an entry in the *Annals of the Four Masters*, assembled in the 1630s, describes how an earlier Ó Domhnaill chief returned from fosterage in Scotland in 1258 and, in the course of an address to his people, quoted a proverb 'in Scottish Gaelic' (*san nGaoidhilcc nAlbanaigh*).[41]

Direct evidence of linguistic divergence is sparse, however, because the vernacular language was not generally used for writing. From *c.* 1200 to *c.* 1650 a single form of Early Modern Gaelic was in use throughout Gaelic Ireland and Gaelic Scotland for writing purposes, and perhaps for wider communication by the cultural and political elite.[42] This form, known as Classical Common Gaelic (or Classical Irish), has been described as the product of a 'medieval exercise in language planning', a remarkable programme of linguistic standardisation carried out under the auspices of the professional bardic schools.[43] Certain linguistic forms were prescribed and others proscribed in the creation of this special 'literary dialect', which did not correspond to any actual spoken form of the language but was nevertheless preserved intact for some four centuries through the authority of the bardic schools. Most of the poems collected here (with the exception of the Songs) give little linguistic indication of their provenance; they could equally well have been composed in

Ireland or in Scotland. By the seventeenth century, if not earlier, Classical Common Gaelic was very different from the Scottish vernacular, and somewhat inaccessible to ordinary Gaels (if not necessarily the aristocracy); the Skye writer Martin Martin, writing *c.* 1695, remarked of the learned bardic poets that 'they furnish such a Stile . . . as is understood by very few'.[44]

As such, the evidence for the development of the distinct Scottish Gaelic vernacular is rather patchy. Useful linguistic indicators can be found in the important fifteenth-century genealogical manuscript known as 'Manuscript 1467' and in the principal written texts from the sixteenth-century Gàidhealtachd, the Book of the Dean of Lismore (an immensely important manuscript, described below, compiled between 1512 and 1526), and Seon Carsuel's (John Carswell) *Foirm na nUrrnuidheadh*, an adaptation of John Knox's *Book of Common Order* (the first Gaelic book to be printed, in either Scotland or Ireland, which was published in Edinburgh in 1567).[45] Indeed, it has been argued that various Scotticisms can even be discerned in the earliest Gaelic text from Scotland, the Book of Deer, which was written *c.* 1150 at the Columban monastery at Deer in northeastern Aberdeenshire (far from both Dál Riata and today's Gaelic heartland: a reminder of how the geography of Gaelic in Scotland has changed over time).[46]

Conversely, songs in the Scottish vernacular that date back to the fifteenth or sixteenth century (the final section of this collection, poems 65–85) were generally not written down before the mid-eighteenth century, and almost certainly reflect linguistic adaptation and modernisation following oral transmission over the course of generations. Some poems here are best described as semi-classical in terms of their language, showing the influence of the literary variety on aristocrats and members of the learned classes. The texts here thus span a spectrum in linguistic terms, from the formal to the informal, from the conservative, even antiquarian, to the innovative.

Writing in Gaelic

Compared to Ireland and Wales, the surviving documents from early Scotland – in any language, even including Latin – are very sparse. While a diverse and extensive array of texts survive from Ireland (mostly preserved in manuscripts written from the twelfth century onwards), including texts that were composed in Scotland (such as poems 1–3, 14 and 30) or that deal with Scottish matters of one kind or another, [47] there are few surviving Gaelic documents that were actually written in Scotland at any time within the period covered in this collection. As noted above, the earliest extant Gaelic text written in Scotland, the Book of Deer, dates from the early twelfth century (at least seven hundred years after Gaelic was first brought to Scotland), and even writings from the sixteenth century, the last stage of the period covered by this collection, are scanty. In part this reflects the increasing marginalisation of Gaelic as a language of power and authority from the twelfth century onwards. By the fifteenth century Scots had become the dominant written language of government and commerce, and writings in Scots from that period are both extensive and diverse; conversely, there are hardly any Gaelic writings from the late Middle Ages, whether official, commercial or artistic in nature. For example, more than a hundred land charters and similar legal documents signed by the Lords of the Isles have survived, written between 1336 and 1490; but of these only one is written in Gaelic, with the rest using Latin or, in a few cases, Scots.[48] Given these deficiencies in the written record, the poems in this collection are overwhelmingly derived from Irish manuscripts, from the sixteenth-century Book of the Dean of Lismore, or from sources that significantly post-date the period of the poems' composition (especially the vernacular songs, which were mostly collected from the later eighteenth century onwards).

Without question, many documents in general and many poems and songs in particular have been lost; the great majority of poems, even formal compositions by learned professional poets, were probably never committed to writing. Especially tantalising are the 'waifs and strays', excerpts or quotations from now-lost poems that are given in later texts, especially the clan histories written (almost always in English or Latin) during the seventeenth and early eighteenth centuries.[49] Even so, there may be some tendency to overstate the extent to which documents have been lost, whether by accident or design; Gaelic writing in late medieval Scotland may simply have been 'an ill-developed art of little consequence'.[50] Even if the role of the language in official and commercial matters was very limited, Gaelic literacy among the aristocracy seems to have been fairly well-established, and the professional learned families maintained a vigorous culture dependent on the written word, with manuscript libraries, such as those of the MacMhuirichs (the leading poetic family) and

MacBheathas (the Beatons, the leading medical family), being passed down from generation to generation.[51]

During the late medieval period, two distinct systems seems to have been used to write Gaelic in Scotland. The style favoured by the Gaelic literati over the centuries (and universally used in Gaelic Ireland) was the *corr-litir* or 'peaked letter' hand originally derived from Latin uncials but most familiar, perhaps, from the Gaelic font (*cló Gaedhealach*) widely used in Ireland until the middle of the twentieth century; its accompanying orthographic system is the direct ancestor of modern Gaelic spelling conventions. The other system, which may actually have been more widely used, at least in some parts of the Gàidhealtachd, bore no relation to the 'standard' system but was based instead on the conventions of Middle Scots, and often written in the distinct 'secretary hand' of the time. The earliest writing in this Scots-based style is a charm contained in a flyleaf to a Book of Hours apparently written in Bute *c.* 1370;[52] an important late variant is the Fernaig manuscript, an invaluable collection of religious and political verse written in Wester Ross in 1689 (the source of poem 11 here). By far the most famous example, however, is the Book of the Dean of Lismore, an extraordinarily important manuscript written at Fortingall in Highland Perthshire between 1512 and 1542. The Book of the Dean is a highly disparate collection of well over two hundred poems, both Irish and Scottish, reflecting the eclectic tastes and predilections of its compilers, Seumas MacGriogair, Dean of Lismore, and his brother Donnchadh; poem 61 explains the nature of the project and provides the title for the present anthology. To the uninitiated reader of modern Gaelic, the Book of the Dean is utterly incomprehensible, and several of its texts have eluded the most painstaking editorial efforts of scholars.[53]

During the period covered by this collection, and indeed until the middle of the eighteenth century, the *printed* word played a very limited role. As discussed in the introduction to poem 9, the first printed book in Gaelic, Seon Carsuel's *Foirm na n-Urrnuidheadh*, was published in 1567, some 114 years after Gutenberg's Bible. This was the only Gaelic book published in Scotland in the sixteenth century. Literate culture, such as it was, remained overwhelmingly manuscript-based; the first secular literary work, Alasdair mac Mhaighstir Alasdair's *Ais-éiridh na Sean Chànoin Albannaich*, was published only in 1751, and only in the later eighteenth century did publishing become reasonably frequent (if still very small in scale relative to more widely spoken European languages). Significantly, Carsuel's book was printed in the Roman font that had been adopted for English-language printing in Lowland Scotland; every subsequent Gaelic book in Scotland followed his example (unlike in Ireland, where the *corr-litir* hand was transformed into the so-called *cló Gaedhealach*), as have almost all hand-written texts produced after the end of the seventeenth century.

SUBJECTS AND FORMS OF COMPOSITION

The poems presented in this volume vary widely not only in terms of the time of their composition but also with regard to their function, form and style. The classifications we have used here (Religion, Panegyric, Elegy, Incitement, Satire and Humour, Love, Ballads, Occasional Verse) give some sense of this diversity, but even these are broad categories; the satires, for example, range from an address to the head of an Irish harper executed for the murder of the son of the Lord of the Isles, which is to some extent a lament for a lost leader, to a mock paean to a potent and prodigious penis (poems 37 and 41 respectively). Our division between the 'Learned Tradition' and the 'Song Tradition' is by no means a rigid one; no firm distinction between 'literary' and 'folk' literature should be assumed.[54]

RELIGIOUS AND SECULAR POETRY

As elsewhere in early medieval Europe, literary and intellectual activity in Gaeldom was largely centered on the Church, with the role of monasteries (most obviously that of Iona) being particularly important in the Gaelic context. Latin was of course the predominant language of the early Gaelic monasteries, but the vernacular was used more frequently and more widely than in other parts of Europe. The early Gaelic literary record (which consists largely of Irish material, as explained above) is overwhelmingly of monastic origin, whether in the form of prose tales such as those of the Ulster Cycle, learned texts on political or literary matters, or religious poetry of different kinds (such as poems 1–3 here). Following reforms to Church structures in the twelfth century, however, the literary role of the Irish monasteries diminished and was largely taken over by secular bardic schools, supported by the aristocracy.

Medieval Gaeldom was a profoundly religious society (although practices of religious observation among the laity were variable) and religious poetry formed an important strand in the corpus throughout the period covered by this collection. The religious poems given here range in date from the seventh century to the end of the sixteenth, and their authors are also very diverse: some are clerics, some professional poets (discussed below), some aristocratic amateurs. The Classical material is largely an expression of mainstream European Catholicism, while the earliest material celebrates the Coptic ideal of monasticism as it developed in these islands. Because the Reformation was only beginning to reach the Gàidhealtachd at the end of the period covered here, little Protestant sentiment is apparent in the religious poems we have included (with the obvious exception of poem 9, a dedicatory poem for a Protestant prayer book). Poem 13, for example, although appended to a Calvinist tract published *c*. 1640, is also attributed in Irish manuscripts to members of the unquestionably Catholic Ó Dálaigh poetic family.

The bardic poets

Although the tradition of formal composition can be traced back over the preceding centuries,[55] Gaelic poetry reached an apogee of sorts during the late Middle Ages, the so-called classical period (*c*. 1200–*c*. 1650). The poetic profession in Ireland, having become separated from the monasteries following the church reforms of the twelfth century, attained a high degree of formal organisation in secular bardic schools, and the technical requirements of poetry became highly regulated, with particularly complex metrical rules. This style of verse has different names: in Gaelic, *dán díreach*, 'strict verse', or *filidheacht na scol*, 'poetry of the schools' or 'poetry of the learned', in English, 'bardic poetry'. The term 'bardic poetry', although irrevocably established in both academic and popular usage, is a misnomer. *Bard* is a technical term in Gaelic, referring to a secondary grade of versifier; it is not simply an ethereal synonym for 'poet', as in English, or the unmarked word for 'poet' as in modern Scottish Gaelic. The trained poets who composed *dán díreach* were not bards, but *filidh* (singular *file*),[56] and would have been affronted to be described as 'bards'. The required professional training for an aspiring *file* took up to twelve years, and was open only to young men (women being entirely excluded) who belonged to professional poetic families. This training, in language, metrics, syntax, genealogy and history, was rigorous and meticulous, and famously required students to compose their works while lying in the dark, and only commit them to writing upon completion.[57]

The bardic poets composed a range of different kinds of poems, with religious works (such as poems 6, 7, 10, 12 and 13 here) being particularly important, but their principal professional function was to produce compositions for their aristocratic patrons, most obviously in connection with major occasions of political significance (births, marriages, inaugurations, deaths, conflicts and crises). Such panegyric poetry fulfilled key social functions, expressing and reiterating shared values, drawing the clan together at times of challenge and crisis; it was very far from idle or meretricious flattery of the particular chief whose virtues and achievements the poet proclaimed. The bardic poets played a key political and social role in Gaelic society, offering advice and criticism on political matters with an immense professional self-confidence secured by their elevated status.[58]

Post-Romantic notions of individual creativity have little relevance in this context; bardic poetry was highly conventional in terms of both form and content. As Eleanor Knott explained, 'native originality was [not] wanting in these . . . men, but it was not required of them. Their duty was not to invent new designs and motifs, but to dispose artistically those which had been preserved from generation to generation by the bardic profession'. In particular, bardic poets often reused and reworked famous lines and phrases so as to achieve a resonance with their audience; the modern concept of the cliché is not always meaningful or helpful here. There was little change in the nature of literary expression over the centuries: according to Knott, the literary style of bardic poetry 'is a flat table-land stretching from the 13th to the 17th century'.[59]

The criteria for assessing the merit of a bardic poem must necessarily differ from prevailing modern understandings; many readers may respond more readily to poems such as 27 and 30 which, above and beyond their technical mastery, express personal despair with controlled and powerful eloquence. A more traditional indicator of esteem might be the extent to which a particular poem was used as an exemplar in the bardic schools or copied and recopied by different scribes over the centuries (as with the works of Muireadhach Albanach Ó Dálaigh, author of poems 6, 14 and 27).

Surviving tracts on the intricacies of metrics and syntax give us considerable insight into the nature of the bardic curriculum, but our understanding of the theory, purpose and process of poetry can to a significant extent be gleaned only by assessing and dissecting the texts themselves: what topics were covered, how imagery and language were used, how form and structure affected meaning and resonance. Unfortunately, scholars working in the field have tended to place more emphasis on the technical (if both fascinating and highly complex) issues relating to metrics and editorial polishing over literary analysis and criticism. This relative inattention may also reflect a negative judgment on the merits of this material; according to William Gillies, some commentators have found it 'insincere, frigid, artificial, unoriginal, unnecessarily obscure, generally dead, and a massive squandering of talent'.[60]

Poem 24, apparently composed for one of the sixteenth century Caimbeul earls of Argyll, is preceded in the manuscript by a fascinating scribal road-map (probably not provided by the poet himself) which lays out the contents of the poem, explaining how the poet makes the key points and addresses the key subjects appropriate to a bardic panegyric, which may have been 'based on some established doctrine which would have been common knowledge to any trained poet':[61]

Atá an dán so ag tráchdadh ar chóig neithibh airidhthe bheanas re hiarrla Earra Ghaoidheal rena onóir do réir sinnsireacht a shean 7 a dhaoine roimhe. An ceád ní .i. gach sdaighle 7 gach onóir budh coir dó d'fhaghail ón rígh 7 ó uaislibh Alban. An dara ní .i. gach tóitheasdal slóigh 7 sochuidhe darab cóir freagra dó an am coguidh no easaonta. An III ní .i. mar ghabhus re a chulaidh chomhlain *et* a dheise chatha uime a measg Ghaoidheal do réir fasuin na nGaoidheal *et* a shinnsior riamh roimhe. An 4 ní .i. mar do-ní síoth iar gcíosughadh gach aicme *et* ar gcosg dá easaonta *et* mar fhógras sé as éagcóir *et* amhail dlighidh *et* lucht déanta uilc feille 7 fionghuile 7 aos gach neimhcheartuis iar cheana. An cúigmhadh ní .i. gach so aimsioracht sine 7 sonuis éireóchus rena linn amhuil as béas d'éirghe re linn na deighríogh *et* na ndeaghuachtaran do thoradh mara 7 tíre do theas 7 d'fheabhas . . . aimsire d'iomad iasg ar inbhearuibh 7 cnuas ar coilltibh *et* do bharr gacha maithis bhudh dheasda.

This poem treats of five particular things which pertain to the earl of Argyll and his honour in accordance with the ancestry of his forefathers and people before him. The first thing is each style and honour which he should receive from the king and the nobles of Scotland. The second thing is each hosting of warriors and followers that ought to respond to him in time of war or unrest. The third thing is how he dons his military apparel and battle-dress amidst the Gaels in accordance with the fashion of the Gaels and all his ancestors before him. The fourth thing is how he makes peace after subduing each sept and checking their dissension, and how he drives out injustice according to prescriptive right, and wrongdoers and perpetrators of evil deeds and of kinslaying, and all other manner of wrongdoers. The fifth thing is every period of pleasant weather and happiness that arises during his reign, as customarily arises under the rule of good kings and nobles, in terms of fruitfulness of sea and land and warmth and excellence of climate, plenitude of fish in estuaries and nuts on trees, and of the best of every goodness besides.[62]

As with the later vernacular panegyric poetry which came into full flower in the seventeenth century (in the work of poets such as Eachann Bacach, Iain Lom and Màiri nighean Alasdair Ruaidh), bardic poetry can be said to have been controlled by a received 'panegyric code', to use John MacInnes' famous term.[63] Specific virtues and characteristics are emphasised: nobility, wisdom, strength, generosity, beauty and so on. Distinct tropes, figures and metaphorical associations and rhetorical figures are used again and again, almost as if reshuffled from poem to poem. The panegyric code of classical verse is similar to, but by no means identical, to the later code described by MacInnes: some tropes common in bardic poetry are rare in vernacular poetry (or vice versa), and some function rather differently. The most systematic overview was given by Eleanor Knott in the 1920s, but a full analysis remains to be made.[64] Classifications, hierarchies and dichotomies permeate the system: a chief's eyes, mouth or hand might be praised, never his nose or his ears, he might be likened to an eagle or a salmon, never to a sparrow or a pike, to an apple-tree or an oak, never to an alder or an elm. One particularly common device, which presents considerable difficulties in translation, might be called 'bardic synecdoche', by which the poet addresses the patron by reference to a part of his body: *a fhabhra donn*, literally 'o dark lashes', *a rosg mall* 'o languid eye', and so on. In light of these well-defined conventions, bardic praise is best understood as an affirmation of the subject's 'fitness for rule', demonstrated in thought which is ultimately a pre-Christian schema linking a temporal lord with the regenerative powers of the earth. In some cases the poem's principal message may be communicated within a handful of quatrains, with the remainder dedicated to the careful, indeed systematic presentation of conventional panegyric images and ideas. This finely textured and formally integrated wrapping was indispensable if the poem was to be considered properly crafted.[65]

The metrical structure of bardic poetry is complex, although we should not overstate the difficulty of composing in at least some of the strict bardic metres once their rules had been familiarised and practised. Several dozen named metres were used, some of them much commoner than others, each with specific requirements as to alliteration, internal and end rhyme and the number of syllables in each line and in the last word of each line, but the pattern of stress, that is to say rhythm, was not regulated. The principles of rhyme are very different from those used in English poetry (and in later Gaelic poetry, in both Scotland and Ireland, in which only vowels are relevant and consonant sounds play no role). In particular, consonants were arranged in several classes corresponding to broad articulatory or phonetic similarities, so that a rhyme could be based on any consonants of the same class; for example, *bh, gh, dh, l, mh, n* and *r* formed one class and *ll, m(m), ng, nn* and *rr* formed another. Perfect rhyme – as between *ionadh* and *iodhan* or *cluineam* and *fuigheall* – required that all the stressed vowels in the words in question be identical and all consonants subsequent to the first stressed vowel (but not necessarily the initial consonant) belong to the same class.[66] The principle of alliteration is much as in English, with the important qualification that all vowels are deemed to alliterate with each other and that the silent letter combination *fh* at the beginning of words is ignored for purposes of alliteration (so that the following vowel or consonant would be taken into account instead).

Among the commonest (and most frequently exemplified in this collection) of the bardic metres are *deibhidhe, rannaigheacht* (*mhór* and *bheag*) and *séadna*.[67] These were elaborations of earlier, pre-classical metrical forms, with stricter structural requirements and additional ornamentation.

Deibhidhe is the commonest, and probably the simplest, of the bardic metres. Each line of the quatrain must contain seven syllables; the last word in the second and fourth lines must have one more syllable than the last word in the first and third lines. The last word in the first and third lines must then rhyme with the unstressed final syllable of the last word in the second and fourth lines (a pattern known as *rinn agus airdrinn*). Two words in each line must alliterate with each other (with the final word in the fourth line alliterating with the preceding stressed word), and two internal rhymes are required between the third and fourth lines.

For an illustration of *deibhidhe*, consider the third verse of poem 23:

> Tugtha d'Albain na sreabh seang
> a cóir féin d'inis Éireann,
> críoch aimhréidh na n-eas mbanna,
> suil bheas aimhréidh eatarra.

There is alliteration between *sreabh* and *seang* in line 1, *inis* and *Éireann* in line 2, *aimhréidh* and *eas* in line 3, and *aimhréidh* and *eatarra* in line 4 (the prepositional *d'* preceding *inis* and the genitival *n-* preceding *eas* being irrelevant). *Aimhréidh* in line 3 rhymes with *aimhréidh* in line 4, as do *mbanna* and *eatarra*; *seang* at the end of line 1 rhymes with *–reann* at the end of line 2, as does *mbanna* with *–arra*.

In *rannaigheacht mhór*, all four lines contain seven syllables and end on a word containing one syllable. (*Rannaigheacht bheag* is identical in all respects except that each line ends with a two-syllable word). The final words of lines two and four rhyme with each other, and the final words of the first and third lines consonate with them (that is, the final consonant is in the same class but the preceding vowel differs). There are at least two internal rhymes in each couplet, and the final word of the third line rhymes with a word in the interior of the fourth line (a pattern known as *aicill*); two words in each line need to alliterate with each other (with the final word in the fourth line alliterating with the preceding stressed word).

For an illustration of *rannaigheacht mhór*, consider the first verse of poem 5:

> Éistidh riomsa, a Mhuire mhór,
> do ghuidhe is liomsa badh lúdh;
> do dhruim réd bhráthair ná bíodh,
> a Mháthair Ríogh duinn na ndúl.

Lúdh at the end of line 2 rhymes with *ndúl* at the end of line 4, and *mhór* and *bíodh* consonate with them. In the first couplet, *riomsa* in line 1 and *liomsa* in line 2 rhyme with each other, as do *Mhuire* and *ghuidhe*; in the second, *dhruim* rhymes with *duinn*, *bhráthair* rhymes with *Mháthair* and *bíodh* forms *aicill* with *Ríogh*. There is alliteration between *Mhuire* and *mhór* in line 1, *liomsa* and *lúdh* in line 2, *bhráthair* and *bíodh* in line 3 and *duinn* and *ndúl* in line 4 (the initial *n*, a marker of the genitive case, being irrelevant).

In *séadna*, the first and third lines contain eight syllables, with the last word of each containing two syllables, and the second and fourth lines containing seven syllables and ending on a one-syllable word. Alliteration is again required in each line (with the final word in the first line alliterating with the following stressed word and the final word in the fourth line alliterating with the preceding stressed word), and two internal rhymes required between the third and fourth lines.

For an illustration of *séadna*, consider the last verse of poem 16:

> Ní fhuil a nÉirinn ná a nAlbain
> Aonghas mar thusa, a thaobh seang:
> Aonghais fháid bhraonghlais an Bhrogha,
> láid, a Aonghais, comha ad cheann.

Seang at the end of line 2 rhymes with *cheann* at the end of line 4, as do *Aonghais* and *Aonghais* in line 3 and line 4, *fháid* and *láid*, *Bhrogha* and *comha*. In line 1, there is alliteration between *fhuil*, *nÉrinn* and *nAlbain* (again, the initial *n*, here prepositional, being irrelevant), in line 2 between *thusa* and *tháobh*, in line 3 between *Aonghais* and *fháid* and between *bhráonghlais* and *Bhrogha*, and in line 4 between *comha* and *cheann*.

Unfortunately, we know relatively little about the performance of poetry in medieval Gaelic Scotland, although public presentation of some kind was the norm with all kinds of verse. In Ireland, the *file* did not present his own poems, but relied upon a *reacaire* or reciter, who chanted or intoned the poem to the accompaniment of a harp or *cruit* (a stringed instrument similar to a lyre).[68] There is some evidence that a somewhat similar division of responsibilities prevailed in Scotland; for example, an account given at the end of the seventeenth century asserts that 'the Bard's office was to rehears [*sic*] what was compiled by the Poets', with the term 'Poet' here corresponding to the *file*.[69] We know still less about how the performance of bardic poems was related to that of other kinds of poetic compositions; different kinds of poets and performers would often travel as part of a *cliar* or 'poet-band', and it appears that an evening's entertainment would involve the presentation of different kinds of poetry, in which the *file*'s work would represent the main event.

Indeed, we know relatively little about the extent to which

formal bardic poetry was composed and performed across the different regions of Gaelic Scotland. While there is no perceptible difference in relation to language and structure between the work of the professional Scottish poets and their Irish counterparts, the volume of the Irish corpus is much greater, as is the number of poetic families and identifiable individual poets. Some scholars have argued that the 'Irish model', with the *file* at the apex of a poetic hierarchy, must also have prevailed throughout Gaelic Scotland, while others have emphasised the gaps in the evidence and suggested that this system may have been effectively confined to areas within the sphere of influence of the Lordship of the Isles, with 'inferior' orders of poets in other regions having more freedom of manoeuvre in the absence of the lofty *filidh*. Nevertheless, there were a number of important families of *filidh* in Scotland (all of which appear to have had relatively recent Irish antecedents), notably the MacMhuirichs, who served the MacDhomhnaill Lords of the Isles and then the chiefs of Clann Raghnaill (see poems 6, 14, 26, 27, 29, 31, 34, 37, 46 and 53), the Ó Muirgheasáins, who served the MacGill'Eathains of Duart and then the MacLeòids of Dunvegan (see poem 7), and the MacEoghains, who served the MacDhubhghaills of Dunollie and then the Caimbeuls (see poems 12 and 13).[70]

Semi-classical poetry

If *dán díreach* was the most formal and prestigious kind of poetry produced in late medieval Gaeldom, it is nevertheless clear that a number of different kinds of styles were being composed during this period and that a number of different kinds of practitioners were active alongside the trained professional poets. The record of surviving manuscripts is heavily weighted in favour of the formal professional material, given its instrumental value to the aristocratic families who commissioned it or its didactic value to poetic trainees, but there was nevertheless a diversity of other styles, particularly works composed in looser forms of the strict metres, complying with some but not all of the technical rules. The most common of these looser forms was known as *óglachas*, while *brúilingeacht* approximated more closely to *dán díreach*. Some of the poets who produced such works (including the authors of poems 21, 22 and 44 here) were professional versifiers of a rank lower than the *file*, others aristocratic amateurs (such as

the authors of poems 28, 40–4 and 48–51). The Book of the Dean
of Lismore, for example, reveals a keen interest in poems
composed by the Gaelic nobility, especially those of the Caimbeul
family (including, significantly, at least one woman) and the
fourteenth-century Irish poet Gearóid Iarla, earl of Desmond. The
subject matter of such poems is diverse and tends to be less
elevated (sometimes considerably less so) than those of the *filidh*;
particularly important are the poems of 'courtly love' (*dánta
grádha*), ultimately of Provençal origin, although modified
somewhat in the Gaelic context.[71] A substantial number of the
poems in this collection (including most of those classified within
Satire and Humour, Love, Ballads, or Occasional Verse), although
still using a form of the classical rather than the vernacular
language, are composed in syllabic metres looser than formal *dán
díreach*; these poems, some of them far from scholarly in nature,
are all included within 'The Learned Tradition' section, which is
necessarily a broad heading. Conversely, some of the texts in the
vernacular (such as poems 66, 68 and 71) bear considerable similar-
ities to the classical poetry in terms of their metrics and rhetoric.

EARLY VERNACULAR SONGS

The last section of this collection consists of vernacular songs,
most of them probably composed in the later sixteenth century.
The oldest surviving songs appear to date to the fifteenth century,
although the authenticity of compositions such as poems 77 and
78 is open to question. These songs were therefore already very
old when they were collected during the later eighteenth century,
an era of intensive collecting activity in the Gàidhealtachd, when
the spirit of the age placed great value on disappearing ancient
traditions and on Scotland's national pedigree.[72] It seems clear
that songs both similar and dissimilar in nature had been
composed and performed steadily over the course of the earlier
centuries, but these have all been lost, and indeed it is beyond
question that only a tiny proportion of the popular compositions
of the fifteenth and sixteenth centuries survived to be gathered by
the collectors of the eighteenth century. In contrast, the surviving
material from the 1640s onwards is much more plentiful. Even in
a conservative culture like that of Gaelic Scotland, oral tradition
does not preserve ancient material indefinitely, and new
compositions tend to push out the old.

The songs here are diverse in character: some are early

waulking songs (which, in some cases, had become transmuted into waulking songs having begun as other kinds of 'songs of occupation'), while others (notably poem 66) are more formal, literary compositions of one kind or another. Structures vary substantially, with some poems seemingly working within early medieval forms and structures; the diversity of the corpus of surviving sixteenth-century material suggests that a variegated song tradition was already well-established by that point.[73] In most cases, the songs are accentual in terms of their metrics (in contrast to the arhythmic syllabic metres used in *dán díreach*), with each line having a defined number of stressed syllables and thus a particular rhythm. However, this feature is by no means universal in the earliest vernacular songs, which continue to show a fidelity to the older syllabic structure.[74] The principles of rhyme in the songs are much simpler than in *dán díreach*; crucially, only vowel sounds are taken into account, so that rhyme structure is a matter of patterned assonance between words containing the same stressed vowel. There are no formal rules concerning alliteration, although it remains a common ornamentation.

Poem 76 shows one common pattern:

> Is mi suidhe an so am ònar
> Air còmhnard an rathaid,
>
> Dh'fheuch am faic mi fear-fuadain,
> Tighinn o Chruachan a' cheathaich

Each couplet throughout the poem has a short *a* sound in the final stressed vowel of the second line (here *rathaid*: *cheathaich*). There is also rhyme between the final stressed vowel in the first line and the first stressed vowel of the second line within the couplet: *ò* in the first quoted couplet (*ònar*: *còmhnard*), *ua* in the second (*fuadain*: *Chruachan*).

In contrast, poem 67 has a rather more complex structure, more similar in metrical terms to classical and pre-classical poetry:

> 'S mithich dhùinne, mar bhun ùmhlachd,
> Dàn bùrduin a chasgairt duit,
> A fhleasgaich bhrìoghmhoir fhliuchas pìosan
> Le d' dhibh spìosair neartmhoraich

Here, there are rhymes between the last stressed syllables of the second and fourth lines (the short *a* sounds of *chasgairt* and *neartmhoraich*); between *dhùinne* and *ùmhlachd* in the first line and *bùrduin* in the second; and then between *bhrìoghmhoir* and *pìosan* in the third line and *spìosair* in the fourth line. There is also *aicill* in most (but not all) of the couplets, as with *ùmhlachd* and *bùrduin* in the first and second lines quoted.[75]

Dating these vernacular compositions is uncertain and imprecise. Some songs, such as 34, 77 and 78, relating to the battles of Harlaw (1411) and Inverlochy (1431), are readily connected to particular circumstances and events, but it is questionable whether they were indeed composed at the time of those events or, if they were, whether the style in which they have come down to us reflects their original form. Other texts are very difficult to date, but evoke a sense of archaism quite distinct from compositions dating from the mid-seventeenth century or later. Although several of the songs were probably or certainly composed by women, the distinct women's voice that is so striking in seventeenth- and eighteenth-century compositions, especially in songs of abandonment, is relatively muted here.

Derick Thomson has summarised the power of these early songs as follows:

> The poems and songs that make the strongest impact arise out of deep emotions, and are tightly structured, sometimes in respect of metrics, sometimes in respect of imagery. The control of vivid visual imagery, interlocked with the emotional drive behind the poem, and conjoined with a spare, non-indulgent structural plan, produces the most striking examples . . .[76]

The Songs may seem more accessible and immediate to many modern readers than the formal bardic poetry, as they more closely approximate to our modern lyric ideal in being concrete, understated and frank.[77]

★

The notes accompanying the poems explain particular points of difficulty and give guidance to further relevant reading. However, this volume is not intended to be an academic edition, so that we have generally not highlighted the editorial issues (metrical and otherwise) that we have tackled ourselves or that previous editors of these poems (whose work we gratefully acknowledge here) have endeavoured to resolve. In addition, the orthography used necessarily varies according to the different stages of the language, and some compromises have been made for the sake of consistency and clarity in a way that may be open to question in various ways. Texts in vernacular Scottish Gaelic are generally spelled according to the newest Gaelic Orthographic Conventions, promulgated by the Scottish Qualifications Authority in 2005, but deviations are necessary in some cases, particularly in texts that show the influence of Classical Gaelic. Personal names are generally given in their (modern) Gaelic form while place names are generally in English.

Wilson McLeod
Meg Bateman

April 2007

Notes to Introduction

1   A more complete selection of early (pre-1350) material is given, in English translation only, in Clancy 1998. Many of these early verse texts are fragmentary, however, and their value is sometimes more historical than literary.

2   This account, given appropriate qualifications and nuances, remains the conventional view, but it has long been challenged, most recently by the archeologist Ewan Campbell, who rejects the theory of Irish immigration because material evidence of Irish contacts during the pertinent period is slight, and who posits a Gaelic-speaking population in Argyll from the Iron Age onwards (Campbell 2001).

3   See Fraser 2006.

4   See Broun 1994.

5   See Clancy & Crawford 2001; Woolf 2001, 34, 41–5; Smyth 1989, 175–238.

6   Nicolaisen 2001, 175.

7   See Barrow 1980; Clancy & Crawford 2001, 81–90.

8   See Murison 1974; MacInnes 1992, 105–6.

9   Barrow 1973, 362.

10   See, e.g., Bannerman 1989; Barrow 1989; Broun 1998; Clancy 2000; Neville 2005; Taylor 1994.

11   See Grant 1991, 200–02.

12   This translation of this much-quoted passage is taken from Grant 1994, 76–7, and Barrow 1980, 146, rather than Felix Skene's version (accompanying his brother William's 1871 edition (p. 38 [Book II, ch. 9]), whose accuracy has been questioned.

13   See Boardman 2005a, 139–40.

14   See Nicholson 1968; Cowan 1997–8.

15   See Broun 1999.

16   See McLeod 2002b.

17   See Bannerman 1977a and 1977b; Thomson 1968b.

18   See MacCoinnich 2002; Macinnes 1993.

19   See Dawson 1994, 2002.

20   Published in W. M. Mackenzie 1932, 5–20 (§ 44, ll. 345–52).

21   Ó Baoill 1979, poem 17 (ll. 1192–3). The irregular spelling here reflects the form in which the poem was originally published in 1707.

22   Simmons 1998, 192 (letter 19). For a discussion, see MacInnes 1981, 1989.

23   See MacInnes 1981, 1989; see also MacCoinnich 2002.

24   See McLeod 2004, 126–8, 136–7.

25   See McLeod 1999.

26   See MacInnes 1989, 92–3; McLeod 2003.

27   On Highland–Lowland interaction generally, see Gillies 1979.

28 Craigie 1944, I, 71.
29 See Gordon 1958.
30 Grant and Cheape 1987, 14.
31 See Stewart 2004; Ternes 2006.
32 MacDonald 1984, 277.
33 See Cameron 1894, II, 154–5.
34 See Herbert 1999; see also Broun 1997, 8–9.
35 See Broun 1999.
36 See McLeod 2004, 40–54; Kingston, 2003; Duffy, forthcoming.
37 See McLeod 2004.
38 Outwith Scotland, and indeed sometimes within Scotland, the term 'Irish' tends to be more frequently used than 'Gaelic' in this context. This usage reflects the Hibernocentric viewpoint of Irish scholars; even so, it is the case that the overwhelming majority of early texts are of Irish rather than Scottish provenance.
39 See Jackson 1951; Gillies 1994b; Ó Buachalla 2002.
40 See Gillies 2006a, 58; Robinson and Ó Maolalaigh 2006, 154.
41 Walsh 1948, I, 72–73; O'Donovan 1856, III, 366 [s.a. 1258]. The annal reference may possibly indicate that a distinct 'Scottish Gaelic' was already perceived in the thirteenth century, but it certainly shows an awareness of such a distinction at the time of writing.
42 Ó Murchú 1988: 246.
43 Ó Cuív 1978.
44 Martin 1934, 177. Note, however, that some complaints concerning the supposed difficulty of understanding bardic verse might be considered 'tendentious or malicious' (Gillies 1988, 255).
45 Ó Baoill 1988; Watson 1937, xxii–xxxii; Thomson 1970, xi–lix.
46 Robinson and Ó Maolalaigh 2006, 154; Ó Maolalaigh forthcoming. This interpretation challenges the conclusion of Kenneth Jackson, principal exponent of the 'Common Gaelic' theory: see Jackson 1972.
47 Notable here are two important historical texts from the eleventh century, the so-called 'Duan Albanach' ('Scottish poem') and 'Prophecy of Berchán', both versified king-lists. See Jackson 1956, 1957; Zumbuhl 2006; Hudson 1996.
48 See Munro and Munro 1986; the solitary Gaelic charter is on pp. 21–3.
49 Examples include two enigmatic couplets on Clann MhicLeòid and a quatrain of an elegy for Ùisdean Friseal of Lovat (†1576) in the Fraser history written by Rev. James Fraser of Wardlaw; lines attributed to the late fifteenth century Irish harper Art (or Diarmaid) Ó Cairbre (see poem 37) in Ùisdean MacDhomhnaill's history of the MacDhomhnaills; a quatrain on the death of Domhnall Gruamach MacDhomhnaill of Sleat (†1537) in the Rev. John MacRa's 'Genealogy of the MacRas'; and an English summary of the final verse of an elegy on Raghnall mac Mhaoil Coluim († c. 1447/8) in Alexander Campbell's account of the

Caimbeuls of Craignish (see Fraser 1905, 40–41, 175; MacPhail 1914, I, 52, 216; Scottish History Society 1926, 228; see generally MacGregor 2002).

50   Black 1994, 127.
51   See Bannerman 1983, 1986; Thomson 1968b.
52   For this text, see Higgitt 2000, 336–45.
53   See Black 1994; Meek 1996; MacGregor 2006a.
54   See Gillies 2006b.
55   See Mac Cana 2004.
56   In later vernacular Scottish Gaelic the term *file* effectively became conflated with that of *bard*, as a somewhat literary word for 'poet'. The latter is now written with an accent (*bàrd*) in Scottish Gaelic, with *filidh* (which has become a rare word) now the singular form in Scottish Gaelic, with *filidhean* used in the plural. Conversely, *file* (plural *fili*) is now the unmarked word for 'poet' in Irish.
57   See generally Bergin 1970, 3–22.
58   See Gillies 1988, 254; Breatnach 1983.
59   Knott 1922, I, li; see also Breatnach 1997.
60   Gillies 1986, 108.
61   Gillies 1986, 111.
62   NLS MS 72.2.2, f. 3a; translation based on Gillies 1986, 111.
63   See MacInnes 1976–78; Black 2001, xix–xxvi. For a schematic chart of the vernacular panegyric code, see Black 2001, 525–7.
64   Knott 1926, I, li–lxiv.
65   See Simms 1987, 70–71.
66   Knott 1957, 4–5.
67   For more detailed discussion and exemplification of the bardic metres, see Knott 1957 and Ní Dhomhnaill 1975.
68   See Matheson 1970, 149–50. William Gillies (1988: 250) points out that given the 'arythmical' form and complex 'word-music' of bardic verse, instrumental accompaniment 'cannot have been intrusive during the recital of the verses'.
69   Reported by Rev. Iain Friseal of Tiree to the antiquarian Edward Lhuyd in 1699 (Campbell & Thomson 1963, 34). Note that there is no indication that there was any overlap in Ireland between the role of the *bard* and the *reacaire*.
70   On the distribution of *dán díreach* in Scotland and the main poetic families, see McLeod 2004, 63–78; see also Mac Cana 2004.
71   See Gillies 1977; Ó Tuama 1988, 1990.
72   See MacInnes 1976.
73   See Thomson 1983, 124–8; 2000, 97.
74   See Ó Baoill 1994, 28; 2003.
75   For a detailed discussion of the metrics of this song, see Ó Baoill 1998, 89–91.
76   Thomson 2000, 114.
77   See Gillies 2005.

RO-RÀDH

Is dòcha nach eil luchd-leughaidh na Gàidhlig ro eòlach air a' mhòr-chuid den bhàrdachd a tha air a cruinneachadh anns an duanaire seo. Ghleidheadh na h-òrain a gheibhear anns an dàrna pàirt den leabhar tro na linntean ann am beul-aithris, agus tha cuid dhiubh gan seinn gu math tric fhathast; gu dearbh, a rèir tuigse mòran Ghàidheal tha iad am measg nan ulaidhean as luachmhoire ann an dualchas na Gàidhlig, agus tha iad ainmeil is iomraiteach air sgàth sin. Ach is dòcha nach eil sin fìor mu na dàin as sine a gheibhear anns a' chiad phàirt den chruinneachadh. Cha do mhair iad air bilean an t-sluaigh, agus cha do ghleidheadh iad anns an aon dòigh; is dòcha nach eil cliù aca ach am measg sgoilearan na Gàidhlig agus cuid de luchd-eachdraidh. Tha diofar bunaiteach eadar a' mhòr-chuid de na dàin anns a' chiad phàirt den leabhar (àireamhan 1–64) air an dàrna làimh agus dàin 65–85 air an làimh eile; is e sin gur e a' Ghàidhlig dhùthchasach Albann-ach a chleachdadh anns an dàrna buidheann agus seòrsachan nas tràithe de Ghàidhlig anns a' chiad bhuidheann (a' Ghàidhlig Mheadhanach agus a' Ghàidhlig Chlasaigeach). Ged nach ionnan Gàidhlig a' Chlèirich Bhig (ùghdar dàin 67) agus Gàidhlig an latha an-diugh, gheibh luchd-leughaidh (agus luchd-èisteachd) Gàidhlig an latha an-diugh grèim air cainnt dhàn 65–85 gun mòran duilgheadais: tha iad, anns an t-seagh sin co-dhiù, 'so-ruigsinneach', rud nach eil daonnan fìor mu bhàrdachd nam Meadhan Aoisean. (Ach thoiribh an aire gun do ghleidheadh cuid de dh'òrain àrsaidh, leithid dàn 57 (agus ann an dòigh eile, dàin 50–52), ann am beul-aithris, agus is dòcha gun do rinneadh tomhas de dh'ùrachadh air cànan nan òran sin thairis air na linntean).

Ach tha sinn gu mòr an dòchas gun tèid luchd na Gàidhlig an sàs anns na teacsaichean as sine, ged is cinnteach gu bheil cainnt nan dàn sin duilich agus doilleir aig amannan. Gu dearbh, air uairean tha a' bhàrdachd fhèin, gu h-àraidh bàrdachd nam filidhean (bàird fhoghlaimte nam Meadhan Aoisean), toinnte, casta agus iomadh-fhillte. Bidh na h-eadar-theangachaidhean feumail an lùib seo, a' tabhann nàdar de dh'àradh, ged nach eil iad daonnan litireil (mar a mhìnichear gu h-ìosal anns an 'Note on Translation'). Tron oidhirp sin, tha sinn an dòchas, gheibh an leughadair Gàidhlig tuigse nas fheàrr air doimhneachd agus leantainneachd litreachas agus dualchas na Gàidhlig.

Wilson McLeod
Meg Bateman
An Giblean 2007

xlix

A NOTE ON TRANSLATION

Every translator well knows the tricky compromises translation demands regarding rhythm, rhyme, prosody, meaning and register. They cannot all be replicated in equal measure from the original. What is claimed for one requires sacrifices in another.

This series of early Gaelic verse from Scotland has opted for translations in verse rather than prose. The sentence structure of prose translations would demand extra words, in particular finite verbs, which are very often absent in the original. In its less strict syntax, verse allows for a closer approximation to the prosodic leanness of much Gaelic poetry.

In the following translations, I have given pre-eminence to rhythm. I have aimed to mimic the stress pattern at the end of each line, depending on whether the final stress falls on the last, second last or third last syllable. The choice of metre had more than technical considerations; it coloured the whole poem. The monosyllabic endings of Muireadhach Albanach's elegy to his wife (poem 27) give a sort of bare lapidary effect compared, for example, to the sinuous possibilities of the *deibhidhe* metres common to satire, the disyllabic endings common to descriptive verse, or the conversational informality of *ae freislighe* in Fionnlagh Mac an Aba's poem (61).

Perhaps some readers will query the importance I attach to rhythm in the translation of poetry that was syllabic in structure rather than stressed. Beyond ensuring that lines are neither too long nor too short, I have ignored exact syllabic count because I believe the ear in English to be largely deaf to its significance. Moreover, as Gaelic has always been a heavily stressed language, stress patterns inevitably form a counterpoint even to syllabic metres.

In achieving a loyalty to rhythm, I have occasionally had to alter the order of lines or words. However, I have tried to keep this to a minimum, as I am conscious of the usefulness of a translation as a crib to the original. It is clear that the poets too required to use chevilles, inversions and no end of kennings to allow them to manoeuvre within the strictures of the metre. I have made only the rare attempt in the translations to echo the complex patterns of internal rhyme, alliteration and consonance.

I must acknowledge the extensive use I made of other translations myself. I would have found my work extremely hard, if not impossible, without them.

Meg Bateman
April 2007

1

ACKNOWLEDGEMENTS

In compiling this volume, we have received assistance and guidance on a wide range of historical and editorial queries, and we would like to express our gratitude to Steve Boardman, Abigail Burnyeat, William Gillies, Anja Gunderloch, Martin MacGregor, Nancy McGuire, Donald Meek, Michael Newton and Domhnall Uilleam Stiùbhart. Our principal debt, however, is to Professor Colm Ó Baoill, who generously answered innumerable queries throughout the process. Any mistakes we have incurred are our own.

We are also grateful to our respective institutions (the University of Aberdeen and the University of the Highlands and Islands Millennium Project; the University of Edinburgh) in relation to periods of research leave which were invaluable in allowing us to take this work forward.

We would like to thank the following copyright holders for generously granting us permission to use their editions of texts: Hugh Cheape (in his capacity as literary executor for the late John Lorne Campbell), Thomas Owen Clancy, William Gillies, Máire Herbert, Ian MacDonald, Caoimhín Mac Giolla Léith, Donald Meek, Michael Newton, Colm Ó Baoill, Pádraig Ó Macháin and Derick Thomson.

Completion of this book has been considerably delayed and the forbearance of Hugh Andrew of Birlinn is greatly appreciated.

ABBREVIATIONS

CMCS	Cambrian/Cambridge Medieval Celtic Studies
CUP	Cambridge University Press
CW	Carmichael-Watson Collection, Edinburgh University Library
DIAS	Dublin Institute for Advanced Studies
EUP	Edinburgh University Press
ITS	Irish Texts Society
NLS	National Library of Scotland
OUP	Oxford University Press
RIA	Royal Irish Academy
SGS	Scottish Gaelic Studies
SGTS	Scottish Gaelic Texts Society
SHR	Scottish Historical Review
SHS	Scottish History Society
SS	Scottish Studies
TGSI	Transactions of the Gaelic Society of Inverness

The Poems

The Learned Tradition

Religion

1. Tiugraind Beccáin do Cholum Cille

Beccán mac Luigdech

Rinn Colum Cille eilthireachd gu saor-thoileach a dh'Alba ann an 563 mar pheanas airson rudeigin ceàrr a rinn e. Chan eil e cinnteach dè bha ann: an e gun do rinn e lethbhreac de shaltair gun chead, no gum b' esan a dh'adhbhraich bàs na h-uiread sa bhatail a dh'èirich air sgàth seo, no gun do rinn e droch dhìoladh air a' cheangal a bha aige ri Dia le bhith ag ùrnaigh airson an taoibh aige fhèin? Co-dhiù, bha buaidh mhòr aige air Crìosdaidheachd ann an 'Alba', 's e sin, Breatainn, mar thoradh air fhuil rìoghail agus a chumhachd spioradail, agus stèidhich e lìonradh de mhanachainnean an sin.

The na 'rannan deireannach' an seo a' sealltainn mar a bha cliù an naoimh air a stèidheachadh beagan dheicheadan as dèidh a bhàis am measg na clèire. Tha am bàrd, Beccán mac Luigdech, a' moladh Choluim Chille air sgàth a chruadail, a fhoghlaim agus a shinnsearachd rìoghail, agus air sgàth na rinn e ann an stèidheachadh nam manachainn. Coltach ri Colum Cille, bhuineadh Beccán do mheur de Chloinn Uí Néill, an teaghlach a bu chudromaiche an Èirinn, agus tha e coltach gun robh e an sàs ann an riaghladh manachainn Idhe anns na 630an mus deach e na dhìthreabhach do Rùm, far an do chaochail e ann an 677, is e an sàs ann am *peregrinatio pro Christo* no 'martre bán'. Thòisich an cleachdadh seo anns na manachainnean Èiphiteach, ach anns an Roinn Eòrpa, ghabh eilthireachd sa chuan àite eilthireachd anns an fhàsach.

Tha oidhirp ga dèanamh anns an eadar-theangachadh pàtranan uaim an dàin a leantail is i a' nochdadh taobh a-staigh nan sreathan, thairis air na *caesurae* agus eadar na sreathan agus na rannan.

To-fed andes   i ndáil fíadat   findáil caingel;
Columb Cille — cétaib landa   lethan caindel.

Caíni rissi: ríge la Día   i ndeüd retho,
ríge n-úasal   ó ro-cinni   céim mo betho.

The Last Verses of Beccán to Colum Cille

Colum Cille took voluntary exile to Iona in 563 as a penance for the wrongdoings that had led to his excommunication. These variously are attributed to his copying of a psalter without permission, the deaths he caused in the ensuing battle or his abuse of his connection with God in praying for the victory of his own side. Through his spiritual and diplomatic prowess he had a strong impact on Christianity in 'Alba', that is Britain, and established a network of monasteries there.

These 'last verses', composed some decades after Colum Cille's death in 597, show the consolidation of the saint's cult among later clerics. The poet, Beccán mac Luigdech, praises Colum Cille for his asceticism, learning and royal blood, and for establishing the monastic life. He also makes constant comparison between Colum Cille and Christ (as did the saint's biographer, Adomnán), speaking of the saint as a light and as peace-maker between God and man, and desiring to be at Colum Cille's right hand in heaven. The image of Colum as an oak tree and the place accorded to poetry may be derived from pagan learning. The poet – like Colum Cille, a member of the powerful Uí Néill kindred in Ireland, albeit a different branch – appears to have been involved in the administration of Colum Cille's monastery in Iona during the 630s and then to have become a hermit on the isle of Rum, where he died in 677, thus fulfilling the monastic ideal of *peregrinatio pro Christo* or 'white martyrdom'. The practice of taking voluntary exile had its roots in Egyptian monasticism, but in European monasticism, withdrawal into the desert is replaced by withdrawal to the sea.

This translation echoes the alliteration of the original over the caesuras, within the line and between lines and verses.

He brings northwards   nearing the Godhead   gathered bright chancels,
Colum Cille,   cells for hundreds,   haloed candle.

Cherished tidings: truth's kingdom   completing my lifetime,
a lofty kingdom,   for He laid out   my life's pathway.

Brississ tóla,   to-bert co crú   cruü glinne
gabaiss foraib   findaib coraib   Columb Cille.

Caindel Connacht,   caindel Alban,   amrae fíadat
fichtib curach   cechaing tríchait   troich-chét cíabat.   8

Cechaing tonnaig,   tresaig magain,   mongaig, rónaig,
roluind, mbedcaig,   mbruichrich, mbarrfind,   faílid, mbrónaig.

Birt búaid n-eccnai   hi cúairt Éirenn   combo hardu,
amrae n-anmae,   ailtir Lethae,   líntair Albu.

Amrae tuire,   teöir lemnacht,   lethnaib coraib,
Columb Cille,   comland gnátho   gnóü foraib.

For muir gáirech,   gairt in ruirich   follnar mílib,
follnar mag ós mruigib réidib,   rígaib, tírib.   16

Trínóit hi seilb   siächt cobluth — caín con-úalath —
úasal la Día,   díambo forderc   fesccur mbúarach.

Búachail manach,   medam cléirech,   caissiu rétaib
rígdaib sondaib,   sonaib tedmann,   tríchtaib cétaib.

Columb Cille,   caindel toídes   teöir rechtae,
rith hi ráith tuir   to-réd midnocht   migne Ercae.

Aiéir tinach,   tingair níulu   nime dogair,
dín mo anmae,   dún mo uäd,   hauë Conail.   24

Cloth co mbúadaib,   ba cáin bethu.   Ba bárc moíne,
ba muir n-eccnai,   hauë Conail,   cotsid doíne.

Ba dair nduillech,   ba dín anmae,   ba hall nglinne,
ba grían manach,   ba már coimdiu,   Columb Cille.

Ba cóem la Día,   díambo hadbae   ail fri roluind,
ropo dorair,   dú forriä   imdae Coluimb.

Colainn crochsus,   scuirsius for foill   finda tóeba,
to-gó dánu,   dénis lecca,   lécciss cróeba.   32

Passions he conquered,   cast asunder   sealed prisons;
over-powered them   with pure habits,   he, Colum Cille.

Connacht's candle,   candle of Britain,   blazing ruler,
rowed in currachs   with a company of pilgrims   past the sea's tresses.

Through the billowing   bellicose margins,   mane-like, seal-rich,
savage, skittish,   seething, white-crested,   welcoming, weeping.

Wisdom's upholder   all over Ireland,   exalted he was;
wondrous his title,   tended is Brittany,   Britain is sated.

Supporting column,   contemplation's milk,   mettlesome customs,
Colum Cille,   consummate practice,   brighter than baubles.

On the boisterous ocean   he implored the Ruler   who rules thousands,
who rules heaven   above smooth moorlands,   monarchs and countries.

In the Trinity's safe-keeping   he sought a currach – courageous his leaving –
aloft with the Father,   ever watched by him,   night and morning.

Monks' shepherd,   mediator of clerics,   keener than any object,
than entries of monarchs,   than moans of sickness,   than serried champions.

Colum Cille,   candle illuminating   legal texts;
the hero's racecourse   ran through the midnight   of Erc's region.

The air's make-peace,   he mollifies the storm-clouds   of surly heaven;
haven of my soul,   safeguard of my creativity,   Conal's descendant.

Declaimed for virtues,   his ways gentle;   galley of treasure,
tide of knowledge,   Conal's offspring,   everyone's counsel.

Crested oak-tree,   soul's fortress,   fast summit,
sun of clerics,   consummate chieftain,   Colum Cille.

Cherished by the deity,   his dwelling was against   an unforgiving cliff-face;
a challenge it was   to uncover the position   of the pallet of Colum.

He crucified his body,   abandoned forever   fair bodies;
bent on learning,   he lay on flagstones,   forsook padding.

Lécciss coilcthi, lécciss cotlud — caíniu bertaib —
brisiss bairnea, ba forfaílid feisib tercaib.

Techtaiss liubru, léicciss la slán selba aithri,
ar seirc léigind, lécciss coicthiu, lécciss caithri.

Lécciss cairptiu, carais noä námae guë,
gríandae loingsech, lécciss la séol seimann cluë.

Columb Cille, Columb boíë, Columb biäss,
Columb bithbéo — ní hé sin in snádud ciäss. 40

Columb canmae, co dáil n-ecco, íarum, riäm,
ríaraib imbaiss, ima-comairc cách fo-n-gniäm.

Guidiu márguidi macc do Eithne — is ferr moínib —
m'anam día deis dochum ríchid re ndomuin doínib.

Día fo-ruigni, rígdae écndairc, hiland lessaib,
la toil n-aingel, hauë treibe Conail cressaib.

Cernach dúbart Día do adrad, aidchib, laithib,
lámaib fáenaib, findaib gartaib, gnímaib maithib. 48

Maith boí hi corp, Columb Cille — cléirech nemdae —
imbed fedbach, fírían mbélmach, búadach tengae.

2. Má Ro-m-Thoiccthi Écc i ndhÍ

Gun urra (am beul Adomnáin)

Tha cliù Adomnáin, a bha mar aba Idhe bho 679 gu ruige a bhàs
ann an 704, stèidhichte gu ìre mhòir air an eachdraidh a sgrìobh
e air beatha Choluim Chille (*Vita Columbae*), ach rinn e obair
chudromach eile a thaobh sgoilearachd agus leasachadh na
h-Eaglais ann an Alba. Am measg nan euchdan sònraichte aige

He forsook bedding, forsook sleeping – sublime doings –
defeated angers, was ecstatic, had sparse mealtimes.

Manuscripts he owned, disowned completely claims of kinship:
in concern for learning he left off battles, abandoned castles.

He discarded chariots, chose currachs, challenger of error;
his exile was sun-like, by sail he released reputation's cables.

Colum Cille, Colum who was ever, Colum who will be,
eternal Colum, not he the safe conduct to cause keening.

Colum, we keep singing, stand behind, before us, until death's meeting,
him we are serving through poetry's injunction which invokes him.

Him I implore, Eithne's offspring – opulence beyond riches –
on his right to bring my soul into heaven's kingdom before any other's.

He wrought for the Ruler a royal requiem within church ramparts,
at the request of angels, Conal's household's heir in vestments

Victorious prayer: to praise the Deity, daily and nightly,
with hands in supplication, splendid alms-giving, and good actions.

Good his body, Colum Cille – cleric of heaven –
a husbandless multitude – melodious true one, tongue triumphant.

If in Iona I Should Demise

Adomnán, abbot of Iona from 679 until his death in 704, is best
remembered as the author of the *Vita Columbae* (*Life of Colum Cille*),
one of the great works of the early Gaelic church, but he was an
immensely important spiritual and scholarly figure in his own right.
Among his achievements is the famous *Cáin Adomnáin* (*Law of the*

bha sgrìobhadh *Cáin Adomnáin* ann an 697, oidhirp a chum dìon
nan neòdrach is nan neoichiontach – boireannaich gu h-àraidh –
ro ionnsaighean an lùib còmhstri no cogaidh.

Tha an dàn goirid seo, anns a bheil Eilean Idhe air a mholadh
mar an t-àite as fheàrr airson fois shìorraidh, air ainmeachadh air
Adomnáin anns a' chunntas *Betha Adamnáin*, a chaidh a
sgrìobhadh mu mheadhan an deicheamh linn.

Chaidh an aon smuain a chur an cèill le Colum Cille fhèin sa
bheannachadh dheireannach aige air a' mhanachainn, air aithris
ann am *Vita Columbae*: 'Huic loco quamlibet angusto et vili non
tantum Scotorum reges cum populís, sed etiam barbararum et
exterarum gentium regnatores . . . grandem et non mediocrem
conferent honorem'.

> Má ro-m-thoiccthi écc i ndhÍ,
> ba gabál di thrócari.
> Nícon fettar fo nimh glas
> fóttán bad fherr fri tiugbás.

3. Mór do Ingantu Do-Gní

Gun urra (am beul Adomnáin)

Tha na rannan seo cuideachd a' nochdadh ann am *Betha
Adamnáin* agus is dòcha gur e an t-aba fhèin a rinn iad. Tha iad
a' tighinn an dèidh earrann anns an eachdraidh anns a bheil
Adomnán a' toirt mìorbhail gu buil air corp Bhruide mhic Bili,
rìgh nan Cruithneach, a chaochail ann an 693, agus a chaidh a
thoirt do dh'Eilean Idhe airson a thìodhlachadh. An dèidh do
dh'Adomnán caithris a dhèanamh air corp Bhruide rè na
h-oidhche, thòisich an corp ri gluasad agus ri fosgladh a
shùilean. Nuair a chaidh a ràdh nach bu chòir duine a chur an
oifis an aba an dèidh Adomnáin mura robh comas aigesan na
mairbh ath-bheothachadh cuideachd, thug Adomnán beannach-
adh do Bhruide, a 'chaochail a-rithist'.

Innocents), promulgated in 697, which strove to protect all non-combatants – and especially women – from attack in the course of warfare.

This short poem is attributed to Adomnán in the mid-tenth-century *Betha Adamnáin* (*Life of Adomnán*), praising Iona as the finest place for eternal rest.

The same contrast between Iona's smallness and fame is made in Colum Cille's final blessing on the monastery, reported in *Vita Columbae*: 'This place, however small and mean, shall have bestowed on it no small but great honour by the kings and peoples of Ireland, and also by the rulers of even barbarous and foreign nations'.

<blockquote>
If in Iona I should demise
it would be a merciful goodbye:
I know under the blue sky
no better sod on which to die.
</blockquote>

Great the Wonders He Performs

These verses also appear in *Betha Adamnáin* and may possibly be the work of the abbot himself. They follow a passage in which the abbot was said to have performed a miracle upon the body of the Pictish king Bruide mac Bili, who died in 693, and was brought to Iona for burial. After Adomnán had watched over Bruide's body through the night, the corpse was said to stir and open its eyes. When it was suggested that no abbot should be appointed to succeed Adomnán unless he too could raise the dead, Adomnán gave a blessing for Bruide, who then 'died again'.

The epigrammatic thought of the second verse, contrasting

Tha stoidhle ghoirid na dàrna rainn, anns a bheil coimeas ga dhèanamh eadar lughad na ciste is meud na rìoghachd, cumanta ann am bàrdachd nam manachainnean aig an àm seo.

Mór do ingantu do-gní,
    in Rí génair ó Mairi:
écc do Bruide mac Bili,
    betha scuabán i mMaili.

Is annam,
    íar mbeith i rríge thuaithe:
ceppán cauë crín dara
    im mac ríg Ala Cluaithe. 8

4. Fil Súil nGlais

Gun urra (am beul Choluim Chille)

Tha an ceathramh seo, a rinneadh, a rèir coltais, anns an aonamh linn deug, air aon de ghrunn dhàn no rannan a chumadh anns na linntean an dèidh bàs Choluim Chille a tha air an cur 'am beul' an naoimh. A rèir dualchais chuir an naomh an rann seo an cèill agus e a' fàgail Èirinn agus a' tòiseachadh fhèin-fhògraidh ann an Eilean Idhe.

Ann am beul-aithris, bhite ag ràdh gun do chùm Colum Cille brat ciarta thairis air a shùilean gus nach briseadh e a mhionnan is e air tilleadh a dh'Èirinn gu Cruinneachadh Droma Ceat ann an 575.

Fil súil nglais
fégbas Érinn dar a hais;
    noco n-aceba íarmo-thá
    firu Érenn nách a mná.

the size of a coffin and a kingdom, is typical of Gaelic monastic poetry of this period.

> Great the wonders He performs,
>   the King who is born of Mary:
> death to Bruide mac Bile,
>   life to little sheaves in Mull.

> Strange,
>   after holding a kingship,
> that a hollow stump of oak
>   holds Dumbarton's king's son.

A Blue Eye Turns

One of many poems or fragments composed in the centuries after Colum Cille's death and phrased as if composed by the saint himself, this quatrain from the eleventh century is supposed to have been uttered as the saint prepared to leave Ireland for Iona. Here as elsewhere, the saint is depicted as plunging himself into deliberate exile.

The tradition developed that when Colum Cille returned to Ireland to the Convention of Drum Cett in 575 he wore a waxed bandage over his eyes so as not to break the conditions of his oath.

> A blue eye turns,
> watching Ireland fade behind,
>   never to see from thenceforth
>   Ireland's women nor her men.

5. Meallach Liom Bheith i n-Ucht Oiléin

Gun urra (am beul Choluim Chille)

Tha e coltach gun do rinneadh an dàn seo anns an dàrna linn deug; seo aon de ghrunn dhàn a rinneadh mun àm seo agus a chuireadh 'am beul' Choluim Chille.

Tha am far-ainm 'Cúl re hÉirinn' (sreath 24) cumanta gu leòr; tuigear gur e nàdar de dh'fhògradh a bha fa-near do Cholum Chille agus e a' fàgail Èirinn gu sìorraidh. A rèir dualchas Eilean Idhe, thog an naomh 'càrn cùl ri Èirinn' air tom anns an eilean, às nach fhaicte sealladh an iar-dheas idir.

Tha coltas nas tràithe air cuspair an dàin seo na tha air a' chànain a chleachdar ann. Mar as trice tha bàrdachd an linn Chlasaigich nas dubhaiche mun t-saoghal, a tha air fhaicinn mar ribe no co-dhiù mar chunnart a bheir an aire air falbh bho rudan spioradail. Ach tha an neach-labhairt an seo a' moladh beatha ann an uaigneas eilein mar shlighe gu Dia air trì adhbharan. Tha na h-eòin, na mucan-mara is sruth na mara a' taisbeanadh cho mìorbhaileach 's a tha an Cruthachadh; chì e mar a tha na tuinn gu nàdarrach a' seinn rin Athair; agus aithnichidh e làthaireachd Dhè sa Chruthaidheachd, chan ann a-mhàin mar an Cruthaidhear ach cuideachd mar an Riaghladair.

Meallach liom bheith i n-ucht oiléin
    ar beinn cairrge,
go bhfaicinn ann ar a meince
    féth na fairrge.

Go bhfaicinn a tonna troma
    ós lear luchair,
amhail chanaid ceól dá nAthair
    ar seól suthain.   8

Go bhfaicinn a trácht réidh rionnghlan
    (ní dál dubha);
go gcloisinn guth na n-éan n-iongnadh,
    seól go subha.

Delightful to Be on the Breast of an Island

This poem appears to date from the twelfth century and is one of a number of poems from this period placed 'in the mouth of' Colum Cille.

The nickname '*Cúl re hÉirinn*' (line 24) is used fairly frequently and reflects the notion that Colum Cille's departure for Scotland represented severance and exile, turning his back on his native Ireland forever. In Iona tradition, the saint is said to have built a '*càrn cùl ri Èirinn*' ('cairn with the back to Ireland') on a hillock on the island, from which the view to southwest – towards Ireland – was completely obscured.

The language of this poem suggests a later date than the theme, which expresses the monastic ideal of island seclusion. Most religious poetry of the classical period was much less optimistic about the world, regarding it as a trap and a distraction from the spiritual (see, for example, poem 11). The speaker finds the island conducive to godliness in three ways: the birds, whales, and tides awaken a sense of awe in him at the wonders of creation; the waves singing to their Father bear witness to nature praising its Maker; and the rhythms of nature give him a sense of God's immanence in the world, not only as Creator, but also the Governor 'who maintains all'.

> Delightful it would be on the breast of an island
>   on a rocky clifftop,
> from there I could often ponder
>   the calm of the ocean.
>
> I'd see her heavy billows
>   on glittering surface,
> as they sang thus to their Father
>   in eternal surging.
>
> I'd see her smooth clean bays and beaches
>   (no mournful meeting);
> I'd hear the call of wondrous seabirds,
>   a cry of gladness.

Go gcloisinn torm na dtonn dtana
    ris na cairrge;
go gcloisinn nuall re taobh reilge,
    fuam na fairrge.   16

Go bhfaicinn a healta ána
    ós lear lionnmhar;
go bhfaicinn a míola mára,
    mó gach n-iongnadh.

Go bhfaicinn a tráigh 's a tuile
    ina réimim;
go madh é m'ainm, rún no ráidhim,
    'Cúl re hÉirinn'.   24

Go n-am-tíosadh congain cridhe
    agá féaghadh;
go ro chaoininn m' ulca ile, —
    annsa a réaladh.

Go ro bheannachainn an Coimdhe
    con-ig uile,
neamh go muintir gráidh go ngloine,
    tír, tráigh, tuile.   32

Go ro sgrúdainn aon na leabhar,
    maith dom anmain;
seal ar sléachtain ar neamh n-ionmhain,
    seal ar salmaibh.

Seal ag buain duilisg do charraig,
    seal ar aclaidh,
seal ag tabhairt bhídh do bhochtaibh,
    seal i gcarcair.   40

Seal ag sgrúdain flatha nimhe,
    naomhdha an ceannach;
seal ar saothar ná badh forrach;
    ro badh meallach!

I'd hear the thunder of the breakers
    against the headlands,
I'd hear a clamour beside the graveyard,
    the sound of the ocean.

I'd see her noble birdflocks
    on the teeming ocean;
I'd see her whales, the greatest
    of all wonders.

I'd see her ebbing and flooding
    in their order;
may my name be — I tell a secret —
    'Back towards Ireland'.

My heart would be succoured
    by gazing at it,
I'd lament my every evil —
    hard to broadcast.

I would bless the Lord Almighty
    who maintains all:
heaven with its pure, loving orders,
    land, shore and water.

On some book I would ponder,
    for the soul beneficial;
a while beseeching beloved heaven,
    a while psalm-singing.

A while plucking dulse from the skerries,
    a while fishing,
a while giving food to the needy,
    a while in a rock-cell.

A while contemplating the prince of Heaven,
    holy the purchase;
a while toiling, nothing too taxing;
    it would be delightful.

6. Éistidh Riomsa, a Mhuire Mhór

Muireadhach Albanach Ó Dálaigh

Chaidh an dàn dùrachdach seo don Òigh Muire a ghleidheadh ann an Leabhar Deadhan Lios Mòr, a chaidh a sgrìobhadh mu thrì ceud bliadhna an dèidh bàs an ùghdair, am file ro-ainmeil Muireadhach Albanach Ó Dálaigh, a bhuineadh do Lios an Doill ann an Contae Shligigh ann an iar-thuath na h-Èireann.

A rèir cunntas dualchasach (a chaidh a sgrìobhadh leis na 'Ceithir Maighstirean' – ceathrar shagartan/sgoilearan Èireannach fo stiùir Mhicheáil Uí Chléirigh – anns na 1630an), b'èiginn do Mhuireadhach teicheadh à Èirinn ann an 1213 an dèidh dha fear Fiond Ua Brolcháin, maor a neach-taice, Domhnall Ó Domhnaill, a mharbhadh le tuagh. Ann an sùilean an fhile cha robh ann an Ua Brolcháin ach sgalag, agus cha robh e den bheachd gum biodh marbhadh a leithid na adhbhar eas-aonta eadar e fhèin agus Ó Domhnaill. Ach chuir Ó Domhnaill feachd air tòir Mhuireadhaigh, gu Gaillimh, Tuathmhumhain agus Baile Àtha Cliath; cha b'urrainn dha tearmann fhaighinn ann an Èirinn idir, agus mu dheireadh fhuair e taic iarlan Leamhnachd (faic dàn 14).

Ged a ghabh Muireadhach am far-ainm 'Albanach' an dèidh greis, tha e coltach gu robh e ga mheasadh fhèin mar fhògarrach ann an Alba. Ann an dàin eile da chuid, tha e a' cur ìmpidh air Ó Domhnaill a thoirt air ais a dh'Èirinn air 'an céad long triallfas tar tuinn' agus a' cur an cèill an eagail nach bi duine sam bith an Èirinn ga chuimhneachadh no ga aithneachadh tuilleadh.

Is e fìor bheag de dh'fhiosrachadh deimhinne a tha againn air Muireadhach. Tha cuid teagmhach gu robh a leithid de dhuine ann an da-rìribh, ach tha e air aon de na filidh as ainmeile a tha ann, air sgàth cumhachd is brìgh a chuid bàrdachd.

Is cinnteach gum b'e duine cràbhaidh a bha ann am Muireadhach, oir ghabh e pàirt anns a' Chòigeamh Cogadh Croise ann an 1218 (na thaistealach seach na shaighdear). Chaidh am file ainmeil Giolla Brighde Albanach maille ris, agus tha grunn dhàn a rinn iad ri linn a' chogaidh croise air tighinn a-nuas thugainn.

O Great Mary, Listen to Me

This heartfelt poem to the Virgin Mary is preserved only in the Book of the Dean of Lismore, which was written some three centuries after the death of its author, the famous thirteenth-century Sligo poet Muireadhach Albanach Ó Dálaigh.

According to the traditional (but non-contemporaneous) account, Muireadhach was forced to flee Ireland for Scotland in the year 1213 after murdering his patron Domhnall Ó Domhnaill's tax collector with an axe. The poet appears to have viewed the attempted tax collection as a gross impertinence and the collector's murder as a triviality, but he badly miscalculated Ó Domhnaill's reaction. After failing to find sanctuary in Ireland, Muireadhach ended up in service to the earls of Lennox, who had their base at Balloch at the south end of Loch Lomond (see poem 14).

Although Muireadhach came to take the byname 'Albanach', he does not appear to have entirely enjoyed his time in Scotland, which seems to have been an exile for him. In one of his poems, he begs Ó Domhnaill to take him back to Ireland on the first boat he sends out; and in another, he worries that after fifteen years away in Scotland he would be entirely forgotten and unknown were he to return to Ireland.

Muireadhach is a shadowy figure of whom little is known for certain. His actual existence as a genuine historical figure has been questioned, but the drama of the traditional story of his life, and the power and range of his surviving poetry, make him perhaps the best-known of all the bardic poets.

Muireadhach's religious conviction is also demonstrated by his participation in the Fifth Crusade, apparently as a pilgrim rather than a combatant, in 1218. His fellow poet Giolla Brighde Albanach joined him in the journey, and several of their poems relating to the crusade have survived.

In this poem Mary is the powerful queen of heaven who has it in her power to grant her kinsman entry to her ale-feast. Her influence with Christ may be sufficient to turn Him from wrath to mercy. As *theotokos*, the bearer of God, her womb is admired as being like the belly of a trout; she is an apple, a royal tree cleft

Anns an dàn seo tha Muire na banrigh air nèamh is an cumhachd aice cead-inntrigidh a thoirt dhan luchd-dàimh aice. Tha de bhuaidh aice fearg Ìosa a thionndadh gu tròcair. Mar an tè a ghiùlain Ìosa na broinn, tha i air a samhlachadh ri breac, ri ubhal, ri stoc craoibhe air a roinn fo thrì, ri crèadh anns a bheil uinge de dh'òr. Tha i na tinne ann an slabhraidh ar slànachaidh, seach gu robh i cho glan 's gun deach am Facal na fheòil innte. Tha i fiù 's na Co-Shlànaighear, aon am measg Cheathrar; tha ceangal ga dhèanamh eadar am math a rinn Muire agus an cron a rinn Eubha. Nochdaidh tòimhseachan Augustain, mar a bha Muire na bean aig a mac agus na màthair aig a h-athair, gus toirt air an inntinn gabhail tro chreideamh ri rud nach tuigear tro reusan. Buinidh tuairisgeul a bòidhchid – a falt, na buill fhada – do dhualchas Gàidhlig a' ghaoil, ach cha threòraich an gaol seo gu staid pheacach e. Aig an deireadh tha an suidheachadh cumanta ann am bàrdachd mholaidh ag èirigh – is am bàrd ag ainmeachadh a dhuais. An turas seo, chan e an t-òr a tha Muireadhach a' sireadh, ach cead-inntrigidh gu talla a mhnà-cinnidh, gu Nèamh.

Éistidh riomsa, a Mhuire mhór,
   do ghuidhe is liomsa badh lúdh;
do dhruim réd bhráthair ná bíodh,
   a Mháthair Ríogh duinn na ndúl.

Sgéal do mháthar meabhair liom,
   'na dheaghaidh atáthar treall,
inghean mhilis mhalach ndonn,
   trilis trom chladhach fá ceann.   8

Anna sein, seanmháthair Dé,
   óa gealbhráthair do ghein rí,
níor ghiall a meadhair do mhnaoi,
   gur fhaoi lé triar d'fhearaibh í.

Rug inghean gach dheighfhir dhíobh,
   geibhidh aca an fhinngheal úr,
teóra inghean a clann chaomh,
   slimgheal a dtaobh, cam a gcúl.   16

in three, clay in which rests an ingot of gold. Mary is a vital link
in the scheme of salvation in being so pure as to conceive the
Word made flesh. She is even seen as Co-Redemptrix, one of
Four Persons, the salvation allowed by Mary linked with the Fall
wrought by Eve. Augustine's paradox of Mary being the mother
of her Father and the spouse of her Son is used to tease the mind
to accept through faith what cannot be understood through
reason. The depiction of her beauty, especially the emphasis on
her hair, and long, slow limbs, accords entirely with the
standards of beauty of native Gaelic love poetry, but here the
love is different because it cannot lead to sin. The whole has
much of the rhetoric of the secular panegyric. The topos of a
poet praising his chief in return for hospitality is clearly
paralleled in the poet's expectation that Mary will pay him for
his poem with entry into her drinking hall. He does not want
gold, but Heaven.

This translation endeavours to reflect the monolithic
simplicity of the original. It should be read as 7–8 syllables per
line rather than with stress.

> O great Mary, listen to me,
>   praying to you should be my zeal;
> on your brother turn not your back,
>   Mother of the great King of all.
>
> Of your mother I recall a tale,
>   often recited for a spell,
> of a sweet-natured dark-browed girl,
>   thick rippling hair about her head.
>
> That was Anne, grandmother of God,
>   from her bright brother came a king,
> no woman knew a greater joy,
>   to three husbands she was wed.
>
> To each good man she bore a girl,
>   by them the fresh bright one begets
> her daughters three, her children mild,
>   slender their form, curling their hair.

Gorma a súile, suairc a ngné,
   a gcuairt nochar chuairt gan ghnaoi,
na sluaigh uile atá ar a dtí,
   trí mná agus Muire ar gach mnaoi.

Tugsad trí fir thoighe a dtriúr
   na trí Mhoire ó nimh na naomh,
gur thráchtmhall torrach an triar
   na gciabh ndrongach snátrom saor.   24

Rugsad trí maca na mná,
   aca roba lia 'sa lia;
(cá seisear mín doba mhó?)
   eisean roba só dhíbh Dia.

Máthair Iacóibh inghean díbh,
   sgiathdóigh ar gach n-imneadh fhuair,
bean díobh Muire máthair Eóin,
   sgeóil nár ghnáthaigh duine i nduain.   32

Tusa Muire Máthair Dé,
   duine níor ghnáthaigh do ghnaoi,
ríghbhile arna roinn ar thrí,
   Rí fírnimhe id bhroinn do bhaoi.

Mise ar bhar n-aithnibh ar-aon,
   id dhaighthigh agus id dhún,
a anam, a Mhuire mhór,
   a ór buidhe, a abhall úr.   40

A bhiadh, a éadach ar h'iocht,
   a chiabh ghéagach mar an ngort.
A Mháthair, a Shiúr, a Shearc,
   stiúr go ceart an bráthair bocht.

Bráthair dhamhsa do Mhac mór,
   a shlat mhallsa, a Mháthair shaor,
deaghbhráthair cóir ar bhar gcúl,
   seanmháthair úr róibh a-raon.   48

Blue their eyes, courteous their ways,
    visiting them was no trip without cheer,
all peoples try to seek them out,
    'Mary', the name of each of them.

Three husbands the three maids took,
    the three Maries from heaven of the saints,
slow-footed and pregnant grew the three
    of the noble clustering heavy-tressed hair.

Three sons the women bore,
    by them did their number grow;
where is a greater gentle six?
    Of them the youngest one was God.

One of the girls, the mother of James,
    found protection from every care;
another Mary was the mother of John,
    tidings no-one has mentioned in verse.

You, Mary, Mother of God,
    no-one ever knew your joy,
a royal tree divided in three,
    heaven's King was in your womb.

May I be guided by you both
    into your good house and your fort,
O great Mary, O my soul,
    O golden apple, apple-tree new-grown.

O food, O clothing to dispose,
    O tresses rippling as in a field,
O Mother, O Sister, O Love,
    your poor brother rightly steer.

A brother to me is your great Son,
    O noble Mother, O languid branch,
to shelter your good brother is right
    your gentle grandmother, recall.

Go ndearna m'ionghaire ar h'Fhear,
  a fhionnMhuire, a earla tiogh,
iomdha im chridhe crithir dhubh,
  mithigh dul dá nighe aniogh.

A Mháthair Dé, déanam síodh,
  ósa ghlédhonn gné do chiabh,
ciúnaigh h'fhearg, a Mhoire mhór,
  a ór dearg i gcoire chriadh.   56

Do nimh thánaig, a thaobh geal,
  a láraig, saor mar an sriobh.
Cá beag liom do dhúthchas damh,
  a chúlchas ghlan fhionn, ót Fhior?

A Thríonóid, a Mhuire mhín,
  tuile gach glóir acht bhar nglóir;
a Cheathrair, caistidh rém dhuain,
  ní geabhthair uaibh aisgidh óir.   64

A ÓghMhuire, a abhra dubh,
  a mhórmhuine, a ghardha geal,
tug, a cheann báidhe na mban,
  damh tar ceann mo náire neamh.

Do chloinn Dáibhíodh thú, a mhall mhór,
  gan chrann mar thú rébhar dtúr,
do chloinn Abhrán h'urla claon,
  gabhlán craobh gcumhra ar do chúl.   72

H'Fhear is do Mhac ar do mhuin,
  geal a ghlac is geal a righ,
t'Fhearathair réd thaobh as-toigh,
  ag soin taom d'ealathain t'Fhir.

Dalta iongnadh dot ucht bhán,
  agus dot fhult fhionnghlan úr,
do Mhac agus t'Fhear ar-aon,
  a shlat shaor gheal ar do ghlún.   80

Until I left my herding to your Spouse,
    O bright Mary, O luxuriant hair,
many a dark swamp was in my heart,
    it is time I went and washed it today.

Mother of God, let's make peace,
    O great Mary, calm your rage,
whose tresses are most rich in hue,
    red gold ingot in a vessel of clay.

From heaven His white side came,
    and thigh, noble like the burn.
How can I deem our shared inheritance small,
    O bright pure hair, through your Spouse?

O Trinity, O Mary mild,
    base is every glory but yours,
O Four Persons, hear my lay,
    not from you a gift of gold.

O Virgin Mary, O dark brow,
    O mighty bush, O garden gay,
of all women the most beloved,
    give me heaven despite my shame.

Of David's race you, great languid one,
    no tree like you when you are searched;
of Abraham's race your flowing locks,
    forking fragrant branches in your hair.

You carry your Spouse and your Son,
    bright is His hand and His arm,
your Spouse and Sire held close,
    manifest your Husband's art.

A miraculous child for your breast,
    for your pure fair fresh hair,
your Son and Father both
    on your knee, O noble bright branch.

Do bhábhair dias aobhdha ann
   dábhar gcaomhna ó ghlionn do ghlionn,
Mac malachdhubh dóidgheal donn,
   óigbhean trom anathlamh fhionn.

Do-ní sé casadh do chiabh,
   do dhuadh é ar t'asal dá dhíon,
do bhas, a ógMhuire úr,
   do chas cúl ródbhuidhe an Ríogh.   88

Tú do shíor doba shámh leis,
   is do chíogh bán ar a bhois,
an uair do nightheá an gcraoibh gcais,
   do lightheá an mbais gcaoimh 's an gcois.

Fraoch buidhe ar h'úrbharr mar ór,
   a Mhuire shúlmhall, a Shiúr,
cíoch geilmhín trom as do thaobh,
   Leinbhín saor donn agá diúl.   96

Mairg do oiligh h'earla glan,
   doiligh, ór ní dhearna cion;
munab ionnraic do bhrú, a Bhean,
   ní headh cnú ar fionnshlait i bhfiodh.

Easbach clann ladrann do luadh,
   a lagbharr fleasgach cam claon,
amharas dob olc an chiall ort,
   a chiabh chladhsholas chaomh.   104

Do bhrú aníos ba lomlán leat,
   mar bhíos a bhronnlár 'san bhrioc,
an Coimdhe 's gan loighe lat,
   Mac Moire do-roighne riot.

Acht tú féin, a Mhuire mhór,
   nochar léir do dhuine dhaor,
suaimhnighe ar fhear, a fholt fiar,
   nach biadh is bean olc ar-aon.   112

You were a lovely pair
   being protected from glen to glen,
a dark-browed, bright-handed Son
   and a young woman, stately, fair.

He would twist and curl your locks —
   your burden, on the ass in flight,
your hand, O young fresh Mary, curled
   the grooved yellow hair of the King.

With Him you were always mild,
   with your fair pap in his palm,
when you washed the fruitful branch
   you would kiss the soft foot and hand.

A golden blaze around your head,
   Mary, sister of the languid eyes,
from your side, a full smooth white breast,
   suckling it, a bright noble child.

Woe is the one who scorned your pure head,
   though hard, for you have done no wrong;
if your womb, Lady, is not chaste
   no nut on bright branch grows in the wood.

Vain to mention children of thieves,
   O soft curling ringleted locks;
you, it were a mistake to doubt,
   O shining gentle trenched head.

Your belly rises up full
   like the belly of the trout;
without ever lying with you
   the Lord made Mary's Son.

O great Mary, but for you
   it would not be clear for a man in bonds;
now it is easier for him, O waving hair,
   not to lie with an evil woman as one.

Cosmhail h'aonMhac réd chúl gcam,
   a shaorshlat an dá shúl chorr,
do ghlaca ag an Ghiolla shiong,
   is t'ionga fhionn data dhonn.

Coinnleach gormshúileach do ghruadh,
   abhra donnghlúineach 'gá dhíon,
geilghéagach leabhair do lámh,
   dán neimbréagach dleaghair dhíom.   120

Glan fallán buidhe do bharr,
   mar mhuine camán fád cheann,
glan do bhas chaoilmhéardha chorr,
   a chas donn shaoirdhéanmha sheang.

Ní dheachaidh d'ég h'aithghin mhná,
   do shaighthin — ní bréag — ní bhia,
níor bhlas beathaidh bean mar thú,
   a bhrú gheal i ndeachaidh Dia.   128

Tugaidh dhún leabaidh is lionn,
   a chúl ris nach teagaimh tonn,
an bhréigfhleadh ar nach bí ceann,
   nárab leam í a dhéidgheal donn.

Guidheadh go hán h'abhra dubh,
   ar ghrádh bhar n-anma, a ghrádh glan,
a Mhuire, ní héadmhar h'Fhear
   fád ghuidhe, a gheal déadghlan, damh.   136

A fholt buidhe cladhach cam,
   a Mhuire na malach seang,
ná leig do bhreith oile ionn,
   feith lionn do chroidhe fár gceann.

Déanam feis, a mheardha mhór,
   dod deis dealbhdha, taobh ré taobh,
gabh m'fhorthain deaghrann is duan
   uam, a ghealmhall shochraidh shaor.   144

O noble branch of the two round eyes,
    your only Son takes after your curling hair,
the slender Boy has your hands,
    and your bright red-coloured nails.

Glitters your blue-eyed face,
    thick lashes shade your cheek,
bright long-fingered your hand,
    I owe you a poem without lie.

Pure healthy yellow your hair,
    tendrils round your head like a bush,
pure your soft slim-fingered hand,
    O slender, strong well-fashioned foot.

There never died a woman like you,
    your equal will never be — no lie,
nor tasted life a woman like you,
    O pure womb where God entered in.

Give me a bed and ale,
    O head which earth corrupts not,
that false feast which has no end,
    O white tooth, not it my lot.

O pure love, for love of my soul,
    let your dark lashes plead,
O Mary, not jealous your Spouse,
    O white tooth, of your prayer for me.

O ringleted trenched yellow hair,
    O Mary of the slender brows,
leave me to no other judge,
    keep your heart's ale till I come.

Let me celebrate, O great swift one,
    by your side your shapely form;
accept my abundant verse and a lay,
    O noble languid bright joyous one.

Ná rabh bean acht tusa im thigh,
gomadh tusa bhus fhear air,
na mná fallsa ad-chiú 's na cruidh,
a bhfuil damhsa riú ná raibh.

Gan sbéis i gconaibh ná i gcrodh,
ná i sgoraibh, a ghéis ghlan,
easbhaidh chorn cáich is a gcon,
orm is a sgor mbláith 's a mban.   152

Tógaibh an malaigh nduibh dhúin,
is an aghaidh mar fhuil laoigh,
tógaibh, go ros faicinn féin,
an gcéibh ródaigh slaitfhinn saoir.

Tógaibh dhún an bonn 's an mbois,
agus an cúl donn go ndeis,
'gus an súil n-ógcruinn ngéir nglais,
réd chéibh dtais go bhfóbrainn feis.   160

Éistidh.

7. Ná Léig mo Mhealladh, a Mhuire

Maol Domhnaigh mac Mhaghnuis Mhuiligh

Seo dàn eile don Òigh Muire à Leabhar an Deadhain, a
rinneadh, is dòcha, anns a' chiad phàirt den t-siathamh linn
deug. A rèir na làmh-sgrìobhainn is e Maol Domhnaigh mac
Mhaghnuis Mhuiligh a rinn e, ball den teaghlach ainmeil bhàrd,
Clann Uí Mhuirgheasáin, a bha a' frithealadh Clann
MhicGill'Eathain Dhubhaird agus a-rithist Clann MhicLeòid na
Hearadh agus Dhùn Bheagain.

Bha an t-ainm Maol Domhnaigh cumanta anns an teaghlach
agus bha file eile air an robh an t-ainm seo air na h-Albannaich
mu dheireadh a rinn cuairt bhàrdail a dh'Èirinn. Chuir Maol
Domhnaigh ceithir bliadhna deug air fhichead seachad ann an

No woman but you in my house —
      over it may you be host;
to false women I see may I not cleave,
      nor to what is mine to own.

With no regard for hounds or herds
      or studs of horses, O white swan,
or others' drinking-horns and stock,
      without their women and their dogs.

Raise to me your dark brow
      and your face like calf's blood,
raise, so that I might see
      the noble bright combed locks.

Raise to me your foot and palm
      and the rich heavy glossy head
and the young round sharp blue eye
      so with your soft tresses I may feast.

O Mary, Protect Me from Deception

This poem to the Virgin Mary, also preserved in the Book of the
Dean of Lismore but probably dating from the early sixteenth
century, is attributed to the poet Maol Domhnaigh mac
Mhaghnuis Mhuiligh (Maol Domhnaigh son of Magnus of
Mull). Maol Domhnaigh appears to be the earliest-attested
member of the Ó Muirgheasáins, one of the great hereditary
bardic families of Gaelic Scotland, who first served the
MacGill'Eathains of Duart and later the MacLeòids of Harris
and Dunvegan.

  A later Maol Domhnaigh Ó Muirgheasáin, was one of the last
Scottish poets to sojourn in Ireland, said to have spent some
thirty-four years in Ireland before returning to Mull about 1642.

Èirinn, agus thill e do Mhuile mu 1642. A rèir a' bhàird ainmeil
à Contae Chiarraí, Piaras Feiritéar, thadhail Maol Domhnaigh
air a h-uile sgoil bàrdachd air feadh na h-Èireann, a' toirt eòlas
agus ealain asta: 'gadaidh bláith gach blátha a-muigh / don
bheich is meadh Maol Domhnaigh'.

Tha an dàn seo na ùrnaigh do Mhuire cho math ri bhith na
earalachadh do chàch a bhith a' sireadh a dìon. Tha an t-uirsgeul
ann an rannan 10–21 a' dearbhadh cho èifeachdach 's a tha i, leis
mar a spìon i peacach à Ifrinn gus cothrom eile a thoirt dha air
an t-saoghal. (Tha na h-uirsgeulan seo cumanta anns a'
bhàrdachd chlasaigich agus gu dearbh ann an litreachas Eòrpach
nam Meadhan Aoisean anns an fharsaingeachd).

Tha rannan 6–9 a' mìneachadh mar a shàbhaileas Muire a
luchd-dàimh a chionn 's gu bheil i cho faisg air Dia. Chan eil
teansa againn idir ann an cùirt lagha a chionn 's nach urrainn
dhuinn *éiric* (no luach fala) Ìosa a phàigheadh, ach a rèir seann
laghannan nan Gàidheal, thèid aig Muire air ar fiachan a chur
mu choinneimh na tha aicese air Ìosa as dèidh dhi a ghiùlan agus
altram. Tha ar piuthar mar sin comasach air fiachan na treubha
a phàigheadh.

Ná léig mo mhealladh, a Mhuire,
    a mháthair Ríogh, déanaidh dáil;
ní fhuil mo chroidhe gan cheannsa,
    cuir, a Mhoire, leamsa láimh.

Ar mo théarma má tá fuireach
    ní fada fós bhias gan teacht;
sul tí mo ré ar iúl éagcóir
    stiúr mé i gcéadóir tréd cheacht.   8

Teach Ifrinn, árus na bpeacthach,
    pian 'na measc ní méanair scéal;
fear an tighe ar tí mo mheallaidh —
    bí im chridhe is beannaigh mo bhéal.

Mé ort ag iarraidh mo mhúinte,
    a mháthair Ríogh, a ghruaidh mar ghrís [   ]   14

According to a contemporary Irish poem, the poet visited all the famous bardic schools from one end of the country to the other, 'like a bee stealing honey from every flower'.

This poem serves both as a prayer to the Virgin and an exhortation to others to seek out her protection whose efficacy is demonstrated in the *uirscéal* or narrative apologue (in stanzas 10–21) of her snatching a sinner from hell in order to give him a second chance to redeem himself. (Such *uirscéalta* are common in medieval Gaelic verse and indeed in many other medieval European literatures; this particular story is not a common one, but it is unlikely to be of purely Gaelic origin).

The poem is based on the assumption, that, while in terms of justice, mankind's case is hopeless, in terms of our connections with our sister Mary we can be saved. The construction is probably based on early Irish law, where the kin-group as a whole was responsible for the crimes of its individual members. By this account, the blood-money we owe Christ for the Crucifixion can be set against the debt Christ owes His mother for bearing and nursing Him. In this poem, we do not stand a chance in a court of justice, but Mary will able to use her influence as a woman to divert justice and so save her kinsfolk.

O Mary, protect me from deception,
    Mother of the King, come to my aid;
my heart is not without tameness,
    Mary, steady me with your hand.

If my life is to be extended,
    it won't be long till it comes to an end;
before my life takes the path of injustice,
    through your teaching show me the way.

The House of hell, the house of sinners,
    the torment among them is no pleasant tale;
the lord of that house is trying to deceive me —
    reside in my heart and bless my lips.

Mary, I'm asking you to teach me,
    O Mother of the King, O cheek like embers [   ]

Is eagal liom lá na hagra,
   a inghean Anna an fhoilt tais;
i n-aghaidh Dé ní fhoil aighneas,
   goir mé óm aimhleas ar m'ais.

Ná léig ceart do chor fána anmain,
   abair nach cóir is cóir lat;
ó tá fearg Dhé ris gach duine,
   ná hearb mé, a Mhuire, réd Mhac.   24

Tagra cáich gan chead a mháthar
   do Mhac Mhuire gá fearr (geis)?
Do-ní glan duine ar n-a dhamnadh
   dá rabh Muire ag labhradh leis.

Is í is caisléan do chloinn Éabha
   ar fheirg Íosa i n-uair an Bhráith,
a mháthair is í ar n-adhbha,
   is í ar láthair chabhra cáich.   32

Biaidh sí ar ar leath Lá na Coinne
   gar gcosnamh go cian ní bhia —
ar sleagh cé do bhí 'na bhánucht —
   bean do-ní dánucht ar Dhia!

Taom dána, dleaghair a chumhdach,
   fan cóir creideamh dá cígh cáidh
is aithnid damh ón Óigh uasail;
   cóir a char i gcluasaibh cáigh.   40

Fear roimhe agá raibh deirbhshiúr,
   do dhearbh a leabhraibh lucht fis,
do bhí an ní uile ar a aonghuth
   is í ag luighe i gcaomhthach a chnis.

Gidh bé do bhiadh agá theagasc,
   níor thairbhe dhó, doirbh an stair,
níor chuir ria bheó uadh an n-inghin;
   truagh an ceó do imthigh air.   48

I fear the Day of Accusation,
  O daughter of Anna of the soft hair,
against God there is no pleading,
  from my iniquity call me back.

Do not let my soul be brought to justice,
  say that in your opinion the law is not fair;
since every man evokes God's anger,
  do not entrust me, Mary, to your Son.

What profit it the Son of Mary
  to accuse anyone without her consent?
The condemned man He pardons
  if Mary were to speak on his behalf.

She is the fortress of Eve's children,
  against the anger of Jesus at Doom;
His mother is our stronghold,
  she is the place of help for all.

She will be on our side on the Appointed Day,
  and though our spear was in his fair breast,
she will not need long to defend us,
  a woman who makes bold with God.

I know a tale of the noble Virgin,
  justifying faith in her pure breast,
a striking story, worthy of preserving,
  it is right to bring it to the ears of all.

There was once a man who had a sister,
  learned men have proven it from books,
everything was as he wanted,
  with her lying beside his skin.

Whoever tried to teach him
  was not successful, hard the tale,
all his life he never renounced the woman,
  wretched folly had him overcome.

Do smuain an fear, fuar an t-inntleacht,
   ar eagal díomdha Dhé bhí
páirt ré máthair Dhé gur dhéanta
   gur ghnáthaigh sé déarca dhí.

Cion ria dheirbhshiair de dhruim uabhair
   gach uair do-níodh, fa nós bras,
do-rad anóir uair san afráil;
   fuair ón Bhanóigh athbháidh as.   56

An tráth do-chuaidh dá chorp dhaonna
   díoth beathadh do bhí 'na ghair,
bheith 'na ghiall dó ag an diabhal —
   cró na bpian do hiadhadh air.

Lúisiféar nior lámhair a fhastódh
   i nIfreann is é ar n-a dhrud;
fear ina dhuine uair éigin
   Muire uaidh a-réigin do rug.   64

An t-anam is í do cheartaigh
   sa chorp chéadna do chleacht sé;
Síol Ádhaimh is í do fhuascail,
   do cháraigh si an uarsain é.

Fuair a-rís ó inghin Anna
   d'éis a bháis, mar bhraittear dún,
fear an chuil a ré (riompa)
   gur chuir sé a chionta ar gcúl.   72

Níor glacadh ris acht réim naomhtha,
   do ní ar thalamh ní thug spéis;
do dhíol iar n-uair a olc roimhe,
   níor smuain olc oile dá éis.

Fuair bás, nochar bheag an claochlódh
   an chuairt tánaise, (ba treall),
gé do bhí an fear uair i n-anchás
   fuair neamh i n-athbhás dob fhearr.   80

The man thought, cold his planning,
   that, for fear of the anger of the living God,
he would gain the favour of God's mother
   and so to her he'd give alms.

For every time he sinned with his sister
   because of pride, he gave at mass
an offering — a cocky habit —
   and in return won the Virgin's love.

When he left his human body
   when deprivation of life was near,
on becoming a hostage to the Devil,
   the realm of torments closed around him.

Lucifer did not dare to engage him
   even after he was incarcerated in Hell;
the man who had once been a human
   Mary grabbed from the Devil by force.

In the body it used to inhabit
   it was she who corrected the soul,
she who released the Seed of Adam,
   she made right his wrong.

After his death, the man of incest,
   we are told, got back his early life
before sinning from Anne's daughter
   so that he could renounce his sins.

Only a righteous path did he follow,
   he had no regard for worldly things;
after a time he redeemed his early evil;
   thereafter he considered no further sin.

The second visit lasted but a season,
   and what a difference when he died,
though the man had once been in extremis
   at his later, better death he gained heav'n.

Fearta mar do fríoth i leabhraibh
   luach a dhéirce — dia do bhail —
tug ria taobh i dtoigh na glóire,
   ag sin taom na hÓighe air.

Ag déanamh uilc ó aois leanaibh
   go Lá an Bhrátha dá mbeith an chlí,
Muire as a láimh nocha léigfe
   duine ar ndáil a dhéirce dhí.   88

Mar do léigfeadh lá dá éigin
   m'anam ré bás mar bhláth slat,
gé tú riamh is cealg im chroidhe,
   do bhiadh fearg Mhoire ria Mac.

Saoilim féin go bhfuighbheam cabhair
   cosc a fheirge madh áil lé;
gé tá Rí an chruinne go créachtach
   dob í muime dhéarcach Dhé.   96

Ar mhéad a-tú í n-easbhaidh eólais
   éigin a rádh riot, a rosg mall,
truagh, a Mhoire, muna mhúine
   sluagh na gcroidhe núidhe a-nall.

   Ná léig.

As found in books, it was miracles
— the reward for his alms, abundant grace —
that brought him to her side in the house of glory,
what happened to him was the Virgin's deed.

Though the body were engaged in evil
from time of childhood to Judgement Day,
No-one who ever gave her charity
would Mary let slip from her grasp.

Though I always have deceit in my bosom,
Mary would be angry with her Son,
if on the Day of His Wrath He abandoned
my soul to death like the blossom of the bough.

I believe that I myself will get succour
if she wishes to check His rage;
although the King of the world is wounded,
she was the kindly mother of God.

Because I am so lacking in knowledge,
I must say to you, O languid eye,
it were sad, Mary, were you not to guide us
— the pure-hearted hosts — across.

8. Seacht Saighde Atá ar mo Thí

Donnchadh Óg

Tha an dàn seo à Leabhar an Deadhain a-mach air cuspair ainmeil, na seachd prìomh pheacannan. Chan eil dad a dh'fhiosrachadh againn mun bhàrd Donnchadh Óg, fiù a shloinneadh.

Gheibhear tionndadh eile den dàn seo ann an Làmhsgrìobhainn MhicRath, a chaidh a sgrìobhadh le Donnchadh nam Pìos MacRath ann an Inbhir Ìonaid ann an Ros an Iar ann an 1689–90; anns an làmh-sgrìobhainn seo is e ainm 'Eoin Carsual' (ùghdar dàin 9 agus 52 agus eadar-theangair a' chiad leabhair Ghàidhlig) a tha ga chur mu choinneimh an dàin.

Thèid an t-anam neoichiontach a ghonadh tron chorp, smuain a mhìnichear gu samhlachail an seo, agus bun gach peacaidh stèidhichte anns a' chorp, leisge anns na h-uilt, an tnùth anns an t-sùil.

Thèid na h-ùrnaighean anns an rann mu dheireadh nam bacadh fiosaigeach an aghaidh nan gath, mar na seann *loricae*. Tha na h-àireamhan air an taghadh anns an t-sreath mu dheireadh gus dùnadh a dhèanamh leis a' chiad fhacal.

> Seacht saighde atá ar mo thí,
>   tá gach saighead díobh 'gam lot,
> ag teacht eadram agus Dia,
>   ó's é sin as mian lem chorp.
>
> A h-aon díobh an t-saighead fhiar,
>   an mian dá gcomhainm an craos:
> minic do mheall í mé an phóit,
>   air ní thánaig fós an aos.
>
> An dara saighead an drúis,
>   sin an chúis dá bhfuilim daor;
> ó lot na saighde nó a gó
>   ní fhuilim beó uatha ar-aon.
>
> An treas saighead díobh atá
>   i n-altaibh mo chnámh a stigh:

8

There Are Seven Arrows in Pursuit of Me

This poem from the Book of the Dean of Lismore deals with the familiar topic of the seven deadly sins. Nothing is known of the poet Donnchadh Óg ('Young Duncan') – not even his surname.

A different version of the poem appears in the late seventeenth-century Fernaig manuscript, written by Donnchadh MacRath at Inverinate in Wester Ross, where it is attributed to 'Eoin Carsual' (i.e. John Carswell), author of poems 9 and 52.

The idea that the innocent soul is wounded through the wiles of the body is given graphic representation here, the poet placing the seat of all sinning in the body, the joints, for instance, causing sloth, and the eye, greed. The physical placing of the prayers between the speaker and the darts recall the earlier *loricae*. The numbers chosen in the final line allow closure with the first word of the poem.

There are seven arrows in pursuit of me,
    each one of them is wounding me,
coming between me and God,
    for that is my body's wish.

One of them is the crooked dart,
    the passion whose other name is greed,
often have I been seduced by drink,
    I, on whom age has not yet come.

The second arrow is lust,
    a matter to which I'm enslaved;
I can survive neither the wound
    nor the blemish of that dart.

The third arrow of them all
    is lodged in the joints of my bones:

cha léig an leisge dá deóin
   mise ar slighidh chóir ar bith.   16

An ceathramh saighead an t-sainnt,
   a Dhé, mairg i nd'fhuair í guin;
fortacht cha nfhaghaim rém ré,
   go ragha cré ar mo mhuin.

'N cóigeamh saighead don ghlaic chuirr
   díomas do chuir riom go h-olc,
maille rém anam do chrádh,
   agus ó nach slán mo chorp.   24

Dhíobh an seiseadh saighead gharg,
   chuireas fearg eadram is cách:
Críost do chasg na n-urchar dhíom
   ó nach bhfaghaim díon go bráth.

An seachtmhadh saighead an t-súil,
   formad is tnúth ris gach ní:
na séid sin i bhfaghmaoid cion,
   annta sin cha nfhuil ar mbrígh.   32

An ghlac soin i leith nach cóir,
   is mór mhilltear leis an arm:
char thilg duine dhíobh nár bhuail,
   char bhuail duine riamh nár mharbh.

Cuirim Paidir aoinMheic Dhé
   is Cré na nOstal go beacht
eadram agus guin na n-arm
   is cóig salm nó sé nó seacht.   40

   Seacht.

it is against the will of sloth
    to let me enter any good path.

Avarice is the fourth dart,
    woe to the one, O God, it wounds,
relief I'll not get while I live,
    not till I am heaped with earth.

From the dismal quiver the fifth dart
    is pride that has vexed me sore,
as well as injuring my soul,
    my body is not healed from it.

Of them the seventh brutal dart
    sets anger between me and other men;
may Christ check those outbursts from me
    since I will get no protection till Doom.

The seventh arrow is the eye,
    envy and covetousness for each thing:
those treasures in which we delight,
    not in them will we find our strength.

That quiver on behalf of that which is not good,
    many are those ruined by its darts,
it never cast one at a man it did not strike,
    it never struck a man it did not kill.

I carefully place the Apostles' Creed
    and the Prayer of God's only Son
between me and the wounding of those darts
    and five, six or seven psalms.

9. Adhmad Beag

Seon Carsuel

Tha an t-'adhmad [dàn] beag' seo a' nochdadh aig toiseach a' chiad leabhair a chaidh fhoillseachadh anns a' Ghàidhlig, *Foirm na n-Urrnuidheadh* (1567), a bha na eadar-theangachadh (no na 'Ghàidhealachadh') air a' *Book of Common Order* aig Eaglais na h-Alba. 'S dòcha gun tàinig Carsuel thairis air cruth beannachaidh an dàin seo bho eisimpleirean de *dhánta grádha* aig an robh freumhan Eòrpach.

Ged a chaidh an leabhar fhoillseachadh ann an Dùn Èideann, chleachd Carsuel a' Ghàidhlig Chlasaigeach, dualchainnt litreachail na h-Alba agus na h-Èireann, agus tha e follaiseach gu robh e fa-near dha an leabhar a sgaoileadh air taobh thall Shruth na Maoile cuideachd, mar phàirt den iomairt airson an creideamh Leasaichte a thoirt do dh'Èirinn. Anns an ro-ràdh aige tha Carsuel a-mach air na duilgheadasan a bha aig 'Gaoidhil Alban agas Eireand' agus tha e a' cleachdadh nan cruthan 'sinne', 'òirnne' is mar sin air adhart.

Rinneadh leabhar Charseuil fo sgèith Ghill'Easbaig Dhuinn, còigeamh iarla Earra Ghàidheal (†1575), a bha air aon de na ceannardan a bu chudromaiche ann an iomairt an Ath-leasachaidh ann an Alba anns an fharsaingeachd agus anns a' Ghàidhealtachd gu sònraichte. Bha 'Ua nDuibhne' (no Ó Duibhne) na thiotal dualchasach a bhite a' cleachdadh mu choinneimh ceannard nan Caimbeulach; ann an sinnsearachd nan Caimbeulach bha an Duibhne seo sia ginealaich air thoiseach air Cailean Mòr (is cha robh ceangal sam bith aige ri Diarmuid Ó Duibhne, gaisgeach na Fèinne).

> Gluais romhad, a leabhráin bhig,
>   go h-Ua nDuibhne rig ad réim;
> chomh luath is fhúicfeas tú an cló,
>   'na áras dó soirbhidh sén.

> 'Na dhiaidh sin siubhail gach tír
>   ar fhud Alban go mín mall,
> acht ort ó nach bfuil a bfeidhm,
>   ná tabhair céim i ngort Gall.

8

A Little Poem

This dedicatory 'little poem' appears at the beginning of the first book published in Gaelic, Seon Carsuel's *Foirm na n-Urrnuidh-eadh*, a translation (or rather adaptation) of the Book of Common Order, which appeared in 1567. Carsuel may well have come across the basic valedictory form of the poem as a motif in courtly love poems.

Although published in Edinburgh, Carsuel's work was written in the common literary language of Scotland and Ireland and was plainly intended for circulation on the far side of Sruth na Maoile as well. The introduction speaks of the challenges facing '*Gaoidhil Alban agas Eireand*' and is phrased in the first person plural. As such, the reference in the third stanza to the distaste of the Irish friars is not mere rhetoric; the book was meant to be put to practical use in the competition between Reformation and Counter-Reformation.

The book was produced under the patronage of Gill'Easbaig, fifth Earl of Argyll (†1575), one of the leading figures in the Scottish Reformation and the first Highland chief to take up the Protestant faith: hence the reference in the first stanza to Ua nDuibhne (a traditional honorific for the leader of the Caimbeuls of Argyll).

Carsuel held several church offices in Argyll prior to the Reformation and in 1560 was appointed Superintendent of Argyll, a new office established by the Reformed Church, and then became Bishop of the Isles in 1565. He died *c.* 1572.

> Go far little book,
> > reach the earl of Argyll in your course;
> as soon as you leave the print,
> > in its own home, make haste there.
>
> After that, journey to every land
> > in Scotland, gentle and sedate,
> but since there is no point,
> > do not enter the land of the Gall.

Dá éis sin taisdil gach tond
  go crích Éireand na bfond bfial;
gé beag ar na bráithribh thú,
  gluais ar amharc a súl siar.

Gach seancha gan seanchus saobh,
  gach fear dáno nár aomh bréag,
cumand eadrad agas iad,
  a leabhráin bhig, biadh go h-éag.   16

Gach neach do ghrádhaigh an chóir
  do tsíol Ádhaimh róimh ní guais,
aca sin déna do nid,
  romhad a leabhráin bhig gluais.

Gluais.

10. Dursan mh'Eachtra go hAlbuin

Fearghal Óg Mac an Bhaird

Bhuineadh Fearghal Óg Mac an Bhaird do aon de na
teaghlaichean fhilidhean a b' ainmeile ann an Còigeamh Uladh
agus choisinn e sàr-chliù dha fhèin aig deireadh an t-siathamh
linn deug agus toiseach an t-seachdamh linn deug. Cleas bhall
eile den teaghlach, rinn e dàin do Chlann Uí Dhomhnaill,
uachdarain Thír Chonaill, agus tha e coltach gun do lean e an
luchd-taice aige gu na Dùthchannan Ìosal an dèidh 'Teitheadh
na nIarlaí' (1607), nuair a dh'fhàg prìomh-uaislean Uladh an
dùthaich airson tearmann fhaighinn air Tìr-mòr na Roinn
Eòrpa.
  Is dòcha gun do rinneadh an dàn seo mu 1581, nuair a
thadhail Fearghal Óg air Dùn Èideann, Earra Ghàidheal agus
Muile. Tha e coltach gun deach e do Dhùn Èideann an lùib
misein phoilitigich aig Aodh Ó Domhnaill gu Rìgh Seumas VI;
bha ceangal làidir eadar Clann Uí Dhomhnaill agus rìghrean
Alba bho shean. Chithear anns na cunntasan rìoghail gun deach

After that travel every wave
    to Ireland of the generous lands;
though the friars have little love for you,
    go west that they may see you.

Every storyteller without false tale,
    every brave man who conceded no lie,
a communion between you and them,
    Let it be forever, O little book.

There is nothing to fear from any one
    of Adam's seed who loves the right,
with them make your nests,
    go far little book, go.

Go.

A Hardship My Journey to Scotland

A member of one of Ulster's pre-eminent families of professional poets, Fearghal Óg Mac an Bhaird was one of the major Irish *filidh* of the late sixteenth and early seventeenth centuries. Like other members of his kindred before him he served the Ó Domhnaills of Tír Chonaill, and appears to have followed his patrons to the Low Countries following the famous 'Flight of the Earls' in 1607, when the principal Gaelic Irish nobility left the country in the wake of the English conquest.

The poem may well have been composed around 1581, when Fearghal Óg visited Edinburgh, Argyll and Mull. His visit to Edinburgh appears to have been part of a diplomatic mission by Ó Domhnaill to King James VI; the Ó Domhnaills had long maintained strong links to the Scottish kings. Remarkably, an entry in the royal Treasury Accounts for that year records a payment to 'fergall og Irische poet'.

Although this poem is sometimes read as demonstrating the

'fergall og Irische poet' a phàigheadh airson nan seirbhisean aige.

Ged a tha cuid a' tuigsinn bhon dàn seo gu robh an seann chàirdeas eadar Gàidheil na h-Èireann agus na h-Alba a' briseadh air sgàth an Ath-leasachaidh, is dòcha gu bheil am file a' cur an cèill nam faireachdainnean aige an dèidh dha buaidh na h-eaglais ùir Phròstanaich fhaicinn air baile Dhùn Èideann seach nan tuigsean aige air suidheachadh na Gàidhealtachd.

Gheibhear sealladh gu math eadar-dhealaichte air turas Fhearghail Óig do dh'Alba ann an dàn 45, a rinneadh, a rèir coltais, le fear a bha a' suirghe air an aon bhoireannach.

> Dursan mh'eachtra go hAlbuin
> dá dtánag — tuar iomarduidh —
>   ó mhínÉirinn ghéigthe ghloin
>   séitche ríghFhéilim Reachtmhoir.
>
> Do ghrádh an domhuin diombuain
> tánag tar tuinn tráichtfhionnfhuair
>   go fionnAlbuin trá óm thoigh;
>   lá an iomarduidh budh huamhoin.   8
>
> Eagail liom lá an tsléibhe
> mar thánag — tuar aithmhéile —
>   lem dhán luachmholta tar lear
>   ó chlár ghruadhchorcra Gaoidheal.
>
> Baoghlach leam a agra orm
> teacht go hAlbuin na n-órchorn;
>   i gcrích sgaithfhinn na ngort ngeal
>   ní chaithim corp an Choimdheadh.   16
>
> Dar m'éigse do mealladh mé;
> dámadh liom Alba uile
>   uch, a Dhé, mo lorg tar lionn
>   is mé gan ord gan Aifrionn.
>
> Rugas díogha deimhin liom
> do thréigeas ord is Aifrionn
>   — ar n-éag gá dál as docra? —
>   do ghrádh na séad saogholta.   24

early breakdown of relations between Scottish and Irish
Gaeldom as a result of the Reformation, the poem is best
understood as reflecting the poet's shock on visiting Edinburgh,
where the Reformation had taken a firm hold, rather than an
assessment of the state of affairs in the Gàidhealtachd, where the
new church took far longer to make significant inroads.

A very different aspect of Fearghal Óg's visit to Scotland can
be seen in poem 45, seemingly composed by a love rival of his.

> A hardship my journey to Scotland
> where I came — presaging sorrowing —
> > from gentle Ireland of pure branches,
> > spouse to king Feilim the Lawmaker.
>
> I came for love of the fleeting Earth
> over the wave of white cold beaches
> > to fair Scotland a while from my home;
> > a matter for dread on the Day of Terror.
>
> I dread the Day of Doom
> as I crossed the sea — what sorrow —
> > with my art of praising for gain
> > from the Gaels' purple-cheeked country.
>
> I fear reproach for having reached
> Scotland of the golden goblets;
> > in the fair-flowered land of bright fields
> > I do not receive the Lord's Body.
>
> By my art have I been deceived;
> but were Scotland mine entirely
> > it would still be woeful for me to be here,
> > deprived, O God, of mass and office.
>
> I am convinced I took the dregs,
> — after death what state is more bitter? —
> > I have abandoned clergy and Mass
> > for love of worldly riches.

Dámadh liom uile a hór bog
dá bhfhaghuinn a bhfuil d'argod
  i gcrích bhraonuair na mbeann bhfionn
  do b'fhearr aonuair an t-Aifrionn.

Ní chreideann Alba fa-ríor
go dtig tonn d'fhuil an Airdríogh
  san abhluinn mar as dleacht dí
  adhruim don reacht do-rinne.   32

An gcuala Alba an fheóir chuirr
ar imthigh air fan abhluinn
  fear go nglór dhiabhluidhe dhoirbh;
  do shlógh iarnuidhe ioffoirn.

An t-Íobhal úd, ráidhim ribh,
do-chuaidh lá do na laithibh
  go teach Dé re dearbhadh uilc;
  fa neamhghlan é ag a iodhbuirt.   40

Dá theampall mar tháinig sin
ar an altóir an uairsin
  do-chí sé an abhluinn re ais;
  adhruim don té dan teaghdhais.

Tre fhochuidbheadh don fhear ghráidh
do fhiafraigh — dia do dhiombáidh —
  séad ar n-adhradh druim ar druim
  créad do b'adhbhar don abhluinn.   48

'Anuas eidir fheóil is fhuil
tig go dearbh', ar an deachuin,
  'barr órbhuidhe taobh mar thuinn
  laogh óghMhuire san abhluinn.'

D'éiliughadh cainte an chléirigh
tug sáthadh dian díchéillidh
  dá sgiain chaoil ghairbhghil ghreanta
  san mbairghin gcaoimh gcoisreactha.   56

If all her gold belonged to me,
if I got hold of all the silver
    in this cool dewy land of peaks,
    hearing Mass but once would be better.

Scotland, alas, does not believe
a wave of the King's blood enters
    into the wafer as is ordained;
    but I cleave to the law He enacted.

Has Scotland of the smooth grass heard
what befell a man concerning the wafer,
    a man of harsh diabolical words,
    a man who belonged to Hell's iron legion?

This Jew, I am telling ye,
once upon a time departed
    to the house of God, intent on evil;
    he was unfit for making sacrifice.

When he came to His church,
there beside him on the altar,
    he sees the Host;
    I cleave to the Head of the household.

Mockingly he enquired
of the cleric — how distressing —
    of what the wafer was made,
    treasure adored through ages.

'Verily, in flesh and blood,
there descends', said the deacon,
    'the golden hair, the foam-white breast
    of the Virgin's Child to the wafer'.

To test the cleric's speech
he made a lunge, sharp and clumsy,
    at the gentle consecrated Host
    with his keen, bright, engraven weapon.

Bainne fola druim ar druim
tig an uairsin as an abhluinn
   — mór bhfáidh ler fíoradh an céim —
dar bháidh an t-Íobhal ainnséin.

A mbíodh innte i n-aghaidh Dé
do bháidh fós — fíor an fínné;
   deimhin liom gur mhuidh a-mach
   an fhuil ós chionn na cathrach.   64

Oiread na mara-so a-muigh
do chuir san abhluinn uasuil;
   séala an ghráidh an bhais do bhean
   dámadh áil lais do léigfeadh.

Mór dtír nach í Alba a-mháin
nach creideann fós — fáth tochráidh —
   don bhairghin go mbí 'n-a fuil
   's í fa ainglibh 'n-a hiomdhuidh.   72

Tánag san tír nach adhair
don abhluinn ghil ghrásamhail;
   mó do mheall an saoghal sinn
   baoghal 'n-a cheann ní chuirim.

Fearr bheith thiar ó thigh go tigh
do sheirc naomhchuirp Dé dhúiligh
   ná ríghe 's a beith a-bhus;
   don bhreith fhíre do fhéachus.   80

Ó nach faicim é innte
an corp diadha doimhillte
   fairche ghrianfhuinn na ngéag gcuir
   iarruim gan mh'éag i nAlbain.

Do sheirc chuirp Íosa d'fhéaguin
slán ó Albain úirghéaguigh
   fairche fhiar na n-úrchros ndonn
   siar dom dhúthchos go ndeacham.   88

Then out of the Host
blood gushes in billows
 and drowned the Jew —
 a tale scholars attest to.

The blood I know surged out
over the city — the witness is truthful —
 and drowned there
 all the enemies of the Almighty.

With blood the volume of the sea
He filled the revered wafer;
 had He wished He could have left unharmed
 the hand that touched love's token.

Scotland is not the only realm
that does not believe — what torment —
 the blood to be present in the bread,
 that couch encircled by angels.

I came to a land that does not revere
the pure, grace-giving wafer;
 greatly has the world deceived me,
 I know of nothing more dangerous.

To survive as a beggar in the west
for love of God's holy Body
 were better than being a king here;
 I have seen the truth of this judgement.

As nowhere can I see
in this sunny wooded country
 the incorruptible Body of God
 I pray that in Scotland I die not.

I long to see the Body of Christ
so farewell to Scotland of fresh saplings;
 let me depart for my home in the west
 a rough land of brown pure crosses.

Guidhim Mac Dé más deóin lais
dom breith go hÉirinn n-iathghlais
agus saorMhuire a súil dil;
a naomhghuidhe dhúinn dlighthir.

Ar bhás pheacaigh san tír thoir
bíodh an Coimdhe dom chobhoir,
    's an ógh naomh buime na mbocht
    craobh darab duille an diadhacht.   96

Go bhfaghom tar iomad mh'olc
coim im dheaghaidh tre dhúthrocht;
    dul fa a géagaibh is dleacht damh,
    teacht dá déagain ní dursan.

Do chaoi Peadar puirt nimhe
fa pháis an Uain ainglidhe;
    uchán, do ba géar a ghal,
    a shruthán déar ní dursan.   104

    Dursan.

11. Creud fan d'Tharlamar an Tùrsa?

Eòin Stiùbhart

Tha trì dàin air tighinn a-nuas thugainn a tha co-cheangailte ri Eòin Stiùbhart, duine-uasal às an Apainn. Tha a dhà dhiubh sin air an gleidheadh ann an Làmh-sgrìobhainn MhicRath, agus chaidh an treas dàn, air a bheil an tiotal 'Faoisid Eoin Stiùbhairt', fhoillseachadh an lùib *Adtimchiol an Chreidimh*, an dàrna leabhar Gàidhlig ann an clò (*c.*1630).

Is e tàire air an t-saoghal an cuspair as cumanta ann am bàrd-achd dhiadhaidh na Gàidhlig Chlasaigich. Thèid giorrad na beatha a thoirt gu ar n-aire, cho math ris na cunnartan a thig an lùib cus bàidh dhan t-saoghail; bu chòir dhuinn aithreachas a

I beseech God's Son if He so wills,
and — it is right to urge her piously —
    noble Mary, my people's fond hope,
    to bear me to Ireland of green meadows.

From a sinner's death in the east
may the Lord protect me,
    and the holy Virgin, nurse of the poor,
    the branch of the Godhead's scion.

Despite my abundant sin when I die
may I win protection through piety;
    going into her arms is right,
    approaching her is no hardship.

Peter who is in Heaven's house
wept for the angelic Lamb's Passion;
    Ah, bitter was his cry,
    his stream of tears was no hardship.

A hardship.

Why Have We Met With Sadness?

This is one of two poems in the Fernaig manuscript attributed to Eòin Stiùbhart, a nobleman of the late sixteenth century from Appin in north Argyll. A third poem, entitled 'Faoisid Eoin Stiùbhairt' ('Eòin Stiùbhart's Confession'), was prefixed to *Adtimchiol an Chreidimh*, a translation of Calvin's *Catechismus Ecclesiae Genevensis* – the second book to be published in Gaelic (*c*.1630).

    Contempt for the world is the dominant theme of Classical Gaelic religious poetry. We are reminded of the shortness of life, and how attachment to the world imperils the soul; we are urged

ghabhail fhad 's a tha an cothrom againn, agus cobhair os-
nàdarrach a shireadh.

Is dòcha gum b' ann bho shearmanachadh eadar-nàiseanta a
thàinig na h-ìomhaighean an toiseach. Ged a tha an fheallsan-
achd gruamach, nì iad bàrdachd mhath leis mar a dhaingnicheas
iad cho breòite 's a tha a' bheatha.

Creud fan d' tharlamar an tùrsa?
 's nì h-ann fo shùil ach blàth brèig;
gun an saoghal ach na sgàil mheallaich,
 mar neulan geala na grèin.

Mar an dealt ri là ciùin
 no 'n sneachd is dlùithe bhios geal;
toradh nan duill' air a' chrann:
 nì mair daoine sionn ach seal.   8

An ròs is cùbhraidh, no 'n lilidh,
 am plumas no 'n siridh dearg,
gur geàrr a bhios iad fo bhuaidh:
 siud meadhair an t-sluaigh gu dearbh.

An samhradh, ge mòr a theas,
 's am foghar, thèid às gu luath;
crìonaidh gach lus tha 'm magh gorm-ghlas:
 mar sin thèid solas an t-sluaigh.   16

Ach 's èibhinn leis gach neach an dàil
 fhaighinn gu àilgheas a' chuirp;
's lèir dhuinn mar an dall
 nach eil duill' air crann nach tuit.

Nì d' fhàs air an talamh suas
 de dhaoine no chroinn no bhuar,
de dh'aon nì nach crìon fa dheòidh:
 mo sgeul bròin a bhith ga luadh!   24

Adhbhar tùirse, is adhbhar bròin,
 gun tuigse bhith de ghlòir Dhè;
gun smaointinn bhith air ar crìch:
 O, Rìgh nan rìgh, cobhair mi!

to repent while there is time, and supernatural help is sought. The forms given to these reflections probably came from the international preaching repertoire, and though they may make for a gloomy theology, they are inherently poetic in their rueful reminder that all must change.

Why have we met with sadness?
    All we see is a false bloom;
the world is a deceptive shadow
    like white clouds before the sun.

Like dew on a calm day,
    or the brightness of the densest snow;
like the foliage of the tree,
    men last but a spell.

The sweetest rose or lily,
    the plum or the cherry red,
they are in season but a moment:
    indeed is a forewarning to man.

Summer, though great its heat,
    and autumn too, pass swiftly by;
every herb on the lush plain withers,
    and so it is with mankind's day.

But everyone wants more time
    to spend on the body's delight;
it is as clear to us as the blind
    that there is no leaf on tree but falls.

Nothing has grown from the ground,
    neither trees nor men nor beasts,
nothing that in the end will not fade:
    my sorry tale to tell!

A cause of sadness and grief,
    not to understand the glory of God;
not to be mindful of our end,
    O King of Kings, come to my aid.

Do bhì triùir dam ionnsaigh gu teann:
  an saoghal 's an sannt 's an fheòil;
Dhè, dìon-sa mise bhon triùir;
  's a Rìgh nan dùl, na leig leò.   32

Dhè, dìon-sa mis' bhon triùir
  do bhì air mhiann feall is brèig,
agus cobhair mi de ghnàth;
  neartaich mo ghràdh 's mo chreud.

    Creud.

12. Is Mairg Do-Ní Uaille as Óige

Athairne MacEoghain

Chaidh an dàn seo fhoillseachadh an cois an leabhair *Adtimchiol an Chreidimh* (faic gu h-àrd), agus tha cuid den bheachd gur e Athairne MacEoghain (*fl.* 1600?) a rinn e. Bha Athairne air aon de na buill mu dheireadh den teaghlach seo, a bha am measg nam prìomh theaghlaichean bàrdail ann an Gàidhealtachd Alba. Tha e coltach gu robh iad mar fhilidhean dùthchasach Chloinn Dubhghaill Dhùn Ollaidh an toiseach, ach uaireigin anns an t-siathamh linn deug rinneadh ceangal eadar Clann MhicEoghain agus na Caimbeulaich, a bha a' sìor fhàs nas cumhachdaiche. Chan eil ach glè bheag de bhàrdachd nan Eoghanach againn, na measg marbhrann air Eòin (mac Ailein) MacDubhghaill (*fl.* 1451), an dà dhàn spioradail a tha gan clò-bhualadh an seo, agus grunn dhàn molaidh is mharbhrannan a rinneadh, a rèir coltais, le Niall, mac Athairne, eadar na 1620an agus na 1640an.

Is mairg do-ní uaille as óige,
  as iasachd deilbhe, a deirc ghlais,
a cruth séimh, a suidhe aoibhinn,
  a céibh bhuidhe chaoimhfhinn chais

Three have wounded me sore:
    the world, greed and the flesh;
God, protect me from the three,
    Lord of all life, don't let them be.

Lord, protect me from the three
    who were intent on treachery and deceit,
succour me at all times;
    strengthen my love and belief.

Woe to the One who Takes Pride in Youth

This poem, one of several prefixed to *Adtimchiol an Chreidimh* (see above), has been attributed to Athairne MacEoghain (*fl.* 1600?), one of the last members of the MacEoghain bardic dynasty, one of the leading poetic families in Gaelic Scotland. The MacEoghains appear first as hereditary poets to the MacDubhghaills of Dunolly, but during the sixteenth century they entered the service of the Caimbeuls of Argyll, by then the dominant political force in Gaelic Scotland. Relatively little work by MacEoghain poets has survived, other than a fifteenth-century elegy on Eòin (mac Ailein) MacDubhghaill preserved in the Book of the Dean of Lismore, the two religious poems given here, and some well-crafted panegyrics and elegies apparently composed by Athairne's son Niall between the 1620s and 1640s.

Woe to the one who takes pride in youth,
    in a borrowed form, in a grey eye,
in a graceful figure, in a comely face,
    in shining soft yellow curling locks.

Dá dtiobhradh Dia dhuit, a dhuine,
   — daoine meallta mheallas siad —
déad mar an gcuip is taobh taislim,
   duit a-raon is aisling iad.   8

Duille an bheatha bhudh bláth bréige,
   baoghal an chuirp cur rén íoc,
ná déan uaill fa cheann na cruinne,
   gearr go buain a duille dhíot.

Dá bhfuighe fós, ní fáth díomais,
   duille an bheatha nach buan seal,
cuimhnigh réd ré dála an duine,
   gurb é námha an uile fhear.   16

Cuimhnigh ar chnuasach na ngráineóg,
   guais dod thionól bheith mar bhíd,
ní bhfuil achd pian ann dot anmuin,
   ná iarr barr don talmhuin tríd.

Ubhall ar gach bior dá mbearaibh
   beirid don taobh dá dtéid siad,
ar ndul ón choill fhádbhuig fhéarchruinn
   fágbhuid fa bhroinn éanphuill iad.   24

Fúigfighthear leat loise an t-saoghail
   mar so, a chuirp, ag cosg do mhian,
fa bhéal na h-uaighe an t-anam,
   sgéal as truaighe, a chalann chriadh.

Gach bhfuarais d'ór agus d'ionnmhus,
   d'eachaibh 's do bhuaibh, giodh beart chlé,
ní léigfighthear lat díbh, a dhuine,
   achd brat lín don chruinne ché.   32

Ainbhfios an chuirp cuid da uabhar,
   eagal dúinn a dhul ós aird,
daor re dhaoirmheas uaill na h-óige,
   buain re h-aoibhneas móide is mairg.

    Is mairg.

If God should have given to *you*, O man,
    — only deluded people do they deceive —
teeth like foam and a slender waist,
    to you alone they are a dream.

The petals of life are false blossom,
    it is dangerous for the body to aim to buy them,
do not take pride on account of the world,
    all too soon will you be stripped of its leaves.

If even so you gain — no cause for pride —
    the petals of life that do not last,
always keep in mind the state of man
    that makes the world a foe to every one.

Remember the hedgehogs' hoard,
    dangerous for your garnering to be as they,
it will only entail your soul in pain,
    from it do not expect the fruit of the earth.

With an apple on the tip of every spine
    they carry them to a special place,
leaving the soft-turfed smooth-grassed wood
    they leave them buried in a hole.

Likewise will *you* leave worldly pomp,
    O body, quenching your desires,
with the soul at the mouth of the tomb,
    the most wretched of stories, O body of clay.

All you have acquired of gold and wealth,
    of horses and cows, though it were a wicked deed,
you will not be allowed any of them with you,
    but a linen shroud of this world, O man.

The body's ignorance is part of its pride,
    we are terrified at the thought of death,
pride of youth is ignoble, to be despised,
    to be concerned with happiness is all the greater woe.

      Woe.

13. Mairg Dar Compánach an Cholann

Athairne MacEoghain

Seo dàn eile a dh'fhoillsicheadh an cois *Adtimchiol an Chreidimh*,
air a bheil an tiotal 'Gearan ar Truaillightheachd na colla'.
A-rithist, chan urrainn cus earbsa a bhith againn gur e Athairne
MacEoghain a rinn e.

Gu tric anns na Meadhan Aoisean thèid an corp agus an
t-anam a riochdachadh mar chàraid phòsta, an corp ri burraidh-
eachd agus an t-anam a' fulang fo ainneart. Thèid an ìomhaigh
air ais gu Plato, agus an t-anam sìorraidh ga fhaicinn mar rud
nas fheàrr na an corp, a dh'atharraicheas agus a gheibh bàs.

Mairg dar compánach an cholann,
   comann fallsa ní fuath lé;
guais thall a cionta fam chomhair,
   tiocfa am bhus omhain é.

Gach grádh riamh do radas díse,
   níor dhíol uirre ar fhuath na bpian;
do fhill mo ghrádh 'na fhuath oram,
   lán dár bhfuath an cholann chriadh.   8

Fuath m'anma is annsacht na colla,
   comann meallta mairg do-ní;
mé dá toil congbhaidh an cholann,
   foghlaidh mar soin oram í.

Ní díol ceana an cholann mheabhlach,
   giodh mór an toil tugas dí;
minic nach buan críoch a cumainn,
   ní fríoth acht fuar umainn í.   16

Lór dom theagasg gé táim aimhghlic
   ré h-uchd an bháis, giodh breith chruaidh,
na h-uilc san teine ga dtéaghadh,
   's na cuirp eile d'fhéaghadh uainn.

Woe to the One Whose Companion is the Body

Another poem prefixed to *Adtimchiol an Chreidimh*, and headed 'Gearan ar Truaillightheachd na colla' ('A Complaint about the Corruption of the Body'). Again, the ascription to Athairne MacEoghain is uncertain.

A common construct in the Middle Ages was to see the body and soul as a mismatched couple, the bullying body being the downfall of the weak, vulnerable soul through its attachment to the world. Ultimately the idea is Platonic: that the eternal soul is superior to the body which undergoes change and dies.

> Woe to the one whose companion is the body,
>   a cheating union she does not condemn,
> her transgressions are a danger to me yonder,
>   a time will come which will be bad.
>
> Every love I ever gave her,
>   was not enough despite fear of pains;
> she returned my love to me with hatred,
>   full of hate for me is the body of clay.
>
> What my soul detests is dearest to the body,
>   woe to the one who makes a false alliance;
> the body keeps me as her plaything,
>   thus she is a foe of mine.
>
> No requital for love is the treacherous body
>   though great the love I gave to her;
> often the end of her association is not distant:
>   round me I found her only cold.
>
> Enough of my teaching though I am foolish
>   at the brink of death, though the judgement is harsh,
> the wicked in the fire burning
>   and the other bodies being seen by us.

Ré h-uchd an bháis is beart chunntair
  an claochlódh truagh tig dá ghné,
an corp ré h-athaidh na h-uaire
  olc an acmhainn uaille é.   24

Na súile i n-aimsir an éaga
  adhbhar biodhgtha mar bhias siad,
— gá beag dúnn ón Rígh mar rabhadh? —
  do-chím cúl ar aghadh iad.

Do-chím an béal dearg ar ndubhadh
  's an déad cailce 'na chnáimh ghorm,
mo thoil ní fhuigheam ón uabhar,
  ní chuireann soin uamhan orm.   32

Mo mhian féin is aimhleas m'anma
  eagal dúinne dul ós aird,
fuair an cholann cuid na deise,
  romhall do thuig meise a mairg.

    Mairg.

The wretched change that comes in its appearance
    at the brink of death is a dreadful thing;
at that moment in time the body
    is ill equipment for pride.

The eyes in death's season
    will become a cause of shock;
— the King sends us no small warning —
    I see them back to front.

I see the red mouth darkened,
    the chalk-white teeth as ugly bone,
yet that does not fill me with horror —
    let me not get my wish from pride.

My desire is my soul's downfall,
    I am afraid for my life's end;
the body got the better portion,
    too slow did I comprehend its woe.

    Woe.

THE LEARNED TRADITION

PANEGYRIC

14. Mairg Thréigeas Inn, a Amhlaoibh

Muireadhach Albanach Ó Dálaigh

Bha na filidh air leth mothachail air an inbhe aca agus na duaisean a bhuineadh dhi. Bha an fhèin-mhoit seo air leth nochdaidh ann am Muireadhach Albanach (faic an ro-ràdh ri dàn 6).

Rinneadh an dàn seo do Amhlaoibh, mac Alúin, dàrna iarla Leamhnachd (†1217), agus tha e soilleir gu robh dàimh stèidhichte eadar Muireadhach agus an neach-taice seo; air sgàth sin tha e a' sùileachadh roghainn cruidh, each agus fearainn. Ann an rann 19 (sreathan 73–76) tha e a' toirt iomradh air 'duan' eile a rinn e do Amhlaoibh, dàn nas foirmeile na an 'laoidh' a leanas, ach gu mì-fhortanach cha tàinig an 'duan' a-nuas thugainn.

Tha dàn eile againn fhathast, ge-tà, a rinn Muireadhach do Alún mac Muireadhaigh, ciad iarla Leamhnachd, agus a rèir coltais rinneadh an dàn seo *c.* 1200, grunn bhliadhnaichean mus do theich am file à Èirinn, rud a dh'innseas dhuinn gu robh dàimh mhaireannach eadar Muireadhach agus iarlan Leamhnachd.

Mairg thréigeas inn, a Amhlaoibh,
an ghuirt uaine ubhallmhaoil,
　　giodh mór do ghnaoi 'gus do ghráin
　　ní lór mur taoi 'gum thógbháil.

Fiche loilgheach budh dleacht damh,
searraigh urlomha Alban,
　　rogha gach fóid challúir chaoimh
　　ód mhallshúil óig, a Amhlaoibh.　　　8

A Amhlaoibh, a fhabhra donn,
ní buidheach inn dot fhearann,
　　bheith aguibh ar Aird na nEach,
　　mairg do chagair mo chuibhreach.

Woe to Him Who Neglects Me, Amhlaoibh

The poem expresses the professional poets' strong sense of entitlement to material rewards from their patrons; and no poet was more renowned for his elevated sense of self-worth than Muireadhach Albanach (see introduction to poem 6).

This poem is addressed to Amhlaoibh, son of Alún, second earl of Lennox (†1217), and makes clear that Muireadhach was well-established in service to this patron – hence his elevated expectations of cattle, horses, and choice land. In stanza 19 (lines 73–76) he refers to an earlier, apparently more prestigious poem (*duan*) to Amhlaoibh that has preceded the current, less formal lay (*laoidh*), but unfortunately this has not survived.

An earlier poem by Muireadhach for Alún mac Muireadhaigh, first earl of Lennox, has also survived, and appears to date from *c.* 1200, well before the poet's famous flight from Ireland, thus suggesting a relationship of some years' standing with the earls of Lennox.

The translation mimics the *deibhidhe* metre of the original where the final word of the second line of the couplet forms an off-rhyme with the final word of the first line. The stressed syllable in the first line therefore rhymes with an unstressed syllable in the second rhyme, the second word of necessity being a syllable longer than the first.

> Woe to him who neglects me, Amhlaoibh,
> of the green orchard of appletrees,
>> although great your charm and your malice,
>> not sufficient are your retaining-fees.

> Twenty milch cows should be my pay,
> swift foals from Scotland,
>> from your stately young eye, Amhlaoibh,
>> the choice of gentle land, fresh-hazelled.

> I'm not thankful for your land,
> O Amhlaoibh, O dark lashes,
>> being retained by you at Aird nan Each,
>> woe on your plan to ensnare me.

Ní currach ní criathrach bog
do dhleisinn d'fhagháil agad,
    cuid don chill do dhligh duine,
    a ghil fhinn, dá almhuire.   16

Munab áil leat ar mo laoidh
crodh is fhearann, a Amhlaoibh,
    bean th'fhearann is íoc an crodh,
    ní dhleagham dhíot do dhomhan.

Cuir fiche loilghioch ar láimh
go ndearnoinn t'fhearann d'fhágbháil,
    sirfead ionadh, a chiabh cham,
    ór siobhal riamh do-rónsum.   24

Do thogras imtheacht uile
uaibh, a chneasbháin chúlbhuidhe,
    do bhoing ré hÉirinn n-ealaigh
    go cloinn méirsheing Muireadhaigh.

Ní neach uaibh, a fholt na raon,
do fhosd mé acht an mórmhaor,
    tearc don tsluagh nár fheall orm-sa
    acht an sduagh sheang shúlmhall-sa.   32

Fiche bó ionnlaogh áloinn
dhamh ód ghnúis mur gheallámhoinn,
    baile saor a Srath Leamhna,
    rath taobh ris an tighearna.

Buar is mean is mál bracha
fuair meisi ó mhac Arbhlatha
    maith an fear agá bhfoghar
    mean is braith is bóthoradh.   40

Maith an treas a-táthar sonn,
dá airghi d'airghibh agum,
    a Dhé do mheisnigh mheathaigh,
    dá sheisrigh do sheisreachaibh.

It isn't marshland or soft fen
I deserve to get as payment;
    my due is part of the churchland,
    O bright one, for his foreigner.

If you think my poem is not worth
land and cattle, Amhlaoibh,
    then keep your land and sell the cattle,
    I'm not claiming all your property.

Put twenty milch-cows aside
so that I might leave your country,
    I will seek another post, O curling ringlets,
    for I've always enjoyed travelling.

O white-skin, O yellow-hair,
I've wished to leave you altogether,
    to make for Ireland of the swans,
    to the slender-fingered kin of Muireadhach.

Not one of your people, O smooth hair,
engaged me but the morair,
    rare was the man who did not play me false
    excepting the languid-eyed, slender pillar.

Twenty lovely cows in calf
for me from your face like embers,
    stock beside the chief,
    a noble homestead in Strath Leven.

Cattle, meal and malted barley
was what I got from the son of Arbhlaith,
    good the man from whom I got
    meal and malt and livestock.

Good the situation here:
for herds I have two cow-herds,
    O God who strengthened the weak,
    of horses I have two plough-teams.

Ó 'd-chualuis, a chúl na sgath,
mur fuair mé mórmhaor Leamhnach
    fásaidh, a chúl barrlag bog,
    tnúdh agas farmad ionnad.   48

Cuimhnigh clann chúlchas Chonghail,
maith th'aignedh rét ollamhnaibh,
    clann Ghofraidh cuimhnigh 'mad chuing,
    a Mhuimhnigh shochraidh shéaghainn.

Cuimhnigh ós cionn do leanna
Lughaidh mór mac Oillealla,
    cuimhnigh Oillill, a athair,
    ós an mBoirinn mbraonsgathaigh.   56

Cuimhnigh Corc mór mac Leamhna,
cathuidhe na claoinTeamhra,
    eineach Cuirc Chaisil cuimhnigh
    an fhuilt mhaisigh mhíondruimnigh.

Do iadhsad 'mád t'aighidh ngil
na Muimhnigh is na Mainigh,
    na Mainigh is na Muimhnigh
    airigh agas athchuinnghidh.   64

Dá ttugthá uile dod aoidh,
a dhuine óig, a Amhlaoibh,
    atád sáirfhir, a bharr bog,
    a-nall ré a n-áirimh iomad.

Muinntior h'athar aithnidh damh
is muinntior mhaith do mháthar,
    re sloinneadh liom-sa um laoidh,
    a choinneal fhionn-sa, a Amhlaoibh.   72

Má thugas duan 'na duain bhinn
dhuid, a Amhlaoibh, a hÉirinn,
    do laoidh, a rí, a-nos do-ním,
    ní bhí fros gan a froisín.

Since you heard, O burnished hair,
how I found Lennox's morair,
    in you, O soft tipped wisps,
    have grown jealousy and envy.

Recall Conghal's ringletted kin,
good your attitude to your men of learning;
    recall Clan Gofraidh under your yoke,
    beautiful distinguished man of Munster.

Recall over your ale,
great Lughaidh, son of Ailill,
    recall Ailill, his father,
    over the Burren with showers, shadowy.

Recall great Corc, son of Leven,
warrior of Tara-slope,
    recall the honour of Corc of Cashel,
    he of the beautiful, smooth-ridged hair.

They have surrounded your bright face,
the men of Munster and the Maine-men,
    the men of Maine and the Munstermen,
    acknowledge them and make supplication.

If you thought about them all,
O young man, Amhlaoibh,
    you'd see surrounding you, soft hair,
    there are excellent men to be counted.

Your father's family are known to me,
and your mother's noble people;
    there to be named by me in my lay,
    O white candle, you, Amhlaoibh.

If I brought a tuneful poem
to you, Amhlaoibh, from Ireland,
    your lay, O prince, do I make now,
    there was never rain without its shower.

Ní bhí bó álainn gan oigh,
ní bhí gamhnach gan ghamhain,
  duan mholta linn gona laoidh,
  a chorcra fhinn, a Amhlaoibh.   80

A Amhlaoimh, a chais chorcra,
a chara 's a chomhalta,
  th'éigeas baird as binn a laoidh,
  mairg thréigeas inn, a Amhlaoibh.

15. Domhnall mac Raghnaill, Rosg Mall

Gun urra

Is e cuspair nan rannan seo (nach do dh'fhoillsicheadh roimhe)
Domhnall mac Raghnaill mhic Shomhairle, a bha beò anns a'
chiad phàirt den trìtheamh linn deug. Is ann bho Dhomhnall a
fhuair Clann Domhnaill a h-ainm, ach a dh'aindeoin sin, is e fìor
bheag de eòlas deimhinne a tha againn air Domhnaill fhèin. A
rèir nan annalan Èireannach, bha e an sàs ann an creach-mara
air Doire Cholm Cille ann an 1212, maille ri bràthair tighearna
Ghall-Ghàidhealaibh. Tha cuid de sgoilearan den bheachd gur
esan 'Mac Somurli rí Airir Goidil' a chaidh a mharbhadh ann am
Béal Átha Seanaigh ann an Tír Chonaill ann an 1247 agus e a'
sabaid às leth Mhaoilsheachlainn Uí Dhomhnaill an aghaidh
Mhuiris Mhic Gearailt, tighearna Shligigh, ach tha tomhas de
theagamh anns a' chùis.

Chan eil dad a dh'fhiosrachadh mun ùghdar, ach faodar a
bhith gu ìre mhath cinnteach gum buineadh e do iar-thuath na
h-Èireann, agus e ag ainmeachadh àiteachan no aibhneachan
ann an Tír Chonaill, Ros Comáin agus Maigh Eo.

Chan fhaighear an dàn ach ann an làmh-sgrìobhainn a chaidh
a sgrìobhadh anns an dàrna pàirt den t-seachdamh linn deug leis
an fhile ainmeil Niall MacMhuirich. A rèir coltais tha toiseach
an dàin air chall, oir chan eil an sreath mu dheireadh na
dhùnadh ceart, agus chan eil am 'blas' ceart air a' chiad shreath
(tha iad, mar as trice, pongail agus ealanta). Tha iomradh anns

Never was fine cow without calf,
nor heifer without issue,
    a praise poem of mine has its lay,
    O flushed fair one, Amhlaoibh.

Amhlaoibh, O regal head of curls,
my friend and my foster-brother,
    sweet is the lay of your learned poet,
    woe to the one who neglects me, Amhlaoibh.

Domhnall mac Raghnaill of the Stately Gaze

This incomplete poem, never published previously, appears to address the eponymous founder of Clann Domhnaill, Domhnall mac Raghnaill mhic Shomhairle, who flourished in the early thirteenth century. Despite giving his name to such an illustrious kindred, Domhnall is a shadowy figure about whom relatively little is known. According to the Irish chronicles, he participated in a seaborne raid on Derry in 1212, together with the brother of the lord of Galloway. He may also be the 'Mac Somurli rí Airir Goidil' ('king of Argyll'), killed at Ballyshannon in Tír Chonaill in 1247 while fighting on behalf of Maoilsheachlainn Ó Domhnaill against the Norman lord of Sligo, Maurice Fitzgerald, but historians disagree about this identification.

The author of the poem is unknown, but the various geographical references in the text suggest strongly that he belonged to the north-west of Ireland.

The poem survives only as a late copy, in a manuscript from the late seventeenth century written by Niall MacMhuirich, last of the great MacMhuirich poets who served first the Clann Domhnaill Lords of the Isles and then the Clann Raghnaill chiefs of Uist and the Rough Bounds. The beginning of the poem is almost certainly missing, but there is no way to tell how many stanzas may have been lost. The citing of the second couplet of verse 3 in the Irish Grammatical Tracts (which date from c. 1500) supports an early date for the poem.

na tràchdasan gràmair (bho *c.*1500) air an dàrna leathrainn de
rainn 3 a' toirt taic dha na cinn-latha thràth dhan dàn seo.

Tha am bàrd a' dèanamh sodal ri Domhnall, ga mholadh mar
rìgh Èireann, is esan à Innse Gall de shliochd Gall-
Ghàidhealach. Bu chòir dha bhith na chèile aig Banbha. Tha an
dà rann mu dheireadh nas pearsanta na an àbhaist, agus an
coimeas aige eadar a bhith a' cur bàrdachd ri chèile agus a bhith
fighe snàithle de dh'fhuaim air leth freagarrach seach gun do
lean e riaghailtean na meadrachd gun smal.

Domhnall mac Raghnaill rosg mall
    ní tost da ghlannluing mar Gholl;
trí buadha as a mbearar geall:
    cuanna seang leabhar a long.

Gairid leinn i luing an rígh,
    sinn na cuir is an séagh saor;
ar luing gasdaine go ngádh,
    basgaire rámh trom re taobh.   8

A stargha lais cona loinn
    sa darna bhais chalma chuirr,
a leathgha san láimh ar-aill,
    láidh tairr a deabhtha ar a druim.

Áluinn an sgiath, sgiath an rígh,
    taraill da thriath is da threóir,
nathair sheang ag tuighe a taobh
    's a hearr caolbhuighe na beóil.   16

Deabhuidh Leath Mogha maith linn,
    flaith an bhrogha ó thuinn go tuinn;
deargfaidh óigfhear fhala Finn
    rinn fhogha iomdha Chóigidh Chuinn.

Is long do sdiúireadh gan sdiúir,
    urradh a fhonn, ge madh áill,
a ghort do roinn ris an rígh:
    is tocht do sgín chroinn go cnáimh.   24

The poet appears to be making a flattering claim that Donald, a Hebridean of mixed Irish and Scandinavian descent, should claim suzerainty over Ireland, through the suggestion that he should be Banbha's husband. The final two verses strike a more personal note than usual, and considering his near-flawless adherence to the rules of *rannaigheacht mhór*, his metaphor of weaving the poem from a pure thread of sound is appropriate. Even so, the poet's claim in the final stanza to have spent half a year working on this poem is probably not to be taken literally.

Domhnall mac Raghnaill of stately eye,
    no rest for his bright ship, like Goll;
three virtues from which a wager is won,
    comely slender long his ship.

Our time feels short in the king's ship,
    ourselves, the heroes and the noble hawk, (?)
our own sprightly ship at risk,
    the beating of oars, heavy at her side.

He has his targe with his blade
    in one strong tapered hand;
his second lance in the other hand,
    he throws the belly of the fight on its back.

The king's shield is a handsome shield
    that came to its lord as his guide;
a slender serpent covering its sides,
    with its thin yellow tail in its mouth.

Leath Mogha's war makes us glad,
    the fort lands stretch from coast to coast;
the youth of the blood of Fionn will make red
    many a spearpoint of the province of Conn.

It is to steer a rudderless ship,
    for a lord of lands, even if he wish it,
to share his domain with the king:
    it is the coming of a wooden knife to bone.

A Bhanbha, bean d'Albain é,
    an fear do gharguidh a gnaoi;
gan flaith, a Bhanbha, na bí —
    cá tarbha rí maith gan mhnaoi?

Fíor fhear níor ghabh Oileach úr,
    fan ngroidheach ngeal ro ghabh riar;
níor ghabh Raithteamhair na ríogh
    fear fíor mun flaitheamhain fial.   32

A ghnúis ri Teamhra na ttonn,
    cúis ga tearrla do fhuinn fhionn,
madh nacha bí craobh na crann
    do-chí barr caomh ós do chionn.

Rugais Domhnall dúin aniar
    na súl ngorm mall is mín gaol
[

                                   ]   40

As esan an chraobh chas dhonn,
    saor a bhas agus a bharr;
an tOirghiallach, ní locht leam,
    na cheann gort goirmfiadhach Gall.

Soillse dreach í Cholla chaoimh
    is deach ina tonna an chuain;
fada don chas bhinn ón Bhúill
    nach sill an tsúil ghlas a ghruaidh.   48

Ó Ghothfruigh ó hÁmhlaibh Fhinn,
    a ghallmhaoir ó thuinn go tuinn,
fleasga donna a ndiaidh an Ghoill
    do chloinn Bhriain is Cholla is Chuinn.

Ionair dhonna ag díon bhur cnis,
    a shíol mar shíol Colla chais;
céadshúgh bhar n-iorar aneas
    mar mheas iubhair ghéagúir ghlais.   56

O Banbha, Scotland's wife —
    the man who roughened her face;
O Banbha, be not without a prince —
    what profit a good king without a spouse?

Fair Oileach did not take a true mate,
    though she extracted a claim from the white stud;
Tara-fort of the kings did not take
    a true husband for the generous head.

O countenance facing Tara of the waves,
    a matter has arisen in a fair land,
a plain where there is neither branch nor tree,
    which sees a fine crop over your head.

Domhnall brought us from the west,
    he of the tender blue eyes of gentle love,
[
               ]

He is the dense goodly tree,
    noble its stock and its crown;
I find it no fault that the Oirghialla man
    should be head of the Galls' green-swarded fields.

Colla's gentle descendant, his face
    is brighter than the waves of the sea;
the curly-headed, sweet-voiced one from the Boyle
    feels it long since the grey eye beheld his cheek.

Descendant of Gofruigh, descendant of Amhlaibh Fionn,
    his Hebridean stewards from sea to sea,
following the Hebridean are stout youths
    of the progeny of Brian and Colla and Conn.

Sturdy tunics protecting your skin,
    O seed like the seed of ringletted Colla,
the first juice from your shores to the south
    like the fruit of the fresh-branched green yew.

Cuma do bhuidhe na bharr,
    é mar dhuille na ccnó corr;
fiathfruighthear leat do Bhé Bhinn
    nar fhionn mac Dé no nar dhonn.

Do-ghéan go h-álainn a aoir
    eadar Mhálainn agus Muaidh;
cuiléan déidgheal ag Derbh-áil,
    gráin éigneadh ngeal ar a gruaidh.   64

Uair go Domhnall dúinn ag dul
    go sduaigh na súl nglan ngorm mall,
uair go Leamhain dúinn ag dol
    rún con a ndeaghaidh dá dhamh.

Do-ghéan saoirsi maisidh mín
    daoibhsi is do bhur n-aisil óir;
dá ráithe dhamh risin duain,
    ga h-uaim do snáithe ghlan ghlóir.   72

16. Ceannaigh Duain t'Athar, a Aonghas

Giolla Brighde Mac Con Midhe(?)

Tha am marbhrann seo, a rinneadh am meadhan an trìtheamh
linn deug, air leth cudromach air sgàth adhbharan eachdraidh a
bharrachd air feadhainn litreachais. Is e glè bheag de litreachas
Gàidhlig a thàinig a-nuas thugainn bhon rè seo, agus gheibhear
bhon dàn seo sealladh beòthail brìoghmhor air saoghal
morairean-mara Innse Gall.

Is e cuspair an dàin Aonghas Mòr MacDhomhnaill (†1296),
mac Dhomhnaill mhic Raghnaill, cuspair dàin 15. Is e fìor bheag
de dh'eòlas a tha againn air beatha Dhomhnaill, ged as ann
bhuaithe a shìolaich an cinneadh as ainmeile ann an Alba. Tha e
coltach gun do rinneadh an dàn a leanas goirid an dèidh bàs
Dhomhnaill, oir tha am file ag iarraidh pàigheadh airson dàn a
rinn e dha. Is dòcha gur e am file Giolla Brighde Mac Con

There is a yellow sheen in his hair
    like the foliage around smooth nuts;
let Bé Bhionn be asked by you
    if the Son of God was fair or brown.

His satire will I defuse
    between Malin and Moy —
Dearbháil's white-toothed whelp,
    the hatred of fierce fights on her cheek.

Whenever I go to Domhnall,
    to the prince of the bright blue stately eyes,
whenever I go to the Lennox,
    I am as keen as a hound in pursuit of two stags.

A beautiful refined work of art
    I will make to you and to your golden parts;
I have spent two seasons on the poem,
    weaving it from a pure thread of sound.

Pay For Your Father's Poem, Aonghas

This thirteenth-century elegy is of significant interest in both literary and historical terms. Very little literature relating to Gaelic Scotland has survived from this period, and this poem gives a vivid and evocative sense of the world of the Hebridean sea-lords.

The subject of the poem is Aonghas Mòr MacDhomhnaill (†1296), son of the Domhnall from which Gaelic Scotland's most illustrious family takes its name, and to whom the previous poem is addressed. Surprisingly little is known of Domhnall's life, however, and the date of his death is not known for certain; this poem was evidently composed shortly after Aonghas' succession, as the poet is essentially endeavouring to collect his father's debt. It has been suggested that the author may be the

Midhe à Tír Eoghain, a rinn marbhrann don cheann-chinnidh
Maoilsheachlainn Ó Domhnaill an dèidh dha bàs fhaighinn aig
blàr Bhéal Átha Seanaigh ann an 1247; a rèir nan annalan
chaidh 'Mac Somhairle Ticcherna Airerghaoidheal' a
mharbhadh air an aon bhlàr, agus tha cuid de sgoilearan den
bheachd gur ionnan Domhnall agus am 'Mac Somhairle' seo.

Ged a bha ceanglaichean làidir eadar Gàidheil na h-Alba agus
Gàidheil na h-Èireann anns na Meadhan Aoisean, tha an dàn
seo a' sealltainn dhuinn gur leisg le cuid de dh'aos-dàna na
h-Èireann tighinn a dh'Alba.

Ged nach do dh'atharraich cainnt is meadrachd an 'dàin
dhìrich' thar nan linntean, faodar a ràdh gu bheil an dàn seo
'tràth' na ghnè. Mar eisimpleir, tha am file a' cur cuideam làidir
air an t-sinnsearachd Lochlannaich aig Aonghas ann an dòigh
nach sùilichte ann an dàn bhon t-seachdamh linn deug.

Ceannaigh duain t'athar, a Aonghas,
    agad atá teach an ríogh:
as tú fréamha is bláth an bhile,
    adéara cách dlighi a dhíol.

Agad do fhágaibh a láithreach,
    leat gach lúireach, leat gach séad,
a áit a luirg 's a chloidhmhe corra
    dhuit 's a fhoirne donna déad.   8

Leat slabhraidh caola con t'athar,
    gach arg cumhdaigh ar do chuid,
a thoighi 's a cháin gan chomhroinn,
    táin is groighe Dhomhnuill duid.

Agad do fhágaibh gá thiomna
    gach teach ó Mhuile go Maoil;
leat a longa uadh, a Aonghais,
    a stuagh Droma craobhghlais Chaoin.   16

pre-eminent Ulster poet Giolla Brighde Mac Con Midhe, who composed an elegy on Maoilsheachlainn Ó Domhnaill following his death at Ballyshannon in 1247, where Aonghas Mòr's father Domhnall, subject of the unpaid-for poem referred to here, may also have been killed.

Although cultural links between Gaelic Scotland and Gaelic Ireland were strong during the late medieval period, the poet's evident desire to avoid journeying to Scotland to present his poem raises interesting questions about the degree of interaction between Irish poets and Scottish patrons. Similar expressions of unease can also be seen in several Irish poems from later centuries.

Although composed according to the same form of language and metre that remained in use by the classical poets until the end of the seventeenth century, this poem is palpably early in some respects. In particular, the poet refers to Aonghas' illustrious Norse ancestors in a way that was later to pass from fashion, as Clann Domhnaill and other Hebrideans came to assert a more exclusively Gaelic identity.

> Pay for your father's poem, Aonghas,
> > since the house of the chief is now yours;
> since you are the roots of the tree and the flower,
> > everyone will say you ought to pay.

> To you he has left his castle,
> > yours every breast-plate, yours every gem,
> his land, his followers, and his pointed weapons
> > are yours, and his brown ivory pieces for chess.

> Yours are your father's slender dog-chains,
> > every treasure chest(?) is part of your lot,
> his houses and tribute without division,
> > yours Domhnall's cattle-herds and his studs.

> In his will he has left you
> > every house from Mull to Kintyre,
> Aonghas, he has left you his galleys,
> > O pillar of green-branched Druim Caoin.

Leat a oiriocht 's a eich luatha,
    leat a bhiataigh gan bhuain díot:
as tú an mac as ceann dar gcathuibh,
    as lat ar gheall h'athair d'íoc.

Adaimh go ndlighi díol mh'éicsi,
    a onchú Banna, a bharr nocht:
gabh sgéal eile mona admha,
    do-bhéar th'eire d'agra ort.   24

Tnúth leamsa éadáil na n-ollamh
    uait, a leómhain Locha Cé:
gá fios an tnúth cáir, a chara,
    do mhúch gráin an mhara mé.

Coire dhá Ruadh, a rí Tuama,
    atá eadroinn, eagail linn,
Coire Bhreacáin blagh dar gconair,
    do ghabh creatán omhain inn.   32

Ní lugha as cás Coire Bhreacáin
    do bheith romhainn, a rí Ceóil:
a uabhar an tann as teasbhach
    ag sduaghadh crann seasmhach seóil.

Canaim ar omhan an anfaidh,
    a fhir Chola, charuid mná,
tar an gcuan go Aonghas Íle
    truagh nach aonros tíre atá.   40

An dara cos 'gá cur romhum,
    a rí Leodhais, isin luing,
an dara troigh thiar ré taca,
    ag triall soir, a dhata dhuinn.

Dobadh olc meisi ar mhuir ngáibhthigh
    do ghabháil ráimhe, a rosg gorm:
bím ar abhainn chiúin ar creathaibh,
    mar ghabhuim sdiúir eathair orm.   48

Yours his assembly and his swift horses,
    yours his hospitallers who cannot be taken away,
as you are the son at the head of our battles,
    it is yours to pay what your father has pledged.

Acknowledge that you ought to pay for my poetry,
    O hound of the Bann, O uncovered hair;
if you do not acknowledge it, tell another story,
    but I will lay your burden of accusation on you.

I envy the high-poets the treasure
    they gain from you, O lion of Loch Cé;
who knows if it is justified envy —
    I am stifled by dread of the sea.

Coire Dhá Ruadh lies between us,
    O king of Tuam, I'm afraid;
on our course lies Corryvreckan,
    I am beset by a seizure of fear.

Not less the difficulty that Corryvreckan
    lies before me, O king of Ceól,
as its exuberance in sultry weather
    will warp firm masts of sails.

I say, out of dread of the ocean,
    O darling of women, O man of Coll,
over the sea to Aonghas of Islay
    it is a shame there is not one point of land.

While I put one foot before me,
    O king of Lewis, into the ship,
the one behind I point westwards,
    when I go east, O pleasant one.

I would make a poor oarsman,
    blue eye, on a perilous sea;
even on a calm river I tremble
    when in charge at the helm.

Gá córughadh budh cóir orum
    ní fheadar ré ttocht tar tuinn:
ní fheadar an budh fhearr suidhe,
    eagal leam luighi san luing.

As é mo ghreim ghabhuim chugum
    chongmhas an loing, a fhlaith Fáil:
go nach brisi tolg na tuinne,
    misi is bord na luingi um láimh.   56

Fiarfaighthior 'nar fearann dúthaigh
    déanamh na loingi, a fhlaith Gall:
ní mór as léir as don fhairrgi
    don thsléibh chas as airde ann.

Dámadh tír go turgbháil gréini,
    gáibhthighi leam dar do láimh,
a bhfuil, a Aonghais, go hAlbain
    do mhuir bhraonghlas bhalgaigh bháin.   64

Targuidh h'athair, aobhdha an bréagadh,
    mo bhreith um luighi 'na luing:
peall fúinn ó Albain go hÉirinn
    targuidh dúinn ó céibhfinn Cuinn.

Mo ghoid as gan a fhios agum
    do fhóbair rí na rosg ngorm
cealg ro cogradh 'gon mhór mhíolla
    codladh iar n-ól fhíona orm.   72

Miosguis leam na laoidheng seólta,
    slat do luingi nochar lúb:
a mheic Domhnaill a Céis Cairrgi,
    do ghéis tonndruim fairrgi fúd.

Bualadh cladaidh, creacha minca,
    mian libhsi ar an luchtsa thall:
meinic ón linnsi lán fala
    lámh re hInnsi glana Gall.   80

I cannot calm myself as I ought to
    when crossing the waves;
I do not know if I'd be better sitting,
    but I'm afraid to lie down.

It is my grip that holds the ship together
    as I drag her towards me, O prince of Fál;
so the waves won't break the ship asunder
    I grasp the gunwale in my hand.

People have to ask, in my native district,
    what a ship is like, O king of the Isles;
from there little of the sea is visible
    even from the highest steep hill there is.

Even if land reached as far as the sunrise,
    most dangerous, I'd swear by your hand,
is the sea, Aonghas, from here to Scotland,
    grey-sprayed, down-pouring, white.

Your father offered, delightful enticement,
    to carry me, lying in his ship:
a couch under me from Scotland to Ireland
    Conn's fair-haired descendant offered me.

Stealing me away without my knowledge
    was attempted then by the prince of the blue eyes;
treachery was plotted by the gentle ruler
    when I was sleeping after wine.

A foolish dislike of the sailing galleys:
    the sail-yard of your ship was not bent,
O son of Domhnall from Céis Cairrge,
    though the ocean's wave-back roared below.

Striking land, more frequent forays,
    is your desire on yonder folk;
from now, there will often be a blood-tide
    washing the fair Hebrides.

Tánaguis a ttimchiol Éirionn:
    uathadh tráigh nach ttugais bhú:
seoltar lat longbhárca leabhra,
    dobhránta, a shlat Teamhra, thú.

Do Loch Fheabhail, d'Iorras Domhnann,
    dírioch uaibh a hInnsibh Gall:
caladh Iorruis, is fuar fíre,
    do fhionnais sluagh Íle ann.   88

Sluagh Íle leat láimh lé hÁroinn,
    d'fios a lámhaígh go Loch Con:
bearar 'gon tsluagh fhinnsin Íle
    buar a hInnsibh míne Modh.

Corcum-ruadh ráinig bhur gcobhlach
    Corca Baisginn ar a brú:
Ó Bhun Gaillmhi go Cúil gCnámha
    maighre súir gach trágha thú.   96

Oighre Manannain mac Domhnaill
    fá Dhun Balair do bhí a throid:
ó ttánuic, a shlat gheal Ghabhra,
    an mac do bhean Banbha a broid.

As uaibh táinig Colum Cille
    dar gcabhair thairis fo thrí:
fir Éirionn do dhíol an duainsi,
    léighionn do shíol uaibhsi í.   104

Bhar seanathair síol gColla
    Coirbre Lifiochair, laoch Mis:
do bhás uí Chuinn catha Gabhra
    druim ratha Banbha do bhris.

Turcuill, Íomhair. agus Amhlaoimh
    iomad, a laoich Locha Riach,
tonn bhrátha an talmhan ar troimnimh,
    damhradh Átha coillghil Cliath.   112

You have sailed all round Ireland;
    rare the shore where you took no cows;
slender long ships you sail in,
    otter-like, O sapling of Tara, you.

To Loch Foyle, to Erris Domhnann,
    from the Hebrides, your course is straight;
in the harbour of Erris, a true preparation,
    you discovered the hosts of Islay there.

The hosts of Islay were with you by Aran
    to test their shooting as far as Loch Con;
taken by those fair-haired hosts of Islay
    are the cattle of smooth Innse Modh.

Your fleet has reached Corca Baisginn
    and Corcomroe as well;
from Bun Gaillmhe to Cúil Chnámha
    you are a salmon searching every strand.

Manannán's heir is the son of Domhnall,
    around Dún Bhalair he waged war,
where he came from, bright scion of Gabhair,
    the son who plucked Ireland from her chains.

From you, Colum Cille came over
    three times to our aid;
the men of Ireland have paid for this poem —
    with its learning that has spread here from you.

Your grandfather was of the line of Colla,
    Cairbre Lifeachair, warrior of Mis;
from the death of Conn's descendant of Gabhair
    the back of Ireland's prosperity broke.

Torcuil, Íomhar and Olaf are around you,
    O warrior from Loch Riach,
the world's wave of doom for vehemence,
    warrior-band of Dublin of the bright hazel trees.

Clanna Somhairle, síol nGofraidh,
   ór ghin tú, nár thaisigh bhú,
a lubhghort cuir. a chraobh abhla,
   saor gach fuil ó a ttarla thú.

Síol gCeallaigh iomad a hÉirinn,
   Oirghiallaigh a hInnsibh Liag,
na craobha caibhniosa ad-chluine,
   do thaidhliossa uile iad.

                          120

Ní fhuil a nÉirinn ná a nAlbain
   Aonghas mar thusa, a thaobh seang:
Aonghais fháid bhraonghlais an Bhrogha,
   láid, a Aonghais, comha ad cheann.

    Ceannaigh.

17. Fuaras Aisgidh gan Iarraidh

Tadhg Óg Ó hUiginn

Tha an dàn molaidh seo leis an fhile Chonnachtach Tadhg Óg Ó hUiginn do Alasdair (mac Domhnaill) MacDhomhnaill, Rìgh nan Eilean, a chaochail ann an 1449, ùidheil air sgàth an t-seallaidh a tha e a' toirt dhuinn air an dàimh eadar Alba is Èirinn anns an rè seo. Bha Tadhg Óg air aon de na filidh a bu chudromaiche anns a' chòigeamh linn deug; rinn e mòran dhàn spioradail a bharrachd air a' bhàrdachd molaidh do chinn-chinnidh Chonnacht is Uladh. Chaochail e ann an 1448 agus chaidh adhlachadh ann am manachainn an Átha Leathain ann an Co. Mhaigh Eo.

A rèir naidheachd a bhàis ann an Annalan Uladh, b'e Tadhg Óg 'oide scol Erenn 7 Alban a n-dán', ach chan eil e idir cinnteach gu robh ceangal an da-rìribh aige ri Alba, oir tha reatraig molaidh den t-seòrsa seo gu math cumanta anns na h-annalan.

The House of Somhairle, the race of Gofraidh,
    from whom you came, who never hoarded kine;
O planted herb garden, O branch of apples,
    noble the blood from which you sprung.

Ceallach's race around you from Ireland,
    the Oirghialla from Innse Liag,
the related branches you hear of —
    I have paid court to them all.

There is no Aonghas in Ireland or Scotland
    to compare with you, O slender form,
Aonghases of the sod of the Brugh, dew-dappled,
    send goods, Aonghas, to you.

I've Received A Present I Didn't Request

This panegyric composed by the Connacht poet Tadhg Óg Ó hUiginn for Alasdair (mac Domhnaill) MacDhomhnaill, third Lord of the Isles (†1449), is particularly interesting as evidence of the relationship between Gaelic Scotland and Gaelic Ireland during the later Middle Ages. Tadhg Óg was one of the most prominent bardic poets of the fifteenth century, composing for a range of leading families in the north and west of Ireland, including Ó Néill, Ó Domhnaill, and Ó Conchubhair chiefs. A considerable number of his religious poems have also survived. He died in 1448 and is buried in the monastery of Áth Leathan (Strade), near Foxford, County Mayo.

In his death-notice in the Annals of Ulster, Tadhg Óg is described as 'preceptor of the schools of Ireland and Scotland in poetry' (*oide scol Erenn ₇ Alban a n-dán*). The evidence of this poem, however, must cast doubt on the extent of his connection to Scotland, as the poet goes to great lengths to avoid journeying to Scotland in response to Alasdair's invitation.

Tha grunn dhàn againn le filidh Èireannach anns a bheil iad
a' cur an cèill nàdar de dh'an-fhois a thaobh suidheachadh nan
Gàidheal ann an Alba – gu bheil e annasach no mì-nàdarra gu
bheil Gàidheil beò taobh a-muigh Èireann. Tha Tadhg Òg a'
dèanamh coimeas eadar MacDhomhnaill agus gaisgich ainmeil
ann an dualchas nan Gàidheal a thill a dh'Èirinn an dèidh
dhaibh seal a chaitheamh ann an Alba, gu h-àraidh Colla Uais
agus a bhràithrean.

Fuaras aisgidh gan iarraidh
gearr bhias i n-a baoithdiamhair;
    truagh nach fuil mo theagh re thaoibh
    an fear do chuir an chomaoin.

Séad re iarraidh má uair neach
ní cneasda nach biadh buidheach;
    créad acht anáir an asgaidh
    séad d'fhagháil nar iarrasdair.   8

Tug d'annsacht damh — dia do shéan —
iarla Rois, rí na n-oiléan
    rem fhaisgin nachar fhuirigh
    gan aisgidh dom ionnsuidhidh.

Tugas d'annsacht d'iarla Rois,
gé fhuilngim i n-a éagmhois,
    súil d'Albain nach éasgaidh liom
    ga féasgain ó ardaibh Éireann.   16

Caidhe séad dá sirfeadh mé
re ré codhnaigh Chinn Tíre
    dá rabh i ngoirmInnse Gall
    nach foighbhinnse a char chugam.

This is one of several poems by Irish poets – including poem 23, by Tadhg Óg's kinsman Tadhg Dall – in which the very existence of Scottish Gaeldom is presented as somehow unnatural, a form of exile, with a return to Ireland being the only proper course of action. The poet compares MacDhomhnaill's situation to that of famous warriors from the Gaelic past who returned from Scotland to conquer Ireland, most notably the fourth-century king Colla Uais, legendary progenitor of Clann Domhnaill, who fled to Ireland with his brothers Colla Dhá Chríoch and Colla Meann, and then reconquered Ireland from the usurper Muireadhach Tíreach. Colla Uais, the oldest of the 'Three Collas', then chose to return to Scotland, but Tadhg Óg here urges his descendants to return to their homeland.

> I've received a present I didn't request,
> not long will it remain a foolish secret;
>> sad my house is not beside him,
>> the man who initiated the intimacy.
>
> If a person gets a gift through asking,
> it would be churlish not to show gratitude;
>> however it is a greater honour
>> to get a gift that is not solicited.
>
> The earl of Ross, the Lord of the Isles,
> showed me such love — sufficient the omen —
>> that he could not wait to see me
>> without sending me a present.
>
> I have given such love to the earl of Ross,
> though I am not with him,
>> that gazing at Scotland gives me no joy
>> as I behold her from the heights of Ireland.
>
> Whatever gift I could desire,
> while he is lord of Kintyre,
>> of all that is in the green Hebrides,
>> that I couldn't get to be sent to me.

Fuaras ó rígh rátha Floinn
séad i gcomhartha chumoinn
   a-tá oirne nach hé sin
   a bhfoighbhe mé dá mhaoinibh.　　　　24

A chorn gen gur chuindigh mé
ar Mac nDomhnaill Dúin Bóinne,
   do dhligh mé an corn do chuindghidh;
   a shir sé orm athchuintghidh.

Do Mhac Domhnaill na ndearc mall
mó an tiodhlagudh dá dtugam,
   an corn gémadh aisgidh óir,
   a n-aisgthir orm 'n-a onóir.　　　　32

Cé a-tá i n-aisgidh mar budh eadh
agam ó onchoin Gaoidheal,
   ní liom do-chuaidh an cornsa;
   fuair dá chionn mo chumonnsa.

An deoch do cuentheá sa gcoirn
i dtigh óil airgnigh Loghoirn
   ní bhíodh ann aga hibhe
   acht clann ríogh nó ridire.　　　　40

Do bhí uair budh iongnadh lat
— deacair cuirm do chur ionnat —
   bheith i dtoighibh óil gan fhíon,
   a shoidhigh óir an airdríogh.

An corn an tráth tugadh dham
le sluagh n-Alban do b'iongnadh
   d'ollamh nachar aithnidh dháibh
   bronnamh a aithghin d'fhagháil.　　　　48

Aithnim is dom iarraidh soir
tháinig thugam an cornsoin;
   re chois a mbliadhna do bheinn
   iarla Rois acht nach roicheim.

I received from the king of Flann's Fort
a jewel in token of the affection
    between us, which is not all
    I will win of his riches.

Though I never requested his drinking horn
from MacDhomhnaill of the Boyne's fortress,
    it was my right to ask for it
    as he asked me to make some petition.

Greater than the cup — though a gift of gold —
is the gift of what I am giving
    to MacDhomhnaill of the stately eyes
    in honour of what to me is given.

Though I got this cup free, as it were,
from the wolf of the Gaels,
    it doesn't seem that way to me:
    he received my love as payment.

The drink you used to pour in the cup
in the plundering drinking hall of Logharn,
    only the children of kings and knights
    would be there to imbibe it.

Once it would have seemed strange to you,
O golden vessel of the High-King,
    to be in drinking halls without wine —
    to fill you with beer is difficult.

When I was given this cup,
it amazed the people of Scotland
    that a poet they didn't know
    should receive such a present.

I recognise it is to entice me east
that that cup came hither;
    would that I were with the earl of Ross
    this year, but I cannot manage.

Tuigim féin nach dolta dhamh
d'iarraidh cruidh i gcrích n-Alban
    gen go mbeadh cuan oile ann
    acht Coire Dhá Ruadh romham.   56

Cúis oile nar áirimh mé
bhacas díom dul thar fairrge:
    ar n-aireine re hiath Cuinn
    ag triath dhaighfhine Dhomhnuill.

Síol gColla Uais nochan fhuil
acht ar amhsaine i n-Albain;
    a chairte ciodh nach osglann
    cion ga aicme ar Alostrann.   64

Créad 'ma bhfuilngeann flaith Íle
gan aoghaire an airdríghe?
    Iongnadh ubhall abhla Cuinn
    d'fhulang Banbha gan bhuachuill.

Mithidh dhóibh dlúthughadh rinn;
is é a n-adhbhar a hÉirinn
    na sluaigh a hinnsibh Alban
    a sinnsir uainn d'ionnarbadh.   72

Gaol re huaislibh aicme Cuinn
a-tá ag seabhcaibh síl Domhnuill;
    nach truagh ealta dar n-éanaibh
    uann ar eachtra i n-oiléanaibh.

Colla Dhá Chríoch is dá chloinn
a bhfuil d'Oirghiallaibh againn;
    ar gColla Uaisne is dá fhuil
    na dronga as uaisle i n-Albuin.   80

Síol éachtach Colla Dhá Chríoch,
síol Colla Uais madh eissíoth,
    is dearmhad dáibh leath ar leath
    muna dhearnad báidh bhráithreach.

I feel that I cannot go
to seek riches in the land of Scotland,
    without there being another way
    than by the Coire Dhá Ruadh whirlpool.

Another matter I haven't told
that prevents me crossing the ocean:
    that our precincts in the land of Conn
    may come to belong to kin of Lord MacDhomhnaill.

The tribe of Colla Uais
is only on campaign in Scotland;
    though his charters do not reveal
    the full love Alasdair's people bear him.

How can Islay's lord
suffer the kingdom to be without ruler?
    Strange that an apple from Conn's tree
    would allow Banbha to lack a shepherd.

The people from Scotland's isles —
it is time for them to join us;
    their ancestors being expelled
    is the cause of their absence from Ireland.

Related to the nobles of Conn's race
are the hawks of Domhnall's kindred;
    is it not sad that a flock of our birds
    should be away on exploit on islands?

From Colla Dhá Chríoch and his scion
all our Oirghialla are descended;
    from Colla Uais and his blood
    come the noblest families in Scotland.

If there be discord between the mighty seed
of Colla Dhá Chríoch and Colla Uais's descendants,
    it is wrong for them to be in two halves,
    not to express brotherly affection.

Leis Banbha do bhuain a glas
an tí dá dtabhrad ceannas;
 moille a thabhaigh ag teacht rinn,
 tearc 'n-a aghaidh fa Éirinn.   88

Triur eile 'n-a éagmhais sin
Mac Domhnaill dheargas craoisigh
 targaidh do thealaigh na bhFionn
 a hAlbain d'fhearaibh Éireann.

A hAlbain is eadh ro ghabh
mac Eithne dara mac Tuathal
 Cró Fiachaidh rob séad samhail
 ar n-éag d'Fhiachaidh Fhionnalaidh.   96

Do bhí i n-Albain — ard an rian —
Mac Con fa mac do Mhaicniadh
 fa chuing nó gur chuir Lughaidh
 fuil Chuinn mar do-chualubhair.

Aithris a ndearna is tír thall
Colla Uais nar ob chomhlann
 faghair ó bhfuil ar a shliocht;
 a-noir do thabhaigh treiseacht.   104

Slighe an trír tháinig a-noir
do ghabháil Fhódla a hAlbain
 tiocfa réalda cinidh Chuinn
 sa slighidh gcéadna chuguinn.

Sléachtain dó do dhlighfeadh sibh,
a shíl Cuinn, a chlann Éibhir,
 ó a-tá ar breith don uasain Eóin
 bheith uasaibh dá bhur n-aindeóin.   112

Ní bhia tír re taobh chalaidh
dá n-ullmhaighid Albanaigh
 gan líne bárc ar a broinn
 ó tracht Íle go hAroinn.

To free Banbha from the bonds of her chains
behoves the one to whom they give headship;
    his delay in claiming her is to our cost:
    there are few in Ireland will oppose him.

MacDhomhnaill who reddens a spear,
another three, in his absence,
    of the men of Ireland will come
    from Scotland to the Fair Men's fortress.

From Scotland indeed Eithne's son,
whose son was Tuathal,
    seized Fiachaidh's Fold — an identical course —
    on the death of Fiachaidh Fionnalaidh.

Mac Con, MacNiadh's son,
was, noble the way, in Scotland
    until Lughaidh, as you have heard,
    brought Conn's race into subjugation.

Colla Uais who never refused a fight
came over from the east to seize power;
    those of his race that are found in yonder land,
    let them emulate his action.

The path of the three that came from the east
from Scotland to seize Fódla
    will be taken by the star of Conn's race —
    by the same course he will reach us.

It should behove you to prostrate yourselves,
O race of Conn and children of Éibhear,
    for it is ordained that that grandson of Eòin
    is to be over you, even if you oppose it.

When the Scots are preparing to come
there will be no land beside harbour
    without its row of moored ships
    from Islay's strand to Aran.

Géabhaidh Mac Domhnaill Dúin Breagh
ráth Logha ar lorg a shinnsear;
do-ghéabha Lios Eamhna as
sgéala dearbha an fios fuaras.   120

Fuaras.

18. Fíor mo Mholadh ar Mhac Domhnaill

Gun urra

The e coltach gun do rinneadh an dàn goirid làidir seo an lùib coisrigeadh Eòin (mac Alasdair) MhicDhomhnaill (†1503), mu 1450. Chaidh an dàn a ghleidheadh ann an Leabhar Dearg Chloinn Mhuirich, an cois tuairisgeul fhada, bhuadh-fhaclach air mar a chruinnich uaislean Innse Gall airson Eòin a chur an oifig. Aig deireadh a' mhòr-thachartais seo 'do chan an file' facail an dàin. Chan eil ainm air a chur mu choinneimh an 'fhile' seo, ach faodar gabhail ris gur e ball de Chloinn Mhuirich a bha ann.

Tha e anabarrach inntinneach gu bheileas a' cur uiread de chuideam air àiteachan agus ainmean Èireannach, fiù 's nuair a bha 'Tighearnas nan Eilean' aig àirde. Chithear an seo am meas agus an luach a bha Gàidheil Alba a' cur air Èirinn.

Is e meadrachd caran tearc a tha air a chleachdadh an seo, rannaigheacht bheag bheag, anns a bheil ceithir lidean anns gach leth-loidhne, uaim anns gach leth-loidhne san dàrna loidhne, agus cuideam ga chur air an dàrna lide mu dheireadh.

Fíor mo mholadh   ar Mhac Domhnaill
Cur le gceanglaim   cur gach comhlainn.

Croidhe leómhain   lámh nár tughadh
Guaire Gaoidheal   aoinfhear Uladh.

MacDhomhnaill of Dún Breagha will seize
the Fort of Lugh as did his forebears;
   the Fort of Eamhain he will also gain,
   sure the news I'm in receipt of.

True My Praising of MacDhomhnaill

This short but vivid poem appears to have been composed for
Eòin (mac Alasdair) MacDhomhnaill (†1503), last Lord of the
Isles, in connection with his inauguration, around 1450. The
poem is preserved in the Book of Clanranald, which gives a
lengthy, florid account of this inauguration (similar in many
respects to lines 117–56 of poem 24), at the end of which the
poet is said to have 'sung these words' to 'certify' (*dearbhadh*)
Clann Domhnaill's determination to stand firm against their
enemies, with Eòin as their leader.

The poet is not named, but it might be assumed that he was
a MacMhuirich, as this family served as hereditary poets to the
Lords of the Isles.

The poet's reliance on almost exclusively Irish terms of
praise, for the most important of Scottish chiefs at the height of
the Lordship's power, demonstrates the continuing prestige of
things Irish in the Scottish Gaelic mindset.

The metre is fairly uncommon, *rannaigheacht bheag bheag*,
with four syllables per phrase, ending with a stress on the
penultimate syllable.

True my praising	of MacDhomhnaill,
hero I'm bound to,	hero of every conflict.
Heart of a lion,	hand that reproached not,
Guaire of the Gaels,	sole champion of Ulster.

Aoinfhear Uladh	táth na bpobal
Rosg le rugadh	cosg na gcogadh.
Grian na nGaoidheal	gnúis í Cholla
Fa bhruach Banna	luath a longa. 8
Cuiléan confaidh	choisgeas foghla
Croidhe connla	bile Banbha
Tír 'na teannail	deirg 'na dheaghaidh
A bheart bunaidh	teacht go Teamhair.
Measgadh Midhe	onchú Íle
Fréimh na féile	tréan gach tíre.
Níor éar aoinfhear	no dáimh doiligh
Craobh fhial oinigh	ó fhiadh n-Oiligh. 16
Níor fhás uime	acht ríoghna is ríogha:
Fuighle fíora	fíor mo mholadh.

19. Ceannas Gaoidheal do Chlainn Cholla

Ó hEanna

A rèir coltais rinneadh an dàn seo, a tha na mhìneachadh air eachdraidh is craobh-sgaoileadh Chloinn Domhnaill, mu mheadhan a' chòigeamh linn deug. Coltach ri dàn 18, is math a dh'fhaodte gun do rinneadh e do Eòin mac Alasdair agus e a' gabhail ceannas nan Domhnallach *c.* 1450. Tha an dàn ag ainmeachadh sinnsirean Eòin suas gu Colla Uais, an gaisgeach Ultach a bha beò (mas fhìor) anns a' cheathramh linn.

Bha sinnsearachd riamh air leth cudromach do na Gàidheil. Gu dearbh, bha eachdraidh chliùiteach an teaghlaich a' dearbhadh còraichean is ceart a' chinnidh agus a cheannaird. Mar sin, cha robh fìorachas is cruinneas eachdraidheil cho cudromach ri feumalachdan poilitigeach. Chithear mar a chaidh eachdraidh

Sole champion of Ulster,   welder of the peoples,
eye which engendered   the quelling of warfare.

Sun of the Gaels,   face of Colla's descendant,
around the Bann's borders,   swift his galleys.

Hound of fury   who checks raiding,
heart steadfast,   great tree of Banbha.

The land is a blazing   beacon behind him,
his ancestral mission   to go to Tara.

Meath's confusion,   wolf of Islay,
root of bounty,   each land's defender.

He refused no-one,   nor pleading band of poets,
generous branch of honour   from the land of Oileach.

None grew up round him,   but kings and queens,
true these judgements,   true my praising.

The Supremacy of the Gaels for Clann Cholla

This poem celebrating the pedigree of Clann Domhnaill appears
to date from the middle of the fifteenth century and, like poem
18, may well have been presented to Eòin, last Lord of the Isles,
at his inauguration *c.* 1450. The poem names Eòin's forefathers
back to Somhairle (Somerled), the founder of the Lordship of
the Isles according to Gaelic tradition, and then traces his
ancestry all the way to Colla Uais, the fourth-century Ulster
warrior-king.

   Genealogy played a crucial role in the late medieval
Gàidhealtachd. A distinguished pedigree located a chief in Gaelic
history and tradition, and connected him to other prominent
kindreds past and present: it was the most powerful means of

nas glòrmhoire a chruthachadh, ùidh air n-ùidh, nuair a dh'fhàs cinnidhean fa leth (na Caimbeulaich, mar eisimpleir) na bu chudromaiche agus na bu chumhachdaiche.

Mar sin tha gu leòr de cheistean a thaobh cruinneas na h-eachdraidh a tha ga toirt seachad anns an dàn seo. Is cinnteach nach eil an liosta shinnsirean idir fada gu leòr; chan eil ach ceithir ginealaich dheug eadar Eòin agus Colla Uais, ged a tha mu mhìle bliadhna eatarra. A bharrachd air sin, tha na h-eachdraichean den bheachd gun do rinneadh sàr-Ghàidheil de theaghlach aig an robh ceanglaichean ri Lochlann a bha co-dhiù a cheart cho làidir.

Chan eil fiosrachadh cinnteach againn mu ùghdar an dàin seo, Ó hÉanna. Tha cuid de sgoilearan den bheachd gur dòcha gum buineadh e do theaghlach foghlaimte a bha stèidhichte ann an Co. Doire, agus gun tàinig a shinnsir a dh'Alba mar phàirt de 'thochradh nighean a' Chathanaich', na fir-dàna a thugadh seachad an lùib posadh Áine, nighean a' chinn-chinnidh Ultaich Cú Maige na nGall Ó Catháin, ri Aonghas Óg MacDhomhnaill († *c.*1329), aig toiseach a' cheathramh linn deug.

Ceannas Gaoidheal do chlainn Cholla —
   cóir a fhógra:
siad arís 'na gcathaibh céadna,
   flatha Fódla.

Ceannas Éireann agus Alban
   an fhuinn ghrianaigh
atá ag an dreim fhuiligh fhaobhraigh
   cuiridh cliaraidh.   8

Fuair ceannas na haicme uile,
   Eóin a hÍle,
fuair Alasdair, flath na féile,
   rath na ríghe.

expressing the chief's importance and natural right to rule. Above and beyond formal record-keeping, genealogy often involved a degree of creative embellishment and outright invention, and it was not uncommon for families to be fitted with a more prestigious Gaelic pedigree as their political importance grew.

The accuracy of the genealogy given in this poem is thus open to considerable doubt. Without question, the number of generations back to Colla Uais is far too short; scholars have disagreed, however, as to whether Clann Domhnaill can properly be connected back to Irish forebears, or whether the professional genealogists of the late Middle Ages grafted a distinguished Gaelic pedigree on to a kindred once identified as distinctly Norse in origin.

Nothing concrete is known of the poet Ó hÉanna. Some scholars have speculated that he might have been connected to a learned family of that name in County Derry, and that an ancestor of his might have formed part of *tochradh nighean a' Chathanaich*, the celebrated wedding-party of Áine, daughter of the Ulster chief Cú Maige na nGall Ó Catháin, which came to Scotland about 1300 in connection with Áine's marriage to Aonghas Óg MacDhomhnaill († *c.*1329).

The headship of the Gaels for Colla's descendants —
    it is right to proclaim it:
they are again in their same battalions,
    the princes of Fódla.

The headship of Ireland and of Scotland,
    of the sunny regions,
is held by that host, bloody, sharp-bladed,
    heroic, poet-surrounded.

Eòin from Islay won the headship
    of the whole kindred;
Alasdair, prince of bounty,
    won the benefit of kingship.

Domhnall, Eóin agus dá Aonghus
   'inán fhial fhaoilidh:
ceathrar do bhean riar do ríoghaibh,
   's dár ghiall Gaoidhil.   16

Domhnall is Raghnall don ríoghradh
   riamh nár tughadh:
Somhairle nár mheall a moladh
   ceann na gcuradh.

Ceathrar ó Shomhairle shúl-ghorm,
   suas go Suibhne:
ceathrar sin nárbh fhóill n-innmhe,
   cóir a gcuimhne.   24

Seisear ó Shuibhne — ríomh rathmhar —
   go rígh Colla,
fíon aca fá bhruachaibh Banna
   a ccuachaibh corra.

Dá n-áirmhinn a dtáinig uime,
   d'uaislibh Ghaoidheal
béim ar éan-ghlúin uaidh go hÁdhaimh
   ní fhuair aoinfhear.   32

Ag so treas do ghinealach Ghaoidheal
   mar do gheallas:
an dream-sa ris nár chóir coimeas,
   's dár chóir ceannas.

Ceannas.

Domhnall, Eòin and two called Aonghas,
　　of welcoming bounty:
four charged with the office of kingship,
　　to whom the Gaels submitted.

Domhnall and Raghnall in kingship
　　never softened:
Somhairle who earned his reputation,
　　leader of heroes.

Four men from blue-eyed Somhairle,
　　up to Suibhne:
four who never fell short of their standing,
　　it is right to recall them.

Six from Suibhne — a favourable number —
　　up to king Colla,
they had wine around the Bann's meadows
　　in horned goblets.

If I were to enumerate all the forebears
　　of Gaelic nobles,
a blight on any generation back to Adam
　　no man has found.

Behold the rank of the progeny of Gaels
　　as I have promised:
that host beyond all comparison,
　　who deserve headship.

　　　　Headship.

20. Cóir Feitheamh ar Uaislibh Alban

Gun urra

Chithear gu soilleir anns an dàn gun urra seo à Leabhar an
Deadhain mar a thuig na filidh an cumhachd: bhathar a' tuigsinn
nan aoir mar inneal fìor-chunnartach, agus mar sin bha e
cudromach rabhadh a thoirt seachad an toiseach. Tha dàin anns
a bheil am file agus an ceann-cinnidh a' trod (an da-rìribh no
mar chleas litreachais) air leth cumanta; gheibhear eisimpleir eile
ann an dàn 25.

Is e cuspair an dàin seo Eòin (mac Shir Roibeirt) Stiùbhart;
is math a dh'fhaodte gur ionnan Eòin (mac Shir Roibeirt) agus
an t-Eòin a dh'eug aig Gart, faisg air Loch Raineach, ann an
1475, a fhuair brosnachadh ann an dàn 35 madaidhean-allaidh
a mharbhadh. Gu mì-fhortanach, chan eil dad a dh'fhiosrachadh
againn air ùghdar an dàin seo no air filidh eile aig an robh
buntainneas ris na Stiùbhartaich.

> Cóir feitheamh ar uaislibh Alban;
>   's í an fhoidhid do-gheibh gach méad;
> más í lann líomhtha do-chímíd,
>   go ngabh an díomoladh éad.
>
> Ní cóir fearg i dtús gach agra,
>   gé cluineann neach ní nach dóigh;
> 'n uair thá gach rath riamh i ndeacra,
>   ní math ciall gan fhreagra cóir.   8
>
> An t-adhbhar fá bhfuil mo thagra,
>   ní math glór gan chiall ré chois,
> má tá brígh i ndán na n-innsge,
>   do-chím tráth dhá h-innse nois.
>
> Ag so Gaoidheal do chloinn Ghaltair
>   ag réir fileadh, feirrde a ghné:
> gé tá mise ar dál ó a bhronnadh,
>   's ciste dámh is ollamh é.   16

It is Right to Serve the Nobles of Scotland

This anonymous poem from the Book of the Dean of Lismore is a fine example of the bardic poets' sense of power: the threat of wounding satires was something taken very seriously, and as such a warning was always given. Poems relating to disputes, real and stylized, between poet and patron are very common; another example is poem 25 below.

The poem addresses Eòin (mac Shir Roibeirt) Stiùbhart; although the matter is not certain, this is probably the Eòin who died at Garth, near Loch Rannoch, in 1475, who, in poem 35, is urged to hunt down wolves. Unfortunately, we know nothing of the author, nor of any other professional poets who composed for the Stiùbhart family.

It is right to serve the nobles of Scotland;
    forebearance it is that wins every gain;
if what I see is a sharpened weapon,
    the slander will produce a grudge.

At the start of an appeal anger is not fitting,
    even if one hears something untoward;
when all the good-will one has gained is in danger,
    being reasonable without satisfaction is not right.

The matter that concerns my appeal,
    — speaking without reason is no good —
if there is any strength in the poem of confessions,
    I see now is the time to tell.

Here is a Gael of Walter's kindred,
    satisfying poets to the betterment of his name:
though I am separated from his bounty,
    he is treasure-chest to poets and learned men.

A Eóin Stiúbhairt a crích Raithneach,
　a lámh Gaoidheal as fearr buaidh,
gabh, a laoich as solta i gcagadh,
　laoidh mholta agus bagar uaim.

Tángas chugad, mheic Shir Roibeirt,
　a Eóin Stiúbhairt na rosg ngorm;
beir, a chleath nach mion fá mheabhair,
　breath, is sin do-gheabhair orm.　　　　24

[　　　　　　　], a thaca maithean Alban,
　riomsa, a Ghaoidheil nach mion moirn,
a thuir, a bharr ghaisge ghéagdha,
　lean an aiste chéadna oirn.

Gabh do rogha, a mheic Shir Roibeirt,
　t'fhaladh riom giodh beag mo thort:
[　　　　　　　　　　　　　　　]
　's mé do-bheir cliar chogaidh ort.　　　　32

Más í do chomhairle bhunaidh
　bheith 'gam eiteach, a fholt réidh,
a lámh thréan na nGaoidheal soinnimh,
　fa séan aoir id choinnibh é.

A Chú Chulainn cloinne Ghaltair,
　Eóin lér oirbhire neart soirbh,
a shlat as tréan gnúis ré caille,
　nocha déan cúis faille oirbh.　　　　40

Ní bhia tú ar shuain ná ar shiorram
　gan aoir liomsa, a thlacht tláith;
ní h-aithnid leis an éan ealtna
　an t-saighead ghéar ghreanta gháidh.

Ní bhia mé i gcomaoin t'fhaladh,
　giodh deacair linn dul fán nós;
acht fá-ríor ar bhéad an bhagair
　don mhéad díona tá agad fós.　　　　48

Eòin Stiùbhart from the bounds of Rannoch,
　　most effective hand among the Gaels,
accept, O warrior, cheerful in warfare,
　　a poem of praise and a threat from me.

I've come to you, son of Sir Roibeart,
　　O Eòin Stiùbhart of the eyes of blue;
give judgement, O pillar not small in intellect,
　　and you will find I'll abide by it.

[　　　　　], O support of the nobles of Scotland,
　　to me, O Gael of no small love,
O tower, O flourishing flower of valour,
　　the same attributes have clung to me.

Take your choice, O son of Roibeart,
　　Your grudge against me though small my fault;
[　　　　　　　　　　　]
　　I will bring against you a band of war.

If it is your considered opinion,
　　to refuse me, O smooth hair,
it is a sign for me to make you a satire,
　　O mighty hand among the fortunate Gaels.

Eòin, the Cú Chulainn of Walter's children,
　　who deems strength easily won a reproach,
O branch who turns fierce face to damage,
　　I will not take you unawares.

You will not be asleep or resting
　　not having received my satire, soft attire,
the bird in the flock does not notice
　　the deadly sharp whittled dart.

I will not be beholden to your malice,
　　though it is hard for me to behave like this;
but alas, for the way my threat will damage
　　all that you have to call your own.

Déar-sa riotsa, a mheic Shir Roibeirt,
a Ghaoidheil nach críon fán chrodh,
fa mó an díoth dhuit mo theagmháil
ná síoth agus beagán domh.

Nárab tusa thollas oram:
nimh na n-aoir ní an cogadh soirbh;
's fearr dhuit gach radháil ón teine
ná a gabháil mar eire oirbh.   56

Gé dhéana mé, mar as cosmhail,
do cháineadh mar dubhradh linn,
beag an fiach mo mhart ré mhaoidheamh,
a thriath shlat na nGaoidheal ngrinn.

Beag an geall duaise rér n-aoir-ne
m'anam-sa fá h-éiric chronn;
beag a bhrígh gach mac ag m'athair,
a shíl shlat ó chathach Chonn.   64

Ní h-amhail sin atá tusa,
a mheic Ghaltair as fearr ciall,
a lámh thréan ó fhine an domhain,
nach d'éar file romhainn riamh.

Math mo dheadhail ré mo dhíomdha
orad do thaobh séad is [   ]
do dhá bhos mar aol gan [   ]
's an chos nár aom [   ].   72
Leór nimh mo theangadh gan ghríosad:
mairg do ghríosadh í rém linn;
a dhéad as geal, rún as gartha,
is fearr gan súgh nathrach sinn.

I will say to you, O son of Roibeart,
    O Gael who is not mean with kine,
greater were the damage to you to strike me
    than to grant me peace and and some small reward.

Let it not be you who goads me:
    the venom of satires is no easy war;
better for you being scorched by embers
    than to take that burden on.

Though I should do it, as is likely,
    dispraise you, as I have said,
my carcase is little to boast of,
    O lord of the scions of the fine Gaels.

Small the promise of pay for my satire,
    my life under the blood price of spears,
of small substance is each son of my father,
    O seed of the scion from the warrior Conn.

Not like that are you,
    O son of Walter of the keenest mind,
O mighty hand of the tribes of the world,
    who never refused a poet before.

It would be good for me to part with my anger
    against you regarding jewels and [   ],
your two hands like lime without blemish,
    and foot that never attracted [   ].

My tongue's venom is sufficient without goading;
    woe to the one who ever kindles my ire;
O white tooth, O warmest affection,
    we are better without the venom of the snake.

21. Lámh Aoinfhir Fhóirfeas i nÉirinn

Giolla Críost Brúilingeach

Rinneadh an dàn seo am meadhan a' chòigeamh linn deug ri
linn cuairt bàird Albannaich, Giolla Críost Brúilingeach, air
ceannard Èireannach, Tomaltach Mac Diarmada, triath Mhaigh
Luirg ann an Co. Ros Comáin, a dh'eug ann an 1458. Tha e
follaiseach gu robh meas aig Giolla Críost air Mac Diarmada, oir
ann an dàn eile leis a tha air a ghleidheadh ann an Leabhar an
Deadhain tha e a' moladh fialaidheachd Mhic Dhiarmada agus
a' dèanamh dìmeas air spìocaireachd Mhag Uidhir, triath Fhear
Mhanach.

Ann an rannan 9 agus 10 (sreathan 33–40) tha Giolla Críost
a' moladh Mhic Diarmada le tuairisgeul air an torrachd nàdarra
a chithear na rè. Seo cleas a tha cumanta agus gu math àrsaidh.

Is e far-ainm seach sloinneadh a tha ann am 'Brúilingeach'; a
rèir coltais bha Giolla Críost ri bàrdachd a chleachd a'
mheadrachd ris an abrar 'brúilingeacht', seòrsa nach robh cho
toinnte ris na siostaman a chleachd na filidh. Leis mar a tha
Giolla Críost ag iarraidh clàrsach air Mac Diarmada, faodar
tuigsinn gur e clàrsair proifeiseanta a bha ann. Is dòcha gum
buineadh e do Chloinn Mhic an Bhreatnaich, a bha nan
clàrsairean do Rìghrean nan Eilean; bhuineadh an teaghlaich ri
Leim ann an Eilean Ghiogha, agus ann an Leabhar an Deadhain
tha na Griogaraich a' cleachdadh an tiotail 'Bard in Leymm' mu
Ghiolla Críost.

Anns an dà rann mu dheireadh tha am bàrd a' bruidhinn ri
bean Thomaltaigh, Caitilín inghean Bháiteir a Búrc, a
bhuineadh do aon de na teaghlaichean Gall-Ghàidhealach a bu
chudromaiche ann an Cúige Chonnacht. Tha seo cumanta ann
am bàrdachd an linn seo, agus gheibhear eisimpleir eile dheth
ann an dàn 25.

> Lámh aoinfhir fhóirfeas i nÉirinn
>   ar anbhuain Ghaoidheal is Ghall,
> flaith na bhfear is bile bonnbhláith,
>   cridhe geal is connbháil ann.

One Man's Arm Can Halt in Ireland

This poem from the mid-fifteenth century shows a Scottish poet, Giolla Críost Brúilingeach, visiting the court of an Irish chief, Tomaltach Mac Diarmada, of Moylurg in County Roscommon, who died in 1458. In another poem in the Book of the Dean of Lismore, Giolla Críost draws a satirical comparison between the generosity of Mac Diarmada and the stinginess of Mag Uidhir, lord of Fermanagh.

In stanzas 9 and 10 (lines 33–40), the poet uses the ancient trope of connecting natural bounty to the king's just rule. This common device is also used in poem 24 (as noted in the extract from the manuscript quoted in the Introduction). Its converse, the depiction of nature grieving following the king's death, is seen in poem 31.

'Brúilingeach' is not a surname but seems to suggest that Giolla Críost specialised in poems composed in the *brúilingeacht* metre, a looser metrical form than that used by the *filidh*. Given his request that Mac Diarmada reward him with a harp, it appears that Giolla Críost was a professional harper; he probably belonged to the hereditary Mac an Bhreatnaich (Galbraith) harpers, who were based at Leim in the Isle of Gigha, as the Book of the Dean refers to him as 'Bard in Leymm'.

The last two stanzas of the poem are directed to Tomaltach's wife, Caitilín, daughter of Bháiteir a Búrc (Walter Burke), who belonged to one of the leading Anglo-Norman – but rapidly Gaelicised – families of Connacht. Such addresses to the patron's wife are common in bardic poetry of this era; another example appears in poem 25.

> One man's arm can halt in Ireland
>   the torment of foreigner and Gael,
> a prince of men and scion white-footed,
>   a bright heart which offers aid.

Ar eineach agus ar aithne
   's ar eangnamh i n-iath an fhéidh
giolla glaccaomh, bile Banbha,
   macaomh tighe Teamhra tréin.   8

Eólach dhomhsa iarla uasal,
   fhóireas Éirinn ar chath cliar;
bradán Sionna na sreabh solta,
   giolla geal do sgoltadh sgiath.

Aithnid domhsa an féinnidh fuileach,
   an fear-soin chongbhas a ghaol;
ciabh fhollán ghlan ag an ghiolla,
   Mongán na mban sionga saor.   16

Lugh Lámhfhada mór mac Eithleann
   airdrí líonmhor Locha Cé;
Íoth seólach ar buaidh a bhéimeann:
   leómhan do chuain Éireann é.

Ar Thomaltach caomh na Cairrge
   do chuir mé m'aithne 'na aoibh;
gabhthar mo laoidh ar m'fhéis romhainn
   go rígh Céise Corainn chaoimh.   24

Mac Diarmada ó Mhuigh Luirg líonmhoir,
   lánchara ceall agus cros;
[   ]
   flaith ar mbuain ar bháire a bhos.

Mac Diarmada is a réim roimhe,
   rí na Cairrge i gcruas a chuilg;
fear is iomdha dá fhuil bhríoghmhoir
   tighearna ar Muigh líonmhoir Luirg.   32

Cruithneacht dearg ar maghaibh míne
   fá Thomaltach chosnas Chéis;
bídh ar clár collbhán uí Cholla
   lomlán a droma ar gach déis.

Renowned his generosity and reputation,
 his prowess in the haunts of the deer,
hero of the house of mighty Tara,
 smooth-palmed youth, Ireland's sacred tree.

I am acquainted with a noble chieftain
 who saves Ireland from poets' strife;
salmon of the Shannon of calm currents,
 a shining youth for cleaving shields.

I know the blood-shedding champion,
 that man who protects his kin;
the youth has clean and shining tresses,
 a Mongán among slim noble girls.

Like long-armed Lugh, great son of Eithliu,
 is Loch Cé's high-king of numerous hosts;
by dint of his blows he is as Ioth on the oceans,
 amongst Ireland's cubs, he is a lion.

Well do I know the good spirits
 of gentle Tomaltach of the Rock;
in return for this feast let my poem be recited
 to dear Céis Corainn's lord.

A true friend of churches and crosses
 is MacDiarmada of thronging Magh Luirg
[   ]
 here he is the pre-eminent prince.

MacDiarmada with his reign before him,
 king of the Rock by the temper of his sword;
many a man of his vigorous forebears
 has been lord of the populous plain of Lorg.

Under Tomaltach's sway, Céis's protector,
 wheat grows red on gentle plains,
in the white-hazelled realm of Colla's descendant
 each ear of corn bends with its weight.

Lacht milis ag buaibh i mbuailtibh,
   branar fa féaraighe fonn;
fá h-árainn mhín is fá monadh
   tír álainn fá toradh trom.   40

Míolchoin gharga ar iallaibh órdha
   ag Tomaltach 's ceann ar cách;
sguir go moch san aonach uallach
   mán loch bhraonach bhuadhach bhláth.

I gcrích Mheic Dhiarmada doinndeirg,
   dearg agus donn craobh na gcrann;
[   ] ar chúl an chragaidh,
   gach meas go h-úr abaigh ann.   48

An chúirt as aoibhne ar druim domhain
   dún Mheic Dhiarmada as geal gné
i gcaisteal fionn na gcloch mbuadha
   ós cionn Locha cuanna Cé.

Cuirn is cuaich is copáin chumhdaigh
   i gcúirt líonmhoir Locha Cé;
ibhthear fíon san chonnphort chnuasaigh:
   is longphort ríogh uasail é.   56

Iomdha a theaghlach álainn uasal,
   a éideadh 's a eachradh ard;
iomdha sleagh is lann is lúireach,
   agus fear mall glúineach garg.

Gabhaidh uime an t-earradh maothshróill
   Mac Diarmada as nósmhor neart:
sé mar tharbh tuinne i ndruim tóra,
   lé bhuille cóir cródha ceart.   64

Dúinidh uime an cotún daingean,
   do dhíon an ríogh ó Ráith Cé;
an t-ór dearg ar crois a chlaidhimh,
   fearg ar a bhois raighil réidh.

The fallow land is of the lushest,
  cows yield sweet milk in folds,
in both its gentle fields and moorland
  it is a beautiful land under heavy crop.

Fierce deerhounds on gilded leashes
  are owned by Tomaltach, lord of all;
horses in the morning in proud assembly
  round the mild dewy healing loch.

Within the bounds of good MacDiarmada
  the boughs of trees are brown and red;
[   ] behind the crag in shelter
  every fruit is ripe and fresh.

In all the world the most joyful assembly
  is the fort of MacDiarmada of sparkling façade
within the fair castle of gemstones
  above the loch of elegant Cé.

Horns, quaichs and engraved goblets
  in the thronging court of Loch Cé;
wine is quaffed in that place of garner:
  it is the palace of a noble king.

Numerous are his noble retainers,
  his vestments and his high-headed steeds;
numerous his spears, swords, breast-plates,
  his solemn men, fierce and strong-kneed.

He pulls around him his shift of fine satin,
  MacDiarmada far-famed for his force:
like a thickset bull on the backs of the routed,
  with well-judged, mighty, unerring blow.

He closes around him the cotton wadding
  that protects the king from the Ráth of Cé;
red gold makes up his sword's cross-hilt,
  in his smooth regal palm there is rage.

Sgian chaisdearg ar an chrios chumhdaigh,
   cathlúireach má chéibh na gcuach;
clogas ós cionn sgabaill sgiamhdha
   mán mhionn abaigh niamhdha nuadh.   72

Sleagh fhada ag an mhílidh mhaiseach,
   Mac Diarmada Muighe hAoi;
sgiath eangach ar chuairt na gcuradh,
   searrach suairc ar fulang faoi.

Tánaig mise, maith an t-adhbhar,
   dot fhios a hAlbain, ó 's cóir,
mád teist, a Chonnachtaigh chaisghil,
   a Thomaltaigh mhaisigh mhóir.   80

Tánag d'iarraidh athchuinge oraibh,
   a hAlbain, a fholt mar ór,
ar an chuan ghagánach ghailbheach
   uar bhradánach mhaighreach mhór.

Cláirseach ar leath dom dhán damhsa
   tabhair mar iarraim, a rí;
ghnúis mar bhláth na habhla abaigh,
   ó's ní tharla agaibh í.   88

A mheic Chonchobhair chuain Chairrge,
   cubhaidh riotsa díol na ndámh;
tá cuid do sgéimhe dá sgríobhadh;
   Éire dhuid ar líonadh lámh.

Inghean Bháiteir a Búrc Breaghdha,
   bean nósmhor neamhghann má ní;
folt cladhach cúlghlan na gcéibheann:
   rogha úrbhan Éireann í.   96

Deárna álainn fhada fháinneach
   ag Caitilín na mbas mbán;
dearg a h-imle solta saora,
   's ingne corcra laomdha a lámh.

      Lámh.

On his tooled belt hangs a red-hafted dagger,
  a breast-plate encircles the one of the curling mane;
a helmet above the decorated mantle
  guards the shining fresh jewel in its prime.

A long spear is wielded by the lovely hero,
  MacDiarmada of the Plain of Aoi;
a cornered shield he bears on exploit,
  a well-trained colt carries his weight.

I have come with good reason from Scotland
  to visit you, fittingly drawn by your fame,
O white-footed man from Connacht,
  O Tomaltach, beautiful and great.

I have come to you from Scotland
  to crave a boon, O hair like gold,
over the huge, wave-cleft, chill ocean,
  abounding with salmon and grilse in shoals.

A remarkable harp for me, for my poem,
  since you possess such a thing,
you with skin like apple blossom,
  grant it to me as a gift, O king.

Son of Conchobhar of the haven of Carraig,
  fitting for you the rewarding of poet-bands;
the details of your beauty are being recorded,
  may Ireland be yours for your filling of hands.

Bháiteir a Bhúrc of Breagh's daughter,
  a lady never niggardly with her store,
with her shining ridged hair in long tresses
  of Ireland's young women she is the choice.

A hand, long ringed and lovely,
  has Caitilín of the white palms;
red her lips, noble and comely,
  and the painted polished nails of her hands.

22. Gabh Rém Chomraigh, a Mheic Ghriogóir

Fionnlagh An Bard Ruadh

Tha ceithir dàin le Fionnlagh an Bard Ruadh (no Fionnlagh Ruadh an Bard) do Eòin Dubh MacGriogair Ghlinn Sreith (†1519) air an gleidheadh ann an Leabhar an Deadhain, maille ris an aoir a rinn Fionnlagh air Ailean (mac Ruairidh) MacDhomhnaill (dàn 38).

Mar a thuigear bhon tiotal aige, b'e bàrd a bha ann am Fionnlagh agus cha b'e file. Tha an diofar ri fhaicinn ann am meadrachd an dàin seo (*óglachas* seach *dán díreach*) agus ann an grunn fhoirmean bho chainnt dhualchasach na h-Alba nach cleachdte anns a' chànan chlasaigeach.

A rèir coltais bha Fionnlagh air a bhith air chuairt; is math a dh'fhaodte gun deach e a dh'Èirinn, oir ann an dàn molaidh eile do Eòin Dubh, 'Fhuaras mo rogha theach mhòr', tha e a' toirt iomradh air cùirt Aodha Mhic Diarmada (ann an Co. Ros Comáin). Bha Aodh, a ghabh ceannas a chinnidh an dèidh bàs Thomaltaigh an Einigh (cuspair dàin 21) ann an 1458, na cheannard gu ruige *c*. 1478. Uime sin feumaidh gun do rinn Fionnlagh a chuairt eadar na bliadhnaichean sin.

Gabh rém chomraigh, a Mheic Ghriogóir,
   fáilte rinn ré teacht id cheann;
thugas lámh fá riar gan aighne,
   a ghrádh chliar 's a chraidhe cheall.

Ní cneasda corruigh ar chongbháil:
   brat thar gach cúis théid tar ceal;
druim ré dalta badh chiall cheilge,
   's gan Dia leantain feirge ar fear.

8

Grant Me Your Patronage, MacGriogair

This is one of four poems composed by Fionnlagh, an Bard Ruadh, to Eòin Dubh MacGriogair of Glen Strae, who died in 1519. All four, together with Fionnlagh's satire on Ailean (mac Ruairidh) MacDhomhnaill (poem 38), are preserved in the Book of the Dean of Lismore.

The poem is composed in *óglachas*, a loose form of the strict metres of the time, and Fionnlagh uses several vernacular Scottish forms that would not appear in a more formal poem. His title indicates that he was a *bard* rather than a *file*, without the training and status of the latter.

Evidently Fionnlagh had angered MacGriogair in some manner, and after a period away from his court, he was seeking to return, with this poem sent as a sort of peace offering. The apologue Fionnlagh uses to bolster his case is somewhat confusing. Conall Clogach is known to Gaelic tradition as the son of a sixth-century king of Ireland who was punished by Colum Cille after Conall caused Colum Cille and his party to be pelted with clods of earth. Colum Cille caused twenty-seven bells to be rung against Conall – the by-name Clogach means 'of the bells' – whom he cursed and deprived of his royalty, senses, memory, and understanding. However, Fionnlagh's invocation of Conall Clogach seems rather different, as the historical Conall Clogach lived several centuries after Conchobhar, the legendary king of Ulster who appears, together with great warrior Cú Chulainn, in the famous Ulster Cycle of heroic stories. Fionnlagh appears to cast Conchobhar in the role of Colum Cille.

> Grant me your patronage, MacGriogair,
>   give me welcome when I come;
> I have offered a hand in peace without a pleader,
>   O heart of churches and darling of bards.
>
> It is not kind to nurse one's anger
>   — a cloak over every matter that's past —
> to reject a fosterling would seem like treason,
>   not even God pursues his wrath on a man.

Usaide a mhathadh 'g cor cuarta
    gur h-annamh gheibhthear dhá cair;
traothaidh fá dheóidh fearg gach flatha:
    ní feóidh a dhearg 's cathamh air.

Fadódh corruigh 's gan mé ciontach,
    a Mheic Ghriogóir na lann ngorm,
gé táim seal a muigh ar th'uamhan,
    do lean dá mhuin uabhar orm.   16

Gé bé neach lér cuireadh eadrainn
    aimhleas bréige nach buan sgeamh,
a bhréag fá dheóidh dobadh díomhaoin:
    créad acht sgeóil far bhfiorghaol sean?

Dalta Chonchobhuir ríogh Uladh,
    Conall Clogach nár mhath ciall,
a fhreagradh amhra mán fhosadh;
    beagnach samhla dhomhsa a thriall.   24

Ó Chonchobhar as an Chraobhruaidh
    ní bhfaghadh cairde 's a thuaith;
fá dhiamhraibh gan locht a liosa,
    bliadhain gan tocht d'fhios a shluaigh.

Giodh mór a mhuirn ar [   ] fhearainn,
    Conall Clogach do chleacht ciall:
do bheacht, is cha b'fhardal céille,
    teacht go a ardfhlath féin dá riar.   32

Mar soin mise i ndiaidh mo thrialla
    ó Mhac Griogóir na n-arm nocht;
ni tuar so mo thriall ó a chóisir,
    duan 'na chomhdháil, duais gan locht.

Díomhaoin do neach a rádh riomsa
    sgarsain ré hEóin na rosg ngorm;
mo thriall, a bhranáin na nGaoidheal,
    dá líon anáir aoibheal orm.   40

It is easier to forgive with him on circuit,
    as fault with him is rarely found;
every prince's anger eventually lessens,
    but an ember cannot cool when fanned.

I was guiltless when anger was kindled,
    though I stayed away with dread of you;
because of that my pride was wounded,
    O MacGriogair of the blue blades.

Whatever man set between us
    harmful lies whose barking will not last,
in the end his lie proved idle:
    it is but a tale of your kinsmen of old.

The foster-son of Conchobhar, King of Ulster,
    Conall Clogach of little sense,
noble was his response about yielding,
    his trials are almost a symbol of mine.

From Conchobhar of the Craobhruadh
    he could get neither respite nor his folk,
in lonely places without the people of his stronghold,
    he was a year without going to see them.

Though in his land he took great pleasure,
    Conall Clogach who practised sense,
decided, from no lack of wisdom,
    to go to his overlord to make peace.

Likewise am I after my journey
    away from MacGriogair of the naked blades;
this is no foreboding that I forsake his banquet,
    but with a poem to greet him, a faultless gift.

It is idle for a man to advise me
    to part from Eòin of the blue eyes;
my being away, O prince of the Gaels,
    for all the honours, burnt me like a coal.

[   ]
[   ]
chuiris srian fa ádh na hAlban
    ag riar dhámh is bhard is bhocht.

Mairg do bhiodhbhaidh teacht it aghaidh;
    ionann duit is do bhaidhbh chliath;
ni dáigh ód shith acht fir ghonta,
    ód láimh ghil a sgoltas sgiath.   48

Baránta na h-aosa dána
    Mac Griogóir a bhronnas ba;
urra dhámh is fear na sealga,
    a lámh gheal a dheargas ga.

                    Gabh rém chomraigh.

23. Fada Cóir Fhódla ar Albain

Tadhg Dall Ó hUiginn

Bha Tadhg Dall Ó hUiginn air aon de na filidh Èireannach a bu
chliùitiche anns an dàrna pàirt den t-siathamh linn deug, agus
tha mu lethcheud da chuid dhàn air tighinn a-nuas thugainn.
Rinn e dàin do ghrunn luchd-taice ann an taobh a tuath agus
taobh a deas na h-Èireann, Ó Domhnaill, Ó hEadhra, Mac
Uilliam Búrc, agus Mac Suibhne nam measg. Chaidh a mhurt
ann an 1591, a rèir coltais le cuid de Mhuinntir Eadhra, a bha
diombach ris an fhile air sgàth aoir sgaitich a rinn e.
    A rèir coltais is e an dàn a leanas, a rinneadh do Shomhairle
Buidhe MacDhomhnaill (†1590), ceannard Chloinn Domhnaill
Aontrama, an aon phìos bàrdachd a rinn e do cheannard
Domhnallach, ach is math a dh'fhaodte gun do rinn e dàn do
bhean Shomhairle Bhuidhe, Máire inghean Chuinn Uí Néill,
cuideachd.

[

]
you have reined in the prosperity of Scotland
   by satisfying poet-bands, bards and the poor.

Woe to a foe who thinks to confront you,
   you are like Badhbh, goddess of wars;
only the wounded emerge from your onslaught,
   from your white hand that cleaves shields.

A guarantee for the men of learning
   is MacGriogair who rewards with cows;
patron of poet-bands and a fine huntsman,
   O white hand that reddens spears.

Long has Fódla Had a Claim on Scotland

Tadhg Dall Ó hUiginn was one of the pre-eminent Irish poets of
the later sixteenth century, and approximately fifty of his poems
have survived. He composed for a range of patrons in the north
and west of Ireland, including Ó Domhnaill, Ó hEadhra, Mac
Uilliam Búrc, and Mac Suibhne chiefs. His career was cut short
by his murder in 1591, supposedly at the hands of six members
of the Ó hEadhra clan, who were outraged at a particularly
wounding satire the poet had composed.

The following poem to Somhairle Buidhe MacDhomhnaill
(†1590), chief of the MacDhomhnaills of Antrim, appears to be
Tadhg Dall's only surviving composition for a member of Clann
Domhnaill, but he may well be the author of a poem to
Somhairle Buidhe's wife, Máire, daughter of Conn Bacach Ó
Néill.

That poem to Máire and the following poem explore similar

Gheibhear anns an dàn do Mháire agus anns an dàn a leanas tèamannan is ìomhaighean cumanta a thaobh tilleadh nan Gàidheal a dh'Èirinn. An lùib seo tha Tadhg Dall a' cleachdadh chan e a-mhàin sgeulachd nan Colla (faic an ro-ràdh ri dàn 19) ach cuideachd trèigsinn na Ròimhe le Julius Caesar.

Bu chòir an dàn seo a thuigsinn ann an co-theacs poiliteagach Còigeamh Uladh anns na deicheadan mu dheireadh den t-siathamh linn deug. Bha Clann Domhnaill a' sìor dhol an neart, rud a bha na chùis-iomagain do na Sasannaich agus do chinnidhean Gàidhealach na sgìre, gu h-àraidh Clann Uí Néill. Bha filidh Chloinn Domhnaill a' feuchainn ri còir is suidheachadh nan Domhnallach a neartachadh.

Bha Somhairle Buidhe (bràthair athar Dhomhnaill Ghuirm MhicDhomhnaill, cuspair dàin 32, agus Aonghais mhic Sheumais nan Ruaig, cuspair dàin 25) air aon de na ceannardan a bu chudromaiche ann am poileataigs Uladh anns na deicheadan mu dheireadh den t-siathamh linn deug, oir bha e furasta dha àrmainn a thoirt a dh' Èirinn air sgàth nan ceanglaichean a bha aige ri cinn-chinnidh Innse Gall agus an cuid àrmann.

Fada cóir Fhódla ar Albain,
anois am a hiomardaidh,
   a cóir féine acht go bhfagha
   ní dóigh Éire i n-aontamha.

Atá re hathaigh d'aimsir
cóir ag an chrích Albainsin
   ó Ráth chneasaolta Chobhthaigh,
   fáth easaonta d'Albanchaibh.   8

Tugtha d'Albain na sreabh seang
a cóir féin d'inis Éireann,
   críoch aimhréidh na n-eas mbanna,
   suil bheas aimhréidh eatarra.

Créad an chóir nuaidhese aniodh
atá ag crioch cloinne Míliodh,
   mná tá aguibh innis damh,
   fa n-aguir inis Alban?   16

themes about the Scottish Gaels' return to Ireland, themes
familiar from earlier panegyrics by Irish poets to Scottish
patrons. Here the poet invokes not only the three Collas (see the
introduction to poem 19) but draws a classical analogy to
Caesar's supposed abandonment of Rome.

The poem should also be understood in the political context
of late sixteenth-century Ulster: the MacDhomhnaills were
consolidating their power in the northeast of the country, to the
consternation of both the English authorities and the native
Gaelic aristocracy, especially the Ó Néills, long the dominant
force in the region. Taken together with later works to Somhairle
Buidhe's son Raghnall, created first Earl of Antrim in 1620, this
poem should be understood as an attempted defence of the
MacDhomhnaills' presence in Ireland.

Somhairle Buidhe (uncle of Aonghas, subject of poem 25,
and of Domhnall Gorm, subject of poem 32) was one of the key
players in Ulster politics of the late sixteenth century, a role
made possible by his ability to draw Hebridean military power
into Ireland.

Long has Fódla had a claim on Scotland,
now is the time to insist on it;
    so long as she gets her own right
    it is unlikely Ireland will remain mateless.

For a long space of time
that land of Scotland has owed taxes
    to Cobhthach's lime-skinned fort;
    a cause of disagreement to the Scottish.

Scotland of the shallow streams
should deliver her dues to the isle of Éire,
    rolling land of sparkling cascades,
    lest there be discord between them.

What new right today
has the land of Míl's children —
    tell me if you know —
    by which she claims the isle of Alba?

An cháin trom do bhí ag Balor
ar Éirinn dá hátaghadh —
    dúsgadh faghla dí a dhéanamh —
    Banbha an í do aigéaradh?

Nó an iad na hoiléinse thoir
atá idir Fhódla is Alboin,
    'sgach eang bha fhionnmhagh Íle,
    nó Ceann sriobhghlan seinTíre?   24

Ní héinní dá saoileann sibh
atá ar cuimhne ag crích Éibhir,
    acht ní is truime re a thabhach,
    sí uime dob easbhadhach.

Na trí Colla, críoch a sgéal,
clann Eochaidh díomsoigh Dhoimléan,
    déanamh dóibh ar fhiadh nAlban,
    triar ris nár chóir comhardadh.   32

Dias don triúr do theacht i lle
go crích Bhreagh na mbeann sídhe;
    rogha an tsluaigh i Moigh Mhonaidh
    ó shoin uainn ar n-anamhain.

Iongna do fhuilngeadar féin,
fir mhaordha na n-arm n-aighmhéil,
    Colla 'sa shéinshliocht ó shoin,
    a n-eighriocht orra d'easbhoidh.   40

Créad fa tiobhradh clann Cholla,
ar son ar fhás eatorra,
    tar magh mbarrúrchas mBanbha
    tal d'andúthchas allmhardha?

Cia an rí ar a bhfuil Banbha ag brath
d'fhuil Cholla na gcolg bhfaobhrach?
    má rug rogha d'fhóir Alban,
    cóir a cora ó chomhardadh.   48

That heavy tribute Balor raised,
to which Ireland was submitted,
    — for Banbha to do it would provoke strife —
    is that what she would claim?

Or is it the islands in the east,
between Ireland and Scotland,
    and every piece of Islay's fair plains,
    or ancient Kintyre of the clear rivers?

It is none of those things you surmise
that Éibhear's country thinks of,
    but something that is harder to exact,
    something she has been deprived of.

The three Collas, the end of their tale,
the children of proud Eochaidh Doimléan,
    they made for the land of Alba,
    three who would brook no rivalry.

Two of the three returned from there
to Bregia's land of the fairy mountains;
    the choice of the host remained
    ever since in the Plain of Monadh.

It is strange that they allowed themselves,
the stately men of the destructive weapons,
    Colla and his ancient lineage ever since
    to be deprived of their inheritance.

Why should Colla's sons,
owing to whatever rose between them,
    give support to a strange foreign land
    before the rippling cropped plains of Banbha?

What king does Banbha expect
of the blood of Colla of the whetted weapons;
    if she made a choice from the sept of Scotland
    it would rightly free her from rivalry.

Rogha leannáin Leasa Cuinn,
Somhairle mhac Meic Domhnuill;
    brath céile do Mhoigh Mhonaidh
    's re bhfoil Éire ag anamhain.

Géag thoraidh Teamhrach na bhFionn,
grian gheal i ndeaghaidh dílionn;
    craobh shéanta d'abhlaibh Íle,
    réalta shamhraidh shoishíne.   56

Éinghein shochair shíl gColla,
lámh ionnarbas eachtronna;
    toradh abhallphóir fhóid Bhreagh,
    cabharthóir na gcóig gcóigeadh.

[   ] cúis doilghe,
gur aguir sí Samhairle,
    críoch Bhanbha fa bhróin Danar
    tarla a gcóir gan chríochnaghadh.   64

Deileóchaidh Éire is é a shuim
roighne curadh chlann nDomhnuill
    re síothmhagh n-arsaidh nAlban
    gasraidh fhíochmhar fhionnardghlan.

Sgéal bheanas le crú Cholla
do léigh sinn i seanrolla
    budh naoidhe um' dheóidh fa dheireadh
    an t-aoighe sgeóil sgaoilfidhear.   72

Urra an sgeóil sgaoilfidhear duit —
Séasar an t-airdrí ordhruic,
    re líon gliadh d'ágaibh áille
    do fhágaibh fhiadh Eadáille.

Gluaisid reompa ón Róimh anoir
go hEasbáin an fhóid iobhraigh;
    líon eachtra dob fhearr obar,
    ní ar cheann teachta tángadar.   80

The choice of sweethearts from Conn's garth,
Somhairle, son of MacDhomhnaill;
    the expected mate from Monadh's Plain
    is he for whom Éire is waiting.

Fruitful branch of Tara of the fair,
bright sunshine after a deluge,
    propitious bough of the apple trees of Islay,
    summer star presaging clemency.

Most fortunate issue of Colla's seed,
a hand that banishes strangers,
    fruit of the apple-tree of the sod of Bregia,
    mainstay of the five provinces.

[   ] a matter of distress,
until she made a claim on Sorley,
    Banbha's land troubled by Danes,
    their claim still not concluded.

From Scotland's ancient peaceful plain
Éire, in short, will sunder
    the choice hero of Domhnall's clan —
    fierce fair pure tall heroes.

A story which touches on Colla's tribe
I read in an ancient parchment,
    it will be fresh to the very end,
    the strange tale which will be broadcast.

The hero of the tale which will be told to you,
is Caesar, the illustrious high-king,
    with a full complement of splendid heroes
    he departed the land of Italy.

They proceeded from Rome in the east
to Spain of the yew-strewn country,
    a band of adventurers of the best work,
    they followed no envoy.

Grádhaighis iarthar Eórpa
Séasar na sluagh ndíleónta;
   ón Róimh do aontaigh anadh,
   'sníor aontoil dóibh dealaghadh.

I gcionn aimsire ar n-anmhain,
lá éigin d'éis tionnabhraidh —
   dáil chabhra an rí dhá rochtain —
   do-chí amhra n-iongontaigh.   88

Dar leis féin fuair 'na fhochair,
'na mnaoi áluinn iolchrothaigh,
   an Róimh ag ríomh a dochar,
   gníomh budh cóir do chronochadh.

Frais do dhéaraibh re a dreich ngil,
fuilt sgaoilte go sgéimh thuirsigh
   'gun Róimh ag éagcaoine a huilc,
   cóir éagcaoine fá n-éabhuirt.   96

'Níor chubhaidh riot', ar an Róimh,
'mo bheith mar bhím i gcéadóir';
   id dheaghaidh gan dál gcabhra
   fám lán d'fhearaibh allmhardha'.

'Caomhna longphuirt nách libh féin,
iongna duit, a óig airmghéir,
   'sdo thír féin arna faghuil,
   dá béim dhíbh ag danaruibh'.   104

Dob iad orfhuighle Shéasair:
'a Róimh an mhúir mhínghréasaigh,
   fár mbreith soir nó ar mbeith i bhus,
   bheith ar do thoil do thriallus'.

'Adéaruinn riot,' ar an Róimh,
'tabhair leat lion do thionóil,
   tiomsuighidh bhur n-óig áille,
   d'ionnsuighidh fhóid Eadáille'.   112

Caesar, of the unassailable hosts,
loved the western part of Europe;
    he agreed to stay away from Rome,
    but they did not all agree on separation.

After remaining away a while,
one day after dozing,
    a visitation to help the king appeared —
    he sees a wondrous vision.

It seemed that he found at his side,
in the form of a beautiful supple woman,
    Rome recounting her wrongs,
    a matter fit for deploring.

With showers of tears down her bright face,
locks loosened in distraught appearance,
    was Rome lamenting her wrong,
    fit is it to lament what she spoke of.

'You should not think it meet', said Rome,
'that I am as I am at present,
    in your absence with no hope of succour,
    overwhelmed by foreigners.'

'To cherish a fortress that is not your own
is astonishing of you, young man of sharp weapons,
    while your own land lies ravaged,
    being lopped from you by barbarians'.

These were the words of Caesar:
'O Rome of the finely chiselled rampart,
    whether carried east or being here
    I have always tried to please you'.

'I would say to you', said Rome,
'bring with you your full army,
    gather your young beautiful heroes
    to invade the soil of Italy.'

'Ná bí ní as fhaide ag anmhain,
nár dhuit do theagh tionnabhráidh —
   giodh eagail aighthe orthuibh —
   d'aithle a eagair d'allmhorchuibh'

Laochradh Ghréag, gasradh Eórpa
rug leis, fa tráth taisbeónta,
   do dhíon na síothRómha soir,
   gníomh dob fhíorchóra ar fhéachoin.   120

Do shaor Séasar, is sé a shuim,
d'éis na n-ainbhreath do fhuluing,
   ó neart saobhchath slóigh dhanar
   Róimh na n-aolchloch n-éagsamhal.

Do-bhéara Banbha, bean Chuinn,
do bhreith na Rómha romhuinn,
   a fear féin ó Mhoigh Mhonaidh,
   ag soin céill a gcualabhair.   128

Ar aghaidh mheic Mheic Domhnuill,
feadh éagcaoine a hanfhorluinn,
   do-chí an Bhanbha bhfairsing bhfinn
   d'aisling suil tarla i dtoirchim.

Mac Alastoir d'fhurtacht cháigh
tiocfa, mar tháinig Séasáir,
   don dulasa fa Bhóinn Bhreagh,
   slóigh nách urusa d'áireamh.   136

Sluagh Shéasair mar rug fan Róimh —
tre Ghort Luirc, líon a dtionóil,
   tiocfa Séasair clann Cholla,
   barr do dhéasaibh díoghloma.

Fásfaidh coill a ciomhsaibh trácht
do chrannaibh seólta síothbhárc,
   ó Mhuaidh shéadoírdhreic bhinn bhaoith
   go Binn Éadoirmheic Éadghaoith.   144

'Tarry not a moment longer,
shame on you, your house of slumbering,
   though you be frightened to face them,
   the matter was brought about by foreigners'.

The heroes of Greece and the warriors of Europe
he took with him, a time for a spectacle,
   to defend peaceful Rome in the east,
   a deed that was considered righteous.

After her suffering of false judgements,
Caesar, in short, delivered
   Rome of the extraordinary limestone castles
   from the aggressive power of the horde of barbarians.

Banbha, wife of Conn, will bring,
just as Rome did earlier,
   her own mate from Monadh's plain,
   that is the meaning of what you've been hearing.

Before him, MacDhomhnaill's son sees,
intent on bewailing her sorrows,
   the fair generous Banbha,
   in a vision before he fell to slumbering.

Alasdair's son, to succour others,
will come, as did Caesar,
   this time to Bregia's Boyne,
   with hosts not easy to number.

As Caesar's army captured Rome
through Lorc's field, with full muster,
   so will come the Caesar of the race of Coll,
   the topmost wheat ear of the gleaning.

A wood will grow by the strands' edge
of masts of stately rigged vessels,
   from the illustrious sweet lightsome Moy
   to Binn Éadoir, son of Éadghaoth.

Díolfaid a gcóir re crích Bhreagh,
géabhthar leis lorg a shinsear
　　thort soir go seanráith dTeamhrach
　　don mhoigh eangbhláith ildionnach.

Don Cholla Uais ór fhás sibh
má tá nár chreid Críoch Éibhir,
　　do bhí sí ag seinshliocht Cholla,
　　eighriocht i nách ionronna.　　　　　　　152

Cia an t-éinrí áirimhthear lionn
nár ghabh airdcheannas Éirionn,
　　ó Cholla go Gaoidheal nGlas,
　　más laoidheadh orra an t-eólas?

Na trí Cholla, gan chead dúin,
tugsad Éirinn tre iomthnúidh —
　　curaidh glanchuain bhréidghil Bhaoi —
　　ar chathbhuaidh éignigh éanlaoi.　　　　160

Cuirfidh Samhoirle 'sé a am,
ní choimheóla um chrích bhFréamhann,
　　crois orra go horlamh uaidh,
　　connradh na gColla an chéaduair.

Fa Chaisiol, fa Chruachain Aoi,
fa Almhain an fuinn ghéagnaoi,
　　's fa ráith n-eachradhghlan nOiligh
　　seanchonnradh cháich crosfoidhir.　　　168

Críoch Bhanbha i mbun na suirghe
don chrois chuirfeas Samhoirle,
　　fuair anois tóir dá tabhach,
　　Bóinn don chrois budh céadfadhach.

　　　　　　Fada.

He will pay back his ancestors' debt
to the land of Bregia, and in their footsteps
    he will take the blossomy, undulating plain,
    eastwards to the ancient fort of Tara.

Though you have sprung from Colla Uais,
Éibhear's land gave that no credit;
    Banbha mated with the ancient line of Colla:
    she is an indivisible inheritance.

Can we count a single king
who did not accept the headship of Ireland,
    from Colla to Gaidheal Glas,
    if mentioning them gives guidance?

The three Collas, without our leave,
forsook Ireland through envy,
    for one day's hard-won victory in war,
    the warriors from Baoi of bright sails and pure harbours.

Somhairle, it is due time,
will speedily declare a revocation;
    he will not fulfil, concerning the Frewin land,
    the first contract of the Collas.

Concerning Cashel and Cruacha Aoi,
and the freshly wooded Hill of Allen,
    concerning Oileach with its faultless studs,
    the ancient covenant of all will be annuled.

Because of the annulment Somhairle will instate
the land of Banbha is engaged in mating;
    a hunting party has come to collect her,
    the Boyne will feel its revocation.

24. Maith an Chairt Ceannas na nGaoidheal

Gun urra

Tha an dàn seo air leth cudromach air grunn adhbharan litreachail agus eachdraidheil. Chan urrainnear a bhith cinnt-each cò an t-iarla Gill'Easbaig a tha fa-near: an ceathramh (1530–58), an còigeamh (1558–75) no an seachdamh (1584–1638). Is dòcha gum buineadh an t-ùghdar do Chloinn MhicEoghain, na filidh a fhreastail air na Caimbeulaich anns an t-siathamh agus anns an t-seachdamh linn deug, ach chan eil dearbhadh ann.

Bha cumhachd nan Caimbeulach air taobh an iar na Gàidhealtachd a' sìor dhol am meud anns an t-siathamh linn deug, an dèidh sgrios Rìoghachd nan Eilean, agus tha an dàn seo ag àrd-mholadh an inbhe ùire. Cha robh an caochladh seo na adhbhar-gàirdeachais do nàimhdean nan Caimbeulach, agus tha e coltach nach do chòrd an dàn a leanas ris na Domhnallaich agus an cuid bhàrd.

Tha an dàn seo na shàr-eisimpleir de bhàrdachd molaidh nam filidh. Gu dearbh, faodar a ràdh gu bheil e nas fhaisge air an àbhaist (àbhaist Èireannach) na a' mhòr-chuid de na dàin ann an Leabhar an Deadhain. Tha an ro-ràdh ris an dàn anns an làmh-sgrìobhainn (faic an ro-ràdh ris an leabhar seo) air leth luachmhor, oir tha e ag innse dhuinn gu mionaideach mar a bha am file a' coileanadh prionnsabalan a' chòid molaidh.

> Maith an chairt ceannas na nGaoidheal,
> greim uirthe géb é 'ga mbí;
> neart slóigh san uair-si do arduigh:
> cóir is uaisle a n-Albuin í.
>
> Ceannas Ghaoidheal Mhoighe Monaidh
> maith an chairt chuirthear lé;
> cíos ó shluagh goirm-greanta Gaoidheal
> tuar oirbhearta d'aoinfhear é.
>
> Ceannas Ghaoidheal maicne Míleadh
> mana ratha, ní réim mion;
> lucht coingleaca ós cách do chongbháil
> tuar oirbhearta d'fhoghbháil d'fhior.

8

The Headship of the Gaels is Good Charter

This anonymous poem, composed in the middle or late sixteenth century, is important for a range of literary and political reasons. The subject is Gill'Easbaig Caimbeul, earl of Argyll, but it is not clear whether this is the fourth (1530–58), fifth (1558–75) or seventh earl (1584–1638). It may be the work of a member of the MacEoghain family, who served the Caimbeuls as hereditary poets during the sixteenth and seventeenth centuries, but this is by no means certain.

During the sixteenth century the Caimbeuls steadily consolidated their power in the West Highlands, following the demise of the Lordship of the Isles, and this poem is a forthright defence of their newly won supremacy. This situation gave no pleasure to the Caimbeuls' many enemies, of course, and Clann Domhnaill leaders and the poets who served them appear to have taken some offence at this poem.

The poem is an outstanding example of bardic praise-poetry in the classical style – rather more so than the generally more idiosyncratic poems found in the Book of the Dean of Lismore. Particularly illuminating is the introductory note in the manuscript summarizing the contents of the poem and explaining the significance of its constituent parts (quoted in the Introduction).

The headship of the Gaels is good charter,
    whoever gets a grip of it;
now it has exalted the power of a people,
    it is Scotland's richest right.

The headship of the Gaels of the moor of Monadh,
    good the charter's claim;
tribute from the Gaelic host of blue-burnished weapons,
    a sign of magnificence for any man.

The headship of the Gael of Míl's descendants,
    providence's sign, no small sway;
a right above all others' to retain warriors
    is an eminent attainment for any man.

Cuirfead ceisd ar fhear a n-eaglais
  fa fhuil Ghaoidheal na n-iodh n-óir:
cía 'ga bhfuil ó chóir a gceannas,
  na slóigh ó thoil theannas tóir?   16

Fuaisgheólad féin fáth na ceasda
  chuirthear orm, cruaidh an chíos:
ceannas Ghaoidheal 'na chéim cleachtuidh
  ag aoinfhear d'fhéin Bhreatuin bhíos.

Giolla Easbuig iarla Ghaoidheal
  glacuis ceart ceannais an t-sluaigh;
do bhí riamh ó chóir 'na chartaigh
  riar an t-slóigh gan antoil uaidh.   24

Do ceangladh a gcairt a shinnsear
  sealbh na nGaoidheal do dhul dó;
leis buaidh an duluinn 's na daoine,
  urruim shluaigh: cá maoine is mó?

Ceannas Gaoidheal oiléin Alban
  aige arís, bu ríoghdha an chairt;
do dhearbh gríos a ghruadh a ttachar
  cíos a shluagh ar Achadh Airt.   32

Damhna meanma do Mhac Cailín
  codhnach Gaoidheal ris do rádh;
annamh tóir no raon nach réidhigh
  an chaor shlóigh nár fhéimigh ágh.

Leis ó chóir, budh cheannas ríoghdha,
  rogha a seabhac sealg a sliabh;
rogha a ccolg is a ngreagh ngoile
  ar lorg a sean roimhe riamh.   40

Rogha an lúireach 's a lann leabhar
  leis 'na chóir, budh cheannas buan;
congnamh sluaigh is each is éididh:
  buain a chreach ní fhéidir uadh.

To a man of the church I will ask a question
    about the blood of the Gaels girt with gold —
who of right holds their headship,
    of the hosts who love to press pursuit?

I myself will resolve the root of the question
    that is put to me — tricky the task:
the headship of the Gaels in its practised progress
    belongs to but one of Britain's battling men.

The right to the headship of the host has been taken
    by Gill'Easbaig, earl of the Gaels;
the people's tribute was always his by his charter,
    and aroused in them no rage.

It was bound into the charter of his forebears
    that the Gaels' inheritance should go to him;
his the people and their animals' produce,
    his the host's reverence — what greater wealth?

The headship of the Gaels of the island of Alba
    is his again, royal the deed;
the flush of his cheeks in conflict has proven
    his hosts' tribute on the Field of Art.

A cause for cheer to MacCailein
    that he be styled Lord of the Gaels;
rare the chase or skirmish that is not sorted
    by that blazing leader that shrinks not from strife.

His by rights — a royal headship —
    the pick of their hawks hunting their moors,
the pick of their swords and of their spirited horses,
    as his people had always claimed before.

The pick of their breastplates and broadswords,
    — an enduring headship — is his by right;
assistance with hosts, with horses and armour
    are his spoils forever that none can wrest away.

Leis rogha a séad 's a ccorn ccumhduigh,
   cíos a n-inbhear, iasg a loch;
báird a múr tar ghairbhe a nglaistréan,
   daingne a ndún 'sa gcaistéal chloch.   48

'S é 'na airdbhreitheamh ós Albain,
   onóir oile 'ga thaobh tais;
a ttigh an ríogh gur bhean bráighe:
   fear dhíobh gacha láimhe leis.

Aireómhad fós cuid d'a cheannas,
   cosg feilli is snádhmadh síodh;
is beag do chrothuibh nach ceartuigh
   cet crochuidh fá reachtuibh ríogh.   56

Cur dligheadh fá dhortadh fola,
   fuasgladh braighdeadh ó chuing chruaidh;
dligheadh caingne is díon daoine
   daingne an ríogh an taoibhe tuaith.

An uair goirthear a ghairm thionóil
   teaguid uime gasruidh Ghall;
gairg fhir ó chrích ghairbh na nGaoidheal,
   gan díoth airm ar aoinfhear ann.   64

Cóir ar tús ag cur san chaithréim
   Clann Domhnaill chuige ón tír thuaith;
na fearchoin as dána an doghruinn,
   ealchuing ágha an chomhluinn chruaidh.

Aireómhad féin, feirdi a eachtra,
   ármuinn uaisle Innsi Gall,
tig don nós sin deabhtha is doghruinn:
   ceathrar tóisigh fhoghbhuim ann.   72

Clann Ghiolla Eóin na n-éacht n-aigmhéil
   iadhuidh uime crosfhál colg:
siad 'na cheann ó mhíonmhuigh Muile:
   ríoghruidh teann na mbuille mborb.

His the pick of their jewels and engraved goblets,
　　the tribute of their estuaries, the fish of their lochs,
the bards of their mansions over their fierce young warriors,
　　the firmness of their forts and castles of stone.

He is the high justiciar over all Scotland —
　　another honour for his soft side;
he took off hostages in the king's fortress,
　　one of them with him in either hand.

I will enumerate now one aspect of his headship:
　　the halting of deceit and binding of peace;
few are the wrongs that are not righted
　　by bringing them under the ordinance of the king.

Setting statutes with regard to bloodshed,
　　releasing captives from callous yokes,
judging cases, protecting people,
　　the king's power in the north.

When his mustering call is sounded
　　Lowland lads gather round,
fierce men from the Gaelic Rough Bounds,
　　with not one man lacking in arms.

Right that Clann Domhnaill be placed in the vanguard
　　who come to him from the northern land,
those valiant hounds, boldest in battle —
　　buoyant bulwarks in bitter strife.

I myself will enumerate, the better for his exploits,
　　the worthy warriors of Innse Gall,
raised in that custom of conflict and battle:
　　four leaders I find there.

Clann Gill'Eathain, of the deed of daring,
　　closes round him, a hedge of crossing spears;
they join him from Mull of the mild pastures,
　　that royal steadfast band of baleful blows.

Sirthe slóigh fan gcéad ghairm chuige
  ó Cheann-tíri na bhfeadh bhfiar;
tig a h-Íle d'uaim a h-eachtra
  líne sluaigh rér dheacra diall.   80

Clann Raghnuill uime ar dhóigh deabhtha,
  díorma roimhear léitmheach laoch;
ní réidh a n-eachtra ar uair bhfeidhme:
  ealta sluaigh na meirgeadh maoth.

Fine Leóid na mbratach mbodhbha
  bíd 'na ttionól, ní thriall mall;
raon da n-eólus soin fa anbhuain,
  Leódhasuigh caor armshluaigh ann.   88

Go Mac Cailín ceann an tionóil
  tig a Barraidh 'na mbróin bhuirb
ealta sluaigh gan fhuireach n-uaire;
  drong fhuileach is cruaidhe cuilg.

Clann Fhionghuine ar inneal troda
  teaguid go laoch Locha Long;
feirrde a eachtra d'uaim na n-oirear
  ealta sluaigh na ccloidheamh ccorr.   96

Iadhar uime duimhneach d'ógbhuidh
  an dáil deabhtha ar diúltadh síodh;
fál tuagh is lámha gan loige
  don t-sluagh dhána is groide gníomh.

Tig le meanma go Mac Cailín
  cúirt deaghlaoch nach seachnann sioc;
coille chuir a fadchlúimh féile
  d'fhuil Artúir is Béine Briot.   104

Teaghlach garbh fá Ghiolla Easbuig
  da fhuil féin, budh feirrde a bríogh;
a gclú ar cuimhne ní cheileabh:
  crú Duibhne gach deighfhear díobh.

Picked people come at his first summons
    from Kintyre of the sloping fields;
from Islay comes at the announcement of his action
    a race of people for whom submission is sore.

Clan Raghnaill gather round him ready for warfare,
    a troop of warriors right bellicose, bold;
not gentle their action in the season of service,
    those fighting bands of the ensigns of silk.

Tribe of Leod of the belligerent banners
    are gathering — no milling march;
a battle under their leadership would not linger,
    Lewismen are there, a blazing armed host.

To MacCailein, head of the muster,
    comes from Barra, as a fierce band,
a host of men impatient for the onset,
    a blood-keen throng of most deadly darts.

Clann Fhionghain arrayed for warfare
    come to the hero of Loch Long;
better is his expedition to unite the coastlands
    for that warrior-band of the sharp swords.

Round him crowd a press of young warriors
    ready for battle having refused peace;
a hedge of hatchets and axes without weakness
    have the bold band of speedy deeds.

There come with spirit to MacCailein
    a court of worthy warriors that shun not frost,
a wood that spread its far-spreading foliage
    of the blood of Arthur and Béine Briot.

A stalwart household around Gill'Easbaig
    of his own blood, the better its might;
their fame is fabled, I will not conceal it:
    each mettlesome man is of Duibhne's blood.

A fhoirneadh a measg a mhíleadh
do Mhac Cailín is tús teinn;
[   ] a reacht 'ga maoidheamh maraidh,
do neart Ghaoidheal gabhuidh greim.   112

Gabhthar leis a lár na nGaoidheal
go grinneal ghliadh mur as dú,
mana ratha da dheirc dhosuigh,
beirt chatha le chosain clú.

Le séan buaidhe fán mbeirt ghaisgeadh
gabhuis léinidh shéaghuinn shróil,
d'uaim ghrinn budh dheacra do dhéanamh,
go sgim ealtan éanuigh óir.   120

Triobhus donnsróil gan chlaon ccumtha
cuirthear uime, móide a mhuirn;
ceann an t-sluaigh ó Inbhear Abha,
go sduaim inghean bhrogha Buidhbh.

Gabhuis tráth fan troightheach mboinngeal
dá bhróig chumtha uachtair óir,
nach bacann léim lúith no lámhaigh:
a chéim cúil ní tháruidh tóir.   128

Cuirthear cotún choiléir órdha,
do h-innleadh do ghréis ó 'n Ghréig,
fá leóghan lonn Locha Fíne:
sonn catha gach tíre a ttéid.

Gabhuis lúirigh leabhuir lonnruigh
Lochlannuigh nguirm ttaobhghil dtréin;
cruaidh sgeine ní mhill a mháille,
rinn sleighe nó gáinne ghéir.   136

Gabhuis sgaball beannchor bodhbha
do bhí ag Eachtair mór mac Prímh:
a sgéal ó 'n Traoi liom a línibh,
do bhí ag Fionn 's níor mhílidh mín.

His mustering amid his soldiers
    for MacCailein is the start of his force;
his ordinance lasts to boast of:
    he takes control of the strength of the Gael.

He goes himself among the Gaels
    as the basis for exploits as is right;
in his eyes, thickly lashed, a lucky omen
    is the battle-gear with which he found fame.

As a charm for victory under his armour
    he puts on his beautiful satin shirt
of fine needlework, hard to accomplish,
    a flock of birds embroidered in gold.

Breeches of brown satin without false shaping
    are put upon him, greater his cheer;
head of the host from Inverawe
    from the dignified daughter of Badhbh's fort.

Two shapely shoes now with golden uppers
    he has put on his fair-soled feet
that hinder not a leap of limbering nor casting,
    pursuit never overtook his backward step.

There is placed a hauberk with golden collar,
    wrought with embroidery from Greece,
about Loch Fyne's lion, impetuous,
    champion of every country where he goes.

He has put on a long lustrous corselet
    from Norway, blue bright-sided tough;
temper of knife has not maimed his mailcoat,
    nor point of spear nor piercing dart.

He dons the shoulder cape, peaked and warlike,
    worn by great Hector, Priam's son
(its tale I have from Troy in writing);
    worn too by Fionn, no gentle giant.

Dúintear uime ré h-uchd catha
   crios cathbuadhach nach taobh tóir,
do dhearbh buaidh gach taobh 'na tiomchall,
   go sgin chruaidh go n-iomchur óir.   144

Cloidheamh ré thaobh, móide a meanma,
   mur mac an Luin an ghleó gill,
nó colg cruaidh Osgair no Fhearghuis:
   buaidh chosgair ar ghealbhois ghrinn.

Gabhuis go gliaidh Giolla Easbuig
   a n-aice an chuilg sgáth an sgéith;
budh réalta sluaigh go séan bhfoghla
   buaidh a h-éan d'a comhdha a ccléith.   152

Teagar chuige a bhfreasdal féinneadh
   feilm chatha go séala sróil;
'ga mbí cinnte an eóil iorghuil,
   a h-eóin impe ar iomdhing óir.

Ar ndul dó 'na dheisi chatha
   budh céim curadh dul 'na dháil,
ar mbuain tuinne a chraoisich comhluinn
   's taoisich uime ar fhoghluim áigh.   160

Mar sin téid a cceann a churadh
   cuiléan leóghuin Locha Long;
damhna teithidh ré gleó Gaoidheal,
   beithir bheó na ccaoilshleagh ccorr.

Ar tteacht dó 'na dheisi chatha
   ní chongbhuidh cách a ghort ghliadh;
ní éir ó shin aon 'na aghaidh
   do-bheir taobh ré cabhair chliar.   168

Ar ngabháil ceannais gach cinnidh
   ceangluidh síothchain 'na síth bhuain;
congbhuidh ó shin reacht is riaghuil,
   do-bheir ceart gan iarraidh uaidh.

There is closed about him before battle
    a triumphant girdle that prohibits pursuit,
that ensures victory on every side around it,
    with a tempered knife with handle of gold.

A sword by his side, the greater his spirit,
    like Mac an Leoin, battle's bet,
or the steely sword of Oscar or Fergus,
    triumph of slaughter in his winsome white palm.

Gill'Easbaig has taken for the fighting,
    next to the sword, the shelter of a shield;
a host's guiding star with omen of pillage
    should have the virtue of its birds to protect it in strife.

A shelter for him in warding off warriors,
    his helmet of battle with a satin seal
which in the fray affords firm guidance;
    birds on a surrounding wedge of gold.

A stalwart's step to go to face him
    once he has donned his battle dress
and plucked the sheath off his spear of combat
    while leaders surround him in school of war.

Thus goes he at the head of his heroes,
    the whelp of the lion of Loch Long;
a cause for fleeing before the Gael's fury,
    a living lightning bolt of slender spears.

When he has donned his dress of battle
    none can sustain his field of fray;
thenceforth no-one will rise against him
    who has respect for poets' praise.

When he has gained each clan's headship
    he makes a treaty of permanent peace;
thenceforth he maintains law and order,
    dispenses justice by them unthought.

Ceanglaidh sé gan cheilg da chéile
   curadh-uaisle Innsi Gall;
léigthear do thoil géill a geimhlibh:
   ní fhuil dréim ri oighribh ann.   176

Glóir na n-éan fá oighre Artúir,
   an éanfhoghar is ceól crot;
gan ghaoth ré bun a fuacht earraigh
   ag cur cuart fá cheannuibh cnoc.

Ré linn leómhuin Locha Fíne
   fiodhbhuidh lúbtha ó chnuas na ccrann;
tig do 'n teas air thí a tadhaill
   nach bí eas ar abhainn ann.   184

Táinig d'iomad iasg na n-inbhear
   gan úidh duine ar déanamh lín;
lór d'a mholadh, mana reachta,
   toradh mara ag teacht a ttír.

Ealbha fhiadh is beich dam buaidhreadh
   fo bhun gach beinne, is tuar tnúidh;
larga tuar o tharbha taguidh
   fá dhual arbha abaigh úir.   192

Cloidheamh cruaidh cosnamh an lagha
   nach lúbann le cealgadh cáich,
d'a ngoirthear iarrla ó Earr-Ghaoidheal,
   ar cceann riaghla, ar n-aoinfhear áigh.

Do-ní iarrla aicmi Duibhne
   díobra feille is fógra an uilc;
croidhe mear gan chungach céille,
   fear do chumhdach cléiri ar chuilt.   200

Do fhoghluim tú as do thosach
   na trí tréidhe is fearr ag flaith:
iomchar goimhe gu h-uair feadhma,
   croidhe cruaidh is meanmna mhaith.

              Maith.

Without treachery he ties together
 the warrior lords of Innse Gall;
at his will, sureties are released from shackles,
 no-one attempts to rival his heirs.

The voices of birds round the heir of Arthur,
 the birdsong is the harmony of harps;
without wind at the source of its spring coldness
 whirling around the heads of hills.

During the lion of Loch Fyne's era
 trees are bent from the branches' fruit;
as a result of the heat which comes with his visit
 no waterfall is found on any stream.

The fish of the estuaries are so abundant
 that no man thinks to make a net;
sufficient his praise, a portent of his fitness:
 the produce of the sea swimming to shore.

Herds of deer by bees bothered,
 a cause for envy, at the foot of each hill,
the slopes — a sign of coming produce —
 under shooks of ripe comely corn.

A firm sword for upholding order
 which is called the earl of Argyll,
who is not swayed by anyone's seduction,
 our chief ruler, our only man of war.

The earl of the sept of Duibhne is successful
 in expelling evil and banishing crime;
a mettlesome heart with no narrowness of prudence;
 a man to equip poets with a quilt.

You have learned from your youth upwards
 the three qualities best in a chief:
to endure a grudge to the hour of action,
 a steadfast heart and a mettlesome mind.

25. An Síth do Rogha, a Rígh Fionnghall?

Gun urra

Tha an dàn seo, a rinneadh faisg air deireadh an t-siathamh linn deug, a' cleachdadh stoidhle breug-throid eadar am file agus a neach-taice, ach tha e follaiseach gur e cleas litreachail a tha fanear dha, agus am file ga chleachdadh mar dhòigh air moladh a thoirt don cheann-chinnidh airson a fheartan.

Chan eil dad a dh'fhiosrachadh againn mu ùghdar an dàin seo, ach tha e a' cleachdadh an fhacail 'dùthchas' an co-cheangal ri Contae Aontrama (sreath 56). Is e cuspair an dàin Aonghas (mac Sheumais nan Ruaig) MacDhomhnaill (†1614), a bhuineadh do Chloinn Iain Mhòir (Clann Domhnaill Ìle), bràthair Dhomhnaill Ghuirm agus Alasdair Charraich (a tha air an caoidh ann an dàn 32) agus mac bràthar Shomhairle Bhuidhe (cuspair dàin 23). Bha Aonghas cuideachd gu mòr an sàs ann an iomairtean is creachan ann an Còigeamh Uladh, mar a thuigear bhon dàn.

Is e an tiotal a tha am file a' cur air Aonghas 'rí Fionnghall', abairt a tha a' toirt urram do dhualchas Lochlannach nan Gàidheal Albannach, agus nan Domhnallach gu sònraichte. Ged nach eil am facal 'Fionnghall' ga chleachdadh ann an Gàidhlig an latha an-diugh, bha e anabarrach cumanta ann am bàrdachd fhoghlaimte an t-seachdamh linn deug agus bhite a' cleachdadh an tiotail 'Rìgh Fionnghall' ann an òrain agus ann am beul-aithris an àite 'Triath nan Eilean'.

An síth do rogha, a rígh Fionnghall,
   no an fraoch cogaidh, a chúl slim?
A rígh, i ngach taobh toibhgheas comhtha
   coimhdheas araon orta inn.

Do-ghéansa, a rígh fréimhe Colla,
   cogadh bhus guais dod ghruaidh mbrioc;
a ghnúis gan fhíoch nar éar comhrag,
   no do-ghéan síoth ro-ghrod riot.   8

Is Peace Your Choice, O King of Hebrideans?

This poem from the late sixteenth century is cast in the form of a dispute between poet and patron, but its stylised nature is very clear as the poet moves to bluster to outright praise of his subject for his military exploits.

We know nothing of the author, but he appears to have come from Ulster. The subject of the poem is Aonghas (mac Sheumais nan Ruaig) MacDhomhnaill (†1614) of Dunyveg in Islay, brother of Domhnall Gorm and Alasdair Carrach, whose deaths in 1586 are lamented in poem 32, and nephew of Somhairle Buidhe, subject of poem 23. Like his relatives, Aonghas was actively involved in the Irish campaigns of the day, as the poem relates.

The poet addresses Aonghas as *rí Fionnghall*, literally 'king of the fair foreigners', a title that harks back to the Norse heritage of the Hebrides in general and of Clann Domhnaill in particular. The term *Fionnghall* is very common in bardic poetry of the seventeenth century, and is seemingly extended to mean the territory inhabited by Scottish Gaeldom rather than simply the Gaels themselves. The now-dominant term *Gàidhealtachd* does not appear until the very end of the seventeenth century, yet *Fionnghall* has now been almost entirely forgotten by Gaelic speakers.

Is peace your choice, O king of Hebrideans,
    or is it wrath of warfare, O smooth locks?
O king, in every place you levy tribute
    I am just as ready for your attack.

I will make, king of the stock of Colla,
    warfare dangerous to your dappled cheek;
O gentle face that never refused combat,
    or I will make with you prompt peace.

Ní locfa mise, a mhic Shéamuis,
    síth no cogadh rét chneas tláith,
's réd dhearc mar néimh óir ar oighridh,
    's réd throighidh séimh mboinnghil mbláith.

Do-ghéan síth no sitheam cogadh,
    a chúl fiar na bhfáinneadh ccruinn,
gan cur a bhfad ort, a Aonghuis,
    rét fholt lag, réd chaolbhais ccuirr.   16

Ní éarfuinn tú um tabhairt ccogaidh
    dod chúl mbachlach mar bharr fraoich:
sibh anois tar m'fhíoch ní éarfuinn
    fá síoth dod bhois mhéarchuirr mhaoith.

Dá mbeinn ag troid atá leatrom,
    a fhlaith Rois, ar do rosg gorm;
ní fhuil leatrom a ccúis cogaidh,
    a ghnúis dhearccorr, aguibh orm.   24

[   ] aimsim fear mo ghualann,
    a ghruaidh ghoirte mar ghné an smuail,
is mairg do bhiadh ar tí mo throide:
    riamh is in tí as foide uaim.

Ní díon ormsa, a airdrí Fionnghall,
    feilm no aibíd iaruinn tigh:
do sgiath gríobh-chorcra ar do chlé-láimh
    ag díon t'ochta, a ghné bháin-ghil.   32

[   ] rom ríoghruidh Fionnghall
    umud 'nan éanfál arm nocht,
[   ] ar súil let beith am baoghal,
    is breith dhúinn a m-aonar ort.

Ó chuan Leódhuis go Loch Eireais
    eagla romhad, a rosg gorm,
is t'eagla ar chách um Bhóinn mbraonghlais,
    gan sgáth roimh, a Aonghuis, orm.   40

I will not refuse, O son of Seumas,
    peace or war with your soft skin,
with your eye like ice with gold gleaming,
    and with your smooth gentle fair-soled foot.

I will make peace or rush into warfare,
    O cascading, curling, ringleted hair,
without going on about it to you, Aonghas,
    with your soft hair, with your slender pointed palm.

I would not refuse you in making warfare
    with your curly hair like the top of a mane:
I would not refuse, despite my anger,
    peace with your soft pointed-fingered palm.

If we were fighting, you would have the disadvantage,
    O prince of Ross, O iris blue;
you have no advantage in the matter of warfare,
    over me, O countenance with oval eyes.

[   ] I aim at my supporter,
    O flushed cheek like a glowing coal;
woe to the one intent on a quarrel —
    always the one who is furthest away.

I wear no protection, high-king of the Hebrides,
    neither helmet nor thick iron coat;
on your left arm, your shield with purple griffin
    protects your breast, O fair-white form.

[   ] before me a royal band of Hebrideans,
    around you, a united fence of naked blades,
[   ] you thinking to be in danger,
    I have to fight you alone.

From the Minch of Lewis to Loch Eireas
    you are feared, O blue eye,
and all fear you round the Boyne's grey water,
    but I, Aonghas, am not afraid.

Do chreich tusa le tús th'oirbhirt
  Inis Eóghuin, a fholt fionn:
ge atá duit fa chíos ód chéidchion,
  mo throid síos ní léicthear liom.

Ge tá an chreach sin Cairrge Fearghuis
  fá bhfríth guasacht lét ghruaidh mhín,
'n a sgáth uaibh do ghnáth ar Ghalluibh
  gan sgáth let ghruaidh mballaigh bím.   48

Do shaorais, 's ní saorfa oram,
  gach aird dod thír, 's níor taom réidh,
ar sluagh Gall dearg-ghruadh dreachbhláith,
  's ar mear-shluagh clann neamhthláith Néill.

Rugais an Rút le ruaig éanlaoi
  d'fhuil Uí Bhilin gerb fhuil ríogh,
's ní reacainn sin ret chéibh ccúlchais —
  sibh do bhein mo dhúthchas díom.   56

Ge do léigsed laoich an tuaiscceirt
  táinte chruidh lét chaolshról mbreac,
ní canab gó lét ghruaidh mbreicshlim,
  bó dom bhuaibh ní léicfinn leat.

Tír-ígheadh d'ainneoin fhear Muile
  do mhill tusa ó phort go port:
a bhas tseang do shíol na gColla,
  da dhíon dob fhearr th'ollamh ort.   64

'S guth orta le t'anfadh feirge
  fir Mhuile gér mór an goimh:
dob fhearr dod chosg mé 'san Morbhairn
  a rosg mar ghné an ghorm-airm ghloin.

Aird Uladh ó oiléan Leamhna
  go Loch cCuan ge do chreach sibh,
ní bhéartha soir uaim do m'ainneoin
  boin i ndeaghaidh an glainneoi [   ]   72

At the start of your career, you raised tribute
    in Inishowen, O fair hair:
although it is your favourite dependency
    I will not give up my suit.

Although your raid on Carrickfergus
    (which brought danger to your smooth cheek)
keeps the Goill in constant terror,
    I am without fear of your freckled face.

You have guarded — I will not deny it —
    every part of your land — no gentle fight —
from the Lowland host, smooth-faced ruddy,
    and from the valiant merciless host of clan Néill.

You won the Route with a single day's offensive
    from the Mac Uilíns, despite their royal blood;
and I would not mention this to your curly ringlets:
    that you have deprived me of my native place.

Although the heroes of the North let herds of cattle
    depart with your fine dappled banner of silk,
I will not lie to your cheek, smooth and freckled:
    no cow of mine would I let you take.

The isle of Tiree, despite Mull's fighters,
    you have laid waste from side to side;
O slim palm of the seed of the Collas,
    were your poet with you, it would have been safe.

A reproach to you with your fury's tempest
    are the men of Mull, though great their spite;
better had I been in Morvern to check you,
    O eye of the hue of a bright steel blade.

Though you harried the Ards of Ulster
    from Leamhain island to Strangford Loch,
you would not carry east to spite me
    a single cow of mine after [   ]

Do chanuis riomsa, a rígh Íle,
    d'fhocal dil a n-Uaimh an Deirg,
mé ar tí do chogadh do chomhall
    ní do thogadh orm feirg.

Ollamhoin, a onchú Leódhuis,
    da luadh riomsa god rosg glas,
a rígh fuinn Fionnghall, dob amhluadh
    do t'fhionnbharr ccruinn ccamruadh ccas.   80

Dar ndóigh dob é th'adhbhar feirge
    d'ar bfreagradh is niamh grísi ad ghruaidh,
d'iomoid mo ghrádha, a dheirg dhonnbháin,
    nó ar seilg dána d'fhaghbháil uaim.

An tráth nach tturnfadh mo ghoimh-se
    do-ghéanuinn dod dhearg-sa dath:
dearg dod ghruaidh ghealbháin do-ghéanuinn,
    a ghruaidh dhealbhnáir shéaghuinn [   ]   88

Os liom bhias baincheann ban Muile,
    maith an cungnamh cogaidh domh:
anlag ro-thréan inghean Eachainn,
    finnbhean sgoth-mhéar ghealghru [   ]

Liom bia a gruaidh ar gné corcrach,
    's a corrshuil ghlas [   ]
cunlinne budh oirrdheirc d'inghin,
    do inghin Mhic Ghille inmhigh Eóin.   96

You gave me, O king of Islay,
    your true word in Uaimh an Deirg
when I was keen to keep up our quarrel —
    a matter which should arouse my wrath.

To mention poets, O wolf of Lewis,
    to me, with your grey eye,
O King of the Hebrides, it was distressing
    to your bright-topped, auburn, cascading curls.

Perhaps the reason for your anger —
    answering me with your cheek flushed hot —
was the excess of my love, O red-brown fair one,
    or an attempt to get a poem from me.

When my rancour would not lessen
    I would make a colour equal to your red,
red I would make for your fair white visage,
    O shapely modest stately [   ] cheek.

Since Mull's chief lady supports me
    it will be a good help to me in war;
not weak but mighty is Eachann's daughter,
    fair lady, flower-fingered bright-cheeked.

On my side is her cheek of crimson,
    and her round grey eye,
nostrils, fairest for a lady,
    for the daughter of stately MacGill'Eathain.

26.   Clann Ghille Eóin na mBratach Badhbha

Gun urra

Tha na rannan luachmhor seo air Cloinn Ghill'Eathain air an gleidheadh ann an làmh-sgrìobhainn anns a' chruinneachadh aig Ualtar MacPhàrlain an Arair. Tha an làmh-sgrìobhainn sin a' cleachdadh siostam sgrìobhaidh Gallda a tha car doilleir; tha an tionndadh a leanas stèidhichte air an obair deasachaidh a rinn an t-Ollamh Iain Friseal anns na 1930an.

Air sgàth na stoidhle teann a chleachd na filidh, chan urrainn-ear a bhith cinnteach cuine a rinneadh na rannan seo: is math a dh'fhaodte gum buin iad don t-seachdamh linn deug, ach dh'fhaodadh e bhith gu bheil iad gu math nas sine. Tha e na chùis-iongnaidh nach tàinig barrachd bàrdachd den t-seòrsa seo a rinneadh do na Leathanaich a-nuas thugainn, a dh'aindeoin an cumhachd ann am poileataigs agus an cultar Innse Gall; ach anns an aon dòigh, is e fìor bheagan de bhàrdachd a tha againn a rinneadh don chinneadh a bu chudromaiche ann an Èirinn, Clann Uí Néill.

Ged a bha dàimh eadar Clann Mhuirich agus Rìghrean nan Eilean (agus an sin Clann Raghnaill), rinn filidh a bhuineadh don teaghlach ainmeil seo dàin do chinnidhean eile cuideachd, Clann Domhnaill Shlèite agus Clann MhicLeòid nam measg. Mar sin, chan eil e na annas gun do rinn ball den teaghlach an dàn seo do Chloinn Ghill'Eathain.

> Clann Ghille Eóin na mbratach badhbha
>   borb ri a mbiodhbhaidh
> 's mairg don tsluagh ar feadh na Fódhla
>   'gan dáil diomdha.
> Gasraidh gleusda Ghaoidheal dhána
>   óigfhir iomdha
> níor cheil buinne (?) don fhuil bhrais mhearaigh
>   nach tais time.   8
> Iomdha dhíobh ag cosnamh creiche
>   le cruas láimhe;
> neach is fhearr ar cluain na cléire
>   gan [   ].

Clann Ghill'Eathain of the Raven-blazoned Banners

This unusual but important fragment survives only in an eighteenth-century English-language manuscript collected by the antiquary Walter Macfarlane of Arrochar. The text appears there in an awkward 'phonetic' orthography, but the version here is based on an edition made by the late Professor John Fraser.

Because formal bardic poetry was so conservative in its style and language, it is by no means clear when these lines were composed. They may be no later than the second half of the seventeenth century, but they may equally be much older. This poem is particularly valuable because no other bardic poetry on the MacGill'Eathains has survived – a striking gap considering the political and cultural importance of this clan, particularly in the sixteenth and seventeenth centuries.

The MacMhuirichs served as hereditary poets for the Lords of the Isles and then for the chiefs of Clann Raghnaill, but this relationship was not exclusive: members of the family also composed for other prominent families. The existence of a MacMhuirich panegyric on the MacGill'Eathains is thus not inherently surprising, even though the MacGill'Eathains are known to have supported the Ó Muirgheasáin poets on a hereditary basis.

Clann Ghill'Eathain of the crow-marked banners,
    savage to their foemen,
woe to the host throughout Ireland
    who meet with their displeasure.
Agile warriors of the Gaels intrepid,
    young stalwarts,
who hid no drop of the blood, fast and merry,
    of no soft weakness.
Many of them winning plunder
    through skill at fighting,
the best man on the clergy's meadow
    without [   ],

'S a gheobhadh a dhuais o ríoghaibh
　　gan díol taire;
's ionnan d'ar crú as d'ar [　　]
　　's do Choin Roí mac Dáire　　　16
's mairg a thachradh ri am (?) bruinne
　　far gruaim ghráine.

who won his reward from princes
  without niggardliness of payment,
equal to bloody [   ] slaughter
  and to Cú Roí mac Daire,
woe to those they'd encounter
  with belligerent scowling.

THE LEARNED TRADITION

ELEGY

27. M'Anam do Sgar Riomsa A-Raoir

Muireadhach Albanach Ó Dálaigh

Is dòcha gur e Muireadhach Albanach am file as cliùitiche a bha
ann riamh. Rinn e farsaingeachd de dhàin, eadar dàin
phearsanta, dàin spioradail agus dàin molaidh do chinn-
chinnidh ann an Èirinn agus Alba (Ó Briain, Ó Conchobhair, Ó
Domhnaill agus Iarla Leamhnachd nam measg).

Thathar a' cur às leth nam file nach robh faireachdainnean
pearsanta rim faighinn nan cuid bàrdachd, ach chan eil sin idir
fìor a thaobh a' mharbhrainn dhrùidhtich seo, anns a bheil
Muireadhach a' caoidh a mhnà. Chan eil ach beagan fiosrach-
aidh dheimhinne againn mu Mhuireadhach ach is e fìor bheag a
tha againn a thaobh a mhnà, Maol Mheadha, ged a tha e coltach
gun do dh'eug i agus i fhathast meadhanach òg.

Is ann ann an Leabhar an Deadhain a-mhàin a tha an dàn seo
ri fhaighinn. Tha cuid de na rannan anabarrach doirbh agus mar
sin chan fhaighear an seo ach sia rannan deug a-mach à còig air
fhichead.

Uair 's a-rithist mìnichidh am file mar a chaill e an dàrna leth
dheth fhèin an lùib bàs a mhnà. Gu fiosaigeach agus gu
mionaideach seallaidh e nach eil i ann tuilleadh: chan eil i anns
an taigh no anns an leabaidh, agus chan eil a làmh fo cheann-
san. Tha na h-ìomhaighean nitheil seo cumanta ann am bàrdachd
Ghàidhlig gus faireachdainnean agus feartan eas-chruthach a
chur an cèill. Chleachdar ìomhaighean lusail an seo gus a
bòidhchead, a torachas agus a dìlseachd a chur an cèill. Tha a
bòidhchead a rèir slat-tomhais na Gàidhlig (ach nach eil i bàn).

M'anam do sgar riomsa a-raoir,
    calann ghlan dob ionnsa i n-uaigh;
rugadh bruinne maordha mín
    is aonbhla lín uime uainn.

Do tógbhadh sgath aobhdha fhionn
    a-mach ar an bhfaongha bhfann:
laogh mo chridhise do chrom,
    craobh throm an tighise thall.

8

My Soul Parted From Me Last Night

Muireadhach Albanach is arguably the most famous of all the bardic poets, not only because of the dramatic circumstances of his life, described in the introduction to poem 5, but also because of the range and depth of his surviving poetry, which includes not only a wide variety of panegyrics to several different patrons, in both Ireland and Scotland, as well as a number of religious and personal poems. This intensely personal elegy for his dead wife is justifiably one of the most famous poems of the bardic era. Unfortunately, we know even less of Muireadhach's wife Maol Mheadha than of the shadowy Muireadhach; it appears that she died fairly young, after twenty years of marriage and having borne eleven children.

The poem is preserved only in the Book of the Dean of Lismore and contains several stanzas which eluded even Osborn Bergin, perhaps the greatest editor of bardic poetry, and the version given here contains only sixteen of the full twenty-five stanzas.

The poet reiterates how he has lost half of himself in the loss of his wife. Again and again he emphasises her absence concretely and exactly: from the house, from their bed, and, in the final verse, in her hand not being under his head. The diction is typical of Gaelic poetry in its use of concrete images as a short-hand for abstract qualities, e.g. the many plant images of her beauty, fruitfulness and rooted loyalty. The sort of beauty ascribed to his wife is also very Gaelic.

> My soul parted from me last night,
>   a pure body, dearly-loved, is in the grave,
> a stately soft bosom taken from me
>   wound in a single linen sheet.
>
> A beautiful white bloom plucked
>   from the tender, bending stem:
> my heart's darling has drooped,
>   the laden branch of yonder house.

M'aonar a-nocht damhsa, a Dhé,
   olc an saoghal camsa ad-chí;
dob álainn trom an taoibh naoi
   do bhaoi sonn a-raoir, a Rí.

Truagh leam an leabasa thiar,
   mo pheall seadasa dhá snámh;
tárramair corp seada saor
   is folt claon, a leaba, id lár.   16

Do bhí duine go ndreich moill
   ina luighe ar leith mo phill;
gan bharamhail acht bláth cuill
   don sgáth duinn bhanamhail bhinn.

Maol Mheadha na malach ndonn
   mo dhabhach mheadha a-raon rom;
mo chridhe an sgáth do sgar riom,
   bláth mhionn arna car do chrom.   24

Táinig an chlí as ar gcuing,
   agus dí ráinig mar roinn:
corp idir dá aisil inn
   ar dtocht don fhinn mhaisigh mhoill.

Leath mo throigheadh, leath mo thaobh,
   a dreach mar an droighean bán,
níor dhílse neach dhí ná dhún,
   leath mo shúl í, leath mo lámh.   32

Leath mo chuirp an choinneal naoi;
   's guirt riom do roinneadh, a Rí;
agá labhra is meirtneach mé —
   dob é ceirtleath m'anma í.

Mo chéadghrádh a dearc mhall mhór,
   déadbhan agus cam a cliabh:
nochar bhean a colann caomh
   ná a taobh ré fear romham riamh.   40

I am alone tonight, O God,
    treacherous the crooked world you see;
lovely the weight of the fresh form
    that was here last night, O King.

Pitiful to me yonder bed
    covered by my long rug;
Ah, bed, on you I have seen
    a long noble body with tumbling hair.

A person with a gentle face
    was lying on one half of my bed;
the only comparison, the hazel bloom
    to the dark womanly shadow of sweet voice.

Maol Mheadha of the dark brows,
    my mead vessel at my side;
the shadow that has parted was my heart,
    a jewelled flower planted here has dropped.

My body escaped the yoke
    and made off as her share;
I have become a body in two parts
    since the bright lovely gentle one left.

She was one of my feet, one of my sides,
    her complexion like the whitethorn,
no one was more loyal to her than to me,
    she was one of my eyes, one of my hands.

The new candle was half of my flesh,
    harshly have I been treated, Lord;
telling of it I grow faint —
    she was the very half of my soul.

My first love, her big calm eye,
    her bosom, ivory-white and curved;
neither her soft breast nor her flank
    ever touched a man before.

Fiche bliadhna inne ar-aon,
 fá binne gach bliadhna ar nglór,
go rug éinleanabh déag dhún,
 an ghéag úr mhéirleabhar mhór.

Gé tú, nocha n-oilim ann,
 ó do thoirinn ar gcnú chorr;
ar sgaradh dár roghrádh rom,
 falamh lom an domhnán donn.   48

Ón ló do sáidheadh cleath corr
 im theach nochar ráidheadh rum —
ní thug aoighe d'ortha ann
 dá barr naoidhe dhorcha dhunn.

A dhaoine, ná coisgidh damh;
 faoidhe ré cloistin ní col;
táinig luinnchreach lom 'nar dteagh —
 an bhruithneach gheal donn ar ndol.   56

Is é rug uan í 'na ghrúg,
 Rí na sluagh is Rí na ród;
beag an cion do chúl na ngéag
 a héag ó a fior go húr óg.

Ionmhain lámh bhog do bhí sonn,
 a Rí na gclog is na gceall:
ach! an lámh nachar logh mionn,
 crádh liom gan a cor fám cheann.   64

We were together twenty years,
    sweeter our words with every year,
eleven children she bore to me,
    the fresh, lithe-fingered, long branch.

Though I am, I am not,
    since my smooth nut fell,
since parting with my dearest dear
    the drear world is empty and bare.

Since the day the smooth support
    was set up in my house
it was never said a guest had beguiled
    the one of the fresh dark brown hair.

O people, do not make me stop,
    it is no sin that weeping be heard;
my house has been stripped bare
    by the parting of the bright brown glow.

The one who snatched her away in a rush
    was the King of hosts and King of roads;
small the fault of the one with branching hair
    that she left her husband while young and fresh.

Beloved the soft hand that lay here,
    Oh King of churches and bells;
Alas, the hand that never blasphemed,
    it is torment it lies not under my head.

28.   A Phaidrín do Dhúisg mo Dhéar

Aithbhreac inghean Coirceadail

Rinneadh am marbhrann ainmeil seo do Niall Óg (mac Thorcuil) MacNèill Ghiogha, a bha na chonsabal aig Caisteal Suibhne ann an Cnapadal (faic dàn 33) às leth MhicDhomhnaill nan Eilean, agus a dh'eug, a rèir coltais, uaireigin eadar 1455 agus 1472. Tha e follaiseach gur e bean Nèill a bha ann an Aithbhreac, ùghdar an dàin, ach chan eil dad de dh'fhiosrachadh againn seach na gheibhear às an dàn fhèin.

A bharrachd air a luach litreachail, tha am marbhrann seo sònraichte cudromach, oir is dòcha gur e seo an dàn as tràithe a rinneadh (ann an Alba no ann an Èirinn) le bana-bhàrd air a bheil ainm cinnteach. Tha ceithir dàin eile le mnathan-uasal (no is dòcha dìreach aon bhean-uasal) air an gleidheadh ann an Leabhar an Deadhain, ach tha e coltach gun do rinneadh iad beagan dheicheadan an dèidh dàn Aithbhric. Tha e anabarrach inntinneach gu bheil àite nas cudromaiche aig bhana-bhàird ann an litreachas Gàidhlig na h-Alba an coimeas ri litreachas na Gaeilge; tha diofar bheachdan aig sgoilearan air a' cheist, ach is dòcha gur ann air sgàth 's nach robh na filidh fhoghlaimte cho làidir ann an Alba a bha barrachd chothroman aig na bana-bhàird.

Rinneadh an dàn a leanas ann an 'óglachas' de rannaigheacht mhór. Tha Aithbhreac a' cleachdadh ìomhaighean is stoidhle an dàin dhìrich, rud a tha ag innse dhuinn gu robh i eòlach air cleachdaidhean nam filidh, ach faodaidh sinn a bhith cinnteach nach d'fhuair i trèanadh foirmeil, oir cha robh àite sam bith do bhoireannaich anns na sgoiltean bàrdachd.

> A phaidrín do dhúisg mo dhéar,
>   ionmhain méar do bhitheadh ort;
> ionmhain cridhe fáilteach fial
>   'gá raibhe riamh gus a nocht.
>
> Dá éag is tuirseach atáim,
>   an lámh má mbítheá gach n-uair,
> nach cluinim a beith i gclí
>   agus nach bhfaicim í uaim.   8

O Rosary That Woke My Tears

This famous and beautiful elegy was composed for Niall Óg (mac Thorcuil) MacNéill of Gigha, who served as constable of Castle Sween (see poem 33) on behalf of the Lord of the Isles, and who appears to have died some time between 1455 and 1472. The author of the poem is evidently Niall Óg's wife, but nothing is known of her beyond the evidence of this one composition.

This poem is particularly important as it may well be the earliest Gaelic poem – from either Scotland or Ireland – that we can reliably attribute to a named woman. Three poems by aristocratic Caimbeul women (or perhaps just one woman) are also preserved in the Book of the Dean of Lismore, together with a quatrain by a Stiùbhart noblewoman, but these were probably composed some years later, in the early sixteenth century. The greater prominence of women poets in Gaelic Scotland than in Ireland, both during this period and in later centuries, is a subject that has fascinated scholars.

The poem was composed in the formal literary language, in a relaxed version of the strict metres of the time, and using traditional bardic imagery and verbal formulae, thus showing that Aithbhreac was an educated woman; but it should by no means be inferred that she received formal training in one of the bardic schools, which were entirely closed to women.

O rosary that woke my tears,
    beloved the finger that on you did lie,
beloved the kindly generous heart
    that you belonged to till tonight.

For the death of him I am sad,
    whose hand you encircled every hour,
alas I do not hear it move
    or see it lying before me now.

Mo chridhe-se is tinn atá
  ó theacht go crích an lá dhúinn;
ba ghoirid do éist ré ghlóir,
  ré h-agallaimh an óig úir.

Béal asa ndob aobhdha glór,
  dhéantaidhe a ghó is gach tír:
leómhan Muile na múr ngeal,
  seabhag Íle na magh mín.   16

Fear ba ghéar meabhair ar dhán,
  ó nach deachaidh dámh gan díol;
taoiseach deigh-einigh suairc séimh,
  agá bhfaightí méin mheic ríogh.

Dámh ag teacht ó Dhún an Óir
  is dámh ón Bhóinn go a fholt fiar:
minic thánaig iad fá theist,
  ná mionca ná leis a riar.   24

Seabhag seangglan Sléibhe Gaoil,
  fear do chuir a chaoin ré cléir;
dreagan Leódhuis na learg ngeal,
  éigne Sanais na sreabh séimh.

A h-éagmhais aon duine a mháin
  im aonar atáim dá éis,
gan chluiche, gan chomhrádh caoin,
  gan ábhacht, gan aoibh i gcéill.   32

Gan duine ris dtig mo mhiann
  as sliocht na Niall ó Niall óg;
gan mhuirn gan mheadhair ag mnáibh,
  gan aoibhneas an dáin im dhóigh.

Mar thá Giodha an fhuinn mhín,
  Dún Suibhne do-chím gan cheól,
faithche longphuirt na bhfear bhfial:
  aithmhéala na Niall a n-eól.   40

My heart has been smarting and sore
    since this day came to a close;
short was the time I listened to his voice,
    to the conversation of the lovely youth.

Mouth of the most delightful voice,
    whose whims were conceded in every land,
lion of Mull of the white walls,
    hawk of Islay of the smooth plains.

No poet-band left without reward
    the man whose memory for song was keen,
he had the bearing of a prince,
    hospitable, courteous, gentle chief.

Poet-bands coming from Dún an Óir,
    poets from the Boyne to the man of curling hair,
often did they come drawn by his fame,
    not less often they got their desire.

Bright slender hawk of Sliabh Gaoil,
    man who showed his kindness to the Church,
dragon of Lewis of the sunny slopes,
    salmon of Sanas of the peaceful burns.

For want of only this one man
    I am alone, longing for him,
without diversion or kindly talk,
    without gladness or sign of mirth.

Not one man of Clann Nèill
    takes my fancy with young Niall gone;
women lack all happiness and joy,
    I cannot hope for cheer in song.

Sad is Gigha of the smooth soils,
    I see Dún Suibhne standing on its green,
fort of the fine men now without a tune,
    they know the sorrow of Clann Nèill.

Cúis a lúthgháire má seach,
    gusa mbímis ag teacht mall:
's nach fuilngim anois, mo nuar,
    a fhaicinn uam ar gach ard.

Má bhrisis, a Mheic Dhé bhí,
    ar bagaide na dtrí gcnó,
fa fíor do ghabhais ar ngiall:
    do bhainis an trian ba mhó.   48

Cnú mhullaigh a mogaill féin
    bhaineadh do Chloinn Néill go nua:
is tric roighne na bhfear bhfial
    go leabaidh na Niall a nuas.

An rogha fá deireadh díbh
    's é thug gan mo bhrígh an sgéal:
do sgar riom mo leathchuing rúin,
    a phaidrín do dhúisg mo dhéar.   56

Is briste mo chridhe im chlí,
    agus bídh nó go dtí m'éag,
ar éis an abhradh dhuibh úir,
    a phaidrín do dhúisg mo dhéar.

        A phaidrín.

Muire mháthair, muime an Ríogh,
    go robh 'gam dhíon ar gach séad,
's a Mac do chruthuigh gach dúil,
    a phaidrín do dhúisg mo dhéar.   64

        A phaidrín.

Place we used to approach in state,
    which brought us merriment every time,
now alas I cannot bear
    to see it rise up from every height.

If Thou, O Son of the living God,
    hast breached the cluster of nuts on the trees,
Thou hast taken hostage our choicest man,
    Thou hast taken the greatest of the three.

The topmost nut of Clann Nèill
    has been stripped away from the generous men;
often does the choicest of their bunch
    fall down to the MacNèill's last bed.

The most recent, finest of them all,
    the tale of him has cost me dear,
my beloved yokefellow has parted from me,
    O rosary that woke my tears.

Broken is my heart within my breast,
    and will remain so until my death,
longing for the fresh dark-lashed man,
    O rosary that woke my tears.

Mary, Mother, nurse of the King,
    may she protect me far and near,
and also her Son who created all,
    O rosary that woke my tears.

29. Ní h-Éibhneas gan Chlainn Domhnaill

Giolla Coluim Mac an Ollaimh An Fear (Dána)

Ann an 1493 chaidh Rìoghachd nan Eilean arfuntachadh le Pàrlamaid na h-Alba, agus tha an dàn ainmeil seo à Leabhar an Deadhain a' comharrachadh doilgheas na rè sin.

Is àbhaist do luchd-eachdraidh an latha a bhith a' comharrachadh 1493 mar dheireadh Rìoghachd nan Eilean, ach cha do ghabh luchd-taice Chloinn Domhnaill ris na rinn a' Phàrlamaid agus an rìgh. Chuireadh grunn iomairtean air dòigh a chum ath-stèidheachadh Rìoghachd nan Eilean gu ruige 1545, nuair a chaochail Domhnall Dubh, ogha Eòin, a chaidh arfuntachadh ann an 1493.

Tha e coltach gum buineadh ùghdar an dàin, Giolla Coluim Mac an Ollaimh, do Chloinn Mhuirich. Tha dà dhàn a bharrachd le Giolla Coluim air an gleidheadh ann an Leabhar an Deadhain, nam measg marbhrann do Aonghas Òg MacDhomhnaill, a mharbhadh ann an 1490 (faic dàn 37).

> Ní h-éibhneas gan Chlainn Domhnaill,
>   ní comhnairt bheith 'na n-éagmhais;
> an chlann dob fhearr san gcruinne:
>   gur dhíobh gach duine céatach.

> Clann as saoire dár dealbhadh,
>   i roibh eangnamh is ághas;
> clann dárbh umhail na tíorain,
>   i raibh crionnacht is crábhadh.　　8

> Clann chunnail chalma chródha,
>   clann ba teódha i n-am troda;
> clann ba mhíne i measg bantracht,
>   agus ba chalma i gcogadh.

> Clann ba líonmhoire eireacht,
>   dob fhearr eineach is áireamh;
> clann nár chathuigh ar eaglais,
>   clann lérbh eagail a gcáineadh.　　16

There is No Joy Without Clann Domhnaill

In 1493 the Scottish Parliament ordered the forfeiture of the Lordship of the Isles, and this famous poem from the Book of the Dean of Lismore evidently dates from this period. Nevertheless, although modern historians have marked out this 1493 forfeiture as a determinative date bringing the end of an era, it was by no means universally recognised as such at the time, and atttempts to restore the Lordship continued until 1545, when Domhnall Dubh MacDhomhnaill, grandson of Eòin, last Lord of the Isles, died in the midst of preparations for a full-scale rising that was to be launched from his Irish base.

The author of the poem, Giolla Coluim Mac an Ollaimh, appears to have been a member of the MacMhuirich bardic family, hereditary poets to the MacDhomhnaill Lords of the Isles; the title 'Mac an Ollaimh' means 'son of the high-poet'. Two further poems by Giolla Coluim, including an elegy on Aonghas Óg MacDhomhnaill (†1490), are preserved in the Book of the Dean of Lismore.

> There is no joy without Clann Domhnaill,
>   there is no support without them;
> the best people in the whole world,
>   to them every good person is related.
>
> Noblest people of all created,
>   who possess ferocity and valour;
> a people to whom tyrants were humble,
>   in whom resided piety and prudence.
>
> A people kind, brave and mighty,
>   a people hottest at time of conflict;
> the most gentle of men among women,
>   the most intrepid in warfare.
>
> A people of most numerous assembly,
>   of highest honour and highest number;
> a people who never warred against churches,
>   a people who were afraid of slander.

Uaithne ána Alban uaine,
    clann as cruaidhe ghabh bhaisteadh:
'gá roibh treas gacha tíre,
    seabhaig Íle ar ghaisgeadh.

Clann ba mhó is ba mhire,
    clann ba ghrinne is ba réidhe;
clann dob fhairsinge croidhe,
    dob fhearr foidhide is féile.   24

Meic ríogh nár thuill a n-aoradh,
    i roibh daonnacht is truime;
fir allta uaisle fhonnmhor,
    i raibh bronntacht is buige.

Clann dob fhearr feidhm is faisgeadh,
    clann dob fhearr gaisgeadh láimhe;
olc liom giorrad a h-íorna,
    'n bhé lér sníomhadh a snáithe.   32

Niorbh iad na droichfhir bhodhra,
    ná na fir lobhra laga;
ré dol i n-ionad bhuailte
    fir nach cruaidhe na craga.

Clann gan uabhar gan éagcáir,
    nár ghabh acht éadáil chogaidh;
'gar mheanmnach daoine uaisle,
    is agar bhuaine bodaigh.   40

Mairg ó rugadh an fheadhain,
    mairg do dheadhail ré gcaidreabh;
gan aonchlann mar Chlainn Domhnaill,
    saorchlann ba chomhnairt aigneadh.

Gan áireamh ar a n-urdail,
    gan chuntadh ar a nduaisibh;
gan chrích gan tús gan deireadh
    ar eineach agá n-uaislibh.   48

Noble pillars of green Scotland,
    the hardiest of people who received baptism,
who won victory over every country,
    for heroism they were hawks of Islay.

The biggest clan and the most cheerful,
    a people most affable and most refined;
a people of hearts most giving,
    of greatest patience and greatest bounty.

Sons of kings who never deserved satire,
    possessing both gravitas and kindness;
wild men, musical and noble,
    in whom resided generosity and softness.

The best people for service and shelter,
    the best people at handling weapons;
evil to me the skein's shortness
    of the Muse who spun their life-thread.

They were not the deaf villains
    nor the men who were weak and leprous;
for going into a place of bashing
    the rocks were not harder than those heroes.

A people without pride or injustice,
    who lifted cattle only in forays;
whose nobles were men of spirit,
    and whose commoners were long living.

Woe to those from whom they were taken,
    woe to those who have departed their society,
there being no other clan like Clann Domhnaill,
    a noble clan of supportive spirit.

It was impossible to count their number,
    impossible to assess their bounty,
without beginning, end or limits
    to the generosity of their nobles.

I dtosach Clainne Domhnaill
  do bhí foghlaim 'gá fáithneadh,
agus do bhí 'na ndeireadh
  feidhm is eineach is náire.

Ar bhrón agus ar thuirse
  do thréigeas tuigse is foghlaim;
gach aoinní ortha thréigeas:
  ní h-éibhneas gan Chlainn Domhnaill.   56

Dobadh tréan gaoth ag tíorain
  fán aicme chríonna chomhnairt:
gé táid i ndiu fá dhímheas,
  ní h-aoibhneas gan Chlainn Domhnaill.

Na slóigh as fearr san gcruinne
  a muirn a mire a bhfoghnamh;
ní comhnairt bheith 'na bhféagmhais:
  ní h-éibhneas gan Chlainn Domhnaill.   64

Macán láimhe [   ]
  dár saoradh ar gach doghrainn:
gé tá sé dhúinne díleas,
  ní h-aoibhneas gan Chlainn Domhnaill.

       Ní h-éibhneas.

30. Marbhna Fhearchoir Í Mhaoil Chiaráin

Ó Maoil Ciaráin

Anns a' mharbhrann ro-ainmeil seo tha am file Ó Maoil
Chiaráin a' caoidh aon mhic, Fearchar, a bha e fhèin na fhile, a
chaidh a mharbhadh leis na Sasannaich agus e air cuairt bhàr-
dail ann an Èirinn. Is e glè bheag de dh'eòlas a tha againn air Ó
Maoil Chiaráin no air Fearchar; a rèir coltais seo an aon dàn le
Ó Maoil Chiaráin a tha air tighinn a-nuas thugainn, agus chan
eil ach aon dàn le Fearchar, an dàn gràidh cliùiteach 'I mbrat an

In the forefront of Clann Domhnaill
    learning was commanded,
and in their lower orders,
    modesty, action and honour.

Out of sorrow and sadness
    I've forsaken wisdom and learning;
owing to them have I all things abandoned:
    there is no joy without Clann Domhnaill.

Mighty was the blast of tyrants
    against the tribe that was wise and supportive;
though today they be disparaged,
    there is no joy without Clann Domhnaill.

The best people in the wide world
    their joy, their sport, their service;
there is no strength without them,
    there is no joy without Clann Domhnaill.

A Babe in arms [   ],
    may He save us from every evil;
though He to us be loyal,
    there is no joy without Clann Domhnaill.

        There is no joy.

A Great Loss Has Been Brought on Me

This unusual but greatly celebrated poem is a lament by the poet
Ó Maoil Chiaráin for his only son Fearchar, also a poet,
apparently killed by the English while on a bardic visit to
Ireland. We know very little of either father or son; this appears
to be the only one of Ó Maoil Chiaráin's poems that has been
preserved, and only one of Fearchar's own works has survived,
the tender love poem 'I mbrat an bhrollaigh ghil-se' (poem 47).

bhrollaigh ghil-se' (dàn 47). Chaidh earrann den mharbhrann air Fearchar a chleachdadh ann an leabhar-stiùiridh air mead-rachd a chaidh a chleachdadh anns na sgoiltean bàrdachd; chaidh an leabhran seo a sgrìobhadh mu 1500, agus mar sin fao-dar a bhith cinnteach gun do chumadh an dàn seo roimhe sin, ach dh'fhaodadh e a bhith linn no dhà nas sine.

Bha an iomhaigh de dh'Ó Maoil Chiaráin a' caoidh Fhearchair air leth ainmeil ann an dualchas nan Gàidheal, agus bhiodh bàird thar nan linntean gu tric a' toirt iomradh air gus call is mulad a chur an cèill.

Chan eil fiosrachadh againn mun teaghlach bhàrdail seo; tha teans ann gu bheil ceangal eadar 'Lí' ann an sreath 173 agus Beinn Lì ann am Bràighe an Eilein Sgitheanaich, ach chan eil dad a dhearbhadh againn a thaobh sin.

Tugadh oirne easbhuidh mhór,
    cneasghuin na coinnle rom chríon,
mo leanabh óm leas do ládh,
    do beanadh mo lámh dheas díom.

Do folchadh gile a ghruadh mbreac,
    budh buan ar mo chridhe a chnoc,
faríor nocha mhar mo mhac,
    glan an tshlat do bhíodh fám brot.   8

Mo chalann atá gan treóir,
    atá mh'anam isan uaigh,
rem aonmhac ní fhoil mo shúil,
    caolbhrat d'úir ghloin ar a ghruaidh.

Gol a mháthar tar moir mhóir —
    'na toigh atáthar gan treóir —
foghar ghuil mhianaigh í Mhaoil,
    faoidh luin ag iarruidh a eóin.   16

Do-rinne dom chroidhe chrú,
    sinne ionar loighe dhá ló,
teagh úire giodh aige atá,
    faide an lá dhúinne ioná dhó.

For technical reasons it can be concluded that the poem was composed before 1500, but it may well be considerably older.

The poem (or other poems on the same subject) seems to have been very well known to Gaelic audiences, for the image of Ó Maoil Chiaráin mourning for Fearchar becomes a standard reference in later Gaelic poetry – the very archetype of grief and loss.

It has been suggested that the reference to 'Lí' in line 173 might be to Beinn Lì in Braes in Skye, implying a family connection to that district, but this can only be speculation.

A great loss has been brought on me,
    I am withered by the candle's wound,
my child has been cast from my use,
    my right hand has been cut off.

Hidden his bright freckled cheeks,
    its agony lives on in my heart,
alas that my son lives not,
    bright that branch below my cloak.

My body is lacking all strength,
    my soul is in the grave,
I am without hope of my only son,
    a thin cover of fresh soil on his cheek.

His mother's weeping over a great sea —
    everyone without spirit in her house —
the sound of her mourning Ó Mhaoil,
    like a blackbird's cry for her young.

My heart has turned to blood,
    I have not risen since that day;
although his is the house of earth,
    longer for me than him the day.

Mo sheise tar an moir mhóir,
  is meise dom thoigh ón tráigh,
dob é an t-anadh aimhghlic uaim
  sgaradh re a ghruaidh mbaillbhric mbáin.   24

Ránag Magh Fáil fa bhfuil tonn,
  mo dháil tar an muir is mall;
truagh mo thadhall fan bhfiadh bhfionn:
  dar liom do bhiadh m'anam ann.

Baoth mé gan leanmhuin mo laoigh
  tar an ngleannmhuir go ngné ruaidh:
beithear arna thocht gan treóir,
  gan fheitheamh m'eóin dob olc uaim.   32

Ní mhair Fearchar go bhfolt nua,
  iona thocht do mheallfadh mná:
do-chuaidh ar bhfear duasach dhó,
  ní ag cnuasach bó am theagh atá.

Ní thig neach anoir ná aniar
  dom thoigh ré heach ná ré hór:
teagaimh gach fear dána dhún,
  acht an geal úr málla mór.   40

A lucht do mharbh an ngéig ngil,
  is do léig fan arm a fhuil,
níor cháin an fear, níor aor ibh,
  níor libh a thaobh geal do ghuin.

Fada a charaid ó a churp shaor,
  ní anaid an lucht gá luadh;
folt na ngleann bhfionnbhuidhe bhfiar,
  cian dream a ionghuire uadh.   48

Ó Maoil Chiarán mo chaor nua,
  mo ghríanán aoil, mo chraobh chnó,
dream gan shuan am thigh atá,
  na mná 's na fir fa dual dó.

My favourite set off across the sea,
    and I walked home from the shore;
unwise of me to await him at home,
    to part from his fair freckled cheek.

I reached Ireland girt by waves,
    tardy my meeting over the sea,
sad my visit to that fair land
    where I thought my darling was.

Stupid I was not to follow my calf
    over the cloven sea, ruddy of hue:
no-one feels any purpose with him gone,
    wrong was I not to guard my bird.

Fearchar of the fresh hair is no more,
    he whose arrival would delight the girls:
my gifted man has left us,
    he is not gathering cows to my house.

No-one appears from east or west
    coming home with a horse or gold:
every man of learning chances upon me
    but the bright fresh tall gentle one.

You who killed the illustrious branch,
    and let his blood flow about the blade,
the man had not satirised you, made no lampoon,
    you had no right to pierce his fair side.

Far his friends from his noble corpse,
    him the people do not linger to recall;
cascading yellow bright waving hair
    far away are the ones who would watch.

Ó Maoil Chiaráin, my living coal,
    my lime-washed sun-bower, my branch of nuts,
the people in my house cannot sleep,
    the men and women who were his kin.

An tráth do sgaoileadh an sgéal,
   cách dhá chaoineadh nochar cheól,
mar do bhaoi ar tteach doba truagh,
   neach ag caoi uadh, neach a neól.   56

Gol a mháthar fá mór é,
   gur clódh a láthar 's a lí,
tairnig a corp agá chaoi,
   olc don mhnaoi nárbh aimrid í.

As é ar mac ar marbhadh féin,
   an tshlat is amhghar a n-uaigh,
as é a bhás rom béara a n-úir,
   is méala dhúin a fhás uain.   64

Gér bheodha gach deighfhear dhíobh,
   ba neimhsheadh gach deóra dháibh;
a dhíoghail ní headh do-fhuair,
   do-chuaidh do ríoghaibh bhfear bhFáil.

Brígh mo chumhadh ní choisg lionn,
   mo roisg ón dubhadh is dall,
m'ucht 'na chrosradhaigh chnámh lom,
   's a lán trom d'osnadhaibh ann.   72

Ní thráigh mo chumha le ceól,
   nocha dáigh a dula dhíom,
nocha ttoirneann bean mo bhrón,
   ná fleadh ná glór roibheann ríogh.

Do chuir ar maicne fa mhaoith,
   ar n-aicme ní chluin an ccuaich:
a aghaidh óg 's a bhonn bláith
   fá fhód cháich is trom re tuaith.   80

Iomdha tromhuinn goin dá ghrádh
   trém choluinn soir agus siar;
na doighthe ag dubhadh mo ghruadh,
   goithne fhuar chumhadh trém chliabh.

When the news spread
   no music made everyone's wails;
pitiful my household's state,
   someone weeping, another in a faint.

Great the weeping of his mother,
   altered her complexion and health,
racked her body from lamenting him,
   Alas the woman ever conceived!

My son is the death of myself,
   agony, the branch in the grave,
his death will lay me in the earth,
   that I ever begot him is sore.

Though mettlesome every man,
   for a stranger they had no care,
his death went unavenged —
   the Irish princes have reneged.

Beer does not staunch the force of my weeping,
   my eyes are blinded by the grief,
my breast is a grating of bare bones,
   with its full weight of heavy sighs.

Music cannot cause my grief to ebb,
   of its leaving me there is no hope,
no woman can my sorrow allay,
   nor feast, nor the blast of princes' horns.

Our children it has made sad,
   our people hear the cuckoo not;
hard on them his young face
   and smooth foot in foreign soil.

Love for him has caused many a wound
   to pierce my body front and back;
the pangs have turned my cheeks black,
   grief's cold dart pierces my breast.

Atá taobh ar saoirmheic sunn
    fá aoinleic risan ndaol ndonn:
sáidhfidh daol am chneassa a cheann,
    measa leam an taobh do tholl.   88

Turus mo mheic tar muir siar
    do luigh 'na leic ar mo lár:
do-gheabhtha chrodh gan chreic nduan,
    truagh a mheic do dhol re dán.

Mo mhac saor ro ghonsad Goill,
    mo laogh an tslat bhosbhog bhinn;
a mheic, giodh gan bhuar do bheinn,
    is truagh leinn gan do leic linn.   96

Ionmhuin trácht nachar throm lúdh,
    ionmhuin bonn mar bhláth na ccaor,
ionmhuin seangthroigh is bos bhán,
    cos is lámh Fhearchoir ar-aon.

Faríor as é an t-aisdear olc
    ar ttaisdeal ó phort do phurt:
mé uair ag loighe ar a leacht,
    feacht oile 's a uaigh rem ucht.   104

Seanmóir cháich ní théid fam thuinn,
    trésan ngéig ngealmhóir mbláith mbinn:
cách uile dá ccrádh fa a ccloinn —
    gá poinn do dhuine a rádh rinn?

Dar linn ní coimseach ar cciall;
    sinn go toirrseach agá thúr,
mur chubhar ngeal ar áth fhuar,
    am sgáth thruagh gan sheagh gan shúgh.   112

Cumha Í Mhaoil Chiarán am churp,
    ar síadhán atám dá thocht;
gan mo dhul d'éag lé ar a leacht,
    créad nach budh dleacht cré ar mo chorp?

The body of my noble son is here
　　under the same stone as the beetle brown;
a beetle will thrust its head into my skin:
　　but worse for me the body it has already bored.

My son's journey west across the sea
　　has lain like a stone on my heart;
you would have got cows without selling poems —
　　sad, my son, your following that art.

Foreigners have slain my noble son,
　　my calf, the soft-palmed melodious branch;
O son, even were I without cows,
　　it is pitiful your grave-stone is not here.

Beloved the instep that carried little weight,
　　beloved the sole like the flower of the ash,
beloved the slender foot and white palm,
　　the hand and foot of Fearchar, both.

Alas, the journey is bad,
　　my travelling from place to place;
at one time I lie on my back on his tomb,
　　at another his grave is against my breast.

Others' preaching does not touch me,
　　because of the tall white smooth sweet branch;
their own children cause all to grieve —
　　what avails it for anyone to say it to me?

I think I have lost my mind
　　as I sadly seek him out;
like white foam on a cool ford am I,
　　a wretched shadow without strength or sap.

Anguish for Ó Maoil Chiaráin fills me,
　　I wander about in a fit of grief;
though I have not died of it on his tomb,
　　why should clay not duly cover me?

Tug h'úidh ar Dhia riomsa, a Rí,
   ní bhia súil am chionnsa ón chaoi:
an truagh lat mo dhéar, a Dhé?
   féagh mé gan mhac is gan mhnaoi. 120

Easbhuidh goin an ghille shaoir,
   easbhuidh linne a oil a n-úir,
táinig dh'olc an oidhidh fuair,
   a thocht uain gur dhoiligh dhúin.

Bás Fearchuir ag searg ar súl,
   mur cheard gan teannchuir atám;
rug mh'ar agus mh'eagar uam,
   truagh dhamh a leagadh ar lár. 128

Do-roinne an Coimdhe chreich ttruim,
   oirne dá gach leith do ling,
do-rad mé an Coimdhe gan chloinn,
   ní hé a roinn do-roighne rinn.

Níor dhamh dligheadh damhsa Dia,
   mo chlannsa gér chineadh nua:
is mé an tshlat do chuir a cnú,
   atú gan mhac 's ní fhuil mh'ua. 136

Reic a mharbhna as dár laoibh leóin,
   gurab tarbha don taoibh fuair;
is dubhach olc 'na duais dúin,
   rug shúil is chluais is fholt uainn.

Dul ar a lighe gach laoi
   do dhubh mo chridhe is mo chlí;
uaigh Fhearchuir giodh uaine a gné,
   bearrfuidh mé gach uaire í. 144

Bróg tar teach do teilgeadh leam
   ag teacht tar an ndeirggeal ndonn:
do reith fear is do fhéagh ann
   nar bhean tall a béal fá a bonn.

For God's sake, O King, give heed to me,
    weeping will leave no eye in my head;
do you pity my tears, O God?
    Behold me without son or wife.

A loss is the wounding of the noble lad,
    a loss for me his going in the earth;
so much evil has come of his death,
    his leaving us has vexed us sore.

Fearchar's death is shrivelling my eye,
    I am like a smith without tongs,
I am bereft of my tillage and stock,
    sad to me his smiting down.

The Lord has levied a heavy spoil —
    He has attacked me on every side;
without children the Lord has left me:
    no share of them did He make.

Justice has God not dealt me,
    though my children were a young growth;
I am the branch that shed its nut,
    I am without son, and grandson too.

Reciting his elegy is among my days of hurt,
    may it be a benefit to the one who got it;
it is sad that my loss was its reward,
    it has deprived me of eye, of ear and hair.

Going to his grave every day
    has blackened my heart and my form;
though Fearchar's grave appears green,
    I will scold it every time.

I threw a shoe over a house,
    naming the fair rosy one with brown hair;
a man ran over to see
    if it lay with the sole up.

As prap ruguis é uan
  an mac tugais a Dhé dhún;
ón ló teasda an té fá a ttám,
  do shlán, a Dhé, feasda fúm.   152

Mo mhac roba naoidhe nua,
  fá caoimhe ioná gach mac mná;
do cheannach nimhe ar dhigh dhó
  a bhó dhighe am thigh atá.

Cubhránach (?) mo chroidhe am chliabh,
  mo shoidhe gulánach (?) géar,
a ghnaoi fhallsa ag snoighe ar súl,
  súgh mo chroidhe dhamhsa a dhéar.   160

Iomdha rem dhreich srothán síos,
  ochán gan mo bhreith don bhás:
is mé an crann do chuir a chnuas,
  mo bharr suas ní fhuil ar ás.

A adhbhasa um an ccorp ccaomh,
  ním calmasa ort, a uagh;
a bhoth a ndéanadh a dhán,
  och mur tám got fhéaghadh uam.   168

Gan mhac feasda is fada leinn
  ar aba cheasda san chill;
mo bhean nocha bhéara chloinn,
  croinn gan fhréamha budh eadh inn.

Gach uair ghuilim tré fhleisg Lí
  cuirim mur cheisd agá chaoi:
bean an bhaile nár bhac é,
  a Dhé, an raibhe mac 'gan mhnaoi?   176

Och is dubha fhallsa í,
  guth dhamhsa gan dula lé;
anbhann mo chorp is mo chlí,
  is olc dhí nach marbhann mé.

Suddenly You snatched him away,
    the son You gave us, God;
from the day the one I speak of died
    I am finished with You, God, for evermore.

My son was young and fresh,
    fairer than every woman's son;
spite bought our loss of him,
    his milking cow is in my house.

The foam of my heart in my breast,
    my rest is tearful and sore;
seeing him falsely wears out my eyes,
    my tears for him are my heart's blood.

Many a stream courses down my face,
    Alas death fails to carry me off;
I am the tree that shed its fruit;
    my produce has not grown ripe.

O house about his gentle form,
    you leave me without strength, O grave;
O hut, where he used to make his verse,
    Alas, seeing you makes me sad.

With a son no more, time is slow
    in the graveyard on account of grief;
no children will my wife bear now —
    we will be trees without roots.

Whenever I weep for Lí's youth,
    I ask this question through my tears:
the goodwife that did not hold him back,
    O God, did that woman ever have a son?

Alas, it is a treacherous grief
    that reproaches me that I die not of it;
weak my body and my frame,
    it is evil of grief not to kill me.

An filise 's an féar thríd,
  mo chridhise an béal gan bhréig,
an tshaorshlat gan mhuirn gan mhóid,
  caolbhrat fóid ghuirm ar an ngéig.   184

Guilim ar a los gach laoi
  ní fhuilim anos do ní;
as í a mharbhnaidh do mheasg mé,
  a Dhé, is leasg lem anmuin í.

Níor ghabh dhíom an Coimdhe cead
  fan ngníomh — mur do-roighne rug;
diomdhach mé don Rígh do-rad,
  mur do ghad dínn an té tug.   192

Tugadh oirne.

31. Alba gan Díon a nDiaidh Ailín

Mac Muireadhaigh

Seo marbhrann ealanta air an nòs phroifeiseanta, a' caoidh dithis
cheann-cinnidh aig Clann Raghnaill: Ailean mac Ruairidh, a
fhuair bàs *c.* 1503, agus a mhac Raghnall Bàn, a fhuair bàs
c. 1511.

Tha an dàn air a ghleidheadh ann an Leabhar Dearg Chloinn
Mhuirich, a sgrìobhadh leis an fhile Niall MacMhuirich mu
dheireadh an t-seachdamh linn deug. A bharrachd air
eachdraidh ainmeil Chloinn Domhnaill agus Chloinn Raghnaill,
gheibhear anns an Leabhar Dhearg cruinneachadh farsaing de
dhàin chlasaigeach, grunn mharbhrannan nam measg. Rinneadh
a' mhòr-mhòr-chuid dhiubh sin do chinn-chinnidh an
t-seachdamh linn deug (le Niall fhèin agus le Cathal, bràthair
athar), agus is e seo am marbhrann as sine. Chan eil e buileach
cinnteach cuine a rinneadh an ceangal eadar Clann Mhuirich
agus Clann Raghnaill, ach tha an dàn seo a' nochdadh dhuinn
gu robh dàimh air choreigin eatarra beagan bhliadhnaichean an
dèidh arfuntachadh Dhomhnallaich Ìle ann an 1493.

Chan eil fios againn cò rinn an dàn, oir chan eil ainm mu

This poet the grass grows through,
   my darling, the mouth that told no lie,
the noble sapling without love, without oath,
   a thin covering of green turf on the branch.

Every day I weep for him,
   nothing holds my attention now;
his elegy has disturbed me,
   O God, my soul abhors it.

The Lord sought not my leave
   for the deed — as He made, so He took;
I am angry with the King who gave
   for He stole from me the one He brought.

Scotland is Defenceless After Ailean

This poem poem laments the death, in rapid succession, of two chiefs of Clann Raghnaill: Ailean mac Ruairidh, who died c. 1503, and his son and successor Raghnall Bàn, who died c. 1511. The poem is simply ascribed to 'Mac Muireadhaigh' (the classical form of the name MacMhuirich) in the Book of Clanranald, the late seventeenth-century manuscript in which it is preserved. It is not known which member of this famous bardic family composed it; there are several poems in the Book of the Dean of Lismore composed at roughly the same time which appear to be the work of MacMhuirich poets, including poems 29 and 37 in this collection.

Following the demise of the Lordship of the Isles, the MacMhuirichs became hereditary poets to the Clann Raghnaill branch of Clann Domhnaill, and left their base in Kintyre for South Uist. This is the only surviving sixteenth-century poem composed for Clann Raghnaill patrons, but many classical MacMhuirich poems from the seventeenth century have survived, composed not only for Clann Raghnaill chiefs but for other branches of Clann Domhnaill and for Clann MhicLeòid.

choinneimh an dàin anns an làmh-sgrìobhainn seach 'Mac Muireadhaigh'. Chan eil dùnadh ceart air an dàn, agus mar sin tha e coltach gun deach pàirt dheth a chall.

Tha am file a' cleachdadh grunn ainmean bàrdail mu choinneimh na Gàidhealtachd (no is dòcha Innse Gall): Clár Monaidh, Clár Fionnghall, Clár na gColla. Chan aithnicheadh Gàidheil an latha an-diugh na h-ainmean seo, agus gu dearbh cha robh iad riamh cumanta ann am bàrdachd. Ach tha ainmean bàrdail air Èirinn anabarrach pailt, agus gheibhear mòran eisimpleirean dhiubh anns an duanaire seo: Achadh Airt, Clár Fhiontain, Críoch Éibhir, Cró Fiachaidh, Gort Breagh, Iath Chuinn agus eile.

Alba gan díon a ndiaidh Ailín,
    oighreacht Raghnaill na rosg gorm:
mo chor ar n-éag an dá fhear-soin
    crodh dá méad nach easbhuidh orm.

Laoch lér cothuigheadh Clár Monaidh
    mac Mairghréide, ca mó béad?
Ní h-ághur lé díoth budh doilghe,
    gidh é críoch gach oighre éag.   8

Ailín ler coisneadh Clár Fionnghall
    fine Cholla fa chneas mín:
go táinig bás oighre ó nEachaidh
    níor chas oirne an deachaidh dhinn.

Éag Raghnaill as an fhréimh chéadna
    ceannas Ghaoidheal do ghabh súd:
fuair tré éag urruim gach aoinfhir
    géag don choillidh fhaoilidh úd.   16

A very different view of Ailean appears in poem 38, the satire 'Theast aon diabhal na nGaoidheal', where it is claimed that he despoiled churches and had sexual relations with his mother and sister. The survival of poems praising and dispraising the same individual is highly unusual.

One interesting feature of the present poem is its extensive use of poetic names for Scotland and/or the Hebrides: *Clár Monaidh, Clár Fionnghall, Clár na gColla* (Plain of Monadh, Plain of the Fair Foreigners, Plain of the Collas). While there are scores of such names for Ireland in bardic poetry, Scottish counterparts are much rarer, perhaps because the curriculum of the bardic schools placed heavy emphasis on Ireland's early history and mythology, while 'imagining Scotland' seems not to have been a high priority.

Also noteworthy is the lengthy apologue, or illustrative historical story, in which Cathbhadh, the 'druid' of Ulster, laments the death of the great warrior Cú Chulainn. Comparison of the grief after the chief's death to the grief after the death of a famous figure from the Gaelic past is a common motif in formal elegies.

Scotland, defenceless after Ailean,
   became the estate of Raghnall of the blue eyes;
on the death of these two men my condition
   cannot be remedied by wealth, however great.

A warrior who maintained the land of Monadh,
   the son of Mairghréad — what greater loss? —
she has no fear of a harsher bereavement,
   though death is the end of every heir.

Ailean, who defended the plain of the Fionnghoill,
   of the tribe of Colla of smooth skin,
until the death of the heir of Eochaidh's descendants
   we knew not grief from all those that died before.

The death of Raghnall from the same lineage,
   he was a man who took the headship of the Gael;
at his death every man paid him homage,
   he too a branch of that generous wood.

Caoineadh Raghnaill na renn corcra
  cor mo chroidhe ní céim soirbh:
gé bé lá as lugha dá éagnach
  atá a chumha a n-éagcruth oirnn.

Ní fhearr fhuilim tar éis Ailín
  oidheadh Raghnaill, ní roinn mhín:
cinn ar slóigh ar cconchlann ccuradh,
  comhthrom bróin do bhunadh bhím.   24

Cumha na deisi dáil chomhthrom,
  ceannach dúin ar dáil a séad:
ní dhamhna d'fhaicsin a h-ardmhagh
  gabhla gaisgidh Alban d'éag.

Tásg Raghnaill do rochtain inmhe
  d'éis Ailín do b'oirdhearc nós:
do chaith a ré rinn i dteasgadh
  truagh nach sinn do theasda ar thós.   32

Raghnall ar ndul a ndiaidh Ailín
  d'éag éinfhir ní fhuil mo spéis:
ráinig a theisd tar ghníomh Ghaoidheal,
  ní cheisd díobh aoinfhear dá éis.

Ainbhreath an bháis ní bheart chomhthrom
  ar Chloinn Colla nár ghabh geis:
a éag is a oighre a n-éinfheacht
  géag Moirne gan léireacht leis.   40

Cantar uaim re t'ucht mar eala,
  a Ua Ruaidhrí na renn ngorm:
mo mhuirn réd chois, a dhéad dhaithgheal,
  t'éag a nois dá aithbhear orm.

Do theisd go bráth biaidh ar chuimhne,
  conchlann t'einigh — ard an clú —
t'éag 'na charaid re h-éag Ailín
  géag nach ráinig taibhéim tú.   48

Mourning Raghnall of purple spear-points
    the state of my heart is not at ease;
whatever day we least lament him
    his loss is upon us as a figure of death.

I am no better off after Ailean,
    the fate of Raghnall was no gentle lot;
leaders of our host and our band of heroes,
    I feel sorrow for both in equal part.

Our mourning the two is just as gloomy;
    the distribution of their treasures has cost us dear;
we have no cause to look to Scotland's uplands
    now that the forked branch of her heroism has gone.

The tale of Raghnall's death having achieved greatness,
    following Ailean who was distinguished in style;
he spent his time with us doing battle,
    alas that we did not die first.

Since Raghnall has gone after Ailean
    no man's death has given me concern;
his fame surpassed the deeds of the Gaidheal,
    with him gone, they think of no-one else.

No fair action is death's sentence
    on the children of Colla who accepted no ban;
with his death and his heir's together,
    the branch of Moirne is blind.

O grandson of Ruairidh of the blue spear-points,
    I sing a song to your breast like a swan;
O white tooth, my joy to be with you,
    your death now is my reproach.

Your fame will be remembered forever,
    the example of your honour — high praise indeed;
your death, a partner to the death of Ailean,
    a branch untouched by scandal, you.

A chinn-bhile Chloinne Cholla
  críoch bhur n-aisdir, anbha an béad:
a ndearna sibh urra d'argain
  truma ná sin d'Albain t'éag.

Úir gan iodh a h-aithle a éaga,
  oighreacht Raghnaill, ní roinn mhion:
mar táid ar ccroinn chnó gan toradh
  coill dá ló, folamh gach fiodh.   56

Tarrla ar an ghréin do ghlais cumhadh,
  nár chuir bláth tré barraibh géag;
anfadh na síon ann gan iomlaoid
  gníomh barr go bhfhionnmaoid a éag.

'Na aimsir fa ghormfhonn Ghaoidheal
  níor ghuth gort a ngeall re sín:
go fuil d'a éag as a aithle
  gur bhréag muir a tairthe ó thír.   64

Críoch Fhionnghall a n-aimsir Ailín
  oirdhearc do chách an céim rug;
fuair re ré triall da gach taradh,
  tar leam ní h-é an talamh tug.

Foisgéal agam ar Choin cCulainn
  's ar Chathbhadh draoi, diochra an léan;
a chinéal ní fhuair gach aoinfhear:
  deigh-eól uaim sgaoileadh a sgéal.   72

Cú Chulainn do chairdeas Ultach,
  ollamh Teamhra ar ar thuit brón:
an t-éag ar aon ag a sgarrthain
  níor fhéad gaol Chathbhaidh do chlódh.

Urchra an éigse fa Choin Chulainn
  críoch a mbróin ní bheag an cheisd:
ní chumhan gidh cian ó Theamhraigh
  curaidh riamh tarraidh a theisd.   80

O topmost tree of the children of Colla,
    your journey's end, great the harm;
despite all the spoiling you inflicted upon them,
    still graver than that to Scotland, your death.

After his death the soil bears no barley,
    Raghnall's legacy, no slight share,
for our nut trees are devoid of produce,
    our hazels decay, every wood is bare.

The sun is locked so tight in mourning
    that no blossom has come through the tips of the boughs;
the rage of the elements without changing,
    a clear sign in which we recognise his death.

There was no word of famine from bad weather
    during his time in the fertile land of the Gael,
but now as a result of his death it happens
    that the sea has beguiled its fruits from the land.

In Ailean's time the land of the Fionnghoill
    made progress conspicuous to all;
in his lifetime every kind of produce flourished:
    I think it was not the earth that brought it forth.

I have an allegory about Cú Chulainn
    and Cathbhadh the druid, heartfelt the grief;
not everyone has experienced its equal;
    good tidings from me to tell its tale.

Cú Chulainn, dear friend of Ulster,
    and the sage of Tara on whom sorrow fell;
death, having parted each from the other,
    could not overcome Cathbhadh's love.

Keen the wise man's grief for Cú Chulainn,
    no small question the limit of their pain;
I recall, though far from Tara,
    no hero who ever attained his fame.

Brón Chathbhaidh níor chuirthe a n-iongnadh
   d'oidheadh na Con, cneas mar thuinn:
mar tá méad treise mo thoirrse
   d'éag deisi don chloinn-se Chuinn.

Toirse Chathbhaidh fa Choin Chulainn
   'gá mheas rer ccor ní céim tnúith:
urchra dá ghéig fhéinneadh annla,
   éinfhear d'éag ní dhamhna dhúinn.   88

Samhuil an bhróin bhí ar Cathbhadh
   críoch na cumhadh lér thuit sinn:
téid a chumha tar chéill cumtha
   's ní lugha a bpéin urchra inn.

Tar chumha cháigh do chuir Cathbhadh
   céim tar gach bróin, borb an grádh:
ránag mar sin uainn a fhulang
   fuair fa Choinn Chulainn a chrádh.   96

Níor b'fhearr Cú Chulainn do Chathbhadh
   caidreadh Raghnaill na rosg ngorm:
nár muirn on chloinn-se d'fhuil Fiachaidh
   do chuir tuirse d'fhiachaibh orm.

Cú Chulainn nár éitigh iomghuin
   éigeas Fódla, fáth gan bhréig;
Cathbhadh do chuaidh d'éag dá orchra,
   géag mar sduaigh tholcha níor thréig.   104

Dá measda dhúinn tré dhíoth éinfhir,
   éag na deisi, doirbhe an léan:
ní fhaghthair barr bróin ar Chathbhadh:
   am chóir re sgarrthain a sgéal.

Ní fhuil 'na ndiaidh dearmad cumhadh,
   nár chuimhnigh dhúinn dáil a séad:
trom linn a cclaisdin 'ga ccaoineadh,
   dá rinn ghaisge Gaoidheal Gréag.   112

Cathbhadh's grief was no cause of wonder
    for the slaying of the Hound, skin white as the wave;
of the same might is the strength of my sorrow
    for the death of these scions of the race of Conn.

To compare Cathbhadh's sorrow for Cú Chulainn
    with our own state is no enviable course;
so fresh our grief for the branch of heroes
    that no other death causes us concern.

Like to the sorrow felt by Cathbhadh,
    the extent of the mourning that laid us low;
his mourning goes beyond reason
    and not less in pain of loss are we.

Cathbhadh went beyond the mourning of others,
    a step beyond any sorrow, vehement his love;
he underwent torture for Cú Chulainn,
    we have been made to suffer even so.

Not better Cú Chulainn's support of Cathbhadh
    than Raghnall's of the blue eyes;
for my delight in these descendants of Fiachaidh
    sorrow has imposed on me her dues.

Cú Chulainn who refused no battle
    and Fódla's sage, an explanation without lie;
for him, Cathbhadh died of sorrow,
    the pinnacle-like branch he did not forsake.

Were we to measure by the loss of one man,
    the death of the two, harsher the grief;
Cathbhadh's sorrow is not found to be greater,
    a fit time then to part from their tales.

After them, there is no neglect of mourning;
    rather we forgot to share out their wealth;
it is heavy on us to hear them lamented,
    two spear-points of valour of the Gaels of Greece.

Cú Chulainn feithmheóir na Fódla,
  feidhm oirdhearc a n-uair do mhair:
díon a threabh tar chách a ccliathaibh
  do ghabh gach tráth d'fhiachaibh air.

An Cú-sin ag coimhéad Alban
  Ailín éachtach, anbha an béad;
ag díon a h-oinigh 's a h-ardmhagh:
  gníomh doiligh d'Albain a éag.   120

Raghnall ar n-éag tar éis athar,
  aithris na Con 'gá chneas seang:
ag coimhéad críoch Chláir na cColla:
  ní frith dhaibh orra budh fhearr.

Eangnamh Ailín mar Choin Chulainn,
  cródhacht Raghnaill na ruaig ndian;
barr ar bhás gach fir a oighre:
  ag sin cás as doilghe dhíobh.   128

Mairidh go bráth buan a chuimhne,
  cumha a chárad, gidh céim doirbh;
d'éag an dá fhear-soin d'fhuil Éibhir
  ní chuir easbhadh éinfhear oirnn.

Tarras, a Raghnaill, rinn cumhadh
  dod choman, a chneas mar bhláth;
críoch ar a clódh níor chuir m'urchra:
  ní fhuil acht brón cumtha ar chách.   136

Beó bladh a n-aithle gach aoinfhir,
  a Ailín nár [ ] ngliaidh;
gé fíor t'éag, is tú nach teasda:
  féach do chlú budh dheasda ad dhiaidh.

Líon catha 'na chaidreabh teaghlaigh
  timcheall Ailín na n-arm sean;
iongnadh é a n-uaigh ina aonar,
  's mar fuair sé an saoghal re seal.   144

        Alba.

Cú Chulainn, watchman of Fódla,
    a pre-eminent champion while he lived;
the defence of his people in battles
    he always took upon himself at the fore.

That Hound guarding Scotland,
    Ailean of mighty deeds, great the loss,
protecting her honour and her uplands,
    a sore matter for Scotland, his death.

Raghnall dead after his father,
    his slender form, the double of the Hound,
for guarding the bounds of the Plain of the Collas
    none better could have been found.

Ailean's prowess was like Cú Chulainn's,
    so too the valour of Raghnall of the routs;
the misfortune surpassing all misfortunes:
    after the death of a man, the death of his heir.

The memory of him lasts firm forever,
    his friends' mourning, though a grievous affair;
since the death of these two men of the blood of Éibhear
    we have felt no other man as such a loss.

Over you, Raghnall, to your friendship,
    O blossom-like skin, I have made a lament;
my grief set out no end to its suppression,
    the sorrow of others is only faked.

Alive after him, a man's reputation,
    O Ailean who shunned not strife;
though true your death, you have not departed;
    behold, your renown lives on.

A full complement for battle in his household
    around Ailean of the venerable arms;
considering his way of living,
    a wonder he is in the grave alone.

32. Do Loisceadh Meisi sa Mhuaidh

Ó Gnímh

Tha am marbhrann seo, a tha air leth pearsanta na stoidhle agus na fhaireachdainn, a' caoidh Dhomhnaill Ghuirm MhicDhomhnaill, mac Sheumais nan Ruaig MhicDhomhnaill Ìle (†1565), a chaidh a mharbhadh anns an t-Sultain 1586 aig Ard na Riadh, air abhainn Muaidhe mu choinneimh Béal an Átha ann an Co. Mhaigh Eo. Fhuair Domhnall Gorm bàs an lùib àr mì-chliùiteach de Ghàidheil Albannach le feachd Shasannach fo stiùir Shir Richard Bingham; uile-gu-lèir, mharbhadh aon 2,300 fireannach, boireannach agus pàiste, nam measg bràthair Dhomhnaill, Alasdair Carrach. Bha meur de Chloinn Domhnaill air a bhith stèidhichte ann am Maigh Eo bhon cheathramh linn deug air adhart (mar ghallóglaigh) agus bha na Búrcaigh, tighearnan na sgìre, air barrachd fearainn a ghealltainn dhaibh.

Bha dàimh leantainneach eadar filidh Chloinn Uí Ghnímh agus Clann Domhnaill Aontrama anns an t-siathamh linn deug agus aig toiseach an t-seachdamh linn deug. Eu-coltach ris a' phàtran àbhaisteach, tha e coltach gur ann à Alba (Cinn Tìre) a bha an teaghlach foghlaimte seo agus gun do rinn iad imrich a dh'Èirinn. Fhuair an duine as ainmeile den teaghlach, Fear Flatha, cliù airson grunn dhàn anns do rinn e caoidh air sgrios nan uaislean Gàidhealach agus dol-sìos a' chultair fhoghlaimte ann an Èirinn an dèidh Cath Chionn tSáile (1601) agus Teitheadh na nIarlaí (1607).

Chan eil fhios cò an 'Ó Gnímh' a rinn am marbhrann a leanas; chan fhaighear ach an sloinneadh aige anns an làmh-sgrìobhainn. Ach rinn am file Brian Ó Gnímh marbhrann air Alasdair MacDhomhnaill, mac Shomhairle Bhuidhe MhicDhomhnaill (bràthair athar Dhomhnaill Ghuirm agus Alasdair Charraich, agus cuspair dàn 23), a chaidh a mharbhadh leis na Sasannaich ann an creach anns an dearbh bhliadhna, 1586, a thachair an t-àr aig Ard na Riadh; dh'fhaodadh e bhith gur e Brian a rinn am marbhrann air Domhnall Gorm cuideachd.

Scalded Have I Been in the Moy

This unusually personal and passionate bardic elegy laments the death in September 1586 of Domhnall Gorm MacDhomhnaill, son of Seumas nan Ruaig MacDhomhnaill of Islay (†1565) and nephew of Somhairle Buidhe (subject of poem 23), at Ardnaree, along the river Moy across from Ballina, County Mayo. Domhnall Gorm was killed as part of a notorious massacre of Scottish Gaelic settlers by English troops under the command of Sir Richard Bingham; some 2,300 men, women and children, including Domhnall's brother Alasdair Carrach, are said to have died in the slaughter.

The Ó Gnímh family of poets seem to have served the MacDhomhnaills of Antrim on a hereditary basis during the sixteenth and early seventeenth centuries. In a reversal of the usual pattern, the family appears to have originated in Scotland and migrated to Ireland. The most famous member of the family, Fear Flatha, is renowned for his laments on the downfall of the Irish Gaelic aristocracy and the decline of Gaelic learned culture in the years following the disastrous Battle of Kinsale (1601) and the Flight of the Earls (1607).

It is not known which member of the family composed the following elegy on Domhnall Gorm; the manuscript simply ascribes it to 'Ó Gnímh'. Another elegy, attributed to Brian Ó Gnímh and preserved in the late seventeenth-century Book of Clanranald, laments the death of Alasdair MacDhomhnaill (a cousin of Domhnall Gorm and Alasdair Carrach and son of their uncle Somhairle Buidhe MacDhomhnaill, subject of poem 23), and Brian may well be the author of the present poem as well.

The poet explores the paradoxes of grief in the figure of the river Moy. The confidence with which he handles the conceit suggests that he was drawing on the pre-Christian tradition of the goddess of the land, manifest in rivers and other bodies of water, as spouse to the temporal ruler. As the mate of Domhnall, her flooding is an act both of grief and fury at his death. This reflects the nature of the earth goddess as nurturer and destroyer, as spring is followed by winter. The poet both loves and hates the river as the embodiment of the land where his foster-father is buried and was killed. The motif of a river rising to drown her people's foes is as old as Táin Bó Cuailgne, in which Glas Cuinn in Ulster rises against the Connacht army.

Do loisceadh meisi sa Mhuaidh:
a bhfad uaidh — anba an anbhuain —
lá m'uilcsi nírbh fhosgadh damh —
mo losgadh d'uisce is iongnadh.

Ar ccur chaor ttuaithfeal tairrsi
d'uisce fhuar don abhoinnsi,
  mar budh uisge agus é ar goil
  rom thuitsi agus mé ar marthoin.   8

In tráth do bhí ag báthadh cháigh
'n-a tuinn mhir budh mó ttormáin,
  budh mó tteinn, budh treisi sriobh,
  meisi san linn do loisceadh.

Fada an Mhuaidh: do loisc an lionn
ar thulchaibh tuaiscirt Éirionn
  mná bréidgheala — buan an crádh —
  's a héigneadha fuar fallán.   16

Dul d'anfadh in mhara a méid,
sriobh mo loscaidh dá leithéid
  buain srothbhuinne sléibhe riom,
  rothruime as déine dílionn.

Is leis do loisceadh meisi
airde a fras a fuairise,
  tonn do bhí dá geileas ghlan,
  an ní as leigheas dár loscadh.   24

Do loisc lionn [mhór] an tuile
sinn ar n-oighidh éanduine
  ar bhfoscadh ar ghoimh na nGall,
  ar losgadh, ar ndoigh Domhnall.

Ar mbás síorruidhe is sinn beó,
ar ndíothladh uile d'éincheó,
  teacht fan Domhnall Ghormsa ar ghuin,
  ar bhfonnsa comdhonn cumhduigh.   32

Scalded have I been in the Moy
though far away — cruel agony —
    on that day of my suffering I had no escape —
    though strange my burning by water.

After flooding with great billows
of chill water widdershins —
    as if the water boiled —
    the river has felled me, though still living.

When she was drowning all
as a frenzied wave of greatest tumult,
    of greatest tension, of strongest gush,
    it was then I was scalded in the water.

Long is the Moy: the water burned,
on the hills of the north of Ireland,
    women in bright clothing — lasting the pain —
    while her salmon remained cool and healthy.

As the storm at sea increased
so did the stream of my burning,
    the rapid torrent of the hillside striking me,
    overpowering flood, of greatest vehemence.

It is by this that I was burned:
the height of her showers and her coldness;
    by a wave that came from her fair bright falls,
    the thing that should be a balm to our scalding.

The great water of the flood
has burned us with one man's death —
    our shelter from the sting of the Goill,
    now Domhnall is our scald, our torture.

Our eternal death while alive,
the destruction of all by one death-mist,
    coming with the slaying of Domhnall Gorm,
    the noble ring-fence of our protection.

Ar n-áitioghadh tíre ar ttreóir,
ar sciath eadrána ar aindeóin,
    ar ndíoboirtne a-nos a nimh,
    ar líogfhoircli ar ndós díttin.

Cloch mhór gé théid 'n-a tarrsa,
fliuchaidh fraoch na habhannsa —
    leithne linn Mhuaidhe ná in mhuir —
    ar ngruaidhe is inn a n-Ultaibh.   40

Dom shaoradh ar an Muaidh mir
ní díon dúinn ard tar íslibh;
    tug a fearg iomluaighil oirn
    ar thiormghuaillibh Lathoirn.

Do fhliuchadh an Mhuaidh misi
suil táinig a tuilisi;
    ar ndul dí ar druim a coradh
    sí dá tuinn dom thiormughadh.   48

Líonadh abhann d'fhearthain truim
dá ttáinic tuitim Domhnuill;
    [do líon] 'n-a tiormach cumhadh
    síon mhionshruth do mhéadughadh.

Ní hionand ind 's na haibhne
giodh ionand ar n-adhbhairne
    ón dílind as lán gach linn
    's a-tám tirim dá tuitim.   56

Níor bheag d'Ultachoibh re a n-ucht
sruth as é a cCúigeadh Chonnacht,
    dá ccosnamh ar cloinn Domhnaill,
    ag buing m'osnadh n-éagcomhlainn.

Croidhe iaroinn a n-am chatha
reacht liom go héacht ardfhlatha;
    cloch ó ghormmuir théacht fan ttuind
    congmhaidh ar n-éacht san abhoinn.   64

Our settler on the land, and our guide,
our shield between ourselves and discord,
    our rock-bulwark, our protecting tree,
    is now our banishment from Heaven.

Though she is crossed by a great stone,
the seething spray of that river —
    wider now Moy's pool than the sea —
    wettens our cheeks in Ulster.

To save me from the frenzy of the Moy
neither high nor low place gives protection;
    about the parched shoulders of the hills of Larne
    her anger has sent me wildly rushing.

The Moy used to wet me
before this flood came upon her;
    now that she overflows her weir
    she parches me with her billow!

Domhnall's fall came about
with heavy rain filling rivers;
    this weather of swelling streams
    has caused a drought of mourning.

Though our circumstances are the same
we are not the same as rivers:
    after the deluge we are parched
    while every lake brims over.

A stream in Connacht was enough
to oppose the men of Ulster,
    to protect the men of Connacht from Clann Domhnaill
    and make me utter groans of injury.

Until the murder of the high prince,
my decree was a heart of iron in time of battle;
    now a slab on the wave from a frozen blue sea
    holds our lost one in the river.

Meinic na'aigneadh dá fhéachain
mar Mhaol Umha a n-ainfhéachain;
  beirt ghloine fan Muaidh misi:
  mo chroidhe uaim inntisi.

Ionmhuin tiar taisi Domhnaill,
fuath liom a áit éagcomhloinn;
  ar ó nDuach a-tám don tuinn;
  mo ghrádh is m'fhuath don abhoinn.   72

Meisi am dhalta ar Dhomhnall Gorm,
mo leag lóghmhar é, m'órchorn;
  croidhe mo cholla a chroidhe;
  croidhe í Cholla ar ccroidhine.

Ó nár bhuanaigh Dia Domhnall
mairg fhuair dá íoc anbhforlann
  mar fhuair mé miodh a bhuabhall
  nó fhuair é d'fhior éanghualann.   80

Dó ríoghroidh chródha Chláir Rois
a ndiaigh Dhomhnaill mheic Shéamois
  ní léir linn sósar nó sean
  sinn dá lósan do loisceadh.

  Do loisceadh.

Often is my spirit to be seen
in dread guise like Maol Umha;
    I am a glassy figure about the Moy:
    my heart, having left me, is in her.

Beloved in the west are Domhnall's remains,
but I curse the place of his downfall;
    because of Duach's scion I am angry with the wave,
    I both love and hate the river.

A foster-son of Domhnall Gorm am I,
my precious jewel, my golden goblet;
    the heart of my body is *his* heart,
    my own heart is the descendant of Colla's.

Since God mowed Domhnall down,
woe to the one who pays with anguish
    for the mead I drunk from his cups
    or for what I had of him in friendship.

Of the valiant royal stock of the Plain of Ross,
in the absence of Domhnall son of Seumas,
    I have seen no-one, young or old,
    since that day when I was scalded.

      Scalded.

THE LEARNED TRADITION

INCITEMENT

33. Dál Chabhlaigh ar Chaistéal Suibhne

Artúr Dall Mac Gurcaigh

Tha an dàn meanmnach seo, a rinneadh, is dòcha, mu thoiseach a' cheathramh linn deug, a' toirt tuairisgeul air iomairt le Eòin MacSuibhne an aghaidh Chaisteal Suibhne ann an Cnapadal, aon de na daingnichean mara as treasa air costa an iar Alba. Bha smachd aig Cloinn MhicSuibhne air an sgìre seo anns an treas linn deug ach chaidh an arfuntachadh leis na Stiùbhartaich (iarlan Tèadhaich). Ghabh Eòin MacSuibhne taobh nan Sasannach ann an Cogaidhean na Saorsa, agus ann an 1310 fhuair Eòin agus a bhràithrean cairt-fhearainn air Cnapadal bho Eideard II Shasainn air a' chùmhnant gum b'urrainn dhaibh grèim fhaighinn air an fhearann a-rithist. Uime sin bu chòir an dàn seo a thuigsinn mar bhrosnachadh do dh'ath-ghlacadh a' chaisteil.

Ach cha d'fhuair na Suibhnich Caisteal Suibhne no an cuid fearainn ann an Earra Ghàidheal a-rithist; an àite sin, fhuair iad inbhe ùr ann an Èirinn mar 'ghallóglaigh' no àrmainn phroifeasanta ann an seirbheis nan ceann-cinnidh Gàidhealach. Bha ceangal air leth eadar na Suibhnich agus Clann Uí Dhomhnaill Thír Chonaill, agus fhuair iad fearann bhuapa ann an leth-eilean Fánad ann an taobh tuath Thír Chonaill (Co. Dhún na nGall andiugh). Sgaoil meuran eile den teaghlach air feadh na h-Èireann, a' cumail taic ri cinnidhean eile leithid Chloinn Uí Conchubhair, Uí Bhriain agus Mhic Cárthaigh.

Tha am blas Lochlannach a tha ri fhaighinn anns an dàn (gu h-àraidh an ìomhaigh ann an sreath 12, 'Lochlannaigh is ármuinn iad') anabarrach inntinneach. Ged a bha cànan is cultar nan Lochlannach glè làidir ann an Innse Gall aig aon àm, shearg iad thar nan linntean agus chaidh fèin-aithne làn-Ghàidhealach a chruthachadh nan àite. A rèir an Ollaimh Dòmhnall Meek, a thug iomadh bliadhna ann a bhith a' deasachadh an dàin as ùr, tha grunn choltasan rim faicinn eadar an dàn seo agus bàrdachd Lochlannach nam Meadhan Aoisean.

Chan eil dad a dh'fhiosrachadh againn mun fhile a rinn an dàn, Artúr Dall, agus chan eil na sgoilearan cinnteach am b'e Albannach no Èireannach a bha ann.

A Meeting of a Fleet Against the Castle of Suibhne

This highly evocative poem, which probably dates from the early fourteenth century, describes an expedition by Eòin MacSuibhne upon Castle Sween in Knapdale, one of the most imposing sea-fortresses of the west coast. The Mac Suibhnes had control of this area during the thirteenth century but were dispossessed by the Stewart Earls of Menteith. During the Wars of Independence Eòin MacSuibhne took the English side, and in 1310 Eòin and his brothers received a charter to Knapdale from Edward II provided the lands could be recaptured. The poem should be understood as an incitement to this attempted retaking of the castle.

The MacSuibhnes never did regain Castle Sween or their Argyll territories, however, and instead became established as one of the great families of *gallóglaigh* (Englished as 'gallo(w)glasses'), hereditary professional warriors in service to the Gaelic Irish chiefs. The MacSuibhnes were connected primarily to the Ó Domhnaills of Tír Chonaill, and received lands from them in the Fánad peninsula in the north of County Donegal, but other branches of the family spread throughout Ireland, serving a range of leading kindreds including Ó Conchubhair, Ó Briain, and Mac Cárthaigh.

The poem is particularly interesting for its Norse associations. Although Norse language and culture were once firmly rooted in the Hebrides, they faded steadily over the centuries as a more purely Gaelic identity was forged. Here, however, the Norse connection is palpable, especially in the famous line 'Lochlannaigh is ármuinn iad' (12). Professor Donald Meek, who editorially reconstructed the poem over many years, has also noted a number of similarities between this poem and different kinds of Norse compositions of the medieval period.

Of the poet Artúr Dall nothing is known, and scholars have disagreed as to whether he was Scottish or Irish.

Dál chabhlaigh ar Chaistéal Suibhne,
    suairc an eachtra i nInis Fáil;
marcaigh do thráchtadh na tonna,
    glantair bárca donna dáibh.

Fir árda ag eagar na loingse
    ar loime luath leanas cuairt;
ní bhí lámh gan ghalgha gasta
    i n-arradh stargha snasta suairc.   8

Do chotúnaibh is díobh eagrar
    aghaidh na mbárc fá chraoibh liag,
do choradhaibh na gcrios gclárdhonn —
    Lochlannaigh is ármuinn iad.

Do chlaidhmhibh go n-ór is déada
    eagar bhárc na mbréideadh ndonn;
i n-arradh cliath do ghaithibh gealgha,
    sgiath ré fraithghibh leabhra long.   16

Ar sgáth sgiath ar scúdaibh breaca,
    brugh starrach corcra cloch n-óir;
bronnadh ad gcaomh is coiléar
    ar taobh na slat roighéar róimh.

Gaithe gorma i ngualnaibh luathbhárc,
    long 'gá líonadh i n-arradh trácht;
cliath theann dhaingeann do cholgaibh,
    foireann sgiath ré bordaibh bárc.   24

Mná Fionnmhacha i ngrianánaibh loingse,
    leapaidh ard ag inghin mhall;
pealla breaca dáibh 'gá dtarraing,
    leaptha ag mnáibh ré h-éanlaighe ann.

Pealla breaca sróill is sionail,
    is sé sin luachair a long;
badhbh Shuibhne is a threóir toghtha,
    duille shróill chorcra ós gach crann.   32

A meeting of a fleet against the Castle of Suibhne,
　　pleasing the adventure in Inis Fáil;
brown barques are being polished
　　for horsemen who would ride the waves.

Tall men equipping the vessels
　　which proceed swiftly on the plain;
no hand lacks fine war-spear,
　　with an elegant handsome targe.

The prows of the ships, festooned with jewels,
　　are decked out with coats of mail
for the warriors of the brown-faced baldrics —
　　they are Norsemen and brave chiefs.

The brown-sailed barques are furnished
　　with swords of ivory and gold;
alongside a rank of bright spear-points
　　shields are attached to the ships' sides.

Behind shields on painted cutters,
　　juts a scarlet deck-house with jewels of gold;
fair helmets and neck-pieces festooning
　　the sharp jutting yard-arms' sides.

Blue spears in the swift barques' shoulders,
　　a longship being loaded beside the shore;
a dense fence of blades and a rank of shields
　　are being fixed to the planks of the barques.

Fionnmhagh's women in the fleet's sun-bowers,
　　a high-placed bed for a stately maid;
speckled rugs at their disposal,
　　and beds where ladies lie alone.

Speckled rugs of silk and sendal
　　in place of rushes in their ships;
Suibhne's raven, with its power enabled,
　　a red satin pennant on every mast.

Go lámhainn chruaidh, go gcrios codad,
  'nar gcairbh síos 'gá gcur lé cláir,
na séada díreach ann gan iomard,
  do chláraibh chlann bhfionnard bhFáil.

Níor chualas urdál an fhéinnidh
  d'fhear na ndos 'gá gcur ré ceird;
na séada óir ó Eirinn aca,
  don bhróin mhéirsheing dhathta dheirg.   40

Ní lugha leó long dá longaibh
  i mbáthadh na n-each 's na mbó,
gan each, gan bhoin díobh, gan bhronnadh,
  's ni fhoil tír gan lomadh leó.

Ní h-áilseadh leó carbh dá gcarbhaibh,
  a lán daingne 's iontaoibh bhuan;
a gcroinn óir ar bhordaibh aca
  ré h-ardach dóibh i gcaraibh cuain.   48

Iomadh fear lainne is fear lúirich,
  iomadh far lúith go léim cháich,
ré súgh mong na bhfairgeadh bhfeargdhonn
  ré h-áird a long mbeannchorr mbláith.

Cia so lé seóltar an cabhlach
  ar Chaisleán Suibhne Sléibhe Truim?
Fear sreangach nach seachnadh saighde,
  leathchrann sgorach codach Cuinn.   56

Eóin mac Suibhne seól a loingse
  ar druim an chuain, cruaidh an ceann;
croinn a long, dianchorr a n-airde,
  dearbhfaidh tonn i bhfairge bheann.

Gaoth go díreach dóibh 'na ndeaghaidh
  ag caol eagach deireadh trácht,
siúil bhreaca dóibh 'na mbolgaibh,
  uan ag teacht go bordaibh bárc.   64

With firm belts and steel gauntlets
   the straight heroes without reproach
are taken down in our ships on gangplanks,
   from the plains of the tall bright families of Fál.

The likes of the warrior hasn't been heard of,
   a leader of the champions setting them in array;
along with them, the golden warriors from Ireland,
   in the coloured slender-fingered scarlet band.

No small matter to them the loss of one of their galleys,
   with the drowning of horses and cows;
lacking horses and cows and rewarding,
   there is no land they have not laid waste.

Not one of their ships is to be neglected,
   their full strength and lasting trust;
their golden masts resting on crutches,
   ready to be raised in swirling firth.

Many a man with sword and corselet,
   many an athlete out-leaping the rest,
withstands the mane's sap of the angry brown oceans
   striking the gunnel of their smooth high-prowed ships.

Under whose command is the fleet sailing
   against the castle of Suibhne of Sliabh Truim?
A sinewy man who avoided no arrows,
   one of the two piercing lances of the land of Conn.

Eòin MacSuibhne is the fleet's commander,
   a hardy leader on the surface of the sea;
the masts of his ships — their height exalted —
   the wave will test on the mountainous brine.

The wind follows them directly
   at the indented kyle at the end of the strand,
their speckled sails are bulging outwards,
   foam reaches the top-strakes of the barques.

Gabhais Eóin acarsaid aoibhinn
  i n-ucht Chnapadail, cuairt chuain,
an abhra bharrtiugh, dhúnach, dhealbhach,
  laochrach, chrannach, lúthach, luain.

Leinne ag ballachaibh Alban
  feartha fáilte ré ucht slim;
álainn sin a gcorcra connlán,
  sileadh drochta lomlán linn.   72

Fáilte ag sruthaibh Sléibhe Monaidh
  ré Mac Suibhne Sléibhe Mis;
teagaid táinte d' iasc na n-ionbhair,
  dáiltear muireasc rionnlann ris.

Léigid géaga a nglúine fútha,
  feartha fáilte rér bhflaith ceóil;
measa sláinte coll gach calaidh,
  trom a bhfáilte i n-aghaidh Eóin.   80

Teagthair d' aos ealadhan Alban,
  fearaid fáilte ar onchoin Mis;
lucht cáinte ó Mhuir Mhanainn
  do chuir fáilte ó rannaibh ris.

Gnáthach bhí a n-iomarbháidh áine,
  eachtra féine Fhinn a gceóil;
aithnighid an duasach deithbhir,
  mar tá dualach d'einigh Eóin.   88

Do-níd cách i gCaisleán Suibhne
  fá sheabhag Chruachan chruinn bhuirb
suidhe fá thimcheall an scur-soin,
  finnfhear Muighe lusghloin Luirg.

A dhá shleagh thollas taobh námhad,
  mar neimh nathrach guin na gcrann;
caol chlaidheamh ó ghreis uí Ghuaire,
  maolaighthear leis guailne Gall.   96

Eòin has reached a happy haven
   in the breast of Knapdale, a voyage at sea;
the thick shapely eye-lashes, with many strongholds,
   warriors and spears, he is hero-lit and strong.

We are to give at the walls of Scotland
   hearty salutations to his slender breast;
handsome indeed their scarlet party,
   dew falls heavily as we appear.

The streams of Sliabh Monaidh give welcome
   to brave MacSuibhne of Sliabh Mis,
shoals of fish of the estuaries come swimming
   and pointed-scaled fish of the sea.

Branches bend their knees beneath them,
   welcoming our melodious prince;
wholesome hazelnuts of every harbour,
   weighty their welcome laid before Eòin.

The men of art of Scotland are coming
   and welcome the wolf of Mis;
satirists, by means of verses,
   welcomed him from the Sea of Man.

Customary was their pleasant contention,
   the adventure of Fionn's warriors, their songs;
they recognise the lawful bestower,
   as is natural with the generosity of Eòin.

Everyone in Castle Sween nestles
   under Cruacha's hawk of the savage spear,
gathered round that champion,
   the fair man of pure-herbed Moylurg.

His two spears pierce a foe's body,
   like snake venom the wound of the shafts;
the foreigners' shoulders are denuded
   by an attack from Guaire's scion's slender sword.

Ceilbhreamaid oileach Mhic Suibhne,
  ráth soillseach na gcloch do chiam;
is fear nach déan dá gclaiginn cabhair,
  síthdíon dual na bhfalaing bhfiar.

Niamhrach díon do lúirich threabhraidh
  ar sgáth chotúin na sgiath ndonn;
gabhais Reachlann stíomghar, starthach,
  míonbharr, clachbhán, calma, corr.   104

An t-aon chlaidheamh as fearr san Eórpa,
  is sé as leabhra leanas maidhm;
cia sgiath san domhan nach diongbhann
  triath gan omhan Cloinne Cairm?

Eóin mac Suibhne na sleagh gcodad
  lé cholg tana teasbhaigh mhál;
fear na sgiath mboillsgeach mbreacdhonn —
  tairis triath, deacair an dál.   112

Dál.

34. Brostughadh-Catha Chlann Domhnaill, Là Chatha Gharbhaich

Lachlann Mòr MacMhuirich

Tha cruth nàdar de bhrosnachadh (no *brostughadh* anns a'
Ghàidhlig Chlasaigich) air an dàn seo, anns a bheil am bàrd a'
misneachadh curaidhean Chloinn Domhnaill ro Chath
Gairbheach ann am 1411. Is dòcha gur e seo an teacs meadrach-
ail (seach ruisg) as sine a tha againn anns a' Ghàidhlig
dhùthchasaich. Ach tha cuid de sgoilearan an latha an-diugh
teagmhach mu eachdraidh an dàin, air grunn adhbharan, agus is
math a dh'fhaodte gun deach a chumadh na b'anmoiche nuair a
bhathar a' coimhead air ais air 'Linn an Àigh', làithean glòrmhor
Rìoghachd nan Eilean.

Let us salute the rock of the son of Suibhne,
    we can see the shining fortress of stones;
a man who will grant their skulls no mercy
    is the tall defender in flowing cloaks of mail.

A protective breastplate of shining chain-mail
    instead of a wadded shirt with brown plates;
he captured Rathlin, low-topped, jutting,
    smooth-surfaced, white-stoned, precipitous, rough.

The single finest sword in Europe,
    he who furthest pursues a rout;
which shield in the world will not try to repel him,
    the fearless lord of the Kindred of Carm?

Eòin MacSuibhne of the hard lances
    with his slender sword of heroes' heat;
'he man of the shields, embossed, gleaming,
    a loyal lord — difficult to meet.

        A meeting of a fleet.

The Harlaw Brosnachadh

This poem is cast in the form of an incitement to the Clann Domhnaill warriors before the celebrated Battle of Harlaw, fought near Aberdeen in 1411. This may be the earliest surviving metrical text in vernacular Scottish Gaelic – the vernacular being chosen, rather than the formal literary language, for ready comprehension by the troops. Unfortunately, it is now considered somewhat doubtful that the poem is a genuine survival of the early fifteenth century; it may be best understood as a historical reimagining composed at some later date, probably with feelings of nostalgia for the glory days of the Lordship of the Isles, the so-called *Linn an Àigh*.

Tha structar an dàin, a' toirt seachad liosta de cho-ghnìomhairean a rèir òrdugh na h-aibidil, follaiseach gu leòr. Bha dàin den t-seòrsa cumanta gu leòr ann an litreachas nam Meadhan Aoisean.

Is e *Aos-Dàna Mhic Dhomhnaill* am far-ainm a chaidh a chur air a' bhàrd Lachlann Mòr MacMhuirich ann an Làmh-sgrìobhainn MhicLagain, a chaidh a sgrìobhadh anns an darna pàirt den ochdamh linn deug. Chan eil fiosrachadh a bharrachd againn mu dheidhinn, agus cha tàinig dàin eile a-nuas thugainn, ged is cinnteach gum buineadh e don teaghlach ainmeil a chaidh a stèidheachadh (a rèir beul-aithris) le Muireadhach Albanach Ó Dálaigh.

Bha Cath Gairbheach na bhatail (a chuireadh faisg air Inbhir Uaraidh ann an Siorrachd Obar Dheathain) eadar sluagh mòr de Dhomhnallaich fo cheannas Dhomhnaill ((†1422), Rìgh nan Eilean, agus feachd a cho-ogha Alasdair Stiùbhart, iarla Mhàrr, mac Alasdair Mhòir mhic an Rìgh. B'e adhbhar a' chatha an t-strì airson smachd fhaighinn air iarlachd Rois. Tha e coltach nach do bhuannaich taobh seach taobh, ach a rèir dualchas nan Gàidheal bha Cath Gairbheach na bhuaidh mhòr chan ann do Chloinn Domhnaill ach do na Gàidheil anns an fharsaingeachd. Tha tòrr iomraidhean air a' bhatail ann an saothar bàird molaidh an t-seachdamh linn deug agus an ochdamh linn deug, leithid Eachainn Bhacaich, Iain Dhuibh agus Mairearaid nighean Lachainn.

Shabaidich iarrla Mhàrr an aghaidh Chloinn Domhnaill aig Blàr Inbhir Lòchaidh ann an 1431 cuideachd, agus tha dà òran co-cheangailte ris a' bhlàr sin rim faighinn gu h-ìosal (dàin 77 agus 78).

> A Chlanna Cuinn, cuimhnichibh
> Cruas an am na h-iorghaile:
> Gu h-àirneach, gu h-arranta,
> Gu h-athlamh, gu h-allanta,
> Gu beòdha, gu barramhail,
> Gu brìoghmhor, gu buan-fheargach,
> Gu calma, gu curanta,
> Gu cròdha, gu cath-bhuadhach,
> Gu dùr is gu dàsannach,
> Gu dian is gu deagh-fhulang,

8

The alphabetic and alliterative structure of the poem, a lengthy list of adverbs, four for each letter, is obvious. Such alphabetic poems were a popular sub-genre in medieval literature, including 'Altus Prosatur', a Latin abacedarian poem by Colum Cille.

The poet Lachlann Mòr MacMhuirich (described in one of the eighteenth-century McLagan manuscripts as *Aos-Dàna Mhic Dhomhnaill*, 'MacDhomhnaill's high-poet') was evidently a member of the famous family of hereditary poets, and nothing is known of him; no other poems ascribed to him have come down to us. There is some uncertainty in the three manuscript sources as to his authorship, with two ascribing it to another poet.

The Battle of Harlaw involved a large Clann Domhnaill force – said to be more than six thousand strong – under the command of Domhnall ((†1422), second Lord of the Isles, and the forces of his cousin Alasdair Stiùbhart, Earl of Mar, son of the notorious 'Wolf of Badenoch' (†1406). At stake was the contested Earldom of Ross. Although the battle appears to have been something of a standoff, it is remembered in Gaelic tradition not only as a great Clann Domhnaill victory but as a triumph of the *Gàidheil* over the *Goill*. As such, the panegyric poets in later centuries often made a point of praising their patrons by referring to their ancestors' involvement at Harlaw.

The Earl of Mar also fought against Clann Domhnaill at the Battle of Inverlochy in 1431, and two songs relating to that battle are given here (poems 77 and 78).

> Children of Conn, recall now
> courage in time of combat:
> be attentive, audacious,
> agile, ambitious,
> be bold, beautiful,
> brawny, belligerent,
> contumacious, courageous,
> clever, combative,
> deliberate, destructive,
> deadly, enduring,

Gu h-èasgaidh, gu h-eaghnamhach,
Gu h-èidith', gu h-eireachdail,
Gu fortail, gu furachail,
Gu frithir, gu forniata,
Gu gruamach, gu gràineamhail,
Gu gleusta, gu gaisgeamhail,   16
Gu h-ullamh, gu h-iorghaileach,
Gu h-olla-bhorb, gu h-àibheiseach,
Gu h-innill, gu h-inntinneach,
Gu h-iomdha, gu h-iomghonach,
Gu laomsgar, gu làn-ath lamh,
Gu làidir, gu luath-bhuilleach,
Gu mearghanta, gu mór-chneadhach,
Gu meanmnach, gu mìleanta,   24
Gu neimhneach, gu naimhdeamhail,
Gu niatach, gu neimh-eaglach,
Gu h-obann, gu h-olla-ghnìomhach,
Gu h-oirdheirc, gu h-oirbheartach,
Gu prap is gu prìomh-ullamh,
Gu prosta, gu prionnsamhail,
Gu ruaimneach, gu ro-dhàna,
Gu ro-bhorb, gu rìoghamhail,   32
Gu sanntach, gu sèanamhail,
Gu socair, gu sàr-bhuailteach,
Gu teannta, gu togarrach,
Gu talcmhor, gu traigh-èasgaidh,
Gu h-urlamh, gu h-ùr-mhaiseach
Do chosnadh na cath-làthrach
Re bronnaibh bhar biodhbhadha.
A Chlanna Cuinn Cèad-chathaich   40
A nois uair bhar n-aitheanta,
A chuileanan confadhach,
A bheithrichean bunanta,
A leòmhannan làn-ghasta,
A onchonaibh iorghaileach,
Chaoiribh chròdha, churanta
De Chlanna Cuinn Cèad-chathaich —
A Chlanna Cuinn, cuimhnichibh   48
Cruas an am na h-iorghaile.

be eager, expert,
well-equipped, elegant,
be forceful, fitful,
fervent, feisty,
be grim, gruesome,
gymnastic, glorious,
alert, awesome,
intractable, impetuous,
well-accoutred, ardent,
innumerable, incisive,
be lethal, lusty,
swiftly lopping, giving it laldy,
mirthful, mortally-wounding,
mettlesome, military,
be noxious, nasty,
never-daunted, never-fearing,
overwhelming, omnipotent,
outshining, outreaching,
precipitate, prepared,
powerful, princely,
be robust, reckless,
ruinous, regal,
be sharp, sainèd,
steady, sure-hitting,
tight, triumphant,
tenacious, tripping,
youthful and yearning
to beat in battle
the foe's forces.
O Children of Conn of a hundred conflicts
now is your hour for honour,
O warring whelps,
O bulky bears,
O leading lions,
O obstinate otters,
live, courageous coals
of the Children of Conn of a hundred conflicts —
O Children of Conn recall now
courage in time of combat.

35. Beannuigh do Theaghlach, a Thríonóid

Giolla Críost Táilliúr

Tha an dàn sònraichte seo, a rinneadh, a rèir coltais, anns a' chòigeamh linn deug agus a tha air a ghleidheadh ann an Leabhar an Deadhain, a' brosnachadh cur às a' mhadaidh-allaidh anns a' Ghàidhealtachd. Tha am bàrd a' misneachadh Eòin Stiùbhairt (fear de Stiùbhartaich Gharbhchrìochan Pheairt) a chum a' chasgairt seo. Bha gràin mhaireannach aig muinntir na Gàidhealtachd air a' mhadadh-allaidh, agus eagal roimhe, agus mu dheireadh chaidh am marbhadh uile uaireigin mu dheireadh an t-seachdamh linn deug no mu thoiseach an ochdamh linn deug.

Ach is dòcha nach bu chòir an dàn a leughadh gu litireil, agus gur 'daoine briste' no eucoraich a bha anns na madaidhean-allaidh seo. Tha teans ann gu robh am bàrd a' brosnachadh murtairean Sheumais I, a chaidh a mharbhadh ann am Peairt ann an 1437, a bhith air an toirt gu lagh, cleas Iain Luim an dèidh Murt na Ceapaich ann an 1663.

Tha ceithir dàin le Giolla Críost Táilliúr air an gleidheadh ann an Leabhar Deadhan Lios Mòr, ach chan eil dad a dh'fhiosrachadh againn mu dheidhinn. Is e an tiotal iomlan a tha air a thoirt dha ann an Leabhar an Deadhain 'Giolla Críost Táilliúr Bod an Stúic', far-ainm sònraichte.

Beannuigh do theaghlach, a Thríonóid,
    a Rí pharrthais phuirt na liag;
do theaghlach nach gann dod ghuidhe,
    thú féin do dhealbh uile iad.

Is duit do cumadh síol nÁdhaimh,
    do ghruaidh dheirg ar dath na subh;
fhir do bheannuigh port is pobal,
    malluigh do locht cogaidh cuil.   8

Atá conairt chursta chuiléan
    déanamh uilc ar clannaibh ríogh;
go gcluineam ár na gceann nguineach:
    is lán gach gleann duilleach dhíobh.

O Trinity, Bless Your People

This highly unusual poem, preserved in the Book of the Dean of Lismore and apparently dating from the fifteenth century, vehemently urges the destruction of wolves in the Highlands. In particular, the poem calls upon Eòin Stiùbhart (apparently the Eòin of that name who held Garth and Fortingall in Perthshire and who died in 1475; see poem 20) to dedicate himself to eliminating this scourge. Wolves were long perceived as a threat in the Highlands, and successive campaigns of extermination led to their extinction sometime in the late seventeenth century or early eighteenth century.

It may well be that the poem should not be read entirely literally as referring to wolves, however, but to 'broken men' or other outlaws. Association of the wolf with the wild and uncontrolled, 'beyond the pale', is deeply rooted in Gaelic and indeed wider European tradition. Yet it may be too much to read the poem as a direct incitement to the capture of the murderers of King James I, who was killed in Perth in 1437.

Four poems by Giolla Críost Táilliúr are preserved in the Book of the Dean of Lismore, but we know nothing about him. His full title, given in the attribution at the beginning of the present poem, is Giolla Críost Táilliúr Bod an Stúic, literally 'of the prominent (or stiff) penis', though perhaps referring to a prominent placename.

O Trinity, bless your people,
    O Heaven's King of the fort of gems;
your innumerable family beseech You,
    You who have created them all.

For you, Adam's seed was created,
    red like the raspberry his cheeks;
O Man who has blessed place and people,
    curse now the sinful agents of war.

A cursed brood of wolf-cubs
    wreak havoc on the people of the king;
may I hear their pernicious heads are slaughtered:
    they abound in each leafy glen.

An lucht cogaidh ar cloinn Ádhaimh,
  ó nach féadtar bheith 'na dtosd,
'na gcealtaibh choidhche ré chéile,
  feartuigh, Rí na gréine, a gcosg.   16

An lucht cogaidh ar cloinn Ádhaimh,
  do fríoth Luicifeir 'na lúib:
ná léig fois ná díon don droing-se,
  loisg, a Rí na soillse súd.

Malluigh na sealga is an mhortlaidh
  itheas eich, caoirigh is cruidh,
do chuir druim ré fód na faithche:
  sgaoiltear cinn an ghasraidh dhuibh.   24

Atá gasradh mhadadh mhaslach
  ar láthair Inse Alt Airt:
lán trudair iad, tréig, a Thríonóid,
  curstar iad dod mhíondóid bhailc.

Giodh iomdha craiceann chon allta
  againn um chláirsigh 's um chruit,
cha teirce claigeann fuar falamh
  againn ón chuain alla uilc.   32

Athair Chríost, déan sneachta seachainn
  ó Loch Abar go Rinn Friú;
luaith i gConghail dá gcorp cnámhach:
  oircheas olc do rádha riú.

Gion gur éiric sin ar searrchaibh
  do mhac Roibeirt na ruag dte,
álach míonmhór na ngleann ngusta,
  is líonmhor ceann cursta ar cleith.   40

A bhfuil ó Bheinn Ghuilbinn ghreanta
  do mhadradh suas go sruth Toilbh,
bhíos ar sealgaibh síos ag suidhe,
  deargár ó Chríost uile oirbh.

The ones who war on Adam's children,
    always together in their lairs,
since they are incapable of being peaceful,
    O King of the Sun, bring them to halt.

The folk who war on Adam's children,
    Lucifer was discovered in their midst;
allow that rabble no rest or quarter,
    burn them, O King of yonder light.

Curse the hunts and slaughter
    which devour horses and cattle and sheep,
which strewed backs on the sod of the meadow,
    let the heads of the black legion be cleft.

An abusive wolf-pack is on location
    about the meadow of Arthur's Burn;
O God, abandon them, utter abominations,
    let them be cursed by your mighty gentle hand.

Though we have many a wolfskin
    covering up harp or lyre,
not fewer the skulls, cold and empty,
    we possess from that wild evil pack.

Father of Christ send snow past us
    from Lochaber to Renfrew,
ashes in Connel for their bony bodies;
    it is right to speak of them ill.

Though it is no requital for his horses
    — the gentle brood of the lively glens —
for Robert's son of heated clashes,
    there's many a cursed head on a stake.

Every wolf from fair Beinn Ghuilbinn,
    up to the river Tolve,
who hunt by waiting on their haunches,
    may Christ send destruction on you all.

Go gcluininn 's mé i nInbhir Nise
    míolchoin ag sgaoileadh na sgonn;
mairg mán iadh baladh na mbuicneach:
    go n-iadh galar tuitmeach trom.   48

Sgamhach conach aillse is acais
    ar lucht marbhtha na ngreagh nglas;
Mac Dé le croidhe nua [   ]
    snoidheadh an chuain ainmheach as.

Loisg gach saobhaidh tha i Sídh Chailleann,
    a Eóin Stiúbhairt na stéad mbras,
más fíor uaim gur sreathach srannmhor
    an chuain ghreannach ghreannmhor ghlas.   56

Ar ghardha Eóin stéidghil Stiúbhairt
    cha léir dhomh cabar gan cheann,
is iad ar chollaibh cas corrach,
    an chonairt ghlas mhongach bheann.

        Beannuigh do theaghlach.

36. Ar Sliocht Gaodhal ó Ghort Gréag

Gun urra

Is e cuspair nan rannan seo Gill'Easbaig, dàrna iarla Earra
Ghàidheal, ach tha tomhas de mhì-chinnt ann a thaobh dè
dìreach a tha air cùlaibh an dàin. Tha e coltach nach tàinig an
teacsa iomlan a-nuas thugainn, oir chan eil dùnadh ceart ann.

Is e an tuigse as cumanta gun do rinneadh an dàn na
bhrosnachadh do Ghill'Easbaig ro Bhlàr Flodden ann an 1513.
Mar a thachair, chaidh Gill'Easbaig a mharbhadh aig a' bhatail
ainmeil sin, maille ri Rìgh Seumas IV agus iomadh duine-uasal
eile. Ach tha cuid de sgoilearan den bheachd nach eil an dàn co-
cheangailte ri Flodden idir, agus gun do rinneadh e mu
c. 1501–2 gus ìmpidh a chur air MacCailein a thaic a thoirt don
iomairt às leth Dhomhnaill Dhuibh Mhic Dhomhnaill (†1545)

Deerhounds tearing the brutes asunder,
 would that I'd hear it in Inverness;
woe to him wrapped in the stink of goatskins,
 soon he'll be wrapped in epileptic fits.

May murrain, rabies, cancer, poison
 strike the slaughterers of the grey herds;
may God's Son with new purpose
 lop away that misshapen brood.

Burn out every lair that is in Schiehallion,
 O Eòin Stiùbhart of the swift steeds;
so that snarling ugly grey brood, if I'm truthful,
 will lie snoring in serried rows.

On Eòin-of-bright-steeds Stiùbhart's ramparts
 I see no stake without head;
the grey hairy pack from the mountains
 on sharp-pointed hazel staves.

The Race of Gaels From the Land of Greece

This famous poem – or fragment – has conventionally been understood as having been composed for Gill'Easbaig, second earl of Argyll (†1513) on the eve of the Battle of Flodden in 1513. King James IV was killed in that battle, together with a swathe of the Scottish nobility, including Gill'Easbaig himself.

The poem is often quoted by historians but there are many difficulties of interpretation. The poem is evidently incomplete, or more precisely acephalous (missing its proper beginning), for it does not conclude with a verbal echo of the opening line (*dúnadh*), as required in formal bardic poetry. More important, the poem is highly unusual in its political and ethnic worldview, for it seems to present a strikingly conservative view of pana chum ath-stèidheachadh Thighearnas nan Eilean an dèidh arfuntachadh 1493. Tha teans ann cuideachd gur ann ann an 1513 a rinneadh an dàn ceart gu leòr ach gu robh am file a' moladh ionnsaigh, còmhla ri Clann Uí Dhomhnaill, air na Sasannaich ann an taobh a tuath na h-Èireann.

Tha an t-ùghdar a' cleachdadh an fhacail 'Gall' uair is uair tron dàn. Is e prìomh-chiall an fhacail seo ann an Gàidhlig na h-Alba cuideigin a bhuineas ri Galldachd Alba, agus is e 'Sasannach' a chleachdar mu choinneimh muinntir Shasainn. Mar sin, mas ann an lùib iomairt Flodden a rinneadh an dàn, feumar na faclan 'Gàidheal' is 'Gall' a thuigsinn ann an dòigh a tha car àraid: muinntir na h-Alba air fad nan 'Gàidheil' agus muinntir Shasainn nan 'Goill'.

Tha ceist nas doimhne ag èirigh, mar a mhìnicheadh anns an Ro-ràdh, an lùib 'dì-Ghàidhealachadh' taobh an ear-dheas na h-Alba aig deireadh nam Meadhan Aoisean: cuine a rinneadh 'Goill' de mhuinntir na 'Galldachd' ùire seo, ann an tuigse muinntir na 'Gàidhealtachd'? Gu mì-fhortanach, chan fhaighear freagairt dheimhinne air a' cheist seo, air sgàth gainnead is tainead nan tùsan.

Ar sliocht Gaodhal ó Ghort Gréag
ní fheil port ar a gcoimhéad,
    dá dteagmhadh nach b'aordha leat
    sliocht Gaodhal do chur tharat.

Is dú éirghe i n-aghaidh Gall,
nocha dóigh éirghe udmhall;
    faobhair claidheamh, reanna ga,
    cóir a gcaitheamh go h-aobhdha.   8

Ré Gallaibh, adeirim ribh,
sul ghabhadar ar ndúthaigh;
    ná léigmid ar ndúthaigh dhínn,
    déinmid ardchogadh ainmhín,
        ar aithris Gaoidheal mBanbha,
        caithris ar ar n-athardha.

Gaelic solidarity against the English enemy, who are cast as *Goill* (literally 'non-Gaels', thus foreigners), with the entire Scottish nation, Lowland as well as Highland, portrayed as Gaels, and solidarity with Gaelic Ireland repeatedly invoked.

However, it may well be that the association with Flodden is entirely erroneous, and that the poem was composed *c.* 1501–2 in an effort to pressure Argyll into supporting attempts on behalf of his nephew Domhnall Dubh MacDhomhnaill (†1545) to restore the Lordship of the Isles, which had been forfeited in 1493. It is also possible that the poem emerged from Argyll's hosting of the Ulster chieftain Aodh Ó Domhnaill in 1513 and discussions concerning a proposed attack on English interests in the North of Ireland. Under either of these scenarios, the use of the terms *Gàidheil* and *Goill* in the poem is rather easier to understand.

The connection of the Gaels with Greece may surprise the modern reader but this is entirely conventional, reflecting the traditional belief set out in Gaelic 'pseudo-history' that the Gaels came to Ireland (and then to Scotland) by way of Scythia, Egypt, and Spain.

> The race of Gaels from the land of Greece
> will have no place in their power
>> if you should think it no disgrace
>> to ignore the Gaelic lineage.
>
> It is right to rise against outsiders,
> no bungled strike do we anticipate,
>> but swords' edge, spears' tip,
>> rightly plied with spirit.
>
> Against outsiders, I tell ye,
> in case they take our country;
>> let's not throw away our land
>> let us make no gentle warfare;
>>> in imitation of the Gaels of Ireland,
>>> let us watch over our fatherland.

Do-chuala mé go roibh sin
uair éigin Inis Incin   16
    fá smacht ag fine Fomhra:
    racht le bile Bóromha.

Nó go dtánaig Lugh tar linn,
mór bhfian darab maith dírim,
    dár marbhadh Balar ua Néid:
    budh samhladh dhúinn a leithéid.

Seala do Ghallaibh mar sain
ag íoc cíosa as an dúthaigh;   24
    [   ] ar eagal gach cinn,
    mór atá teagamh orainn.

Cia nois ar aithris an fhir
fhóirfeas Gaoidheil ar Ghallaibh,
    rér linne, mar do-rinn Lugh
    taobhadh a chine ó anghuth?

Aithnid domh, dámadh áil leis,
duine dh'fhéadfadh a aithris,   32
    Lughaidh ar feadh na Banbha:
    cubhaidh duit a ionnshamhla.

Ghiolla Easbuig nach d'eitigh d'fhear,
is tú an Lugh fá dheireadh;
    a Iarla Oirir Ghaoidheal,
    bí id churaidh ag commaoidheamh.

Cuir th'urfhógra an oir 's an iar
ar Ghaoidhlibh ó Ghort Gáilian;   40
    cuir siar thar ardmhuir na Goill,
    nach biadh ar Albain achrainn.

Do chuir Lugh nár loc troda
lé chlaidheamh géarr ceannchodad
    Éire fá smacht Gaoidheal nGréag
    [   ]

I have heard that it came to be
that Ireland was once subject
    to a tribe of Fomorians:
    an outrage to the prince of Bóromha.

Until Lugh came across the sea,
with many a band of fine fighters;
    by him was slain Balar ua Néid:
    to us his likes will be an example.

Likewise outsiders for a while
raised tribute from the country;
    fear was put in every one,
    great is our suspicion.

Who now in imitation of that hero
will deliver the Gaels from outsiders
    in our times, as did Lugh
    standing by his race against insult?

I know, were it his desire,
a man who could do likewise,
    Lugh throughout Banbha:
    fitting for you the comparison.

You, who never refused request,
you are the Lugh of the present;
    O Gill'Easbaig, earl of Argyll,
    become an exulting champion.

Send your summons east and west
to the Gaels of the field of Leinster;
    drive the outsiders west over the sea,
    so Scotland may not be in conflict.

With his sharp hard-tipped sword,
Lugh, who never flinched at action,
    gave control to the Gaels of Greece,
    putting Ireland into their power.

Na fréamha ó bhfuilid ag fás,
díthigh iad, mór a bhforfhás,
   nach faighthear Gall beó dot éis,
   ná Gaillseach ann ré h-aisnéis.   48

Loisg a mbantracht nach maith mín,
loisg a gclannmhaicne ainmhín,
   is loisg a dtighe dubha,
   is coisg dhínn a n-anghutha.

Léig le h-uisge a luaithre sin,
i ndiaidh loisgthe dá dtaisibh;
   ná déan teóchroidhe a beó Gall,
   a eó bheóghoine anbhfann.   56

Cuimhnigh féin, a ghruaidh mar shuibh,
go bhfuil orainn ag Gallaibh
   annsmacht réd linn agus pléid
   'nar chinn gallsmacht [   ].

Cuimhnigh Cailéin th'athair féin,
cuimhnigh Giolla Easbuig ainnséin,
   cuimhnigh Donnchadh 'na ndeaghaidh,
   an fear conchar cairdeamhail.   64

Cuimhnigh Cailéin eile ann,
cuimhnigh Giolla Easbuig Arann;
   's Cailéin na gceann, mór a chlí,
   lér gabhadh geall an [   ].

Cuimhnigh nach tugsad na fir
umhla ar uamhan do Ghallaibh;
   cia mó fá dtugadh tusa
   umhla uait an dula-sa?   72

Ó nach mair acht fuidheall áir
do Ghaoidhlibh ó ghort iomgháidh,
   teagair lé chéile na fir,
   's cuir th'eagal féine ar náimhdibh.

Saigh ar Ghallaibh 'na dtreibh féin:
bí id dhúsgadh, a Mheic Cailéin:
   d'fhear cogaidh, a fholt mar ór,
   ní maith an codal ramhór.   80

The roots from which they grow,
destroy them, great their propagation,
    after you let no foreigner be found alive,
    nor foreign bitch to be counted.

Burn their women who are not mild,
burn their uncouth offspring,
    burn their miserable sheds
    and remove the blight of their presence.

Send their ashes down the stream
after the burning of their corpses,
    show no pity to a single one,
    you mighty death-dealing salmon.

During your own time, remember
our suffering, O cheek like raspberry,
    of foreign spite and tyranny,
    expanding their suzerainty.

Remember Cailean, your own sire,
remember Gill'Easbaig in addition,
    after them remember Donnchadh,
    the friendly hunt-follower.

Remember the other Cailean,
remember Arran's Gill'Easbaig;
    Cailean of the heads, great his might,
    who won the stake at [   ].

Remember those men did not submit
out of fear to the Goill,
    why, any more than they,
    should you now pay them homage?

Since only the dregs of the slain
remain of the Gaels from the field of peril,
    bring the men together
    and put fear of yourself in the enemy.

Attack the Goill on their own soil,
rouse yourself, O son of Cailean,
    for a man of war, O hair like gold,
    too long a sleep is no benison.

THE LEARNED TRADITION

SATIRE AND HUMOUR

37. A Chinn Diarmaid Uí Chairbre

Eóin, Deadhan Chnóideoirt

Tha an dàn seo na aoir air cur gu bàs a' chlàrsair Èireannaich
Diarmaid Ó Cairbre, a mharbh an neach-taice aige, Aonghas
(mac Eòin) MacDhomhnaill, a bha na oighre air Rìoghachd nan
Eilean, ann an Inbhir Nis ann an 1490. A rèir na h-eachdraidh
ainmeil aig Ùisdean MacDhomhnaill, rinn Diarmaid am murt le
bhith gearradh sgòrnan Aonghais le sgithinn fhada, an dèidh do
cheann-cinnidh Chloinn Choinnich a ghealltainn dha gun
toireadh e a mhac mar mhnaoi dha nan dèanadh e an gnìomh
gun fhìrinn na cùise a leigeil mu sgaoil an dèidh làimhe. Chaidh
Diarmaid a dhìcheannadh air sgàth na h-eucoir aige agus chaidh
a cheann a chur an àirde gu poblach agus a bhodhaig fhuasgladh
– is e sin ri ràdh, a reubadh bho chèile le eich a ruith gu na
ceithir àirdean.

Tha am bàrd a' cantainn 'rí Íle' ri Aonghas air sàillibh a'
cheangail eadar Rìghrean nan Eilean agus Ìle. Tha cleachdaidh-
ean den t-seòrsa seo cumanta ann am bàrdachd an linn agus cha
bu chòir an tuigsinn gu litireil; air an làimh eile, bha an tiotal
'rìgh' (a' leantainn tuigse nas sine, roi-fhiùdalach air an fhacal)
cumanta anns na h-abairtean urraim 'rí Innsi Gall' agus 'rí
Fionnghall'.

A rèir coltais bha 'Eóin, Deadhan Chnóideoirt' na bhall de
Chloinn Mhuirich, an teaghlach as ainmeile de dh'aos-dàna na
h-Alba. Bha e na chleachdadh cumanta aon bhràthair a dhol an
sàs anns an eaglais agus an fheadhainn eile a bhith ri bàrdachd.

A chinn Diarmaid Uí Chairbre,
   giodh lór th'airgne agus t'uaille,
cha mhór liom méad do dhocra
   gé 'taoi i gcrochadh ré cuaille.

Cha truagh liom fád ghruaig ghreannaigh,
   ná gaoith ghleannaigh dá gairbhe,
cha truagh liom gad id ghiallaibh,
   a chinn Diarmaid Uí Chairbre.

8

O Head of Diarmaid Ó Cairbre

This poem celebrates the execution of the Irish harper Diarmaid Ó Cairbre, who murdered his patron Aonghas (mac Eòin) MacDhomhnaill, heir to the Lordship of the Isles, in Inverness in 1490. According to a seventeenth-century Clann Domhnaill history, Diarmaid committed the murder by slitting Aonghas' throat with a long knife, after the chief of the MacCoinnichs had promised him his daughter's hand in marriage if he carried out the deed and kept his silence thereafter. Diarmaid himself was beheaded for his crime and his head then placed on public display, while his body was drawn and quartered – that is, torn apart by horses running in different directions.

The poem refers to Aonghas as *rí Íle*, king of Islay, Islay being the seat of the Lords of the Isles. This styling is a common poetic convention, not to be taken literally; but the ordinary Gaelic title for the Lord of the Isles was *rí Innse Gall*, king of the Hebrides, or *rí Fionnghall*, king of the Hebrideans, reflecting a traditional, pre-feudal usage of the term 'king'.

Eòin, Dean of Knoydart, appears to have been a member of the MacMhuirich bardic family. It was not at all unusual among siblings of learned families for one brother to enter the clergy and others to pursue a poetic career.

O head of Diarmaid Ó Cairbre,
    though plentiful your pride and possessions,
not plentiful enough your discomfort,
    though you hang suspended from a cudgel.

I do not pity your unkempt tangles,
    however stormy the glen wind blowing through them;
I do not pity the withe between your jawbones,
    O head of Diarmaid Ó Cairbre.

Mairg do smuain do bhéim bràghad
   nach badh námha do chairdis;
och is mairg nár thill t'iachtaigh,
   a chinn Diarmaid Uí Chairbre.

Do milleadh leat rí Íle,
   fear imirt fhíona is airgid,
'gá dtá an trilis úr iarnaidh,
   a chinn Diarmaid Uí Chairbre.   16

Rí Íle na gcorn gcomhóil,
   do chuir onóir ar chairdibh;
mairg do chréacht a chneas niamhgheal,
   a chinn Diarmaid Uí Chairbre.

Ionmhain liom a bhas mhórdha,
   nár dhoichleach óir ná airgid,
's lérbh annsa fleadh is fiadhach,
   a chinn Diarmaid Uí Chairbre.   24

Iarraim ar Rígh na n-Astal,
   an tí fhasgas le [   ],
dá fhurtacht feasda ó phianaibh,
   a chinn Diarmaid Uí Chairbre.

     A chinn Diarmaid.

38. Theast Aon Diabhal na nGaoidheal

Fionnlagh an Bard Ruadh

Air an uachdar tha an dàn seo a' dèanamh gàirdeachas ri bàs
Ailein mhic Ruairidh, ceann-cinnidh Chloinn Raghnaill, a chaochail
ann am Blàr Athaill *c*. 1503. Ach is math a dh'fhaodte gun do
rinneadh e fhad 's a bha Ailean fhathast beò mar nàdar de
bhreug-mharbhrann; chan eil dàin a tha a' dèanamh subhachas
air bàs nàimhdean idir cumanta ann an dualchas litreachail nan
Gàidheal.

Woe to him who comprehended your neck-stroke
    who was not an enemy to your alliance;
 alas and woe to him who ignored not your yelling,
    O head of Diarmaid Ó Cairbre.

By you was destroyed the king of Islay,
    a man who dispensed wine and silver,
fresh and stiff were his tresses,
    O head of Diarmaid Ó Cairbre.

The king of Islay of the cheerful goblets,
    who raised his friends in honour;
woe to him who hurt his bright white body,
    O head of Diarmaid Ó Cairbre.

Beloved to me the palms that were noble,
    that were never mean with gold or silver,
who appreciated both feasting and hunting,
    O head of Diarmaid Ó Cairbre.

I beseech the King of the Apostles
    He who protects by [   ],
to protect him forever from torment,
    O head of Diarmaid Ó Cairbre.

       O head of Diarmaid.

The Chief Devil of the Gael is Dead

The poem appears to celebrate the passing of Ailean mac Ruairidh, chief of Clann Raghnaill, who died *c.* 1503. It may well be that the poem was composed during Ailean's lifetime as a sort of mock-elegy; poems celebrating the actual death of enemies or rivals are not common in Gaelic tradition (the previous poem being something of an exception).

A very different view of Ailean appears in poem 31, where he

Tha sealladh gu math diofraichte air Ailean ri fhaighinn ann an dàn 31, far a bheileas a' dèanamh gaisgeach agus fear-dìona na h-Alba dheth. Is e rud gu math annasach gu bheil dà dhàn againn a tha a' moladh agus a' dì-moladh an aon duine.

Tha an liosta de ghearanan aig a' bhàrd, Fionnlagh, an aghaidh Ailein gu math inntinneach: gu bheil e ri sgrios eaglaisean, sgrìnean agus reiligean, gu bheil e ri feise le a mhàthair agus le a phiuthar, gu bheil e na shaighdear gun sgil gun dìoghras. Tha am bàrd ga shamhlachadh uair is uair ri torc, biast brùideil an-uasal a rèir dualchas nan Gàidheal. Tha an aoir gu soilleir stèidhichte air a' chòd-mholaidh air a chur bun-os-cionn. Tha eisimpleirean de dh'aoir tearc a chionn 's nach robh na daoine air an robh iad ag amas air an cumail.

Tha còig dàin a tha air an ainmeachadh air Fionnlagh air an gleidheadh ann an Leabhar Deadhan Lios Mòr. Chan eil mòran fios againn mu dheidhinn, ach is ann do bhuill de Chloinn Ghriogair a tha na dàin eile aige.

Feumar cuimhneachadh gur e dreuchd no inbhe shònraichte a bha ann am 'bàrd' an taca ris an fhile àrd-nòsach.

Theast aon diabhal na nGaoidheal,
sgéal as cóir do chommaoidheamh,
bhaoi ré daorlot cheall is chros,
an maoltorc mall gan mhathas.

A h-ifreann thánaig ar dtús:
usaide an sgéal a iomthús,
mar thá a bheatha rís ar bail
i gceathaibh ghrís an diabhail.   8

Do nasgadar air fá rinn,
an uair dh'fhág sé teach n-ifrinn,
toidheacht don dún chéadna ar ais,
's a chúl ré réadla pharrthais.

An uair thánaig an torc dubh,
b'iomdha deamhan 'gá chonnradh:
garbh mhothar gacha péiste
shín go h-anbha oilléitigh.   16

is portrayed as a warrior-hero and great defender of Scotland. The survival of poems praising and dispraising the same individual is highly unusual.

The charges mustered against Ailean in Fionnlagh's satire are interesting: he is a despoiler of churches, shrines, and cemeteries, he is a mediocre and reluctant warrior, he has sexual relations with his mother and sister. He is also repeatedly likened to a a boar, a brutal and ignoble animal in Gaelic tradition. The dispraise can be clearly analysed as an inversion of the usual categories of the panegyric code. Examples of satire are relatively rare, for their addressees of course did not aim to preserve them.

Five poems attributed to Fionnlagh are preserved in the Book of the Dean of Lismore. Little is known about him, but his four other poems are addressed to MacGriogair patrons. As explained in the Introduction, his title *bard* is a term of art, referring to a secondary order of professional poets, at a lower level than the highly trained *file*.

The chief devil of the Gael is dead,
news that ought to be celebrated,
    he who desecrated churches and crosses,
    the sluggish boar, bald and meritless.

From hell's quarter he came firstly:
his origin makes the news more plausible
    of how again he is doing well
    in the ember showers of the Devil.

When he left the house of hell,
at the point of his sword they bound him over,
    that to the same place he'd return,
    and keep his back to the stars of heaven.

When the black boar arrived there,
many a demon conspired with him;
    the harsh outcry of every monster
    rose up hugely and hideously.

Ar eagal a bheith gan ní
do-rinneadh do mhac Ruaidhrí
    a chniocht go h-onáireach ann,
    i riocht Chonáin i n-iofrann.

Is cóir an agra thá i ndiu
ag Ailéin ar na diabhlaibh,
    gurab é fa rí orra,
    ar liom, 'na thím eatorra.   24

Is mithigh sgur réd mharbhnaidh,
a shean bheathaigh bhiothcharnaigh,
    mheic Ruaidhrí ón mhúr a mach,
    fhuair ní gan lúdh gan lámhach.

Fá chaithréim do chur i sum
dlighim coinne ré Colum;
    ó's í caithréim t'aoir uile,
    a Ailéin mhaoil mhíoghoire.   32

Do rinn tusa, 's ní h-í a mháin,
creach Íe is reilge Odhráin;
    is tú dhochann go borb ann
    cochall na n-ord 's na n-aifreann.

Is tú bhuair olc Innse Gall,
's tú bhocht a cíos 's a tearmann;
    is tú as gealtach nós a mach,
    lé leantar fós do thosach.   40

Acht aonbhuille ar do láimh chlí,
do bhréithir, a mheic Ruaidhrí;
    ní clos do ghleó ó soin a mach
    is an chros bheó dod mhallacht.

Math an dís fá bhfuil do shlán,
dóibh-sin fós is [tú daltán]
    ó chéadtosach do chagaidh,
    a bhréanchlosach anabaigh.   48

The son of Ruairidh was then made
— for fear he'd lack substance —
    a knight honourably in hell,
    just as was Conán.

Proper the claim that Ailean makes
today upon the devils,
    for he, I think, was their chief,
    for the time he spent among them.

It is time to stop this elegy for you,
you animal, old and portly,
    O son of Ruairidh, from the sea-bound fort,
    who won cattle without spearcast or moving.

To give proper account of his triumph
I ought to meet with Colum,
    for your career is your satire complete,
    O Ailean, bald and impious.

You carried out, and that was not all,
the despoiling of Iona and Odhrán's graveyard;
    it was you who barbarously mutilated there
    the shrine of the gospels and masses.

You stirred up malice towards the Islands,
you impoverished her tribute and her sanctuary;
    you have always had the way of the coward
    which follows on naturally from your origins.

But one blow reached your left side,
on my word, O son of Ruairidh:
    since you were cursed by the living cross
    nothing has been heard of your exploits.

Good the pair whom you defied
and you moreover their fosterling;
    from the very outset of your war,
    you over-ripe and stinking carcase.

Creach eile nach raibh san lagh
ar Fíonán i nGleann Garadh;
    mhalluigh do naomh feartach féin
    do mhaol gealtach, a Ailéin.

Atá mar gach naomh eile
ag díoghailt a oirbhire:
    do chuir Dubhthach lé chúis féin
    an cuthach i ngnúis Ailéin.   56

Do thír dubhach is do shluagh,
do baineadh dhíobh an chnámhthuagh;
    léigid deireadh do mhuirne
    idir Seile is Subhairne.

Ní h-iongnadh a bheith i bpéin:
fada ó b'ionchrochtha Ailéin;
    ná luaidh ar láthair an fhir
    chuaidh go a mháthair 's go a phiuthair.   64

Mithigh a nois sgur dot aoir,
a mheic Ruaidhrí, a ainmhín;
    a Ailéin nach greasann greas,
    caithréim t'easgaine is oircheas.

         Theast.

39. Alasdair, 'ndo Thréig Tú an Ghruaim?

Donnchadh Mac an Phearsúin

Aoir gu math diofraichte à Leabhar an Deadhain. Gu mì-
fhortanach chan eil dad a dh'fhios againn mu ùghdar an dàin, no
mu Alasdair gruamach.

    Tha an dàn seo, mar 'Holy Willie's Prayer' le Burns, a'
magadh air bodach a tha air fàs tuilleadh is sòlaimte na
chreideamh. Is e pàirt den àbhachdas gun gabh am bàrd fhèin,
mas fhìor, ris a' cheangal eadar gruaim agus gràs.

Another raid outwith the law
on Fíonán in Glen Garry;
    your own miraculous saint cursed
    your craven bald pate, O Ailean.

He, like every other saint,
avenges the evil done him;
    Dubhthach, in his own cause,
    set madness in Ailean's visage.

Sad are your land and hosts,
deprived of the bone-axe;
    they put an end to pleasure
    between Sheil and Subhairne.

No wonder he's in torment;
long was Ailean gallows-ripe;
    don't speak of the virility of the man
    who went into his mother and sister.

Time now to cease from your satire,
son of Ruairidh, you hooligan;
    Ailean who does not press a fight,
    fit is the triumph of your cursing.

Alasdair, Have You Given Up the Gloom?

A very different kind of satiric poem from the Book of the Dean of Lismore; we know nothing of this poem's author, or of gloomy Alasdair.

This poem, like Burns' 'Holy Willie's Prayer', ridicules an old man who has become too solemnly religious. It is part of the humour that the poet himself pretends to be convinced of the correlation between gloom and grace.

Alasdair, 'ndo thréig tú an ghruaim,
    nó a bhféad sibh a cur uaibh ar lár?
a nd'fhan sibh 'n bhliadhain gan ghean?
    nó a mbí sibh mar sean go bráth?

Chaoidhche ní nd'fhuaras do ghean,
    ó ataoi tú go sean liath:
más ar ghruaim bhitheas an rath,
    's mór fhuair thú de mhath ó Dhia.   8

40. Créad dá nDearnadh Domhnall Donn?

Sir Donnchadh Caimbeul Ghlinn Urchaidh

Tha an aoir seo, a rinneadh, is dòcha, mu dheireadh a' chòig-
eamh linn deug, a' bruidhinn ri Domhnall Donn Mac an
Fhleisteir, a bha, a rèir coltais, na dhaoine-uasal ann an dùthaich
Chaimbeulaich Ghlinn Urchaidh. Chan eil e duilich drabast-
achd an dàin a thuigsinn; tha cuid de na h-eileamaidean a tha
ann an Domhnall rud beag nas doilleire; is dòcha gu robh
cumhachdan aig na lusan seo a thaobh leigheis no druidheachd.

B'e Sir Donnchadh Caimbeul (1443–1513) mac do
Chailean, às an do shìolaich Caimbeulaich Ghlinn Urchaidh,
agus co-ogha do Chailean, ciad iarla Earra Ghàidheal (†1493);
chaidh Sir Donnchadh a mharbhadh aig Blàr Flodden, maille ri
Gill'Easbaig, dàrna iarla Earra Ghàidheal. Tha naoi dàin aig Sir
Donnchadh air an gleidheadh ann an Leabhar an Deadhain,
agus tha measgachadh de chuspairean aotrom agus aoire ri
fhaicinn annta. Uile-gu-lèir, tha Leabhar an Deadhain a' nochd-
adh gu robh ùidh làidir ann an litreachas aig uaislean nan
Caimbeulach anns a' chiad phàirt den t-siathamh linn deug.

Créad dá ndearnadh Domhnall Donn,
    nó cá poll i roibhe a mhéin?
Nó an bhfuil a fhios ag neach i gcrí,
    créad an ní dhá ndearnadh é?

Alasdair, have you given up the gloom?
   Are you capable of throwing it off?
Is it a year you've been without cheer?
   Are you staying that way for good?

Never have I found you in good form
   since you grew grey and old;
if grace is in proportion to gloom,
   then great the good you have from God.

Of What Was Domhnall Donn Made?

This satirical poem, probably composed towards the end of the fifteenth century, addresses one Domhnall Donn Mac an Fhleisteir, perhaps a member of the local gentry in the territory of the Caimbeuls of Glen Orchy. Although the scatalogical references are not difficult to interpret, some of the elements of which Domhnall is said to be composed are more opaque; these plants may have been understood as having particular medicinal or other properties.

Sir Donnchadh Caimbeul (1443–1513) was the son of Cailean, from whom the Caimbeuls of Glen Orchy descended, and a first cousin of Cailean, first earl of Argyll (†1493); Sir Donnchadh was killed at the Battle of Flodden, together with Gill'Easbaig, second Earl of Argyll. A total of nine poems by Sir Donnchadh, dealing with a wide range of humorous and satirical subjects, are preserved in the Book of the Dean of Lismore. The Book of the Dean reveals a strong interest in literature among the Caimbeul aristocracy of the early sixteenth century.

Of what was Domhnall Donn made,
   or what mud contained his traits?
Or does any mortal know
   from what substance he was formed?

Gach luibh anuasal 'san bhioth,
    chuaidh sin chuige, ceann i gceann:
min tseagail agus lionn ruadh,
    cac madadh agus fual meann.   8

Lán cléibhe do bhuachar bó,
    binid mhór i roibhe toirt;
ros an ghafainn cuid dá mhéin,
    is díthean bréan bhíos i ngort.

Bun an chaisearbháin 's a bharr,
    domblas aoi agus garr marc,
chuaidh mar leó chuige go lór,
    agus cuirm mhór do chac arc.   16

Bréanán brothach agus creamh,
    is lus leamh bhíos 'san lón;
galánach ghabhas a bhéal,
    is olc an néal tá ar a thóin.

Mac an Fhleisteir, giolla an chruidh,
    cuirfe mise dhuibh i gcéill,
is do gach duine á bhfuil ar bhioth,
    gur díbh sin do-rinneadh é.   24

Luighfead ainm Domhnaill Duinn,
    'san talmhain seo a chum Mac Dé
nach faca éan duine a-bhos
    ba dhaoire corp agus cré.

      Créad.

Every base plant that grows
    went towards him, all mixed up,
with rye meal and bile,
    dogs' shit and kids' piss.

A full creel of cow-dung,
    the herb Robert, ever strong,
henbane seed, part of his kind,
    and stinking groundsel from the field.

Root of dandelion and the top,
    gall of liver and horses' dung
were added to him in plentiful supply,
    a great feast of pigs' turds to boot.

Stinking camomile and garlic bulbs,
    and every bitter plant that grows in the marsh;
his mouth emits a foul puff,
    evil the cloud around his rear.

Regarding Fletcher, the cow-herd,
    I make a declaration to you
and to any other living soul
    that from those things he was made.

I will swear by Domhnall's name
    that on this earth that God's Son made
I never saw a mortal man
    who was of baser body and clay.

41. Bod Bríoghmhor Atá ag Donncha

Sir Donnchadh Caimbeul Ghlinn Urchaidh

Dàn brìoghmhor eile le Sir Donnchadh Caimbeul, anns a bheil uaim nam buadhairean a' cur gu mòr ris an àbhachdas. Is dòcha gur ann aig Donnchadh fhèin a bha am bod sònraichte seo; ann an dàn eile de a chuid, 'Mairg ó ndeachaidh a léim lúidh', tha e a' gearain mu mar a chaill e a spionnadh fearail, agus mar sin is dòcha gum bu chòir an dà dhàn a leughadh còmhla. Air an làimh eile, a chionn 's gu bheil am buadhair 'riabhach' ga chleachdadh mu choinneimh Dhonnchaidh, tha teans ann gur ann air an duine-uasal Donnchadh Riabhach MacGille Chonaill (†1526), aig an robh fearann air taobh Loch Tatha, a bha am bod brìoghmhor seo.

Bod bríoghmhor atá ag Donncha,
fada féitheach fíordhorcha,
    reamhar druimleathan díreach,
    sleamhan cuirneach ceirtíneach.

Cluaisleathan ceannramhar crom,
go díoghainn data dubhghorm;
    atá breall ag an fhleascach,
    is e ceannsa (?) go conachtach (?).   8

Maolshrónach mallghormtha glas,
fuachdha forránach fíorchas;
    go cronánach ceannghorm cruaidh,
    móirbhéimneach i measc banshluaigh.

A Potent Prick Has Donnchadh

Another poem by Sir Donnchadh Caimbeul, described by William Gillies as an example of 'anti-courtly' poetry, 'uniting the image-creating techniques and self-conscious seriousness of bardic verse with the bravura, description and hyperbole of the folktale run, to produce what can only be called a *tour de force* of adjectival description'.

The owner of the 'potent prick' praised here is not entirely clear. It might well be the poet himself; another of his surviving poems laments the decline of his potency with the passing of the years, and the two could be read as companion pieces. Alternatively, given that Donnchadh is described as *riabhach* ('grizzled' or 'brindled'), it might be addressed to the Loch Tayside landowner Donnchadh Riabhach MacGille Chonaill (†1526) by a woman, in the same manner that Iseabal Ní Mheic Cailéin (author of poems 48 and 49) praises her priest's sexual prowess in 'Éistidh, a lucht an tighe-se'. (It seems unlikely, though, that a male poet would refer to any penis but his own as *Is annsa linn,* or 'dearest with us' or 'our pride and joy' (line 24)). The translation reflects the original's comically exaggerated use of alliteration.

In the Welsh tradition, many more examples survive of poetry addressed to the genitals, both male and female.

> A powerful prick has Duncan,
> engorged elongated ebony,
>> bulging broad-backed bloated,
>> well-swaddled spouting slippery.

> Big-lugged broad-headed bent,
> capacious colourful cerulean,
>> the knave has a knob,
>> now quiescent, now querulous.

> Smooth-nebbed stately-purple shiny,
> manic thickly matted malevolent,
>> buzzing blue-headed brutal,
>> wallop-wielding among womenfolk.

An fheam tá ag Donncha riabhach,
dar leam, nocha tuilsciamhach —
   síorullamh, a-muigh 's a-mach,
   fíorchruaidh feargach fionnfadhach.   16

Fomhóir fliuchshúileach faitheach (?),
steallach stuaghach starraightheach;
   bannlamh as a bhalg a-mach —
   an fheamlorg airgtheach fháthach.

Go collach, ciabhach, ciorclach,
dona cursta cuisleannach;
   is fada rámhach 's is rod:
   is annsa linn an rábhod.   24

   Bod.

Go súghmhor, sáiteach, salach,
lúthmhor láidir laomcharrach (?),
   ceannramhar borrfadhach borb,
   druimneach deigheól an dubhlorg.

Sreamaillseach soeól an sonn
bhuadhaigheas cath is comhlann;
   go teascaightheach teilgthe te,
   is treabhraighthe fíoch na fleisce.   32

42. Do Chuaidh Mise, Robart Féin

Gun urra

Aoir air nòsan an luchd-chlèire a thaobh feise, a rinneadh mu
thoiseach an t-siathamh linn deug, a rèir coltais, agus a tha air a
ghleidheadh ann an Leabhar Deadhan Lios Mòr.

Do chuaidh mise, Robart féin,
   do mhainisdear an dé a nunn,
agus níor leigeadh mé a steach
   ó nach robh mo bhean mar rium.

Grizzled Duncan's appendage,
in my opinion, is no ornament;
    for every occasion, primed,
      angry adamantine hairy.

The hooded, rheumy-eyed giant,
spurting straining face-jutting
    a cubit out from its bag,
      the corrosive colossal knob-kerry.

Rotund, rough-haired, ring-girt,
amoral accursed apoplectic;
    probing oar-like obsessed:
      our pride and joy, this king-prick.

Stabbing, salacious, sappy,
boisterous bullying glans-blazing,
    fat-headed burgeoning barbaric,
      the ridge-backed expert black bludgeon.

The spunk-sweating worldy warrior,
triumphant in tiff and battle;
    flattening in full flight febrile,
      unstoppable the commotion of the cabar.

Yesterday I, Robert, Set Off

A satire on the sexual mores of the clergy, the point of this anonymous poem from the Book of the Dean of Lismore, probably dating from the early sixteenth century, is obvious.

    Yesterday I, Robert, set off
      to yonder monastery alone,
    but when I arrived I wasn't let in
      because I hadn't brought my wife.

43. Mairg Duine Do Chaill a Ghuth

Donnchadh Mór ó Leamhnacht

Is dòcha gun do rinneadh an dàn-fhacal seo, a tha air a ghleidh-eadh ann an Leabhar an Deadhain, mu thoiseach an t-siathamh linn deug.

Chan eil fiosrachadh sam bith againn a thaobh a' bhàird seo, Donnchadh Mór, seach gum b'ann à Leamhnachd a bha e, sgìre a bha fhathast gu math Gàidhealach na rè.

Mairg duine do chaill a ghuth,
   agus 'gá bhfuil sruth do dhán,
agus nach fhéad gabháil leó,
   agus nach eól bheith 'na thámh.

Agus nach seinn cor ná port,
   agus nach gabh gan locht laoidh,
agus nach sguir dá chruit bhinn,
   agus nach seinn mar as mian.   8

Is mairg nach sguir dá dhring drang,
   agus do-ní a rann do rádh,
agus nach cluintear a chruit,
   agus nach tuigthear a dhán.

'S mairg nach tabhair tóidh dá chéill,
   is nach congbhann é féin slán;
is mairg do-bheir treas go tric
   ar an mheas nach rig a lámh.   16

Dá mbeith mo mhian annsan mheas,
   nach soichinn do dhreap go h-ard,
do ghearrfainn an crann fá bhun,
   gé bé neach ara gcuir mairg.

Mairg.

Woe to Him Who Has Lost His Voice

This epigrammatic poem from the Book of the Dean of Lismore probably dates from the early sixteenth century.

We know nothing of the poet Donnchadh Mór other than his connection to the Lennox, which was still a strongly Gaelic area at this time.

Woe to him who has lost his voice
    yet has a constant stream of songs,
who is incapable of singing them
    but cannot hold his peace.

Who cannot play a reel or tune,
    nor recite a lay without going wrong,
won't stop strumming on his sweet harp,
    and cannot sing as he would like.

Woe to him who keeps on with his din
    and makes to recite his verse;
whose harp is not heard
    nor his poetry understood.

Woe to him who heeds not his sense,
    and doesn't keep himself intact;
woe to him who often makes to grab
    at the fruit his hand cannot reach.

If I desired the fruit
    that I couldn't reach by climbing high,
I would cut the tree at the root,
    whoever would suffer the woe.

Woe.

44. Tánaig Long ar Loch Raithneach

An Bard Mac An t-Saoir

Tha an dàn seo à Leabhar an Deadhain na eisimpleir ùidheil den ghràin-bhoireannach a bha cumanta ann an litreachas na Roinn Eòrpa aig deireadh nam Meadhan Aoisean. Tha an aoir seo, maille ri dàn eile a rinneadh leis an aon bhàrd, 'Créad í an long-sa ar Loch Inse?', a' nochdadh buaidh na h-aoire *Das Narren Schyff* (*Long nan Amadan*) aig Sebastian Brant, a dh'fhoillsicheadh ann am Basel ann an 1494 – deagh chomharra gu robh Gàidhealtachd nam Meadhan Aoisean dlùth-cheangailte ri litreachas agus cultar na Roinn Eòrpa anns an fharsaingeachd.

Tha e coltach gu robh An Bard Mac an t-Saoir beò anns a' chiad phàirt den t-siathamh linn deug. Cha tàinig a-nuas thugainn ach an dà dhàn a tha air an gleidheadh ann an Leabhar an Deadhain. Ach a rèir eachdraidh Chloinn an Tòisich, a chuireadh ri chèile anns an dàrna pàirt den t-seachdamh linn deug, chaidh am bàrd a thoirt am bruid ann an creach air Raineach agus an dèidh sin bha e ri bàrdachd molaidh do cheannardan Chloinn an Tòisich, na measg marbhrann air Fearchar mac Dhonnchaidh (†1514) agus Uilleam mac Lachlainn (†1515). Tha teans ann gu bheil ceangal air choreigin eadar am marbhrann seo agus dàn 69, 'Cumha Mhic an Tòisich'.

'S e aoir air bàta a tha an seo, mar chaochladh air a' mholadh air bàta a chithear ann an dàn 33. Tha an long seo air a h-ainmeachadh *Long na ndrochbhan* agus buinidh i do Mhac Cailein. Cha ghabhadh i a bhith air a togail air na h-adhbharan a tha air an ainmeachadh – duilleagan agus dealgan dris, luachair, moll eòrna, ₇ rl. Tha an sgioba rùisgte gun nàire anns na crainn. Tha am bàta gu soilleir 'urchoideach, ionnsaigh-theach', agus buinidh na boireannaich dhan Diabhal. A dh'aindeoin adhbhar na luinge, lughad an sgioba 's dèinnead na stoirme, tha i a' dèanamh astar mìorbhaileach. Gu soilleir 's e bàta os-nàdarrach a tha againn an seo, fo smachd bhana-bhuidseach. Bheir an dàn nar cuimhne sgeulachdan à beul-aithris far an tèid bana-bhuidsich gu muir ann am plaosg no ann an criathar, is iad a' glacadh èisg thar tomhais. 'S dòcha gu bheil

A Ship Has Come on Loch Rannoch

Together with a companion piece by the same author, 'Créad í an long-sa ar Loch Inse?' ('What ship is this on Loch Inch?'), this unusual poem from the Book of the Dean of Lismore exemplifies the misogyny that permeates much late medieval European literature. It also appears to show the influence of Sebastian Brant's *Das Narren Schyff* (*The Ship of Fools*), published in Switzerland in 1494, another indication that late medieval Gaeldom was readily exposed to the influences of Continental European literature.

The poet, who evidently belonged to the inferior poetic order of *baird*, was probably active in the early sixteenth century. These two poems in the Book of the Dean are his only works that appear to have survived. A history of the Mac an Tòisichs, compiled in the late seventeenth century, reports that the poet was kidnapped in a raid on Rannoch and thereafter composed poems for that clan, including an elegy on Fearchar mac Dhonnchaidh (†1514) and Uilleam mac Lachlainn (†1515). This elegy may possibly be connected to poem 69, 'Cumha Mhic an Tòisich'.

The poem is a satire of a ship, an inversion of the sort of praise of a ship and crew found in poem 33. The ship on Loch Rannoch is named as *Long na ndrochbhan* (the ship of evil women) and is purported to belong to MacCailéin. She is composed of materials impossible for boat building: planks of bramble leaves, rivets of bramble thorns, stringers of rushes, cables of barley husks and so on. The crew of naked women with dyed palms shamelessly expose themselves on the mast. The boat is harmful and hostile, her crew belong to Lucifer. Despite the impossible construction of the boat, the smallness of the crew, and the fierceness of the storm, she is making speedy and pernicious progress. This is clearly a supernatural boat, crewed by witches. It brings to mind traditional tales of witches going to sea in sieves or eggshells who catch unnatural amounts of fish by unnatural means, and also the superstition against women crewing boats, reflected until recent times in the tendency for

plathadh an seo cuideachd den amharas a tha aig iasgairean na
Gàidhealtachd chun an latha an-diugh mu dheidhinn boireann-
aich a bhith aig muir.

Tánaig long ar Loch Raithneach
go h-urchóideach ionnsaightheach,
   go h-aistreach éadtrom earlamh
   fairsing déadlach doidhealbhach.

An long soin do luadhtar linn
níor chum cumadóir romhainn;
   córaide a h-iongnadh d'innse,
   cia a fiodhradh dá foirinnse.   8

Buird do dhuilleógaibh dreasa
ó chorraibh a caoimhshleasa;
   [ardrach bhan as measa madh]
   tairngí dreasa 'gá dlúthadh.

Reanga láir do luachair chrín,
totaí coiseóga cláirmhín;
   ráimh do sgealbaibh raithnigh ruaidh
   ré gráin na fairge fionnfhuair.   16

Crann siuil do chuilcnibh calma
ré muir dúrdha danarra;
   tá slat bhréan ar gcúl an chrainn,
   connlán dúr ar a [   ].

Cáblaí do chaithibh eórna
ar srothaibh 'gá sírsheóladh;
   seól sreabhainn ris an chairbh dhuibh,
   deabhaidh searbh ag na srothaibh.   24

Long na ndrochbhan adeir cách
ris an luing go gcruth neamhghnách;
   cóir tuilleadh san lucht san luing
   ré h-ucht tuinne dá tarraing.

Hebridean fishermen to turn back home if they encountered a
woman on their way to their boats.

A ship appeared on Loch Rannoch,
injurious calamitous,
 roving nimble ready,
 wide daring inelegant.

The likes of that ship
no shipwright made before us;
 all the more reason to describe
 her wonders and her timbers.

Planks of bramble leaves
from the tips of her sideboards;
 [a crew (?) of women of foulest ways]
 bramble thorns, her rivets.

Floor stringers of withered rush,
thwarts of soft-sided grasses;
 oars of russet bracken strips,
 against the malice of the cold white ocean.

The mast is of stout bulrush
to withstand a sea, surly impudent;
 behind the mast is a rotten rope,
 a resentful crew on her [ ].

With cables of barley beard
she endlessly sails the currents,
 a membranous sail on the black ship,
 and the tides in bitter conflict.

Everyone calls this oddly shaped ship
The Ship of the Bad Women;
 the ship ought to have more crew on board
 to drive her against the billows.

Na mná measgacha mórdha
'na deireadh ar drochcomhrádh;
    sál tar a leas annsan luing,
    freastal gan ádh gan urraim.   32

Na mná loma náireach soin
ar leabaidh draighin deacair;
    taom tar a gcois annsan gcairbh,
    brosnadh ar an ghaoith ghléghairbh.

Na mná labhrach ar gach leth
di ar [   ] na cairbhe,
    iona ngurrach ré taobh tonn,
    gaoth [   ] fuighleach focal.   40

Na mná coitcheann corra soin
ós cionn cáich annsan gcrann-soin,
    a ndeireadh ré gaoith na ngleann,
    dlaoi teineadh fá dtimcheall.

Na mná uaibhreacha uile
i dtopchrann na caomhluinge,
    gan [chadódh] gan chairrge dhe
    acht fairrge ag fadódh feirge.   48

Torann tréan annsan mhuir mhóir,
fearg ar iarmhaint an aieoir;
    an cuthach ar cairrgibh clach,
    sruth na fairrge 'gá folach.

Frasa garbha ré gaoith Mháirt,
cairrge loma mán luathbháirc;
    fraoch ar tosgaraibh na dtonn,
    gaoth ag brosnadh má dtiomchall.   56

Anfadh garbh ré gaoith shneachta
'gá gcasadh mán chuideachta
    go muir téacht as nach tig long,
    sál ag téachtadh má dtiomcholl.

The women, drunk and vain,
in the stern gossiping lewdly;
   the brine swamps their thighs,
   a luckless and dishonourable service.

On a painful bed of thorns,
these shameful naked women;
   goaded on by the rombustuous wind,
   bilge wets their legs in the vessel.

On either side of the ship's deck(?)
these garrulous women;
   hunkered down beside the waves,
   the wind carrying(?) snatches of their babble.

Above the others on the mast
are other common odd women,
   their bums facing the wind of the glens,
   and a blaze of fire around them.

These insolent women are all
on the topmost mast of the vessel,
   with neither wrapping nor rock,
   the ocean kindling its anger.

Mighty thunder on the open sea,
in the airy firmament there is fury;
   stony rocks boil,
   the current concealing the vessel.

Boisterous showers before the March gale,
bare rocks around the swift vessel;
   the processions of waves are furious;
   the wind around them hurrying on.

A fierce storm with wind and snow
twists the waves round the cargo
   into a frozen sea no ship escapes,
   with the brine congealing about them.

Idir cheann is chois is láimh
gan díoth díola ar na drochmhnáibh;
ar cích chuan ar cairde a mach
ar fairrge, fríth bhuan bhadach.   64

Tá lán Luicifeir i luing
Mheic Cailéin, Donnchaidh dhearccuirr,
ar ghalraighe ar ghnáth ar dhath,
do mhnáibh na ndeárna ndathta.

45. Cá h-Ainm A-tá ar Fearghal Óg?

Gun urra

Tha e coltach gun do rinneadh an dàn seo air an fhile Ultach
Fearghal Óg Mac an Bhaird (ùghdar dàin 11) le co-shuirigheach
dha. Is dòcha gu bheil ceangal eadar an t-iomradh air Muile
anns an t-sreath mu dheireadh den dàn agus an turas a thug
Fearghal a dh'Alba ann an 1581 (faic an roi-ràdh ri dàn 11).
Dh'fhaodadh e bhith gun do rinneadh an dàn ann am Muile, oir
cha robh buntainneas follaiseach aig an fhile ris an eilean.

Gu mì-fhortanach, chan eil fhios ri fhaighinn a thaobh
ùghdar an dàin seo.

Cá h-ainm a-tá ar Fearghal Óg
cá taobh táinig an sgológ,
    nó cá ceird ré bhfuil an fear?
    do chuir fheirg ar ar n-aigneadh.

Labhuir go fóill re Fearghal:
ná biodh sé re sibheanradh,
    ná géabhadh cogur i gcúil
    's ná déanadh obar iomthnúidh.   8

Ná claonadh súil re suirghe —
beir chuige mar chomhairle:
    ná bíodh sgéal ag orradh air —
    ná cromadh méar ar mhállaibh.

Between head and foot and hand,
these bad women are not without payment;
  storm-stayed on the oceans's breast,
  on a vast waste, watery crested.

Clearly Lucifer's brood is in the barque
of round-eyed Donnchadh, son of Cailean,
  from the sickliness, habits and hue
  of the dyed-palmed women.

What Reputation Has Fearghal Óg?

This poem seems to have been composed by a love rival of the
famous Irish poet Fearghal Óg Mac an Bhaird (author of poem
11). The reference to a visit to Mull in the last line of the poem
corresponds to the evidence of Fearghal's visit to Scotland in
1581 (described in the introduction to that poem), and it may be
that the present poem was composed there, as the poet's
connection to the island seems to have been slight and it would
otherwise seem an unlikely thing to mention.

Nothing is known of the poem's author.

What reputation has Fearghal Óg,
where has the scholar come from,
  or what craft is the man about?
  He has put me in poor humour.

Speak yet to Fearghal:
let him not be dallying,
  nor whispering in an alcove,
  nor doing the work of jealousy

Take this to him as advice:
let his eye not wander,
  let him not lay a finger on gentle maids,
  let no patron have a story against him.

Do-chuala, dá gcreide sin,
gur fhéach Fearghal uair éigin —
do chráidh mo chroidhe dá chionn —
ar mhnáibh an toighe i dtigiom. 16

Ní h-é a-mháin: do dearbhadh damh —
cúis ar bhfeirge re Fearghal —
súil re maluirt, grádh ar ghrádh,
gur amhuirc lámh ar leannán.

Más é gur fhéach uirthe féin,
cá beag a mhéid do mhíchéill?
Rachadh ar dhéar do dháil damh
gan mhéar i láimh do leagadh. 24

Bean is mhionca mharbhas cách,
innis uaimsi don óglách;
an bheansoin dá dtarla a thol,
budh easbhaidh anma d'Fhearghal.

Do-chuala Fearghal, feacht n-aill,
gur marbhadh le mnaoi gcumuinn
a mhac samhla, eacht oile;
do-arla a cheart cosmhuile. 32

Och mo thruaighe féin Fearghal,
marbhthar é gan ainnearbhadh;
ní cás dúinn cré ós a chionn
dá mbé fa úir na h-Éirionn.

Dá gcuirthe sin ar seachrán,
fear dhéanta na ndíreachdhán,
ainm na mná lér marbhadh sinn
a-tá ar adhradh i n-Éirinn. 40

Deaghail bháis na beanadh di,
ná bíodh ag amhurc uirthe;
do mharbh sí duine re dán
do-bhí i Muile 'na mhacámh.

I have heard, if one can believe it,
that once Fearghal ogled at
    the woman of the house that I frequent,
    through it my heart is in torment.

Not only that: it was proven to me —
the cause of my anger with Fearghal —
    that expecting to trade love for love,
    he gazed on the hand of my sweetheart.

If it is true that he looked at her,
what is the extent of his folly?
    It would cause me to weep
    even though he never touched her.

Most often it is a woman kills a man;
tell this from me to the young stalwart:
    the woman on whom his desire fell
    will mean the death of his soul to Fearghal.

Fearghal must have heard at some time
how a man just like him was finished
    on another occasion by a lady-love;
    the very same has just occurred.

He will be killed without a doubt,
alas, I am sorry for Fearghal;
    no matter to me if he's covered with earth,
    as long as it's the soil of Ireland.

If that man were led astray,
the maker of strict poetry,
    the name of the woman by whom we were slain
    would be honoured in all Ireland.

May the separation of death not touch her,
let him not be ogling her,
    though she may have killed a poet
    who visited in Mull in his manhood.

46. Èatroman Muice o Hó

Niall Mòr MacMhuirich

Bha Niall Mòr MacMhuirich (*c.*1550–an dèidh 1613) air aon de
na filidh mu dheireadh a bhuineadh do Chloinn Mhuirich. Tha
co-dhiù ceithir dàin da chuid air tighinn a-nuas thugainn, dán
grádha ainmeil nam measg (àireamh 53). A rèir dualchas an
teaghlaich, bha ochd ginealaich dheug eadar Niall Mòr agus
Muireadhach Albanach, a thàinig a dh'Alba còrr is trì cheud
bliadhna ro linn Nèill Mhòir. Tha e coltach gun do dh'fhàg an
teaghlach Cinn Tìre, far an robh iad nam filidh do Chlann
Domhnaill nan Eilean, mu linn Nèill, no beagan roimhe; thàinig
iad do dh'Uibhist a Deas, far an d'fhuair iad fearann ann an
Stadhlaigearraidh bho Mhac 'ic Ailein.

Anns an aoir seo air a' phìob tha Niall Mòr a' cleachdadh na
Gàidhlig dhùthchasaich seach a' chànain litreachail a chleachd e
ann an dàin eile. Chan eil e idir na annas gum biodh file àrd-
nòsach a' dèanamh dhàn na b' aotruime maille ris na dàin
fhoirmeil aige.

> Èatroman muice o hó,
> Air a shéideadh gu h-an-mhór,
> > A' cheud mhàla nach raibh binn
> > Thàinig o thùs na dìlinn.
>
> Bha seal re èatroman mhuc,
> Ga lìonadh suas as gach pluic;
> > Craiceann sean mhuilt 'na dhiaidh sin
> > Re searbhadas is re dùrdail.   8
>
> Cha raibh 'n uair sin anns a' phìob
> Ach siùnnsar agus aon lìop,
> > Agus maide chumadh na fuinn
> > Do'm b' cho-ainm an sumaire.

A History of the Pipes from the Beginning

Niall Mòr MacMhuirich (*c*.1550–after 1613) was one of the last great MacMhuirich poets. At least four of his poems have survived, including a famous *dán grádha* (poem 53). According to family tradition he was directly descended, through eighteen generations, from the great Muireadhach Albanach Ó Dálaigh, who had come to Scotland more than three hundred years previously. About Niall's time, or slightly earlier, the family migrated from Kintyre, where they had served the Lords of the Isles, to Uist, where they received land at Stadhlaigearraidh in South Uist as hereditary patrons to the Clann Raghnaill branch of Clann Domhnaill.

This satirical poem on the subject of the pipes is composed in the vernacular of the time rather than the formal literary language. Derick Thomson has described it 'as an early example of village poetry almost, featuring its specific characters and using a combination of wit, invective, and bawdry to make its points'. It was by no means unusual for learned poets to produce less elevated 'off-duty compositions' of various kinds.

The bladder of a pig, *o hó*,
blown up to burst,
    was the first discordant bag,
    to come before the Flood.

A spell of using bladders of pigs,
blowing them up with bulging cheeks;
    after that an old wether skin,
    good for making a raucous buzz.

Then there was nothing to the pipes
but a chanter and a mouth-piece,
    and a stick that would hold the notes
    known also as the drone.

Tamall doibh 'na dhiaidh sin
Do fhuair ais-inntleachd inneil:
    Feam fada leabhar garbh
    Do dhùrdan reamhar ro-shearbh.   16

Ar faghail an dùrdain sheirbh
Is a' ghoithinn gu loma-léir
    Chraobh-sgaoil a' chrannaghail mar sin
    Re searbhadas is re dùrdan.

Pìob sgreadain Iain MhicArtair
    Mar eun curra air dol air n-ais
Làn ronn 's i labhar luirgneach,
    Com galair mar ghuilbnich ghlais.   24

Pìob Dhòmhnaill do cheòl na cruinne
    Crannaghail bhreòite as breun roimh shluagh:
Cathadh a mhùin don mhàla ghrodaidh,
    Fuidh 'n t-sùil ghrainde robaich ruaidh.

Ball Dhòmhnaill is dos na pìoba,
    Dà bhéist chursta a' chlaiginn mhaoil:
Seinnidh corr-ghluineach a ghafainn,
    Fuaim truilich an tafainn sheirbh.   32

Do-cheòl do bhi 'n Ifrinn ìochdrach
    Foghar pìoba nan dos cruaidh,
Culaidh a dhùsgadh nan deamhan
    Lùgail do mheòir reamhair ruaidh.

Mar fheasgar an Earrach mìn,
    Mar mhart caoilidh teachd gu tlus,
Thig sgreadadh a' chruim riabhaich
    Mar bhraoim tòine 'n Diabhail duibh.   40

Chuir Bhènus bha seal an Ifrinn
    Mar dhearbhachd sgeul gu fearaibh Dhomhain,
Gur coranaich bhan is pìob-ghleadhair
    Dà leannan ciùil cluas nan deomhan.

But after a while they discovered
a wicked up-grading for the device:
 a long, coarse, sagging rump
 to increase its raucous throaty buzz.

After achieving this coarse droning
and the shrill and terrible reed
 the contraption could then cast wider
 its skirling and its humming.

Iain MacArtair's shrieking pipes
 are like a peewit flying backwards,
full of spittle, loud and lanky,
 a diseased belly like a grizzled curlew.

Of all the world's music, Domhnall's pipes
 are the sickest contraption, stinking in a crowd:
spraying their piss from the rotting bag,
 under the ugly ragged rusty hole.

Domhnall's organ and the drone of the pipes,
 two wheezing beasts from a bald pate:
the lanky heron plays his bent reed
 with the wretched noise of harsh barking.

The cacophony of deepest Hell,
 the blast of pipes of the harsh drones,
a device to waken the devils,
 bending your stubby red fingers.

Like an afternoon in gentle Spring,
 like a starving cow reaching comfort,
comes the grating of the brindled bulge
 like a fart from the Devil's backside.

Venus, who was for a while in Hell,
 sent confirmation to the men on earth
that the dirges of women and the roar of pipes
 are the two darlings of music in the devils' ears.

THE LEARNED TRADITION

LOVE

47. I mBrat an Bhrollaigh Ghil-Se

Fearchar Ó Maoil Chiaráin

Is e an dàn gràidh ealanta seo an aon phìos bàrdachd a tha
againn bho Fhearchar Ó Maoil Chiaráin, file òg a chaidh a
mharbhadh an Èirinn a tha mar chuspair a' mharbhrainn
ainmeil a rinn athair (dàn 30). Is dòcha gur ann anns a'
cheathramh no anns a' chòigeamh linn deug a bha Fearchar beò,
agus is cinnteach gur ann ro 1500. Chan eil dad anns an òran
fhèin a tha ag innse dhuinn gur e Albannach a bha ann, agus tha
e follaiseach gun do rinneadh an dàn ann an Èirinn, is dòcha ri
linn cuairt bhàrdail.

I mbrat an bhrollaigh ghil-se
ní bhiadh an dealg droighin-se,
   dá mbeith, a Mhór bhéildearg bhinn,
   an éindealg d'ór i nÉirinn.

San mbrat-sa níor chóir do chur
acht dealg d'fhionndruine uasal,
   nó dealg iongantach d'ór cheard,
   a Mhór bhionnfhoclach bhéildearg.   8

A fholt lag ar lí an ómra,
a chur id bhrat bhreacórdha,
   a stuaigh chobhsaidh nár chealg fear,
   níor chosmhail dealg don droighean.

Níor churtha, a chnú mo chroidhe,
id bhrat eangach iolbhuidhe,
   a ghruaidh dhearg do-ghéabhadh geall,
   acht dealg do-ghéanadh Gaibhneann.   16

A ghruadh chorcra do char mé,
gan dealg óir acht an uair-se
   ar feadh na huaire, a ghlac ghlan,
   do bhrat uaine do b'annamh.

In the Cloak on This Bright Breast

This elegant love poem is the only known surviving composition by Fearchar Ó Maoil Chiaráin, whose tragic death in Ireland is lamented by his father in poem 30. It is not known when Fearchar lived, though it was probably sometime in the fourteenth or fifteenth century, and certainly before about 1500. Nothing in the poem itself reveals his Scottish origins, and it was evidently composed in Ireland, probably during a poetic *cuairt*.

In the cloak on this bright breast
there should be no brooch of blackthorn
    if, red-lipped sweet-voiced Mòr,
    there were a brooch of gold in Ireland.

It was not right to put in this cloak
anything but a brooch of noble bronze alloy
    or a clasp of gold wondrous-wrought,
    O red-lipped Mòr, sweet-talking.

O wispy hair of amber tints,
a brooch of blackthorn is not fitting
    to put in your cloak of gold checks,
    O steadfast pillar who cheated no person.

Let nothing be put, O kernel of my heart,
in your chequered cloak of many yellows,
    O red cheek which would win a pledge,
    but a brooch made by the smith, Goibhniu.

O rosy cheek which I have loved,
never before did you lack a gold fastening;
    O pure hand, scarce in all that time
    was your green cloak ever without one.

48. Atá Fleasgach ar mo Thí

Iseabal Ní Mheic Cailéin

B'e bean-uasal ann an cùirt Inbhir Aora a bha ann an Iseabal Ní Mheic Cailéin; a rèir coltais b' i bean no nighean Chailein, ciad iarla Earra Ghàidheal (†1493). Bha i air aon de na bana-bhàird Ghàidhealach as tràithe a tha air a h-ainmeachadh. Chan eil fios deimhinne aig na sgoilearan an ionnan 'Iseabal Ní Mheic Cailéin' agus 'Contaois Oirir Ghaoidheal, Isibeul'; tha an t-ainm 'Iseabal Ní Mheic Cailéin' mu choinneimh dàin 48 agus 49 anns an làmh-sgrìobhainn ach 'Contaois [*Countess*, no bantighearna] Oirir Ghaoidheal, Isibeul' mu choinneimh an dàin dhrabasta 'Éistidh, a lucht an tighe-se', anns am faighear 'scéal na mbod mbríoghmhar' agus moladh sònraichte air bod a sagairt phearsanta.

Thòisich an traidisean de *amour courtois* no gràdh cùirteach anns an aonamh linn deug ann am Provence, is dòcha fo bhuaidh bàrdachd-ghaoil na h-Arabais. Sgaoil na nòsan seo air feadh na Roinn Eòrpa thairis air na linntean agus thàinig iad a dh'Èirinn agus a dh'Alba fo bhuaidh nan Normannach. Tha fada a bharrachd eisimpleirean air tighinn a-nuas thugainn à Èirinn na à Alba, ach tha na 'dánta grádha' a tha air an gleidheadh ann an Leabhar an Deadhain anabarrach luachmhor, gu h-àraidh a chionn 's gun cluinnear annta guth soilleir nam boireannach, rud nach fhaighear anns na dàin Èireannach. Tha e anabarrach inntinneach gu robh (a rèir coltais) uiread de shaorsa aig mnathan-uasal na Gàidhealtachd anns an rè ud a thaobh chùisean feise is drabastachd.

There's a Young Man in Pursuit of Me

Iseabal Ní Mheic Cailéin was a high-ranking noblewoman in the court of the earls of Argyll – either the wife (who died in 1510) of Cailean, the first earl (who died in 1493), or his daughter. She is one of the earliest historically attested women poets in the Gaelic world, along with Aithbhreac inghean Corcadail (author of poem 28), who flourished *c.* 1470. She is also one of very few named women to have poems survive in the courtly love genre in either Scotland or Ireland.

The tradition of *amour courtois* or courtly love emerged in the eleventh century in the south of France, probably with origins in Arabic love poetry. It started as an elevation of romantic love and was adapted in feudal Europe to the *mores* of chivalry. The longing of a man for an unavailable, socially superior woman was seen to reflect the longing of the soul for reunification with God. Such a love, uncontaminated by consummation, was seen as ennobling. The courtly love style spread from the troubadours of Provence to the trouvères of northern France and from there to England and into the learned Gaelic circles of Ireland and Scotland. Gaelic examples are more playful than many of their counterparts, as if a combination of tone and motifs, rather than the whole philosophy of chivalrous love had been transmitted. Unlike native Gaelic love poetry, Gaelic courtly love poems are short, elegant and succinct. The motif appears of love as an illness. The tone is often secret and adulterous, the experience made all the more delectable because it is illicit. A woman's name might be encoded in the poem; the poet may envy the gift he sends his lover, for it can touch her while he cannot. The studied manner of this genre, however, produced a backlash, particularly among the Goliards, or student clerics of Europe. This style was also transmitted to Gaelic culture, and plenty of satiric examples exist where the conventions of *amour courtois* are inverted. Bawdry is the most extreme example of this, and examples survive from the House of Argyll in the Book of the Dean of Lismore, including poem 41 here and the poem 'Éistidh, a lucht an tighe-se', probably composed by Iseabal, concerning her priest's sexual prowess. Iseabal's work suggests that aristocratic women at the time were allowed considerable freedom of speech.

Atá fleasgach ar mo thí
    a Rí na ríogh go rí leis!
a bheith sínte ré mo bhroinn
    agus a choim ré mo chneis!

Dá mbeith gach ní mar mo mhian,
    ní bhiadh cian eadrainn go bráth,
gé beag sin dá chur i gcéill,
    's nach tuigeann sé féin mar tá.   8

Acht ní éadtrom gan a luing,
    sgéal as truaighe linn 'nar ndís:
esan soir is mise siar,
    mar nach dtig ar riar a rís.

49. Is Mairg dá nGalar an Grádh

Iseabal Ní Mheic Cailéin

Seo dán grádha eile le Iseabal Ní Mheic Cailéin a' tha a'
cleachdadh ìomhaigh a' ghaoil mar ghalar, cleas a bha air leth
cumanta anns an stoidhle bàrdachd seo. Mar as trice, gheibhear
sealladh bho fhear seach bho bhean, agus am bàrd a'
mìneachadh gu bheil e air leòn a' bhàis fhaighinn, no gur truagh
nach do rugadh dall e, nach fhaighear faothachadh ach leis a'
bhàs fhèin, ach fiù an sin, gun seas an gaol maireann a bhuail e
eadar e agus Dia. Tha co-dhùnadh Iseabail nas saoghalta, ge-tà,
agus i a' dèanamh nàdar de bhagairt air fear a gaoil.

Is mairg dá ngalar an grádh,
    gé bé fáth fá n-abrainn é;
deacair sgarachtainn ré pháirt;
    truagh an cás i bhfeilim féin.

An grádh-soin tugas gan fhios,
    ó's é mo leas gan a luadh,
mara bhfaigh mé furtacht tráth,
    biaidh mo bhláth go tana truagh.   8

There's a young man in pursuit of me,
    O King of Kings, may he have success!
Would he were stretched out by my side
    with his body pressing against my breast!

If everything were as I would wish,
    no distance would ever cause us separation,
though that is all too little to say
    with him not yet knowing the situation.

But it isn't easy if his ship doesn't come,
    for the two of us it's a wretched matter:
he is East and I am West,
    so what we desire can never again happen.

Woe to the One Whose Sickness is Love

Another courtly love poem by Iseabal Ní Mheic Cailéin that plays with the common conceit of love as an illness. The Lilium Medicinae, a medical textbook of 1303, even cites the disease of love as a condition to which noblemen are particularly prone. The conceit describes the poet as fatally wounded by the shafts of beauty; he had rather been born blind; death is the only release possible but, even then, love will stand between himself and God. Other poems of course declare the anthithesis. Iseabal's poem here is interesting in standing somewhere between the two extremes: she does not present herself entirely as the victim, and gathers some self-possession in the veiled threat of the final verse.

Woe to the one whose sickness is love,
    no matter the grounds I might present,
hard it is to get free of its hold,
    sorry the state I'm in.

That love I have given in secret,
    it being better not to declare it,
unless I find relief before long,
    my bloom will grow wan and wretched.

An fear-soin dá dtugas grádh,
   's nach féadtar a rádh ós n-aird,
dá gcuireadh sé mise i bpéin,
   gomadh dó féin bhus céad mairg.

Mairg.

50. 'S Luaineach mo Chadal A-Nochd

Eachann Mòr MacGill'Eathain

Tha cuid air cumail a-mach gun do rinneadh an t-òran seo mu 1520 le Eachann Mòr († *c.*1571), an t-aonamh ceann-cinnidh deug aig Cloinn Ghill'Eathain Dhubhaird agus bràthair Ailein nan Sop (cuspair dàin 67), ach tha gu leòr de theagamh anns a' chùis. Chan eil boireannach sam bith ga ainmeachadh anns an òran fhèin, ach mas e Eachann Mòr a rinn e tha a h-uile teans ann gur e a bhean a tha fo cheist, Mòr, nighean Alasdair (mac Eòin Chathanaich) MhicDhomhnaill Dhùn Naomhaig. B'e Eachann seanair Lachlainn Mhòir, a chaidh a mharbhadh aig Blàr Thràigh Ghruinneard ann an 1598 (faic dàn 74).

Ma chumadh e tràth anns an t-siathamh linn deug, feumaidh gun do rinneadh atharrachaidhean is ath-dhealbhadh air thairis air na linntean. A dh'aindeoin sin, tha coltasan eadar an t-òran seo agus na dánta grádha a bha measail aig na h-uaislean aig deireadh nam Meadhan Aoisean.

'S luaineach mo chadal a-nochd,
   Ge beò mi, cha bheò mo thlachd,
Mo chridh' air searg ann am uchd,
   Air dubhadh mar an gual gu beachd.

'S ann san Earrach an seo shìos,
   Tha 'bhean as meachair' mìngheal cruth,
Deud air dhreach cailce na beul
   'S binne na 'n teud-chiùil a guth.

8

That man to whom I have given love,
(this should not be said out loud)
if he should ever cause me hurt,
may he suffer a hundred times the woe.

Woe

Restless my Sleep Tonight

This song, perhaps dating from *c.*1520, has sometimes been attributed to Eachann Mòr MacGill'Eathain († *c.*1571), eleventh chief of the MacGill'Eathains of Duart and nephew of the infamous Ailean nan Sop (subject of poem 67), but his authorship is a great deal less than certain. Although no woman is named, it is believed to be addressed to his wife Mòr, daughter of Alasdair (mac Eòin Chathanaich) MacDhomhnaill of Dunyveg and the Glens.

The song has almost certainly undergone some degree of change over the centuries, as its language and structure might otherwise suggest a rather later provenance. Derick Thomson has spoken of its 'chiseled elegance', and it shows certain similarities to other courtly verse of the period.

Eachann Mòr was the grandfather of Lachlann Mòr MacGill'Eathain, whose death is lamented in poem 74.

Restless my sleep tonight,
though I live, not so my joy,
my heart has withered in my breast,
has gone black like a lump of coal.

Lying here in the Earrach below
is the gentle woman of soft white form,
teeth like chalk in her mouth,
sweeter than harp-strings her voice.

Mar chobhar an uisge ghlain,
    Mar shlios eala ri sruth mear,
Glan leug mar an cathadh-cuir,
    Dh'fhàs mi gun chabhair ad chean.

Ur-shlat ùr nam fàinne fionn,
    'S do bhàrr air fiamh glan an òir,
Do ghruaidh mar an caoran dearg,
    Air lasadh mar dhealbh nan ròs.   16

Meòir fhionna air bhasa bàna,
    Uchd solais as àille snuadh,
An gaol a thugas duit ra luathas,
    Ochan nan och! 's cruaidh an càs.

Cha dìrich mi aonach no beann,
    Mo cheum tha air lagadh gu trom,
Iuchair na Cist' tha mar spàirn,
    Tha siud cho ìosal ri m'bhonn.   24

Mar ghràinne-mullaich an dèis,
    Mar ghallan san òg-choill' a' fàs,
Mar ghrian ri falach nan reult,
    Cha lèir bean eile air do sgàth.

51. Tha Bean an Crìch Albainn Fhuar

Alasdair (mac Ruaidhrí) MacMhathain

Tha teagamh ann a thaobh eachdraidh agus ùghdar an òrain seo cuideachd; a rèir dualchais b'e Alasdair (mac Ruairidh) MacMhathain a rinn e. Tha e coltach gu robh Alasdair mar cheann-cinnidh Chloinn MhicMhathain Loch Aillse mu thois-each an t-siathamh linn deug; ghabh e pàirt anns an ar-a-mach às leth Dhomhnaill Dhuibh MhicDhomhnaill ann an 1505–06 (faic dàn 29). Ann an làmh-sgrìobhainn bhon naoidheamh linn deug anns an deach an teacs a ghleidheadh thathar ga

Like foam on a pure loch,
    like a swan's flank by a running stream,
a bright jewel like drifting snow,
    I have grown helpless with lack of you.

Fresh shoot of the fair rings,
    your hair burnished bright like gold,
like the rowan berry your cheek,
    flushed like the colour of the rose.

Fair fingers on fair palms,
    bright breast, loveliest of hue,
Alas, sorry is my plight
    to speak of the love I gave you.

I climb neither mountain nor hill,
    my step has grown heavy and weak,
Iuchair na Cist' is too much
    though it is of no great height.

Like the topmost ear of the corn,
    like a sapling growing in the wood,
like the sun blotting out the stars,
    you make other women disappear.

There is a Lady in the Cold Land of Scotland

Although the ascription is somewhat doubtful, this satirical poem on love lost has been attributed to Alasdair (mac Ruairidh) MacMhathain, apparently chief of the MacMhathains of Lochalsh during the early sixteenth century. Alasdair is best known for his participation in the rising of Domhnall Dubh MacDhomhnaill in 1505–06, an attempted restoration of the Lordship of the Isles following its forfeiture in 1493 (discussed in the introduction to poem 29). In the nineteenth-century

ainmeachadh mar 'Admiral Sir Alexander Matheson', ach chan eil e idir cinnteach cò às a thàinig na tiotalan seo.

Am beachd an Urramaich Uilleam MacMhathain, is e dàn measgaichte a tha ann, anns a bheil dà shreath air an cur còmhla, agus sgeulachd nan eun anns na rannan mu dheireadh a' dèanamh mìneachadh air choreigin air a' chunntas air còmhstri a tha ga dhèanamh anns a' chiad cheithir rannan.

Tha bean an crìch Albainn fhuar,
　　ge fada bhuam i gur gearr;
Dé! cha chreidinn air mo chùl
　　gum bitheadh i dhùinn am feall.

Gheibhmid a h-airgead 's a h-òr,
　　gheibhmid sìoda 's sròl gu tiugh
bhon té sin tholl mi le gaol,
　　nach seall rium ach faoin an-diugh.　　　　　8

Bean is dà chridhe 'na cliabh,
　　nar leigeadh sian mi 'na dàil;
'n dara cridhe leam gu lùb,
　　's cridh' eil' air mo chùl dam chnàmh.

Is ionann sin 's mar dh'fhàs a' bhean,
　　an deud geal 's am fabhra rèidh —
a rùin, ged bhiodh tu 'nad thosd,
　　gum bi dhùinne cloch fo sgèith.　　　　　16

Seachd bliadhna 's deacair d'an eun
　　tolladh le bheul anns a' chraoibh;
'n obair sin ged bha i trom,
　　cha do sguir gun d' tholl e taobh.

Ach tuig-se gur mise tè
　　'gan robh fios air beus nam mnà;
on labhair mi le mo bheul,
　　agam féin bha fios mar bhà.　　　　　24

manuscript in which the poem is preserved, Alasdair is styled 'Admiral Sir Alexander Matheson', perhaps because he held some kind of maritime command in the Domhnall Dubh rising. The basis for the title 'Sir' is also unclear.

William Matheson suggests it is a composite poem. If so, the poet may have felt the story of the birds in the last four verses illustrated the war of the sexes of the first four verses. Just as the woman now ignores the poet, so does the woodpecker ignore the starling once he has completed her nest. The logic, though not the biology, is sound.

> There's a lady in cold Scotland's bounds,
>   who though far from me is near;
> God! I would never have believed
>   she would deceive me behind my back.
>
> I would receive her silver and gold,
>   I would receive satin and thick silk
> from one who pierced me with love,
>   who today scarcely gives me a look.
>
> A woman with two hearts in her breast —
>   forbid anything to let me near her!
> one of her hearts to me inclines,
>   the other mocks me behind my back.
>
> Like that has the woman grown,
>   of the white tooth and the fine brow;
> though you might be silent, love,
>   I have a stone below my wing.
>
> For seven difficult years the bird
>   worked with its beak in the tree;
> though the work was hard, he did not stop
>   till he had hollowed out its side.
>
> But I am a woman, understand,
>   who knew women's ways;
> ever since I learned to speak
>   I knew exactly how they were.

Is mise 'n t-snag on fhiudhaidh fhuar,
   's gur h-e 'n duin' ud shuas an druid;
ionmhainn leamsa, a chùil duinn,
   cha mhisde leam ged a thuig.

An uair a b'ullamh an nead
   thàinig an t-snag on taobh thall,
's gun d'fhuadaich i 'n druid don t-sliabh,
   mar nach biodh i riamh sa chrann.   32

52. Trèig t'Uaisle 's Na Bi Rinn

Eòin Carsuel(?)

Tha teans ann gun do rinneadh an dàn aotrom seo, anns a bheil
am bàrd ri nàdar de spaisdearachd le bean-uasal neo-ainmichte,
le Seon Carsuel, ùghdar/eadar-theangair an leabhair dhiadhaidh
Foirm na n-Urrnuidheadh (faic dàn 9). Ach chan eil fianais
dheimhinne againn a thaobh ùghdar no eachdraidh an dàin.

Trèig t'uaisle 's na bi rinn,
   a bhean an fhuilt fhinn nan lùb;
gur fianaiseach sinn a-ghnàth
   bhith ag ràdh gur uasal thu.
'S mùinte dhuit a bhith nad thosd,
   a bhean an fhuilt chochallaich chruinn;
ma bha thusa shliochd Chairbre Chais
   ta mise shliochd Art mhic Cuinn.   8

Sliochd Bhriain Bhoirbh ma ta thu,
   taimse shliochd Nèill nan naoi Ghiall;
ge dubh leat do mhala chaol,
   is duibhe na sin lì an lòin.

I am the woodpecker from the chill wood,
    the starling, that one above;
beloved to me, O brown locks,
    I am none the worse if he finds out.

When the nest was complete
    the woodpecker came from afar
and banished the starling to the hill
    as if he were never in the tree.

Stop Boasting of Your Noble Birth

This satirical anti-courtly-love poem, in which the poet engages in a sort of flyting with the woman he addresses, has sometimes been ascribed to Seon Carsuel (John Carswell), the sixteenth-century cleric best known for *Foirm na n-Urrnuidheadh*, his adaptation of the *Book of Common Order* (see poem 9). His authorship must certainly be open to considerable doubt, however.

Stop boasting of your noble birth,
    O fair lady of the cascading curls;
I will always be able to vouchsafe
    to your being of noble stock.
You are counselled to keep quiet,
    O lady of the round hood-like hair;
though you be of the line of Cairbre Cas,
    I am of the line of Art mac Cuinn.

If you are descended from Brian Boru,
    from Niall of the Nine Hostages am I,
though black you think your slender brow,
    blacker than they the blackbird's hue.

Ge dearg leat do leaca thaobh,
　's leòir deirgead nan caora con;
's ge geal leat do bhràghad bàn,
　's geal an sneachda 's beag a luach.　　　16

Ta 'm buaghalan buidhe fàs
　mas buidhe na 'n t-òr do ghruag;
mas e 's gun cuireadh tu grèis
　sgrìobhainn le peann geòidh gu luath;
mas e 's gun gabhadh tu dàn
　chuirinn le sgeul càch 'nan suain.

53. Soraidh Slán don Oidhche A-Réir

Niall Mòr MacMhuirich

Eu-coltach ris na dàin gu h-àrd, seo dán grádha a rinneadh le file foghlaimte, ball de Chloinn Mhuirich (agus ùghdar dàin 46). Gheibhear ann, is dòcha, sealladh air na nòsan is na riaghailtean neo-dheachdte a chuartaich na gnothaichean seo ann an cùirtean nan triathan Gàidhealach mu dheireadh an t-siathamh linn deug.

　Is e seòrsa de *aubade* a tha ann, òran a tha ga sheinn le dithis leannan agus iad a' dealachadh anns a' chamhanaich. Tha cuid de na h-ìomhaighean is na cleachdaidhean seo a' leantainn stoidhle àbhaisteach nan dánta grádha, ach aig an aon àm tha e a' cur cuideam sònraichte air tuigse agus sàsachadh pearsanta.

Soraidh slán don oidhche a-réir
　fada géar ag dul ar ccúl;
dá ndáiltí mo chur i ccroich,
　is truagh nach í a-nocht a tús.

Though you consider your cheeks are red,
   the redness of the dogberry were enough,
and though you think your throat is white,
   snow is white and little its worth.

The yellow ragwort is void
   if yellower than gold your hair;
if you would embroider a cloth,
   I'd write quickly with the quill;
if you would recite a poem,
   I'd enrapture all with a tale.

Farewell Ever to Last Night

This famous poem is another example of the courtly love tradition, in this instance composed by a trained professional poet. It may convey a sense of the protocol surrounding such matters in a Highland court of the late sixteenth century.

The poem is an *Aubade*, a song sung at dawn by parting lovers. Conventional courtly love motifs, such as the lingering gaze and the exquisite agony of distance and denial, are combined to produce a poem of great tension. The poem seems to cut across the bounds of the genre to express something far bigger about individual fulfilment in the face of society's *mores*. It makes a claim long before the advent of Romanticism for the integrity of experience and memory in the face of disintegration and opprobrium. The appeal to Mary in the final verse is a common conceit in medieval religious poetry, that Mary, being human, has a greater tolerance of man's foibles than does God.

A satirical song on the subject of the pipes attributed to Niall Mòr is published here as poem 46.

Farewell ever to last night,
   far and sharp it recedes;
though I were to be hanged for it,
   sad its beginning were not tonight.

Atáid dias is tigh-se a-nocht
    ar nách ceileann rosg a rún;
gion go bhfuilid béal re béal
    is géar géar silleadh a súl. 8

Tocht an ní chuireas an chiall
    ar shilleadh díochra na súl
cá feirrde an tocht do-ní an béal
    sgéal do-ní an rosg ar a rún?

Uch ní léigid lucht na mbréag
    smid tar mo bhéal, a rosg mall;
tuig an ní-se adeir mo shúil
    is tú insan chúil úd thall. 16

'Cuinnibh dhuinn an oidhche a-nocht
    truagh gan sinn mar so gu bráth,
ná léig an mhaidean is-teach,
    éirigh 's cuir a-mach an lá'.

Uch, a Mhuire, a bhuime sheang,
    ós tú is ceann ar gach cléir,
tárthaigh agus gabh mo lámh —
    soraidh slán don oidhche a-réir. 24

There are two in this house tonight
    whose secret their eyes do not hide;
without their being mouth to mouth,
    keen, keen is the gazing of their eyes.

Silence is what makes sense
    of the intense look of the eyes;
what good is the silence of the lips
    if the eyes tell the tale of their love?

Alas, the hypocrites allow no word
    to cross my lips, O gentle eye;
understand what my eyes say
    as you sit in the corner over there.

'Tonight remember our night,
    alas we will not be ever thus;
do not let the morning in,
    get up and chase away the day.'

Och, Mary, foster-mother slim,
    since you are the patron of every poet,
rescue me and take me by the hand —
    farewell ever to last night.

THE LEARNED TRADITION

BALLADS

54. Arann na n-Aiged n-Imda

Gun urra (am beul Caílte)

Bha Gàidheil Alba agus Èireann anabarrach measail air sgeulachdan is laoidhean na Fèinne bho na Meadhan Aoisean air adhart. Chaidh mòran dhàn a leigeil air Oisean, mac Fhinn mhic Cumhaill, gu h-àraidh an fheadhainn a nochd ann an *Accalam na Senórach*, còmhradh ainmeil a rinneadh eadar Oisean agus Naomh Pàdraig, nuair a bha Oisean air maireann 'an dèidh na Fèinne'. Tha an laoidh a leanas air a thoirt bhon *Acallam*, anns a bheil an laoch Caoilte ga aithris an dèidh do Phàdraig faighneachd dheth 'Dè an t-sealg as fheàrr a fhuair an Fhèinn riamh an Èirinn no an Alba?'

B'e Oisean a' bhunait do 'Ossian' aig Seumas Mac a' Phearsain, agus b'e 'Fingal' a rinn e de dh'Fhionn. A dh'aindeoin nan deasbadan air dè dìreach a rinn Mac a' Phearsain, tha an laoidh seo, agus beartas dualchas na Fèinne, a' dearbhadh nach ann à mac-meanmna Mhic a' Phearsain a thàinig Oisean/Ossian, a dh'aindeoin nam beachdan aineolach a tha fhathast rin cluinntinn an siud 's an seo.

Is e pàirt de 'aoibhneas' Arainn mar a chumas e sealgaireachd ris an Fhèinn, gan cumail ann am biadh agus ri cur-seachadan gaisgeil. Taobh a-muigh nan dàn tràtha a chaidh a dhèanamh leis na manaich agus, a-rithist, taobh a-muigh bàrdachd nam Fuadaichean, tha bàrdachd Ghàidhlig a' toirt dhaoine a-staigh mar phàirt de nàdar; chan eil nàdar air a shamhlachadh mar àite gun daoine.

Arann na n-aiged n-imda,
    tadall fairce rea formna,
ailén i mbiadta buidne,
    druimne i ndergthar gaí gorma.

Aige baetha ara bennaib,
    mónainn maetha 'na mongaib,
uisce uar ina haibnib,
    mes ara dairgib donnaib.   8

Arran's Hunting

Fianaigheachd, or stories and poems relating to Fionn mac Cumhaill and his warriors (the *Fèinn* in Scottish Gaelic, sometimes Anglicised as 'Fians' or 'Fingalians'), was immensely important and hugely popular in both Ireland and Gaelic Scotland from the middle of the medieval period onwards. Many poems were attributed to Fionn's son Oisín (the Irish Gaelic form; Oisein or Oisean in vernacular Scottish Gaelic), most famously *Accalam na Senórach*, the dialogue between Oisín, the only survivor of the earlier heroic age, and Saint Patrick, from which this twelfth-century poem in praise of Arran is taken. The poem is placed in the mouth of the Fenian warrior Caílte, as part of his response to Patrick's question 'What was the best hunt, whether in Ireland or in Scotland, that the Fèinn ever took part in?'

Oisín was of course the Ossian of James MacPherson, and Fingal was his name for Fionn. Whatever the precise nature of MacPherson's reworkings, embellishments, recreations, and reimaginings, the existence of texts like this one, composed centuries before his birth and attributed to Oisín, demonstrate that this figure was by no means a creation of MacPherson's own imagination, as some ill-informed commentators still endeavour to make out.

Part of the 'delightfulness' of Arran is its suitability for human heroic activity and sustenance. Apart from the early stage of eremetic poetry and the late stage of Clearance poetry, Gaelic poetry includes people as part of nature. Nature, with a few exceptions, is not constructed as 'an absence of people'.

> Arran of the many red-deer,
>   ocean reaching to her shoulders;
> island where warriors are nourished,
>   ridge where blue spears are blooded.

> Frisky hinds on her summits,
>   ripe blaeberries in her thickets,
> cold water in her rivers,
>   acorns on her brown oak-trees.

Mílchoin innti is gagair,
   sméra is áirne dub droigin,
dlúith a fraig rena fedaib,
   daim oc dedail 'má doirib.

Díglaim corcra ara cairrcib,
   fér cen locht ara lercaib,
ósa crecaib, caem cumtaig,
   surdgail laeg mbrecc oc bedcaig.   16

Mín a mag, méth a muca,
   suairc a guirt, scél as chreitte,
cno for barraib a fidcholl,
   seólad na sithlong seicce.

Aíbinn dóib ó thicc soinenn,
   bricc fá bruachaib a habann,
frecrait faílinn 'má finnall,
   aíbinn cech inam Arann.   24

55. Gleann Measach Iasgach Linneach

Gun urra (am beul Deirdre)

Ged is dòcha nach do rinn i fhèin e an da-rìribh, tha an dàn seo am beul Deirdre, a tha air aon de na caractaran as iomraitiche agus as brònaiche ann an litreachas Gàidhlig nam Meadhan Aoisean. A rèir fàisneachd a rinneadh aig àm a breith, bha e an dàn dhi sgrios a thoirt do dh'Ulaidh; bha uaislean na cùirte a' moladh gum bu chòir a cur gu bàs, ach an àite sin chaidh a cur a-mach gu daltachd dhìomhair gus an ruigeadh i aois pòsaidh, nuair a phòste i ri Rìgh Conchobhar (caractar cudromach anns an 'Rúraíocht', no seann-sgeulachdan Uladh). Ri linn a dalt-achd, ge-tà, thachair i ris an laoch òg Naoise, agus thug i air a toirt air falbh an aghaidh a' phlana aig Conchobhar. Chaidh an dithis air fògradh an uair sin air feadh na h-Èireann, maille ri bràithrean Naoise agus buidheann mhòr de luchd-leantainn,

Greyhounds running there and mastiffs,
    brambles and dark sloes on blackthorn;
close against the woods her dwellings,
    deer scattered in her oak-groves.

Purple gathering on her boulders,
    faultless grass on her hillsides;
over her crags, a fair cover;
    capering dappled fawns bleating.

Smooth her plain, her swine fleshy,
    lovely her fields — believe the tidings —
nuts atop her woods of hazel,
    long galleys sailing past her.

Delightful for them in fine weather,
    trout beneath the banks of her rivers,
gulls round her white cliff replying,
    delightful at all times is Arran.

Fruitful Glen with Pools and Fishes

This poem is attributed to – or placed in the mouth of – Deirdre, one of the most famous and tragic figures in early Gaelic literature. Prophesied at birth to cause ruin to Ulster, she was spared the death urged by the nobles of the court and sent out to be fostered in secrecy until she reached marriageable age, when she would become the wife of king Conchobhar (an important figure in the Ulster Cycle of tales). During her fosterage, however, she encountered the young warrior Naoise, son of Uisneach, and demanded that he take her and defy Conchobhar's will. The pair then went on the run throughout Ireland – accompanied by Naoise's brothers and a large retinue – and eventually fled to Scotland. A negotiated return resulted in the treacherous killing of Naoise and his brothers, while Deirdre

agus mu dheireadh thall theich iad a dh'Alba. Chaidh aonta a
ruigsinn eadar iad agus Conchobhar ach nuair a thiss iad a
dh'Èirinn chaidh Conchobhar an aghaidh na gheall e: chaidh
Naoise agus a bhràithrean a mharbhadh le foill agus chaidh
Deirdre a thoirt do Chonchobhar. Mu dheireadh, chuir Deirdre
às dhi fhèin an dèidh do Chonchobhar a toirt do rìgh eile,
Eoghan mac Durthachta, an duine a mharbh Naoise às leth
Chonchobhair.

Bha sgeulachd Deirdre air leth measail aig na Gàidheil thar
nan linntean agus chaidh grunn thionndaidhean dhith a thogail
bho bheul-aithris.

Chan eilear buileach cinnteach dè an gleann a tha fo cheist
anns an dàn seo, ach tha ceangal làidir eadar sgeulachd Deirdre
agus Gleann Èite, mar a chithear anns an ath dhàn.

> Gleann measach iasgach linneach,
>   a thulcha corra is áille cruithneacht;
> bheith dá iomrádh damhsa is deacrach,
>   gleann beachach na mbuabhall mbeannach.
>
> Gleann cuachach smólach lonach,
>   buadhach an fhoraois do gach sionnach,
> gleann creamhach biolrach mongach
>   seamrach sgothach barrchas duilleach.
>
> Binn gotha fiadh ndruimdhearg mballach
>   faoi fhiodh darach ós maoil mullach;
> oighe míolla is iad go faiteach
>   'na loighe i bhfalach san ghleann bhileach.
>
> Gleann na gcaorthann go gcnuas corcra,
>   go meas molta do gach ealta;
> parrthas suain do na brocaibh
>   i n-uamhchaibh socra 's a gcuain aca.
>
> Gleann na seabhac súlghorm séitreach,
>   gleann iomlán do gach cnuasach,
> gleann na mbeann sleasach bpéacach,
>   gleann sméarach airneach ubhlach.

8

16

was given over to Conchobhar, and then committed suicide after Conchobhar gave her over to another king, the very man who had killed Naoise at Conchobhar's behest.

The story of Deirdre remained highly popular in the *Gàidhealtachd* down to the nineteenth century and versions of the story – narrated and sung – were collected from oral tradition.

It is not clear which glen is the subject of the poem, but the Deirdre story is strongly associated with Glen Etive in Argyll, which is specifically mentioned in the next poem.

Fruitful glen with pools and fishes,
    its rounded mounds with finest wheat crops,
for me speaking of it is painful,
    glen with bees and horned oxen.

Glen with cuckoos, thrushes, blackbirds,
    precious its cover to all foxes,
grassy glen with cress and garlic,
    with clover and flowers and leafy tendrils.

Sweet the sound of dappled roedeer
    in oak woods below bare headlands,
gentle hinds lying timid,
    hidden in the glen's tall forests.

Glen of rowans with scarlet berries,
    fruit praised by every birdflock;
a tranquil paradise to the badgers
    in peaceful holts with their litters.

Glen of hawks, blue-eyed, crying,
    glen abundant in every harvest,
glen of the terraced, speckled hill-sides,
    glen with brambles, sloes and apples.

Gleann na ndobhrán sliomdhonn smutach
    ós cionn iasgaigh is binn bocach;
is iomdha géis thaoibhgheal shocrach
    's éigne iuchrach re taobh leacach.   24

Gleann na n-iubhar gcas gcraobhach,
    gleann braonach is mín lulghach,
gleann aoldathach réaltach grianach,
    gleann ban sgiamhach bpéarlach bpuncach.

56. Ionmhain Tír an Tír-Úd Thoir

Gun urra (am beul Deirdre)

Laoidh eile a dh'èirich às an sgeulachd ainmeil 'Oidheadh
Chloinne hUisneach', a tha ga chur ann am beul Deirdre. A rèir
na sgeulachd sheinn i an t-òran seo agus i a' coimhead air ais air
Alba an dèidh dhi tilleadh a dh'Èirinn.

Ionmhain tír an tír-úd thoir,
Alba gona hiongantaibh;
    nocha dtiocfainn eisde i-lle
    mana thíosainn le Naoise.

Ionmhain Dún Fiodhgha is Dún Fionn,
ionmhain an dún ós a gcionn,
    ionmhain Inis Draighean de,
    is is ionmhain Dún Suibhne.   8

Coill Chuan!
gus' dtigeadh Ainnle, monuar;
    fá gair liom do bhí an tan,
    is Naoise in oirear Alban.

Gleann Laoigh!
do chollainn fán mboirinn chaoimh;
    iasg is sidheang is saill bhruic,
    fá hí mo chuid i nGleann Laoigh.   16

Glen of sleek-brown, flat-nosed otters
    over fishing grounds, and sweet goat-bleating,
with many a swan, white-sided, gentle
    and spawning salmon beside each flagstone.

Glen of twisted spreading yew-trees,
    dewy glen of tender milch-cows,
sunny glen, lime-white and starry,
    glen of neat girls, pearled and lovely.

A Dear Land

Another ballad connected with the famous story 'Oidheadh Chloinne hUisneach' ('The Violent Death of the Children of Uisneach'), and placed in the mouth of Deirdre. According to the tale, she sang this song on her return to Ireland, looking back toward Scotland.

Beloved land, that land in the east,
Scotland with her wonders;
    I would not have left her for here
    had I not come with Naoise.

Beloved, Dún Fiodhgha and Dún Fionn,
beloved, the stronghold above them,
    beloved, Inis Draighean,
    and beloved too, Dún Suibhne.

Coill Chuan!
which Ainnle, alas, frequented;
    short to me the time
    that Naoise was in Scotland.

Glen Lui!
I would sleep below the fair rock;
    fish and venison and badger fat —
    that was my fare in Glen Lui.

Gleann Masáin!
ard a chriomh, geal a ghasáin;
do-níomaois colladh corrach
ós inbhear mongach Masáin.

Gleann Éitche!
ann do thógbhas mo chéidtigh;
álainn a fhiodh iar n-éirghe;
buaile gréine Gleann Éitche.   24

Gleann Orchaoin!
ba hé an gleann díreach dromchaoin;
nochar uallcha fear a aoise
ná mo Naoise i nGleann Orchaoin.

Gleann Dá Ruadh!
mo-chean gach fear dána dual;
is binn guth cuach ar chraoibh chruim
ar an druim ós Gleann Dá Ruadh.   32

Ionmhain Inis Draighean de
is uisge glan a ghainmhe;
nocha dtiocfainn eisde an-oir
mana thíosainn lem ionmhain.

Ionmhain.

57. Am Bròn Binn

Gun urra

Is e an laoidh seo am pìos as cudromaiche ann an dualchas
Artair ann an Gàidhealtachd na h-Alba. Ged a bha sgeulachdan
is laoidhean na Fèinne fada na bu chudromaiche, sgaoil stuthan
co-cheangailte ri Artar agus Am Bòrd Cruinn air feadh
Gàidhealtachdan Alba is Èirinn. Tha cuid a' cumail a-mach gum
b'e 'Am Bòrd Cruinn' seach 'Am Bròn Binn' a bha mar thiotal
air an laoidh seo an toiseach.

Glen Massan!
tall its garlic, bright its grasses;
 our sleep would be broken
 above the lush estuary of Massan.

Glen Etive!
there I built my first dwelling;
 lovely its wood on rising,
 a sunny fold is Glen Etive.

Glen Orchy!
that was the straight fair-ridged valley;
 no man of his age was prouder
 than my Naoise in Glen Orchy.

Glendaruel!
my love to every man born there;
 sweet the voices of cuckoos on bending branch
 on the ridge above Glendaruel!

Beloved too is Inis Draighean,
and the pure water of its beaches;
 I would never have left the east
 had I not come with my beloved.

Beloved.

The Sweet Sorrow

This ballad is the most famous composition of the Arthurian
tradition in Gaelic Scotland. Although the stories of the Fianna
enjoyed a great deal more prominence in Gaelic tradition,
material relating to Arthur and the knights of the Round Table
also permeated Gaelic Scotland and Gaelic Ireland. The title
given here, 'Am Bròn Binn' (literally the 'Sweet Sorrow') may be
a corruption of 'Am Bòrd Cruinn' (the 'Round Table').

Thàinig an teacsa a chleachdar an seo à làmh-sgrìobhainn a rinneadh anns an ochdamh linn deug ann an Siorrachd Pheairt, ach a rèir coltais tha e stèidhichte air tionndadh na bu shine a rinneadh ann an Innse Gall, is dòcha ann an Uibhist. Chaidh na dusanan de thionndaidhean a chruinneachadh bho bheul-aithris, à Ìle, Tiriodh, Barraigh, Uibhist, an t-Eilean Sgitheanach agus tìr-mòr na Gàidhealtachd. Cleas sgeulachdan is laoidhean na Fèinne, is dòcha gu bheil an stuth a sgaoil tro bheul-aithris stèidhichte air teacsaichean sgrìobhte bho na Meadhan Aoisean.

Tha an sgeulachd a tha ga h-innse anns an tionndadh seo den laoidh caran doilleir ann an àiteachan, agus tha cuid de thionn-daidhean eile nas rèidhe. Nuair a dhùisgeas Artar às a bhruadar, tha Sir Gallabha a' falbh a lorg a' bhoireannaich a chunnaic Artar; tha e a' ruigsinn bun ballachan caisteil agus a' dìreadh slabhraidh dhubh a tha ga cur sìos thuige; tha nighean a' nochdadh agus a' toirt rabhadh do Ghallabha gum bi famhair a' tilleadh agus nach gabh a mharbhadh ach leis a' chlaidheamh aige fhèin; tha an nighean an sin a' tàladh an fhamhair gu cadal le ceòl na clàrsaich, tha Gallabha a' goid claidheamh an fhamhair agus a' gearradh dheth a chinn, agus mu dheireadh tha an dithis a' teicheadh còmhla.

Là a chaidh Artar nan sluagh
Gu tulach nam buadh a shealg,
Chunnacas a' tighinn on mhaigh
Gruagach b'àillidh cruth fon ghrèin.
Cruit an làimh na h-ighinn òig
'S mìlse pòg 's as gile gnè;
Cho binn 's gun do sheinn i chruit,
'S binne 'n guth a leig i lè.   8
'S ann le fuaim a teudan binn
A chaidh an rìgh 'na shuain sèimh;
'S nuair a dhùisg e às a shuain,
Thug e làmh gu luath air airm.
M'an nighinn a sheinn an ceòl
Nach facas a beò no marbh,
Labhair Fios Falaich gu fial,
'Thèid mi fèin ga h-iarraidh dhut,   16

The present text is preserved in an eighteenth-century manuscript of Perthshire origin, but it appears to have been based on an earlier work composed in the Hebrides, probably Uist. Dozens of different versions have been collected, from Islay, Tiree, Skye, Barra, Uist, and the mainland. As with the Fenian material, the versions circulated in earlier tradition may in turn be based on written texts of the late medieval period.

In some versions Sir Gawain sets out to find the girl Arthur saw in his dream. He arrives at the base of a castle and climbs a black chain that is lowered down; the girl warns Gawain that a giant will return who can only be killed by his own sword. The girl lulls the giant to sleep with her harp-playing, Gawain steals the sword and cuts off the giant's head and the two escape. This version, however, has another twist, when the girl dies herself rather than have foolish men kill each other in competition for her.

One day when Arthur of the hosts
went to the knoll of virtues to hunt,
there was seen coming from the plain
a maid of loveliest form under the sun.
A harp was in the hand of the young girl,
of the sweetest kiss and brightest face;
and though sweetly she played the harp
sweeter the voice she let out with it.
It was to the sound of its sweet strings
that the king fell into gentle sleep;
and when from his slumber he awoke
he quickly took hold of his arms.
About the girl who sang the song
who was not to be seen dead or alive,
Fios Falaich generously spoke,
'I'll go myself to fetch her for you,

Mi fèin 's mo ghille 's mo chù,
Nar triùir a shireadh na mnè.'

Dh'fhalbh e le ghille 's le chù
'S le a luing bhrèagh bhrèidgheal àrd.
Bha e seachd mìosan air muir
Mum fac' e fearann no fonn
San leigeadh e 'n long gu tìr.
Chunnaic e 'n aiteal a' chuain   24
Clacha buadhach le biolar gorm,
Uinneagan gloinn' air a stuaigh,
Bu lìonmhor ann cuach is corn.
Bha Sir Ghallabha 'na bhun,
'S an t-slabhraidh dhubh às a-nuas,
'S an t-slabhraidh nach do ghabh crith,
Thug i esan 'na ruith suas.
Chunnaic e 'n nighean mhìn bhlàth   32
An cathair an òir a-staigh,
Streabhan sìoda fo dà bhonn,
'S bheannaich an sonn dha gnùis ghil.
'Na bheannaich Dia thu, fhir?
'S trom an cion thug thu thar tuinn;
Ma tha fear na cloich seo slàn,
Cha d'fhidir e càs no truas.'
'Cùis as fhaide leam nach tig,   40
Còmhrag ris dhèanaim gu luath.'
'Ciamar a dhèanadh tu siud?
'S nach tu laoch as feàrr fon ghrèin,
Is nach dearg arm air an fhear
Ach a chlaidheamh geal glan fhèin.'
'Dùisgeamaid bruidhinn 's traoghamaid fearg,
Suidheamaid cealg mun fhear mhòr;
Goideamaid a chlaidheamh bhon fhear,   48
Sin mar bheir sinn dheth an ceann.'

Chunnaic mi 'n dèidh tighinn on mhuir
Òganach air ghuin le airm;
Bha spuir òir air a chois dheis,
'S bu leòr a dheise 's a dhealbh.
Bha spuir eile m'a chois chlì

myself, my servant and my dog,
the three of us to seek the girl.'

He set off with his servant and dog,
with his lovely tall bright-sailed ship.
He was seven months at sea
before he sighted land or rock
where he could bring the boat to shore.
He saw in the gleam of the sea
a castle of jewels with green cress,
windows of glass in the gable,
with numerous cups and horns within.
Sir Gawain was at its base
with the black chain hanging down,
and the chain that never shook
it took him up at the run.
He saw the gentle kindly girl
on the golden throne within,
with a silk carpet under her two soles,
and the hero greeted her bright face.
'Did God bless you, man?
Great the love that brought you over the wave;
if the man of this castle is fit,
he has known neither pity nor plight.'
'To make a long matter of it doesn't please —
I would do battle with him at once.'
'How would you do that when you are not
the best warrior under the sun
and no weapon can hurt the man
but his own brightly burnished sword.'
'Let's waken talking, let's drain wrath,
let's set a trap for the huge man,
let's steal his sword from the man,
that's how we'll take off his head.'

I saw after coming from the sea
a young man pierced by arms;
he had a golden spur on his right foot
and imposing were his raiment and his form.
He had another spur on his left foot

De dh'airgead rìgh no dh'òr feall;
Thug mise làmh dh'ionnsaigh an spuir,   56
Dè ma thug, cha bu mhath mo chiall;
Thug esan glacadh air airm
Is b'fhear marbh a bhith na neul.
'Fosadh! fosadh! òglaich mhòir,
Mi beò agus am fochar m'airm,
Innis dhomh beachdaidh do sgeul,
Cò thu fèin no ciod e t'ainm.'
''S mi Bile Buadhach nan rath,   64
Agam a bhios teach nan teud;
'N teagamh gum bi mi nam rìgh?
Mu mo choinneamh do bhì Grèig.
'S ann agam fèin a bhios a' bhean
'S àillidh leac 's as gile deud,
'S ann agam a bhios an long
Chuireas an tonn às a dèidh;
'S ann agam fèin bhios an t-each   72
As luaithe bhuail cas air feur,
'S ann agam a bhios an cù
Air nach laigheadh tnùth no treun.'

Ghluaiseadar gu teach air chloich,
'S ann a gheibh thu beachd mo sgèil;
Sin mar mharcaich mi an t-each
Bu luaithe 's bu ghasda ceum.
Marcachd na fairge gu dian,   80
Fàlaireachd air druim a' chuain,
Chunnaic mi cath connachair triùir
Còmhrag dlùth mu cheann na mnè.
Cuiridh mi 'n còmhrag na thosd,
Cuiridh mi an cosg orm fèin,
An triùir bhràithre, mo sgeul truagh,
Còmhrag truagh mu cheann na mnè.
'S mi 'n curaidh nach do ghabh fiamh,   88
Chiad mhac a bh'aig Rìgh na Fraing;
Leam a thuit dìs mhac Rìgh Grèig,
'S iad fèin a mharbh an treas fear.
Mas àill leat mis a thoirt leat,
Treachaid leac do chlann Rìgh Grèig,

made of king's silver or false gold.
I stretched my hand towards the spur,
what if I did, I had no sense.
He took a hold of his arms,
a man in a daze would be dead.
'Peace! Peace! Great giant,
I am alive and near my arms,
tell me, notable your tale,
who you are and what is your name?'
'I am Victorious Bile of good luck,
mine will be the house of strings,
is there any doubt I'll be a king?
Against me, there was Greece,
mine will be the girl
of loveliest cheek and whitest tooth,
mine will be the ship
that leaves the wake behind;
mine will be the steed
whose hoof fastest struck the turf,
mine will be the hound
who was neither grudging nor bold.'

They moved to the house on the rock,
here you will get the proof of my tale.
That is how I rode the horse
of fastest and finest gait,
vehemently riding the sea,
prancing on the ocean's back,
I saw a dog-like fight between three,
a fierce battle for the sake of the girl.
I will bring silence to the strife,
I will carry the cost myself,
the three brothers, my wretched tale,
in bitter strife about the girl.
I am the hero that never took fright,
the first-born son of the King of France;
I felled the two sons of the King of Greece,
they themseves killed the third.
If you would like to take me along
to open graves for the Greek King's sons.

Sin mar a threachaid mi 'n leac
O 's i obair fir gun chèill,
A dhèanamh air chòmhaich mnè,   96
Uaigh a threachaid dha deòin fèin.

Thug ise leum a sìos dhan t-sloc,
'S i bhean ghlic bu ghlaine snuadh;
Leum an t-anam às a corp,
Ochadan a-nochd gur truagh.
Nam biodh agams' an sin lèigh,
Chuirinn e gu feum san uair,
Dhèanainn ath-bheothachadh as ùr,   104
Chan fhàgainn mo rùn san uaigh.
Air sliabh sligh nam briathra ceart,
Air a dheas làimh, a Mhic Dè,
Gun robh mi fèin gu Là Luain.
Sin agaibh deireadh mo sgeòil,
'S mar a sheinneadh am Bròn Binn.

58. Ardaigneach Goll

Fearghus File

Tha an laoidh àrd-aigneach seo, a chaidh a ghleidheadh ann an
Leabhar an Deadhain, a' moladh Ghuill mhic Morna, ceannard
grunn àrmann à Connacht agus prìomh-nàmhaid Fhinn mhic
Cumhaill.

Chan urrainn dhuinn a bhith cinnteach an e duine an da-
rìribh a bha ann am 'Fearghus File'. Tha dàn eile fon ainm seo
ann an Leabhar an Deadhain ann an cruth còmhraidh eadar
dithis; anns an dàn seo is e 'file Féine Éireann' a thathar a'
cantainn ris.

        'Ardaigneach Goll,
           fear cagaidh Finn,
        laoch leabhar lonn,
           fhaghail ní tim.

That is how I tilled the ground
for it is the work of a senseless man
to fight for the reward of a girl,
to dig a grave to please her.

She leaped down into the pit
the wise woman of fairest face.
Out of her body leaped her soul,
Alas and alack it is sad tonight.
If I had had a leech there
I'd have set him to work at once,
I'd have revived her once again,
I would never have left my love in the grave.
On the hill of the road of the true words,
on His right hand, O Son of God,
may I be myself till the day of Doom.
There you have the end of my tale,
about how the Sweet Sorrow was sung.

High-Spirited Goll

This spirited lay from the Book of the Dean of Lismore praises
Goll mac Morna, leader of the Fianna of Connacht and great
rival of Fionn mac Cumhaill.

It is not clear whether 'Fearghus File' was an actual individual
or a literary construct. A second poem attributed to him
preserved in the Book of the Dean is also constructed in the
form of a dialogue; there he is addressed as 'file Féine Éireann'
('poet of the Fianna of Ireland').

'High-spirited Goll,
enemy of Fionn,
warrior tall and fierce,
his foray not faint.

'Saoraineach suadh,
    saorshnaidhte a thaobh;
muireach ar sluagh
    Goll cruthach caomh.   8

'Mac Morna mear
    fá cródha i ngoil,
a chlú fá sean,
    fear geanail sin.

'Ríghfhéinnidh fial,
    ní tim a ghlór,
ní saobh a chiall,
    laoch aobhdha mór.   16

Mar théid i gcath
    réim flatha faoi;
gé mín a chneas,
    ní tais do-ní.

'A mhéad ní mion,
    ós géagaibh tor;
's é as gloine gean,
    oide na sgol.   24

'Ós barraibh beann
    iarras an roinn;
fá h-eagal linn
    a thagra theacht rinn.

'Deirim riot, Fhinn
    na dtrilis ndonn,
bí ar eagla Ghuill
    th'aigneadh go trom.   32

'Gan chur ré mhath
    san chath ní dóigh;
ionnsaightheach cáigh,
    ceannsalach slóigh.

'Noble-valued sage,
    nobly chiselled his side,
chief of hosts,
    shapely gentle Goll.

'Morna's cheerful son,
    bloody in a fight,
his reputation of old,
    an affectionate man.

'Generous warrior-prince,
    not mild his voice,
not erring his sense,
    great warrior of joy.

'When he goes to war,
    princely his course;
though soft his skin,
    not tender his deeds.

'His stature is not small,
    a tower above trees,
he is brightest of mood,
    patron of the schools.

'On the mountain tops
    he demanded the share;
we were afraid
    to counter his claim.

'I tell you, Fionn
    of the brown-coloured locks,
fear of Goll
    will weigh your spirit down.

'Not likely that in war
    he will not add to his sway;
ever on the attack,
    leader of hosts.

'A eineach ní mion,
    fuileach an fear,
duasaidh na sgol,
    uasal a ghean.   40

'Oirdheirc a luadh,
    toirbheartach fial,
trosd catha as buan,
    fos flatha a chiall.

'Duinne 'na fholt,
    bruinne mar chailc,
iomlán má chorp
    lomlán do sheirc.   48

'Éire fá chíos
    budh cóir dhá chúis;
is meanmnach bhíos,
    dealbhach a ghnúis.

'Ní fheil rí ós Goll,
    ní cheilim ort, a Fhinn;
treise ná tonn
    a ghaisgeadh grinn.   56

'Flaitheamhail fios,
    daitheamhail cneas;
ar Gholl ná clis:
    ní slim a threas.

'Bronntach a dháil,
    conbhfach a threóir,
fíreata mín,
    míleata mór.   64

'Dá rádh go bráth
    a ágh 's a fhíoch,
námhach (?) ré cách,
    lámhach an laoch (?).

'His honour is not small,
    bloody the man,
rewarder of poets,
    noble his mien.

'Illustrious his fame,
    generous and free,
a lasting thrust in war,
    his sense, a princely prop.

'Brownness in his locks,
    chest like chalk,
perfect in form,
    overflowing with love.

'Ireland in tax
    is due his style;
mettlesome his ways,
    handsome his face.

'No king is over him,
    I hide it not, Fionn,
mightier than the wave
    is his valour fine-tuned.

'Princely his word,
    of good colour his skin,
don't meddle with Goll,
    not feeble in the fray.

'Generous his gifts,
    fierce his might,
gentle and true,
    soldierly, great.

'Spoken of till Doom,
    his fortunes and wrath;
hostile to foes,
    dextrous the sword.

'Cleath chonas bhuan,
   sonas na bhFian,
mórdhálach cuan,
   iorghalach dian.   72

'Leómhan ar ágh,
   cródha 'na ghníomh,
leabhar a lámh,
   ragha na ríogh.

Sonas 'na ród,
   solas a dhéad;
cuiridh sé léan
   ar gach tréan dá mhéad.   80

'Buan rún an fhir,
   buaidh gcomhraig air;
léidmheach a ghoil,
   éigneach a stair.

'Laoch [   ] lonn,
   neimhneach lé lainn;
tarcaiseach Goll,
   airceasach linn.   88

'Laoch armach mear,
   feargach ré coir;
colg conbhfach air,
   onchú ar ghoil.

'Forghla na gcon,
   roghrádh na mban,
laoich, dámh gan on,
   do ghnáth 'na ghar.   96

'Lé biodhbhaidh rod
   a throd ní tláth;
maoidheamh na gcreach
   a dhreach fá bláth.

'Lasting pillar of war,
      the joy of the Fian,
magnificent and calm,
      terrible, swift.

'A lion for triumph,
      hardy in deed,
long his hand,
      choice of the kings.

'Joy in his path,
      bright his tooth;
however big a man,
      he will bring him woe.

'Enduring in intent,
      his, victory in strife,
daring his fight,
      violent his tale.

'Warrior fierce,
      venomous with his blade;
disdainful is Goll,
      and greedy, I deem.

'Warrior armed and swift,
      fierce against the wrong,
about him a vicious sword,
      a wolf for rage.

'The choice of hounds,
      women's choice love,
warriors ever by his side,
      a band without fault.

'Against a furious foe,
      not faint his fight;
when boasting of raids,
      his complexion blooms.

'Seadhmhar a chruth,
 ághmhar a rath;
ní tréine sruth
 ná a réim i gcath.   104

'Mac Morna as dian,
 fá h-orra a ghéill,
ionnuar a ghlór,
 biothbhuan a thréan.

'Triath meardha mear,
 fial feardha a chor,
gan táir 'na ghar,
 a dháil ar for.   112

'Mac téad as caomh
 nach tréigeadh dámh,
san chagadh ríogh
 nár lag a lámh.

'Uathmhar a cholg,
 is borb a ghleó;
'n uair éirgheas fhearg,
 trian sealga dhó.   120

'Mhic Cumhaill ghrinn,
 comhaill is geall
síoth buan do Gholl
 gan fhuath gan fheall'.

'Anois rém lá
 do ghnáth gan ghó
bheirim gan chealg
 trian sealga dhó'.   128

'Ní tuilleadh ann,
 fearr nás an corr:
grádh t'einigh, Fhinn,
 trian con do Gholl.

'Substantial his form,
   lucky his fate;
no stronger the tide
   than his course in war.

'Mac Morna who is strong
   his pledge ensured,
serene his voice,
   lasting his strength.

'Swift lively lord,
   generous manly his wont,
near him, nothing base,
   his bestowing is observed.

'Son who loves the harp,
   who'd forsake no poet-band,
in the war of the kings,
   not weak was his hand.

'Terrible his sword,
   his onset fierce;
when his anger is roused
   give him a third of the hunt.

'Son of gentle Cumhall,
   promise and discharge
a lasting peace with Goll,
   without hatred or deceit.'

'Now and throughout my day,
   always without deceit,
I will give him without mistake
   a third of the hunt.

'There is something more,
   better than the rest:
for love of your honour, Fionn,
   give Goll a third of the dogs.

'Tréig th'fhíoch, a Ghuill,
  bí síothach rinn:
'nad ré gan mheing
  trian fiadhaigh Finn.'   136

'Geobhad-sa sin,
  Fhearghuis, a fhéil,
is sgaoil mo ghruaim:
  ní fuar mo mhéin.'

'Cara gan cealg,
  béal tana dearg,
eineach 's a lúth,
  a chlú ós ard.'   144

Ardaigneach Goll.

59. Gleann Síodh an Gleann So rém Thaoibh

Ailéin mac Ruaidhrí

Tha an dàn seo am measg nan laoidhean as ainmeile ann an dualchas na Fèinne ann an Alba, agus cha robh eòlas air ann an Èirinn idir. Ach tha an sgeulachd a tha mar bhunait don laoidh air leth ainmeil ann an dualchas na h-Èireann cho math ri dualchas Alba: eachdraidh air teicheadh Dhiarmuid, fear de na laoich as gaisgeile den Fhèinn, agus Gráinne, bean Fhinn agus nighean an rìgh ainmeil Cormac mac Airt. (Tha 'Leaba Dhiarmuid agus Ghráinne' air iomadach clach-truiseil ann an Èirinn fhathast, a' comharrachadh àiteachan far an tug an dithis an oidhche, a rèir beul-aithris). Rinneadh rèite eadar Fionn agus Diarmuid mu dheireadh, ach bha farmad aig Fionn ri Diarmuid fhathast, agus dh'iarr e air Diarmuid a dhol a mharbhadh torc mòr Bheinn Ghulbainn, mar a thathar ag innse anns an laoidh.

    Chan eil fiosrachadh sam bith againn air a' bhàrd seo, Ailéin mac Ruaidhrí, ach tha e coltach gu robh e beò anns a' chiad

'Abandon your anger, Goll,
  with us make peace:
yours, for the rest of your life,
  no mistake: a third of Fionn's hunt.'

'I will accept that,
  Fergus, the kind,
my scowl has dispersed,
  my mien is not cold.'

'Friend without guile,
  slender red lips,
his honour and strength,
  his reputation is high.'

High.

This Glen Beside Me is Glen Shee

This poem is one of the most famous compositions in the Fenian tradition of Scotland; it is not known in Ireland. The story here is built upon an underlying, and greatly celebrated, episode, the story of the elopement by Diarmuid, one of Fionn's most valued warriors, with Fionn's wife Gráinne, daughter of king Cormac mac Airt. (Many standing stones are remembered as 'Diarmuid and Gráinne's bed', sites where the couple slept while on the run). Fionn and Diarmuid were later reconciled, but the treacherous Fionn still harboured his grudge, and sent Diarmuid on a mission to kill the great boar of Beinn Ghulbainn, as narrated in the present poem.

Nothing is known of the poet Ailéin mac Ruaidhrí, who also composed another Fenian poem preserved, like this one, in the Book of the Dean of Lismore, and probably dating from the early sixteenth century.

phàirt den t-siathamh linn deug. Rinn e laoidh eile air an Fhèinn
a tha air a ghleidheadh, mar a tha Laoidh Dhiarmuid, ann an
Leabhar an Deadhain.

Gleann Síodh an gleann so rém thaoibh
   am binn faoidh éan is lon;
minic rithidís an Fhéin
   air an t-srath so an déidh a gcon.

An gleann so fá Bheinn Ghulbainn ghuirm
   as h-áilde tulcha fá ghréin,
níorbh annamh a shrotha gu dearg
   an déidh shealg ó Fhionn na bhFéin.   8

Éisdidh beag, madh áil libh laoidh,
   a chuideachta chaomh so, bhuam,
air Bheinn Ghulbainn 's air Fhionn fial,
   is air Mac Uí Dhuibhne, sgial truagh.

Guidhear lé Fionn, fá truagh an sgealg,
   air Mhac Uí Dhuibhne as dearg lí
dhul do Bheinn Ghulbainn do sheilg
   an tuirc nach féadann airm a dhíth.   16

Lé Mac Uí Dhuibhne nár thréith
   dám bé gun dtorchradh an torc,
geallar rogha lé eól Fhinn;
   is sé easnadh rinn do locht.

A fhíor, fá h-earlamh a dháil,
   Mac Uí Dhuibhne, grádh nan sgol;
ach, so an sgeul fán tuirseach mná
   — gabhar leis do láimh an torc.   24

A dhiongbháil do fhlaith na bhFéin
   dá gcuireadh é as an gcnoc
an seann torc sídhe ba garbh
   do bha aig Balar 'na shealbh muc.

This glen beside me is Glen Shee,
 where birds and ousels sweetly sing;
often did the Fian run
 in this valley behind their hounds.

Below Ben Ghulbainn lies this glen
 of the fairest knolls beneath the sun,
not seldom were its rivers red
 after the hunts of Fionn of the Fian.

Gentle company, listen a while
 if you'd like to hear a lay from me,
about Ben Ghulbainn and generous Fionn,
 and Mac Uí Duibhne — a sorry tale.

Fionn makes the request — sad the deceit —
 that Mac Uí Duibhne of rosy hue
should go to Ben Ghulbainn to hunt
 the boar that weapons cannot kill.

Should it happen that the boar would fall
 by Mac Uí Duibhne's hand — no dolt was he —
Fionn knowingly promises him a choice;
 (it was a weakness that did you the harm).

In truth, his encounter was already planned,
 Mac Uí Duibhne, beloved by poets;
alas, this is the tale which makes women sad:
 he undertakes to contend with the boar.

It would have been worthy of Fionn himself,
 if he had driven it from the hill,
the ancient savage fairy boar,
 which Balar once had in his herd of pigs.

Suidhighidh Fionn as dearg dreach
    fá Bheinn Ghulbainn ghlais an t-sealg;
do fríoth Diarmaid leis an torc;
    mór an t-olc a rinn a sgealg.   32

Ré claisdeacht comhgháir na bhFian
    anoir 's aniar teacht fá ceann,
éirghis an ainbhéisd ó a suain
    is gluaisis bhuaidh air a' ghleann.

    Gleann.

Cuiris, ré faicinn nan laoch,
    an seann torc sídhe air fraoch borb
bu géire na gáinne sleagh,
    bu tréine, is eadh, ná an Ga Bolg.   40

Mac Uí Dhuibhne na n-arm géar,
    freagrar leis an ainbhéisd uilc;
'na taobh réil trom neimhneach gáidh,
    cuirear sleagh an dáil an tuirc.

Brisear a chrann leis fá thrí,
    's a cheann, fa-ríor, ar an mhuic;
an t-sleagh ó a bhais bháirrdheirg bhláith
    racht leis nochar sháith 'na curp.   48

Tairrngis an t-seann lann ó a truaill
    do chosain mór buaidh a n-ár;
marbhais Mac Uí Dhuibhne an phéisd,
    do thánaig féin dá h-éis slán.

Tuitis sbrochd air Fhionn na bhFéin
    is suidhis é 'san gcnoc;
Mac Uí Dhuibhne nar dhiúlt dámh,
    olc leis a theacht slán ón torc.   56

Air bheith dhó fada 'na thosd,
    adubhairt, gérbh olc re rádh,
'Tomhais, a Dhiarmaid, ó a shoc
    gá mhéad troigh 'san torc so atá.'

Fionn of ruddy countenance arranges the hunt
    below Ben Ghulbainn of the green slopes;
Diarmaid was discovered by the boar —
    great the evil of Fionn's deceit.

Hearing the clamour of the Fian,
    coming towards it from east and west,
the great beast rose from its sleep,
    and moved away along the glen.

On seeing the warriors, the ancient fairy boar
    raised a vicious bristle on its skin,
sharper than the tips of spears,
    stronger, indeed, than the Ga Bolg.

Mac Uí Duibhne of the sharp blades
    gives a response to the great evil beast:
into its venomous heavy lustrous flank
    a spear is hurled towards the boar.

His spearshaft is broken by him three times,
    its point, alas, rebounding on the pig;
it irked him that with his smooth rosy-nailed hand
    he hadn't stabbed the spear into its side.

He drew from its sheath the old blade
    which had won great victory on the field;
Mac Uí Duibhne killed the beast;
    he himself came back unharmed.

Dejection fell on Fionn of the Fian,
    and he sat back on the hill, enraged
that Mac Uí Duibhne who refused no poet-band
    had returned from the boar unscathed.

After he'd been silent a long time,
    he said, though it was an evil thing,
'Measure, O Diarmaid, from its snout
    how many feet are in this boar.'

Char dhiúlt é athchuinghe Finn
    — olc linn gan a theacht dá thoigh;
toimhsidh an torc air a dhruim,
    Mac Uí Dhuibhne nach trom troigh.   64

'Tomhais 'na aghaidh a rís,
    a Dhiarmaid, gu mín an torc;
fá leatsa rogha dhá chionn,
    a ghille na n-arm rionn gort.'

Iompóidhis — ba thurus gáidh —
    agus toimhsidh dhaibh an torc;
guinidh an fraoch nimhe garbh
    bonn an laoich bu gharg an dtrod.   72

Tuitidh an sin ar an raon
    Mac Uí Dhuibhne nár fhaomh feall,
'na laighe do thaobh an tuirc
    — ach, sin aidheadh dhuit gu dearbh.

Atá sé an sunn fá chriaidh,
    Mac Uí Dhuibhne, ciabh na gcleacht,
aonmhacámh fuileach na bhFian
    'san tulaigh so chiam fá fheart.   80

Seabhac súlghorm Easa Ruaidh,
    fear lém beirthe buaidh gach áir,
an déidh a thorchairt lé torc
    fá thulchán a' chnoic so atá.

Diarmaid, Mac Uí Dhuibhne fhéil,
    a thuiteam tré éad, mo-nuar!
bu gile a bhráighe ná grian,
    ba deirge a bhial ná bláth cnuas.   88

Fá buidhe fhionnadh 's a fholt,
    fada a rosg barrghlan fá fhleasg,
guirme 's glaise 'na shúil,
    maise is caise a gcúl na gcleacht.

He did not refuse Fionn's request
    — we grieve that he never came back home;
Mac Uí Duibhne, not heavy of tread,
    measures the boar along its back.

'Measure the boar from the other end,
    measure it, Diarmaid, precisely again,
as a reward for this you have a choice,
    young lad of the sharp pointed blades.'

He turned — it was a perilous deed —
    and obediently measures the boar;
the coarse venomous bristle stabs
    the sole of the warrior who was fierce in strife.

Then he falls upon the field,
    Mac Uí Duibhne who never played false,
lying there beside the boar;
    there you behold a truly tragic death.

He is here under the clay,
    Mac Uí Duibhne of the curling locks;
the single bloodiest warrior of the Fian
    lies in this mound we see on his grave.

The blue-eyed falcon of Eas Ruaidh,
    he by whom victory was won on every field,
having been laid low by the boar,
    he lies under the hump of this hill.

Diarmaid, generous Ua Duibhne's son,
    being killed through jealousy, alas;
his breast was brighter than the sun,
    his lips redder than the blossom of fruit.

Yellow was his hair and the beard on his cheeks;
    below his headband his lashes were long and fair;
blueness and greyness were in his eyes;
    lustre and curliness in his ringleted hair.

Binneas is grinneas 'na ghlóir,
   gile 'na dhóid bháirrdheirg bhláith,
méad agus aobhacht 'san laoch,
   seinge is saoire 'na chneas bán.   96

Coimhtheachtach is mealltóir ban,
   Mac Uí Dhuibhne bu mhear buaidh;
an t-Suirghe char thog a súil
   ó chuireadh úir air a ghruaidh.

Imeartaidh éididh is each,
   fear a n-éigin chreach nár chearr;
gille a b'fhearr gaisge is saoi
   — ach, truagh mar ataoi 'sa ghleann.   104

      Gleann Síodh.

Sweetness and delicacy were in his voice,
    whiteness in his smooth rosy-nailed hands;
stature and comeliness were in his form,
    slenderness and nobility below his white skin.

Mac Uí Duibhne of victory swift,
    companion of women and their delight,
Courtship has not raised her eye
    since earth was laid upon his cheek.

Bestower of battle-dress and steeds,
    a man never clumsy in the heat of a raid;
a lad who excelled in valour, and a poet,
    how sad you are like that in the glen!

The Learned Tradition

Occasional Verse

60. Mór an Feidhm Freagairt na bhFaigheach

Giolla Coluim Mac an Ollaimh

Tha an dàn neo-àbhaisteach seo a' dèanamh aoir air seann chleachdadh ris an cante faighe, no *thigging* anns a' Bheurla Ghallda, anns am biodh cuideigin ann an dìth ag iarraidh biadh is rudan eile air daoine eile. Bhathar a' measadh diùltadh na faighe mar neo-fhialaidheachd. Ach bha e furasta gu leòr cus iarraidh agus uallach mì-reusanta a chur air neach-aoigheachd, agus sin cuspair an dàin a leanas.

Gu ìre mhòir, tha am file a' cleachdadh trioblaid na faighe mar chleas a chum moladh fialaidheachd Eòin MhicDhomhnaill, Triath nan Eilean (cuspair dàin 18 agus 19), agus a mhic Aonghas (a tha air a chaoidh ann an dàn 37).

Mar a thathar a' mìneachadh anns an roi-ràdh ri dàn 29, tha e coltach gum buineadh Giolla Coluim do Chloinn Mhuirich.

Mór an feidhm freagairt na bhfaigheach
    thig fá seach,
an drong gus dtigid go h-aidhbhleach
    ar gach leath.

Neach dá n-iarraid bíd go h-aidhbhleach
    seach gach fear:
umhla dár chuir dún i ndaidhbhreas
    gusa bheag.   8

Beagán do shloinneadh na bhfaighdheach
    sloinnfead duibh,
an uair thigid fir na faighdhe
    d'fhaighdhe chruidh.

Bíd go mín cairdeamhail caibhneach
    mar is dluigh,
's an uair chuirthear iad ar chairdeas
    cia nach tuig?   16

Great the Load to Satisfy the Thiggers

This highly unusual poem satirizes the custom known in Lowland Scots as *thigging,* an ancient and occasionally notorious practice by which material goods were demanded by one in need. To refuse a thigger was considered the height of inhospitality. Yet thigging could easily be abused, placing an intolerable burden on the host; such is the theme of this poem.

The treatment of thigging here is essentially an elaborate construct to praise the great generosity of Eòin MacDhomhnaill, last Lord of the Isles (subject of poems 18 and 19), and his son Aonghas (whose death is lamented in poem 37).

As noted in the introduction to poem 29, Giolla Coluim appears to have been a member of the pre-eminent MacMhuirich bardic family.

Great the load to satisfy the thiggers
    who come time and again,
on those on whom they keep descending
    from every side.

The one on whom they make demand dreads them
    beyond all;
it is a subjugation that has almost
    bankrupted this fort.

Something of the nature of the thiggers
    I will recount,
about when the men among them
    come looking for stock.

They are mild kind and friendly
    as is right,
but when they're asked for respite
    who fails to twig?

Gabhaid míghean roimhéin ghairbhe
    agus ruid;
cromaid cnuasuighid a mailghe
    muin ar muin:
'go bráth nocha chara cainge
    sinne dhuid.'

Seagh na bhfaireann bhíos 'nam aigneadh
    tuig go math:
'n uair is léir, giodh olc an mhaidean
    nó go math,
do-níd éirghe ghrad, go raghrad,   24
    Rí na rath.

Cantar leó, 'Cha linn ach aithreach
    ar dtoisg féin;
fíor gach seinbhriathar tá i dtaisgidh
    i mbí spéis:
riocht na ndrochcarad ar aistear
    thig i gcéin.'

Éirghim-se ann sin ar sgáth náire,
    's budh ghnáth bhruid;   32
's do-bheirim dhóibh lán na láimhe
    do mo chuid.

Canaid riomsa le gean gáire
    ré maoin bhuig:
'ar an dáil is mór an bráighe
    thugadh duid;
a h-aon mhac samhla ag mac Ádhaimh
    nocha nfhuil.'   40

Beagán do shloinneadh na bhfhaighdheach
    sloinnfidh mé:
meic Uí Shúiligh, meic Uí Anmoich
    iad i gcéin.

They take the huff, a fit of displeasure,
   and seem peeved,
they hunch, and gather their eyebrows
   one by one,
saying, 'Never again will we support you
   in a dispute'.

Understand well the sort of person
   I have in mind;
whether good or bad the morning,
   as soon as it's light,
they get up, all too quickly,
   O King of grace!

They say, 'Sore our disappointment
   with our journey here;
true the old treasured proverbs
   which are held dear:
sorry the state of unwelcome relations
   who come from far.'

Then I get up, embarrassed —
   it's a common trap,
and get them a handful
   of my things.

They say to me, suddenly cheerful
   with the liberal gift,
'When wealth was distributed, great the uplands
   bestowed on you,
no-one else among all peoples
   got the like.'

Something of the thiggers' lineage
   I will recite:
they were sons of O' Covetous, sons of O' Sluggish,
   way back.

Meic Uí Mhoichéirghe, lá samhraidh
   iarras gréin;
meic Uí Shirthigh, meic Uí Shanntaigh
   iad go léir.   48

Tiogfaid mná dhíobh d'fhaighdhe chaorach
   orm fá seach;
go sonnradhach sanntach sirtheach
   thig gach bean.

Cuingidh diallaid, iasad easrach
   ar a h-each;
beiridh sirtheach nó dhá shirtheach
   lé mar neart.   56

Agus giolla bhíos fá h-aodach
   don treas fear;
agus inilt do-ní daondacht
   ar gach neach.

Mara bhfaghbhaid faighdhe chaorach
   uam le gean,
do-níd bagradh agus fraochach
   gan bheith beag;   64
's é ainm bagartha an dá shirtheach
   fatha fead.

Tiogfaid faighdhigh dhíobh ré shotal,
   Rí na ríogh,
giolla mo ghroighe ré chogar:
   'druid a niar;
innis focal nó dá fhocal
   dhomh go dian: 72

Gá h-each as fearr thá ag an ollamh?'
   's é adeir siad;
'cionnus éirgheas é san tosach?
   créad a fhiach?'

Sons of the Day-Grabbers, who, in summer,
    covet the sun;
sons of Go-Getters, sons of O' Greedy,
    are they all.

Their women approach me one after another
    to get a sheep,
acquisitively, greedily, bent on business,
    comes each wife.

One requests a saddle, a loan of bedding
    for her horse;
she brings with her one or two spongers
    as a prop.

And a man-servant under her garments
    as a third one;
and a female servant who shows kindness
    to every one.

If no sheep I grant them
    in good will,
they make threats and imprecations
    in no small degree:
the name of the threats of the two beggars
    is 'whistle wretch'.

Others will come wheedling,
    King of Kings,
to my stable boy, and whisper:
    'Come over here;
just for a moment,
    I want a quick word:

'Which is the doctor's best stallion?'
    is what they say;
'How does he rise in the forequarters?
    What is he worth?'

Mion lem ghiolla-sa ré bhrosgal
    comunn cliar;
gach each innseas é ré shotal
    gheibh mar bhias.   80

Iarrthar ormsa h-aithle a theagaisg,
    thall 'nar dtoigh,
an t-éineach lúth is lí d'eachaibh
    do bhí ar ghroigh.

Beag nach faighdhe mheic is athar
    í mar sin;
créad a nois do-ghéantar againn
    uime sin?   88

Rugadar ar mba is ar gcapaill
    as ar dtoigh;
's í ciall as fearr atá againn
    triall ré gcois,
go fionnta cóich as fhearr acfhainn
    ré dol ar toisg.

Go taigh Eóin Mheic Dhomhnaill dámhach,
    chorcas rinn,   96
d'fhaighdhe ar an fhear laomhsgar lámhach
    rachaidh sinn.

Gach ní tugamar gus trásta
    cuma linn,
más é mac Eóin, an folt ánbhog,
    íocas rinn.

Giodh ceart cam leat, a rí bearnais
    na n-arm nocht,   104
aithíoc na faighdhe nach dearnais
    do chur ort,

[ ] mé ar do ghealbhois
    a thoirt dhomh;
dod mhuintir-se, a mheic uí Fhearghuis,
    thugas crodh.

At this flattery, my groom has small interest
    in the company of poets;
the scout finds out through his fawning
    about each horse the boy describes.

After this instruction, I am then requested,
    over in my house,
to give the very horse of that description
    that was in the stud.

Thigging is thus put into practice
    by father and son,
what now can be done about it
    by us?

They have taken my cows and my horses
    from the house;
the best counsel we have now
    is to leave as well;
to ascertain which of us has the best endurance
    for going on a quest —

To the thronging house of Eòin MacDhomhnaill
    who reddens spears,
to thig from the man, generous and open-handed,
    we will go.

I'm not worried about what I have given
    up to now,
if it is the son of Eòin who makes repayment,
    of the soft shining hair.

Though you think it perverted justice, O king of notches
    of naked blades,
to charge you with the repayment of the thigging
    you never undertook.

[I ask you] to recompense me
    by your white hand,
it was to your own kin, O scion of Fergus,
    that I gave stock.

Muintir dhuit, agus é i nAlbain,
    gach flath fial;   112
muintir dhuit na fhaighdhigh amhlaidh,
    a fholt fiar.

Dá dtíosadh an fear a Francaibh
    seachad siar,
canaidh é ré do ghnúis dheargglain
    as math niamh:
'Muintir mise d'Eóin óg eargnaidh,
    aige bhiam.'   120

Muintir dhuit ó mhuir go monadh,
    Dia dod dhíon!
gomadh tú ghabhas an soladh
    dlighe a íoc,

Gion gur íocais cion dá ndearnsad
    ar a gceann.
Canaidh riomsa an súlghorm seangbhog,
    ag ól bheann.   128

'Aithíoc na bhfaighdhe nach dearnas
    íocthar leam;
do-ghéabhair uam í go h-earlamh,
    nó ní's fearr;

'Na ba is na capaill do sgaoilis
    as do thoigh,
mara beag lat uam do dh'aoineach —
    bó ar do bhoin —   136
searrach sleamhain seingmhear saoitheach,
    aire ghroigh'.

Adéarainn-se a nois ruaig mholta
    dod ghnúis réidh;
'is tú as cruaidhe i ngreis chrothta,'
    canfaidh mé;

Every generous prince that resides in Scotland
    is of your kin;
related to you the thiggers likewise,
    O cascading hair.

If there came here westwards
    one of the Franks
he would say to your rosy healthy face,
    of good hue,
I am of clever Young Eòin's people,
    him will I join.

From sea to mountain, may God protect you,
    stretch your kin,
may it be you who gets the advantage
    of what is yours to pay,

Though you have not paid off the debt yet
    incurred by them.
The blue-eyed, slender one will address me,
    as he drinks from horns:

'Repayment of the thigging I did not ask for
    will be made by me;
readily from me you will get its equal
    or even more;

For every cow and horse with which you parted
    from your house
from me you will receive, unless you think it little,
    a cow for your cow,
a sleek slender mettlesome thoroughbred,
    a stud of herds.'

Then I would compose a flight of glory
    to your gracious face;
'You are the fiercest in time of combat',
    I will declare.

''S tú as buige do bhronnadh longaidh
  réd linn féin;   144
is tú as fearr fá chlaidheamh corra
  as math féigh.

'Is tú as fearr fát ór 's fát ionnmhas
  do chloinn Chuinn;
ní mó ort ná uisge ionnlaid
  dod bhois chuirr
bhar n-oineach 's bhar ndéirc ré iomlaid
  druim ar dhruim.   152

'Is tú as cruaidhe ag cosnamh tíre
  nach bí id sheilbh;
bheith it aghaidh, a rí Íle,
  mór an feidhm.'

                Mór an feidhm.

61. Duanaire na Sracaire

Fionnlagh Mac an Aba

Faodar an dàn seo, às an tàinig tiotal a' chruinneachaidh seo, a
thuigsinn mar bhrosnachadh do chrìochnachadh Leabhar
Deadhan Lios Mòr. Thathar a' bruidhinn ri Dubhghall (mac
Eòin Riabhaich) MacGriogair, athair Sheumais (Deadhan Lios
Mòr) agus Dhonnchaidh. Thathar a' moladh gum bu chòir
cruinneachadh measgaichte, caochlaideach a chur ri chèile, agus
sin a rinneadh aig a' cheann thall.

B'e ùghdar an dàin seo, Fionnlagh Mac an Aba (†1525),
ceann a chinnidh, agus a rèir coltais bha e a' fuireach ann am
Both Mheadhain ann an Gleann Dochard, mu cheann Loch
Tatha. Bha e am measg grunn uaislean a rinn dàin a chaidh a
ghleidheadh ann an Leabhar an Deadhain, maille ris na
Caimbeulaich a rinn dàin 40–41 agus 48–49. Gheibhear an seo
na sreathan ainmeil 'ná beir duan ar mhísheóladh / go a
léigheadh go Mac Cailéin'; ach chan eil e buileach soilleir a bheil
Fionnlagh a' moladh tuigse MhicCailein air litreachas no air
àbhachdas.

'You are the most liberal at throwing banquets
in your time,
you are the best at handling a pointed rapier
of sharp edge.

'You are the most generous with gold and treasure
of all Clan Conn;
no more to you than the slops from washing
your tapered hands,
the giving of hospitality and bounty,
heap on heap.

'You are the fiercest at winning country
you do not possess;
to fight against you, O prince of Islay,
great the load.'

Great the load.

The Songbook of the Pillagers

This short poem, which provides the title of the present volume, can be understood as an encouragement to the compilation of the Book of the Dean of Lismore. The poem is addressed to Dubhghall (mac Eòin Riabhaich) MacGriogair, father of Seumas (the Dean of Lismore) and Donnchadh, the brothers who colloborated on the Book of the Dean. The suggestion is to produce an eclectic collection, including material from a range of sources, and that is indeed what eventually emerged.

The author of this poem, Fionnlagh Mac an Aba, who died in 1525, was chief of his clan, and appears to have been based at Bovain in Glen Dochart, at the head of Loch Tay. He is one of several Gaelic aristocrats whose compositions are preserved in the Book of the Dean, including the Caimbeul authors of poems 40–41 and 48–49. The poem also makes clear that the Caimbeuls were sophisticated patrons of poetry in its famous lines 'ná beir duan ar mhísheóladh / go a léigheadh go Mac Cailéin' ('don't bring anything inelegant / to MacCailein for perusal'). This suggestion may be ironic, however, the implication being

Duanaire na sracaire,
    dámadh áil libh a sgríobhadh,
fuaras féin don phacaire
    ní dá bhféadtar a líonadh.

Giodh iomdha na h-andaoine
    ar tí millidh na tuatha,
cha nfhaghthar 'na chomaoin-se
    aon réad san domhan uatha.   8

Do bhéasaibh na lorgánach,
    gion go mbeith uatha acht míle,
an teach 'gá mbia a gcomhdháil-sean,
    cha ruig iad é go h-oidhche.

Atá uasal anuasal
    aca 'na chotach cille;
dá mbéasaibh bheith 'g aitheasgadh:
    gidheadh nocha chluinn sinne.   16

Cha bhia mé 'gá sloinneadh-san,
    cha nfhuil agam dá seanchas
acht a mbeith san choinfheasgar
    agus na coin 'na leanmhain.

A Dhubhghaill, a chompánach,
    a mheic Eóin na lann líomhtha,
'gá bhfuil iúl na lorgánach,
    déan an Duanaire sgríobhadh.   24

Sgríobh go fiosach fireólach
    a seanchas is a gcaithréim;
ná beir duan ar mhísheóladh
    go a léigheadh go Mac Cailéin.

that Argyll could be relied upon to have such a sense of humour
as would allow him to appreciate a work containing much
irreverent material.

The Songbook of the Pillagers,
    should you be pleased to write it,
I have myself from the peddlerman
    something that might go to fill it.

Although there's many a character,
    who is set on ravishing the people,
not the slightest jot in recompense
    comes to light of their traditions.

Even if they have but a mile to go,
    it's a habit of the sluggards,
not to reach till the close-of-day
    the house where they will gather.

Theirs by church covenant
    the noble and the simple;
it is their custom to answer back:
    'Pooh, that doesn't concern us.'

I will not recite their ancestry,
    I know nothing of their story
save their appearance at eventide
    with the dogs following after.

O Dughall, my confidant,
    son of Eòin of the whetted weapons,
as you know the ways of the wanderers,
    you write the song-book.

Record knowledgeably and expertly
    their rants and traditions;
don't bring anything inelegant
    to MacCailein for perusal.

Cuimhnigh féin an comunn-sa,
   a Ghriogóir, mar do-chualais,
go bhfuil agam oradsa
   do chuid do chur san Duanair.   32

Ná biodh annsan domhan-sa
   do shagart ná do thuathach
'gá bhfuil ní 'na gcomhghar-san
   nach cuirthear é san Duanair.

Duanaire.

62. Fada Dhomh an Laighe-se

An Barún Eóghan MacCombaigh

Tha an dàn sìmplidh pearsanta seo, a rinneadh, is dòcha, mu
thoiseach an t-siathamh linn deug, a' cur an cèill faireachdainn
uile-choitcheann: cho sgìtheil 's a tha e a bhith anns an leabaidh
air sgàth tinneis. Tha am bàrd a' cumail a-mach gum biodh e
deònach beartas a chaitheamh airson a shlàinte fhaighinn air ais;
tha na rudan a tha e a' sònrachadh a' toirt deagh shealladh
dhuinn air na bha cudromach ann an dualchas Gàidheil a linne.

Tha e follaiseach gum b'e duine-uasal gun trèanadh foirmeil
a bha anns a' bhàrd seo, ach is e glè bheag de dh'eòlas a tha
againn mu dheidhinn. Chan e tiotal laghail a tha ann an 'barún'
ach ainm neo-fhoirmeil a bhathar a' cleachdadh airson cuid de
dh'uaislean aig deireadh nam Meadhan Aoisean. Is dòcha gu
bheil an sloinneadh 'MacCombaigh' – a bha cumanta ann am
Bràghaid Albann agus Gleann Sìdh aig an àm – co-cheangailte
ri sliochd Alasdair Mhòir Mhic an Rìgh (†1406), no 'Madadh-
allaidh Bhàideanach' mar a bha aig na Goill air. Ach chan eil
fianais againn a thaobh càirdeis eadar Eóghan agus Alasdair Mòr.

Fada dhomh an laighe-se,
   allmhurach liom mo shláinte;
bheirinn do luach leaghais bhuaim
   dá mbudh liom na táinte.

Remember, you, this partnership,
  O Griogar, just as you heard say,
that you are obliged to me
  to add your share to the song-book.

Let there not be in the whole wide world
  a single cleric or layman,
who has anything in his repertoire
  that is not included in the Songbook.

    Songbook.

Long Have I Been Bedridden

This simple and personal poem, probably composed in the early sixteenth century, expresses a universal sentiment – the tiresomeness of an illness that confines one to bed. The poet expresses his willingness to part with great wealth in order to regain his health; interestingly for the modern reader, the material things he summons up to express this wish are deeply rooted in Gaelic tradition and mythology.

The poet is evidently an aristocratic amateur, but we know little about him. The title 'baron' is not a formal office but a generic ascription for noblemen of a certain rank; the term is common in the late Middle Ages but its legal and political significance is not entirely understood. The name MacCombaigh – common in Breadalbane and Glenshee at the time – may be associated with the descendants of the so-called 'Wolf of Badenoch' (Alasdair Stiùbhart, Earl of Buchan (†1406), son of King David II), but the poet's connection to this celebrated ancestor is unknown.

    Long have I been bedridden,
      my health has become a stranger;
    I would give in return for recovery
      droves of cattle if I had them.

Táin bó Cuailnge, ceathra throm,
  táin bó Darta is bó Fliodhais
do-bheirinn is an tarbh trom,
  dá mbudh liom, i luach leaghais.   8

Greagh is eachraidh Mhanannáin,
  claidheamh is corn mhic Cumhaill,
dúdach Mhanannáin bheirinn,
  's ga bolga Chon Chulainn.

Ór Éibhir is Éireamhóin,
  's é bheith agam im chomhra,
cruit Chuircheóil do cheileadh brón,
  agus sgiath ríogh na [   ].   16

Long Laoimein nár luime lí,
  's í bheith agam ar cladach,
do-bheirinn-se a h-uile chí
  sul bhiam mar so ré fada.

Fada liom gan Alasdair
  Mac an Tóisigh a theachta;
dh'fhuadaicheadh sé an galar-sa,
  nach beinn mar so ré fada.   24

          Fada.

63. Fuath Liom

Gun urra

Tha an liosta de dh'adhbharan-gràine seo air a gleidheadh ann
an Leabhar Deadhan Lios Mòr agus tha e coltach gun do rinn-
eadh e mu thoiseach an t-siathamh linn deug. Ged a tha gearan-
an a' bhàird caochlaideach nan gnè, chithear annta na luachan a
tha a' nochdadh anns a' bhàrdachd àrd-nòsaich, mar am meas
air creachan, sealg agus aoigheachd. Tha a' ghràin-bhoireannach
a chithear anns an dàn cumanta gu leòr cuideachd.

The Drove of Cooley, hefty animals,
   the Drove of Dartaid and of Flidais,
and the mighty bull I'd deny myself,
   if they were mine, in return for well-being.

The horse studs and steeds of Manannán,
   the sword and the horn of Fionn MacCumhaill,
Cú Chulainn's disembowelling spear
   and Manannán's trumpet I'd surrender.

The gold of Éibhear and of Éireamhón,
   if I had them in my coffer,
Cuircheól's harp that banished despondency,
   and the sword of the king of [   ].

Laoimean's ship of no bareness of character,
   if she were mine on the foreshore,
of all I see I'd give everything,
   rather than be like this much longer.

I feel it long since Alasdair
   Mac an Tòisich has come to see me;
he would banish this malady
   so I'd not be like this much longer.

     Long

I Hate

This idiosyncratic list of pet hates is preserved in the Book of the Dean of Lismore and probably dates from the early sixteenth century. Although the complaints are diverse and seem almost random, they clearly reflect the principal values emphasised in more formal poetry such as esteem for raiding, hunting, and hospitality. The misogynist tone of the poem is also not unusual.

   The reference to distaste for poet-bands that include women

Chan eil e furasta an t-iomradh anns an dàrna rann air 'cliar ara mbí bean' a thuigsinn. Mar as trice bha am facal 'cliar' a' ciallachadh grunn bhàrd agus luchd-ealain de dhiofar sheòrsachan a chaidh air chuairt còmhla; bha cliù sònraichte aig 'Cliar Sheanchain'. Chan eil e idir follaiseach gun do ghabh boireannaich pàirt ann an cliair, ach is cinnteach nach robh àite sam bith aig boireannaich aig sgoiltean proifeiseanta nam file. Is e mnathan-uasal a bha anns na bana-bhàird as tràithe air a bheil eòlas againn (leithid Aithbhric inghin Corcadail, ùghdar dàn 28), agus fiù 's anns an t-seachdamh agus anns an ochdamh linn deug bha tòrr an-fhois ann a thaobh àite bhana-bhàrd leithid Màiri nighean Alasdair Ruaidh agus Mairearaid nighean Lachlainn.

> Fuath liom bheith anmoch ag triall,
>   fuath liom cliar ara mbí bean;
> fuath liom dobrón i dtigh n-óil,
>   fuath liom baile mór gan ghean.

> Fuath liom droichbhean ag fear math,
>   fuath liom flath ara mbí gruaim;
> fuath liom deoch anbhfann 's i daor;
>   fuath liom duine saor gan stuaim.   8

> Fuath liom a chogadh nó a shíth
>   nach léigeann a ní má seach;
> fuath liom ceannphort gan bheith cruaidh,
>   fuath liom sluagh nach déanadh creach.

> Fuath liom bheith fada ré port,
>   fuath liom bheith go h-olc fán bhiadh;
> fuath liom bean éadmhor 's í drúth;
>   fuath liom cú nach marbhann fiadh.   16

> Leasg liom dol i nÉirinn siar
>   ó nach maireann Brian ná Conn;
> fuath liom baintreach gan bheith mear,
>   fuath liom fear 's a aigneadh trom.

in the second stanza is somewhat difficult to interpret. The term *cliar* generally referred to bands of professional poets, often of different ranks in the literary hierarchy, who moved from court to court in search of patronage and hospitality. It is not clear whether women were ever included in such poet-bands, that is, the extent to which this poem refers to an actual rather than hypothetical or imagined source of distaste. We have no evidence of professional women poets in the late medieval period; the early women poets were aristocratic amateurs, and even in the seventeenth century leading women poets like Màiri nighean Alasdair Ruaidh encountered significant resistance from the established orders.

> I hate to be out travelling late,
>> I hate to see a woman among poets,
> I hate depression in a pub,
>> I hate a homestead without cheer.
>
> I hate a good man with a bad wife,
>> I hate a prince who is depressed,
> I hate drink that is weak but dear,
>> I hate a noble who lacks aplomb.
>
> I hate the war and the peace
>> of a man who shares not his wealth,
> I hate a chieftain who is not firm,
>> I hate a host that makes no raids.
>
> I hate to wait long for a boat,
>> I hate being mean about food,
> I hate a woman to be fast and lewd,
>> I hate a hound that kills no deer.
>
> I hate going to Ireland in the west,
>> since Brian and Conn are no more,
> I hate a widow who is no fun,
>> I hate a man whose spirits are low.

Fuath liom cailleach as olc néal
is a teanga go léir luath;
ní fhéadaim a chur i gcéill
gach ní dá dtugas féin fuath.   24

64. Is Fearr Sgíos Cos Bharr Gnímh Ghlain

Gun urra

Tha e coltach gun do rinneadh an dàn goirid seo à Leabhar an
Deadhain anns a' chiad phàirt den t-siathamh linn deug. Chan
eil 'dànfhacail' (dàin bheaga le blas sheanfhaclan orra) den
t-seòrsa seo ro chumanta am measg nan teacsaichean a thàinig
a-nuas thugainn bho na Meadhan Aoisean. Mar as trice, chaidh
dàin a ghleidheadh air sgàth an luach phoilitigich no spioradail,
ach cha robh na buannachdan sin a' buntainn ris na dànfhacail.

Is fearr sgíos cos bharr gnímh ghlain
ná fos agus sgíos meanman;
   mairidh sgíos meanman go bráth:
   cha mhair sgíos cos acht aontráth.

I hate an old hag in a bad mood
    with a tongue too ready to scold,
I seem unable to put into words
    everything that fills me with hate.

Better Tiredness of Feet

Short epigrammatic poems like this one, preserved in the Book of the Dean of Lismore and probably dating from the early sixteenth century, are not particularly common among the literary works of the late medieval period that have survived. Many works, especially formal panegyric poetry, were preserved for political or devotional reasons, but there was little instrumental motive for preserving works of this sort.

Better tiredness of feet from a brave deed
than inertness and tiredness of spirit;
    tiredness of feet lasts but a spell,
    tiredness of spirit lasts forever.

THE SONG TRADITION

PANEGYRIC

65. MhicPhàrlain an Arair

Am Bàrd Laomainneach

Seo aon de na dàin as sine a tha againn anns a' Ghàidhlig
dhùthchasaich (seach a' Ghàidhlig Chlasaigeach). Gheibhear an
seo mòran ìomhaighean is abairtean a tha cumanta anns a' chòd
molaidh a chithear ann am pailteas ann an saothar bàird an
t-seachdamh linn deug leithid Iain Luim, Eachainn Bhacaich
agus Màiri nighean Alasdair Ruaidh.

Is dòcha gun do rinneadh an dàn anns a' chiad phàirt den
t-siathamh linn deug. Bha dùthaich Chlann MhicPhàrlain mu
thimcheall an Arair, mu cheann a tuath Loch Laomainn, agus is
dòcha gur ann do Dhonnchadh MacPhàrlain, an ceann-cinnidh
a chaochail ann an 1547, a rinneadh e, oir is e 'deagh mhac
Dhonnchaidh' a tha am bàrd a' cantainn ri oighre (sreath 41).

Chan eil fiosrachadh sam bith againn mun bhàrd seach am
far-ainm aige, agus chan eil dad de dh'fhianais eile air an obair
litreachail aige.

> MhicPhàrlain an Arair,
>   Làmh àghmhor an einich,
> Fhir as fial ri h-ealaibh,
>   Bu tu riar' gach filidh.
>
> Mhic fhìor-ghlic fhearail
>   Leis an dìolar sgolaibh;
> Laoich chruaidh nach crìon aithne
>   Nì nas buaine d'onoir.   8
>
> Thèid d'eineach 's do nàire
>   Thar fineachd 's ùine;
> Gach filidh ag ràdh siud:
>   Gun sirear 's nach diùltar.
>
> Òlar fìon ad bhaile
>   'S iomad cliar 's luchd-ealaidh
> Air chlàr-dìsle 's fo-rainn
>   Th'air mirean teachd ad choinneimh.   16

To MacPhàrlain of Arrochar

This poem is one of the earliest surviving compositions in vernacular Scottish Gaelic, as opposed to the literary language of the bardic schools. This is also a valuable early example of the 'panegyric code', the complex system of imagery and rhetoric that developed more fully in the praise-poetry of the seventeenth century, in the work of poets like Iain Lom and Màiri nighean Alasdair Ruaidh.

The date of the poem is unclear but it was composed during the first half of the sixteenth century. The MacPhàrlains held territory around Arrochar, by Loch Lomond, and it may be addressed to Donnchadh MacPhàrlain, the clan chief who died in 1547, as the poet refers to his patron's heir as 'son of Donnchadh'.

Of the poet we know only his by-name, and no other works by him seem to have survived.

> MacPhàrlain of Arrochar,
> > renowned hand of bounty,
> man who is generous to learning,
> > you satisfy every poet.
>
> O man wise and powerful
> > by whom schools are supported,
> hardy hero of no mean reputation,
> > yet more lasting is your honour.
>
> Your modesty and reputation
> > spread over kindred and season;
> every poet proclaims this:
> > he who seeks won't be disappointed.
>
> Wine is drunk in your mansion
> > and many poets and men of learning,
> at dice boards with pieces
> > come cheerily to meet you.

Laoich threun dheas lùthmhor,
    Gam fuaighte beachd àghmhor,
Is sluagh teachd fod lùchairt
    Le buaidh-chreich od nàmhaid.

'N cur ruaig dhuts' gu dàna,
    Dan dualchas bhith cliùiteach;
Siud gheibhte 'ad chòir-sa:
    Treun-laochraidh bhorb lùthmhor.   24

'S iomad geur-lann thana,
    Làmh as làidir buille,
Cinn-bheirt chòmhdach chonach,
    Dol an tòs do choimeisg.

An àm truid b'e d'aighear
    Cuirp a bhith fo udhar,
T'fhiùthaidh bhith ga caitheamh,
    'S fir a' lùbadh iubhair.   32

'S an greas gàbhaidh gheibhte
    Den mheas chùbhraidh ubhal;
Laoich chròdha, sàr-làimh dheas
    Ag iomairt nan lùth-chleas.

Dod nàimhdibh-se e b'aithreach
    Dol an dàil do choimeisg;
'N cur a' bhlàir an tainead,
    Dhaibh bu nàir' an turas.   40

D'oighre deagh mhac Dhonnchaidh:
    Làmh ghleusd' air fiùbhaidh;
Fear nach maoim on àr-fhaich,
    Sluagh nach d'fhuiling iompach'.

Lem buidh'near buaidh-chosgair
    Ri guala rìgh sheasamh;
'S math an gnìomh 's an cosnadh
    Gun eagal roimh ghàbhaidh.   48

Powerful sturdy adept warriors
   connected with tales of valour,
and hosts coming to your palace
   with plunder from your enemy.

Bravely pursuing your battles,
   to be renowned is in their nature;
this would be found around you:
   a powerful fierce brave army.

Many a blade, sharp and slender,
   and hand of mighty impact,
rich protective helmets
   in the vanguard of your battle.

In time of strife you delighted
   in seeing wounded bodies,
your arrows made use of,
   and men flexing yew bows.

And there'd be found in pressing danger
   among the fragrant fruit an apple;
brave dextrous heroes
   plying swords agilely.

To your enemies it was distressing
   going to meet you in battle,
their forces growing thinner,
   for them a shameful matter.

Your heir, good son of Duncan,
   a well-trained hand on a weapon,
a man who does not flee from slaughter,
   a host who gives no quarter.

By them is won battle,
   standing at the king's shoulder;
good is the deed and the outcome,
   being fearless before danger.

'N àm luidreadh nam faobhar,
　　Na h-Araraich dhàna
Nach iarr barant saoghail —
　　Lasair cholg a b'ait leò.

Dol gu garbh an toiteal:
　　Srann de phìob air faiche,
Fir len dìolar crosan,
　　Òr-pheall 's e dearg-lasta　　　　　　56
Am barr croinn eang sìoda.

Is garbh-laochraidh sparrta,
　　An sgaball teann dìonach;
B'e miann a' mhic àghmhoir
　　'Oighreachd a bhith lìonmhor.

Ag iomairt an tàileisg
　　Am prionns-lios an fhìona;
Chan innsear beachd m'aigne　　　　　　64
　　Air àrmann na firinn —
De shìolach nam flath e
　　'S de fhreumh nan rìghrean.

Cha bhaoghal na fir
　　'S am foghail a-muigh;
Tha 'n t-Arar air theine
　　Chur faobhair am fuil;

Cha teotha buill ùird　　　　　　　　　　72
　　Air innein nam bolg
Na iomairt an eilg
　　Air mire le feirg.

'S e chualas mar aithris
　　Aig ealaidh gach tìre,
Air teachd chum do bhaile
　　Nach b'ainnis an dìoladh;　　　　　　80

Nis' ortsa, Thriath 'n Arair,
　　Thog mi caithream na firinn,
Is guma cian maireann
　　Do bhan-chèile ghnìomhach.

At the time of blades being walloped,
    brave Arrochar's warriors
who, of their lives want no assurance,
    the flash of swords would be their pleasure.

Going fiercely into battle
    the skirl of pipes on the greensward,
men by whom churches are paid for
    gold saddles fringed with crimson.
silken wings atop each arrow

And fierce armoured warriors
    in tight protective helmets;
it was the fortunate son's intention
    that his land should be thronging.

Playing at the chess-board
    in the royal fort of wine in plenty;
my regard for the true hero
    can never be told of —
he is descended from the princes
    and of the blood of the monarchs.

The men need not fear
    when there is a fray outside;
the laird of Arrochar is fired up
    to put blades in blood.

No hotter the blow of hammer
    on the anvil of bellows
than the play of the noble
    in the frenzy of anger.

This was heard as tidings
    in the songs of every district:
at your homecoming
    payment was no rarity.

Here's to you, O Lord of Arrochar,
    I have raised a truthful clamour,
and may she also be long lasting
    your diligent lady.

66. An Duanag Ullamh

Gun urra

Tha an dàn beòthail seo do Mhac Cailein, a rinneadh anns an
t-siathamh linn deug, cudromach air grunn adhbharan
litreachail agus eachdraidheil. A thaobh an dà chuid cànain agus
stoidhle tha an dàn a' seasamh eadar saothair nam file agus a'
bhàrdachd molaidh a thàinig gu bàrr anns an t-seachdamh linn
deug. Tha am bàrd a' cleachdadh cànan dùthchasach na
Gàidhlig Albannaich, ged tha grunn structaran is fhoirmean
clasaigeach rim faighinn ann cuideachd; agus tha mòran den
ìomhaigheachd gu math coltach ri cleachdaidhean bàird an
t-seachdamh linn deug. Is e 'snéadhbhairdne' an t-ainm a
chleachdar mu choinneimh na meadrachd seo, stoidhle a tha gu
math àrsaidh a bhathar ga cleachdadh gu sònraichte ann an
'crosanachd', a bha na mheasgachadh de mholadh (ann an
rannan) agus de dh'aoir (ann an earrannan ruisg).

Tha dà thionndadh den dàn rim faighinn anns na làmh-
sgrìobhainnean, agus tha e nas fhasa am faicinn a-nis mar dà
dhàn fa leth, oir tha uiread de dhiofaran eatarra. A rèir an
Ollaimh Uilleam MacGill'Ìosa, 'the surviving versions of the
poem all post-date an early contamination between two similar
compositions in the same *snéadhbhairdne* metre'. Uime sin chan
eil e furasta, ma tha e comasach idir, am bun-teacs a lorg.

Tha e coltach gun do rinneadh Tionndadh A do Chailean
Meallach, treas iarla Earra Ghàidheal, goirid mus do chaochail e
ann an 1529 agus gun do rinneadh Tionndadh B do
Ghill'Easbaig, ceathramh iarla Earra Ghàidheal (†1558),
uaireigin an dèidh 1555. Tha diofaran cudromach is inntinneach
eadar an dà thionndadh. Tha Tionndadh A a' moladh Chailein
mar sheirbheiseach dìleas Rìgh Alba agus a' sònrachadh nan
ceanglaichean aige ri cinnidhean tìr-mòr Shiorrachd Inbhir Nis;
ach chan eil iomradh sam bith air an Rìgh ann an Tionndadh B,
anns a bheil am bàrd a' dèanamh gaisgeach cròdha agus fear-
creacha de Mhac Cailein agus a' moladh nan dàimhean aige ri
cinnidhean Innse Gall a-mhàin.

Chan eil dad a dh'fhios againn mu ùghdar na duanaig (nan
duanag?) seo. Am beachd an Urramaich Uilleam MacMhathain,

The Finished Verses

This vivid sixteenth-century poem to the earl of Argyll, which survives in two distinct versions, has very considerable literary and historical value. In several respects it represents an intermediate point between the formal court poetry of the late Middle Ages and the vernacular praise-poetry that became dominant in the seventeenth century. The poem is composed in the Scottish Gaelic vernacular, but it uses a number of older, classical forms more typical of the learned poetry; much of the imagery of the poem is a harbinger of the 'panegyric code' that comes into full flower in the seventeenth century. It is composed in a centuries-old syllabic metre, a traditionally popular form known as *snéadhbhairdne* (marked most obviously by the alternation of long (eight-syllable) and short (four-syllable) lines. This metre was particularly associated with a style of composition known as *crosanachd* or *crosántacht*, which typically combined verse sections praising the subject of the poem with prose sections satirising his enemies. It may be that this poem once had such a satirical prose section, and that the sudden change of subject after line 52 (48 of version B) constitutes a point of hiatus once filled by a prose passage.

Two separate versions are given here; the two are sufficiently different that it is more useful to consider Version B a separate composition, reworked and updated, rather than a mere variant of Version A. It is not easy to untangle them; William Gillies has suggested 'that the surviving versions of the poem all post-date an early contamination between two similar compositions in the same *snéadhbhairdne* metre'.

Version A, which survives in several early manuscripts and was first published in 1776, is apparently addressed to Cailean Meallach, third earl of Argyll (†1529), and was probably composed in the late 1520s. Version B, which is preserved in a single manuscript, is apparently addressed to Gill'Easbaig, fourth earl of Argyll (†1558), and was probably composed in the mid-1550s. Although there is considerable overlap between the two versions, the specific references differ in significant respects: Version A lists allies not only in the Hebrides but also in the

b'e am bàrd aig Eachann Mòr MacGill'Eathain Dhubhaird a
dh'ullaich na rannan seo, an lùib a' phòsaidh (ann an 1557)
eadar a mhac, Eachann Òg, agus Seònaid, nighean Ghill'Easbaig,
an ceathramh iarla. Ach chan fhaighear dearbhadh air seo anns
an teacsa, agus chan eil na Leathanaich a' faighinn prìomhachas
anns an liosta de chàirdean anns an òran.

Tionndadh A

Triallaidh mi le m' dhuanaig ullaimh
  Gu rìgh Ghàidheal,
Fear aig am bi am baile dùmhail
  Sona saidhbhir.

Triath Earra Ghàidheal as feàrr faicinn
  'S as mò maitheas:
Cailean Iarla fo chliùidh
  As fial flaitheas.   8

Abhall uasal farsaing freumhach
  Do 'n cubhaidh moladh;
Crann as ùire dh'fhàs troimh thalamh,
  Làn de thoradh.

Seabhag as uaisle thèid sna neulaibh,
  Crann air chrannaibh;
Mac rath do chum Dia gu h-ealamh
  Don chlèir ullamh.   16

Central Highlands (Friseals and Clann Mhic an Tòisich), and refers to Cailean's service in suppressing a rebellion in the Borders in 1528 on behalf of King James V, while Version B appears to refer to an annual payment agreed in 1555 by An Calbhach Ó Domhnaill, chief of the Ó Domhnaills of Tír Chonaill, in exchange for the earl's military support for An Calbhach's Irish campaigns. Interestingly, Version A presents MacCailein as a loyal royal officer while Version B depicts him more as a traditional Gaelic warlord, making no mention of the king of Scotland.

We know nothing of the poet who composed these 'finished verses', but he may well have been a *bard* in the strict sense, a versifier of somewhat lower status without the polish of formal training in a professional school. According to tradition he was in service to MacGill'Eathain of Duart, but there is no evidence in the texts themselves to confirm this.

Version A

I travel with my finished verses
    to the prince of Gaels,
a man whose thronging household
    is cheerful and wealthy.

Argyll's lord of best appearance
    and greatest bounty:
Cailean, earl most famous
    for generous ruling.

A spreading apple-tree deeply-rooted,
    his praise is fitting;
the freshest tree to break the topsoil,
    laden with produce.

Noblest hawk that flies the heavens,
    tree crowning the forest,
son of fortune God made expertly,
    prepared for the poets.

Mar leòmhann neartmhor nimhneach làidir,
  Ann àm trioblaid thu;
'S beag nach deachaidh Alb' air udal
  Gus na theasraig thu.

'N tràth ghluaiseas Cailean Iarla
  'S a shluagh bunaidh,
Cuirfear leis air fairge o chaladh
  Cabhlach ullamh.   24

Loingeas leathann làidir luchdmhor
  Dealbhach dìonach
As sleamhna slios a dhol san fhuaradh
  Darchruaidh ràmhach.

Togar an sin na geal-chroinn chorrach,
  Suas le 'n lònaibh:
'S iomad ball bhiodh teann gan dèanamh
  Ann àm dhaibh seòladh.   32

Dèantar an stagh dìreach, dualach
  Mun bhràigh thoisich,
Togar na siùil mhòr' le maise
  Le sgoid lìn croiseach.

Dèantar a' chluas sa chìch thoisich
  Dhol san fhuaradh,
Mar steud ro-luath, 's sruth ga sàrach,
  'S muir ga bualadh.   40

Liuthad laoch fulangach meanmnach
  Dòrngheal treubhach,
A dh'iomradh lùb air a h-àlach
  Socrach sèitreach.

'N deagh shluagh lìonmhor fo làn armaibh,
  O 'm barcaibh reamhra,
Air a dheas-làimh daonnan neart nan Guibhneach,
  Aig Rìgh Alba.   48

Like a lion, powerful baneful mighty
    are you in time of trouble:
Scotland almost in jeopardy
    before you saved her.

When earl Cailean processes
    with his attendant army,
he sends out to sea from the harbour
    well-rigged vessels.

Broad robust laden galleys,
    sound and shapely,
of sleekest side against the weather,
    oak-hard, oars in plenty.

The bright erect masts are hoisted
    up with their rigging,
many a taut rope made ready
    at the time of their sailing.

Secured the strong plaited halyard
    to the stem-post,
hoisted the big broad beautiful mainsails
    and small cross-sheet.

The sheet is tied to the forebreast
    driving windward:
like a swift steed, the tide against her,
    and the sea pounding.

Many a patient mettlesome warrior,
    fists clenched courageous,
would row the oars till they crumpled,
    steady panting.

The good host, coming armed and thronging
    from their stout galleys:
Caimbeul strength always on the right hand
    of the King of Scotland.

Le lagh a' cheartais, nuair a b'èiginn,
 Le cruaidh chogadh,
Bhuidhinn sibh buaidh, 's tha sibh òirdheirc;
 Fhuair sibh toiseach.

Nì 'n aithne dhomhsa bhur càirdean
 Ge fairsing m'eòlas,
Ach 's ro-chinnteach leat gun èireadh
 MacLeòid Leòdhais.   56

Fuil Mhic an Tòisich gu h-ullamh,
 Feachd MhicShimidh;
'S mairg air an leigeadh iad am buillean
 Ann àm lann iomairt.

Clann Gille Eòin gu làidir lìonmhor
 On Fhèinn Mhuileach,
An dream thug buaidh anns gach bealach
 'S a b' fheàrr fuireach.   64

Brollach Chlann Domhnaill ort a' feitheamh
 D'an cliù buaidh-làraich
Uaislean Innse Gall gu coimhlion,
 Fir gun fhàilinn.

Fhuair thu siud on rìgh 's gum b'airidh
 Bhith d' àrd-cheannard,
Air fearaibh Alba, 's bhith d' àrd-bhreitheamh
 Nithe 's anama.   72

Atà thu d' àrd-fhear coimhid is glèidhidh
 Air a' chrìch thall;
Ràinig, 's bhuadhaich air ar nàimhdean,
 'S fhuair sibh sìochaint.

Air àrd-chomhairle na h-Alba,
 'S tu 's stiùir uile,
Do cho-mhath nì 'n d'fhuaras 'n seanchas
 O linn Uilleim.   80

When required, with the law of justice,
   with harsh warfare,
you won victory, and you are famous:
   you won the vantage.

I am not acquainted with your allies
   though wide my knowledge,
but it is certain MacLeòid of Lewis
   would rise with you.

Mac an Tòisich blood will stand ready
   and the host of clan Friseal;
woe to those whom their blows beleaguer
   when swords are playing.

Clann Gill'Eathain, numerous and sturdy,
   Mull warriors,
the tribe victorious in every defile
   and who best resisted.

Clann Domhnaill's vanguard, renowned for winning,
   waits on your orders;
all of the Hebridean nobles,
   men without defect.

The king made you, quite rightly,
   high commander
of the men of Scotland and a justiciar
   of church and state matters.

You are the chief guardian and defender
   of the far border;
you came, won over your enemies,
   and achieved concord.

Of all on Scotland's high council,
   you're the helmsman;
your match I've not heard of
   since the time of William.

Ualas, flath nam fear gun choimeas
   Am measg dhaoine;
Cailean na dhòigh-sin gun choimeas,
   An t-Iarl' Aorach.

Ge ro-mhòr d' inbhe, d' ainm 's d' onair,
   'S mò do ghliocas,
Rinn thu buna-stèidh na firinn,
   Is a' cheartais.   88

Rinneadh leat dlighe cheart
   Do lag 's do làidir,
Beannachd gach aon duine ad chuideachd
   Ghall is Ghàidheal.

An t-Athair cumhachdach do d' ghlèidheadh,
   'S am Mac Fìrinn,
An Spiorad Naomh dhìon do nàire
   O rìgh Loch Fìne.   96

Nì 'n d' fhuaras do chomhaith dh'urrainn
   'S nì mò dh'iarras:
A cheann nam fear bu phailte cùram,
   Leat a thriallam.

      Triallaidh.

Tionndadh B

Triallaidh mi le m' dhuanaig ullaimh
   Gu rìgh Ghàidheal,
Fear aig am bi am baile dùmhail
   Sona saidhbhir.

Triath Earra Ghàidheal as feàrr faicinn
   'S as mò maitheas:
Gille Easbaig Iarla fo chliùidh
   As fial flaitheas.   8

Wallace, prince without equal
    among the people,
Cailean likewise without equal,
    Earl of Inveraray.

Though great your status, name and honour,
    greater your wisdom;
you laid the base for the foundation
    of truth and justice.

By you just laws were enacted
    for the weak and mighty;
all in your retinue give you their blessing,
    both Gall and Gàidheal.

May the mighty Father keep you always
    and the Son of Righteousness,
and the Holy Spirit who protected your virtue
    O Loch Fyne's ruler.

I never found a chief to match you,
    no more do I need to,
O leader of the men of gravest duty,
    to you I travel.

        I travel.

Version B

I travel with my finished verses
    to the prince of Gaels,
a man whose thronging household
    is cheerful and wealthy.

Argyll's lord of best appearance,
    and greatest bounty:
Gill'Easbaig, Earl most famous
    for generous ruling.

Seabhag as uaisle thèid sna neulta,
   Crann air chrannaibh;
Mac rath do chum Dia gu h-ullamh
   Do'n chlèir ealamh;

Abhall uasal farsaing freumhach
   Do 'n cubhaidh moladh;
Crann as ùire dh'fhàs troimh thalamh,
   Làn de thoradh.   16

Dias abaich chruithneachd 's i lomlàn
   Am measg seagail:
'S beag nach deachaidh Alba air udal
   An àird air th'eagal.

'N tràth ghluaiseas Gille Easbaig Iarla
   Le shluagh bunaidh,
Cuirear leis air fairge o chaladh
   Ard-rìgh ullamh.   24

Loingeas leathann làidir luchdmhor
   Dealbhach dìonach
Sleamhain sliosrèidh ro-luath ràmhach
   Darchruaidh dìreach.

Togar leò na geal-chroinn chorrach
   Suas le 'n lònaibh:
B'iomdha ball bhiodh teann gan dèanamh
   'N am dhuit seòladh.   32

Dèantar an stagh dìonach dualach
   Do'n mhaoil thoisich,
Togar an seòl mòr leathann maiseach
   'S an sgòdlin croiseach.

Dèantar a' chluas do'n chìch thoisich
   Dol san fhuaradh:
An steud ro-luath, sruth 'ga sàiltibh
   'S muir 'ga bualadh.   40

Noblest hawk that flies the heavens,
    tree crowning the forest,
son of fortune God made expertly,
    ready to reward poets.

A spreading apple-tree deeply-rooted,
    his praise is fitting;
the freshest tree to break the topsoil,
    laden with produce.

Ripe wheat-ear, full to bursting,
    among the rye-stalks:
Scotland almost in jeopardy
    at the height of your anger.

When Earl Gill'Easbaig processes
    with his attendant army,
he sends out to sea from the harbour
    well-rigged vessels.

Broad robust laden galleys,
    sound and shapely,
sleek streamline swift oars bristling,
    oak-hard, deadly.

The bright erect masts are hoisted
    up with their rigging,
many a taut rope made ready
    at the time of your sailing.

Secured the strong plaited halyard
    to the stem-post,
hoisted the big broad beautiful mainsail
    and small cross-sheet.

The sheet is tied to the forebreast
    driving windward:
the swift steed, the tide at her hooves
    and the sea pounding.

'S iomadh laoch fuileachdach meanmnach
    Dòrngheal trèitheach
A dh'iomradh lùb air a h-àlach
    Gu sunndach sèitreach.

Do shluagh lìonmhor leathann armach
    Air bhàrcaibh reamhra:
'S mairg air 'n dèanadh feachd Uí Dhuibhne
    Creach na Samhna.   48

Chan aithne dhomh fad a-mach ort
    'S nì math m'eòlas,
Ach 's ro mhath mo dhòigh as àbhaist
    MacLeòid Leòdhais.

Clann Ghille Eòin gu làidir lìonmhor
    Den Fhèinn Mhuilich,
Dream a thug buaidh anns gach bealach,
    'S a b'fheàrr fuireach.   56

Tigidh Seumas nan Ruag gu d'bhaile
    Gach uair shirinn;
Uaisle Innse Gall an coimhlion,
    Mar adeirim.

Tigidh gu lìonmhor gu d'bhaile
    Le 'n sluagh daoine:
Leat a bhì Alba air a h-àlach,
    'S an Fhraing bhraonach.   64

Cìos as uaisle aig fearaibh Albann,
    Feachd is loingeas:
'S leat-sa sin gu h-umhal tairis
    'N tùs gach conais.

Thig thugad cìos Thìre Conaill
    A bhith bheò-chalma
Conn a-rìs, bu chruaidh a chuibhreach
    Le a shluagh meanmnach.   72

Many a bloody mettlesome warrior,
    fists clenched courageous,
would row the oars till they crumpled,
    exultant panting.

Your hosts, armed and numerous,
    on sturdy galleys:
woe on whom the men of Clan Caimbeul
    make their Hallowe'en plunder.

I cannot fathom your influence
    and my knowledge is not good,
but I am certain these frequent you:
    MacLeòid of Lewis,

And Clan Gill'Eathain, powerful, plentiful
    of the Mull warriors,
a tribe that were victorious in every battle?
    and best resisted;

Seumas of the Routs visits your homestead
    whenever my enquiry;
all the nobility of the Hebrides
    as I stated.

There comes crowding to your homestead
    with their armies:
yours is Scotland and her levy
    and dewy France;

The most tribute of the men of Scotland,
    the most troops and galleys:
those are yours, obedient and pliant,
    in every conflict.

To you comes Tirconnell's tribute,
    ready for battle;
a second Conn, hard his bondage,
    with his spirited army.

An t-Athair cumhachdach do d' choimhead
'S am Mac Fìrinn,
'S an Spiorad Naomh dhìon do nàire
A rìgh Loch Fìne.

Cha d' fhuaras do chomhaith dh'urrainn
'S nì mò dh'iarras:
A rìgh nam fear as pailte cùram,
'S leat-sa thriallas.   80

    Triallaidh.

67. Caismeachd Ailein nan Sop

Eachann MacGill'Eathain, Tighearna Chola (An Clèireach Beag)

Tha e coltach gun do rinneadh an t-òran molaidh ainmeil seo
mu 1537; tha e air aon de na dàin as sine a tha againn anns a'
Ghàidhlig dhùthchasaich (seach a' Ghàidhlig Chlasaigeach),
agus tha structar agus cleachdaidhean an dàin anabarrach
inntinneach air sgàth sin.

Is e cuspair an dàin seo an spùinneadair mì-chliùiteach Ailean
nan Sop MacGill'Eathain – mac Lachlainn Chatanaich, an
deicheamh ceann-cinnidh aig Cloinn Ghill'Eathain Dhubhaird,
agus bràthair an aonamh chinn-chinnidh deug, Eachann Mòr, a
rinn (is dòcha) dàn 50. Tha an dàn seo a' cur cuideam sònraichte
air sgilean seòladaireachd Ailein, rud a tha a' freagradh air an
eòlas eachdraidheil a tha againn air an duine.

A dh'aindeoin a' mholaidh a gheibhear anns an dàn, tha beul-
aithris a' cumail a-mach gun do rinn am bàrd, Eachann (mac
Iain Abraich) MacGill'Eathain, air an robh am far-ainm 'An
Clèireach Beag', an dàn an dèidh do Ailean prìosanach a
dhèanamh dheth; chaidh an t-òran a chumadh airson a shaorsa
fhaighinn.

Ach tha e cinnteach gu robh seòladh na phàirt den chòd-
mholaidh. Nochdaidh rannan mu sheòladh agus a bhith a' toirt
long air tìr anns na rannan ann an sgeulachdan na Fèinne;

May the mighty Father keep you always
and the Son of Righteousness,
and the Holy Spirit who protected your virtue,
O Loch Fyne's ruler.

I never found a chief to match you,
no more do I need to,
O leader of the men of gravest duty,
to you I travel.

Travel.

A War-Song for Ailean nan Sop

This spirited song of praise for the notorious brigand Ailean nan Sop MacGill'Eathain – son of Lachlann Catanach MacGill' Eathain, tenth chief of the MacGill'Eathains of Duart, and brother of the eleventh chief, Eachann Mòr, putative author of poem 50 – appears to date from about 1537; it is one of the oldest surviving poems composed in the Scottish Gaelic vernacular, and its structure and technique are of considerable literary interest.

The poem places particular emphasis on Ailean's seafaring skills, a classic theme in Gaelic poetry and something fully in keeping with his historical reputation. (His sobriquet *nan sop* 'of the wisps' may be derived from his practice of setting burning wisps of straw to buildings in the course of his many raids). The poem is somewhat deceptive, however, for tradition has it that the poet, Eachann (mac Iain Chaim) MacGill'Eathain, nicknamed 'An Clèireach Beag' ('The Little Clerk'), had been taken prisoner by Ailean nan Sop and composed the poem as the price of his freedom.

However, it is indisputable that sailing had become a topos for praise. Sailing and beaching are emphasised in the runs of Fenian tales; sea-faring constitutes an episode in the panegyric

nochdaidh seòladh mar mholadh anns an 'Duanag Ullamh' (dàn 66) agus san 'Iorram Dharaich' (dàn 79), agus mar a chaochladh anns an aoir mun luing anns a bheil boireannaich mar sgioba (dàn 44). Anns an t-seachdamh linn deug dh'fhaodadh seòladh a bhith na phrìomh phàirt de dhàn, mar eisimpleir ann an 'Iorram do Bhàta Mhic Dhòmhnaill' aig Iain Lom agus anns an 'Làir Donn' aig Murchadh Mòr mac mhic Mhurchaidh. Chaidh a leasachadh fiù a-rithist le Alasdair mac Mhaighstir Alasdair ann am 'Birlinn Chloinn Raghnaill'.

B'e an Clèireach Beag an còigeamh ceann-cinnidh aig Cloinn Ghill'Eathain Chola, agus mar sin bha e càirdeach do Ailean nan Sop. Fhuair e ceannas a' chinnidh an dèidh bàs athar, Iain Cam, uaireigin eadar 1542 agus 1558, agus fhuair Eachann fhèin bàs an dèidh 1583. Bhathar ga aithneachadh mar dhuine foghlaimte, cràbhaidh, agus tha dàn eile da chuid air cuspair nan Deich Àithntean air tighinn a-nuas thugainn.

Chan eil e soilleir dè as coireach gu bheil am facal 'caismeachd' ga chleachdadh an co-cheangal ris an òran seo; is math a dh'fhaodte gun deach measgachadh a dhèanamh eadar an dàn seo agus am fonn pìobaireachd 'Caismeachd Eachainn mhic Ailein nan Sop'.

Tha a h-uile leathrann ceangailte tron dàn air fad le comhardadh air *a* san treas lide bhon deireadh (ch*a*sgairt duit: n*ea*rtmhoraich: m*a*sgalach: c*a*daltach etc) agus le aicill.

'S mithich dhùinne, mar bhun ùmhlachd,
    Dàn bùrduin a chasgairt duit,
A fhleasgaich bhrìoghmhoir fhliuchas pìosan
    Le d' dhibh spìosair neartmhoraich;
Noch nar cheilte fion na Frainge
    Na theach meanmnach masgalach —
Shìol uaibhreach nach biodh uaigneach —
    Om biodh sluaigh gu cadaltach;
'S iomadh geòcach ann ad chòsan
    Agus deòraidh aigeantach.
Nuair leigeadh iad a-mach am bàrcaidh
    Far an càball ro-ghasda
Ceanglar umpa, mar bhur n-àbhaist,
    Cuan a b' àird do chasgairt leò —

8

'An Duanag Ullamh' (poem 66) and in 'An Iorram Dharaich' (poem 79), and the converse in the satire of a boat crewed by women (poem 44); in the seventeenth century, sea-faring could become the main focus of praise, as in Iain Lom MacDhòmhnaill's 'Iorram do Bhàta Mhic Dhòmhnaill' ('An Oar-Song for James MacDonald's Galley') and Murchadh Mòr MacCoinnich's 'An Làir Donn' ('The Brown Mare'). The genre is most developed in Alasdair mac Mhaighstir Alasdair's 'Birlinn Chloinn Raghnaill' ('Clanranald's Galley').

An Clèireach Beag was the fifth chief of the MacGill'Eathains of Coll, a cadet branch of the clan, and a distant cousin of Ailean nan Sop. He succeeded his father Iain Cam sometime between 1542 and 1558, and Eachann himself died sometime after 1583. He had a reputation as a scholarly and pious man; a poem of his on the subject of the Ten Commandments has also survived.

The term *caismeachd* usually refers a war-tune and seems inapposite to this poem; it may at some stage have been confused with 'Caismeachd Eachainn mhic Ailein nan Sop', a pipe-tune composed for Ailean's son.

The translation echoes the stress pattern of the original where lines end alternately with penultimate and prepenultimate stress.

It behoves me, as a modest homage,
    to declaim to you some lampooning verse,
O powerful champion who wets goblets
    with your spiced liquor, intoxicant;
in whose flattering household
    French wine was no mystery,
making the hosts grow drowsy,
    a proud tribe not lacking company,
with many a minstrel made welcome
    and lively traveller fitted in.
When they let out their galleys
    from their cables most powerful
that secure them as is your practice
    they may master the roughest seas;

'S nitear sin a rèir a chèile,
   Gun fheum air a h-athdèanamh —   16
Beairt chaol righinn lìonmhor chainbe
   Gun aon snaidhm marcaich oirr'
'N ceangal re failbheagaibh iarainn,
   Droineap nach iarr acarachd:
Sin air dèanamh lughach làidir
   Le spionnadh àrd sa cheart-uair sin,
Gus 'n tugadh air a crannaibh claonadh
   Taobh na gaoithe de cheart-ruigin.   24
Nuair a shuidheadh iad air a crann cèille,
   Gach fear Fèin re dreapaireachd,
A liuthad sodar mhuir anfaidh,
   'S e gu ceanngheal caiteanach,
A bhriotadh gacha taobh d'a brannradh,
   'S e an coimh-ruith re baidealaibh;
Fadadh fradhairc anns na neulaibh —
   Slat o beul a dh'aicinn-sa,   32
A' dol timcheall sruth nan sàilean,
   'S i gu leanbhail tartarach,
'S iomad lùireach 'n ceangal ri h-eàrrach
   'S bogha dearg Sasgannach;
Crainn air an locradh o rinn gu dosaibh
   Le an cinn dhodach fhadghàinneach.
Nuair chunnacadar am fad bhuat
   Na crìochan ris an robh fuath aca-san.   40
Ghlacadar na fuirbidh righne
   Nan dòidibh mìn ladarna;
Rinn iad an t-iomram teann teth tògtha
   Làidir, eòlach, acfainneach.
Thug iad cudrom air na liaghaibh
   'S ràimh gam pianadh acasan;
Chuir iad am beòil mhòr re chèile,
   'S an dà chlèith an t-sracadh sin.   48

and without need to repeat it
 this is done systematically:
a rigging of plentiful fine tough canvas
 with no use of running-knots —
is secured to iron bolt-rings,
 tackle that requires no gentleness;
with brute strength at the right moment
 this is done neatly forcefully,
so the masts are seen bending
 to the rigging's leeward-side.
When they sat on the topmast,
 every hero of them clambering,
the stormy sea was in such motion,
 white-crested and turbulent,
her rail spattered on either bulwark,
 the current racing her bulging sails.
Clear vision up to the heavens —
 I could see her bowsprit jutting out,
skirting the tidal currents
 she's childlike in her clamouring,
with many a shield round her gunwales
 and ruddy bow of the English style,
arrows whittled from point to feathers
 with long-shafted vicious heads.
When they saw in the distance
 the lands of their enemies
oars were grabbed by tough heroes
 in their fists, smooth and resolute;
they rowed hard hot expertly,
 powerfully potently springingly,
pitting their weight against the oar-blades,
 the shafts stressed to breaking-point;
ramming the gunwales together
 and the oar-banks in that massacring.

68. Òran na Comhachaig

Domhnall mac Fhionnlaigh nan Dàn

A rèir an Dr Iain MacAonghuis b'e Domhnall mac Fhionnlaigh nan Dàn, a bha beò anns an dàrna pàirt den t-siathamh linn deug agus a rinn Òran ainmeil na Comhachaig, 'the last of the great hunter-gatherers'. Chuir e seachad iomadach bliadhna anns an fhàsach eadar Gleann Comhann, Raineach agus Bràigh Loch Abar. Gheibhear anns an dàn seo iomadach ìomhaigh, samhla agus beachd-smuain a tha rim faighinn an dà chuid ann an litreachas àrsaidh na Gàidhlig agus, a-rithist, ann am bàrdachd Dhonnchaidh Bhàin Mhic an t-Saoir.

Tha pailteas de dh'ainmean-àite air an ainmeachadh anns an dàn, a' comharrachadh sgìre bho Loch Lìobhann mu dheas gu Spithean mu thuath, bho Bheinn Nibheis mun iar gu Beinn Eallair mun ear. Aig teas-meadhan an òrain tha crìochan Loch Trèig, agus gu h-àraidh Creag Uanach, cnoc aig iar-dheas an locha. Air gualainn Creig Uanaich (no is dòcha Gairbh-bheinne, a tha faisg oirre) tha an t-Sròn, agus is ann an co-cheangal ri seo a tha a' chomhachag ga h-ainmeachadh fhèin mar 'comhachag bhochd na Sròine'.

Ged a bhuineadh Domhnall mac Fhionnlaigh do Dhomhnallaich Ghleann Comhann, bha e dlùth-cheangailte ri Dòmhnallaich na Ceapaich, aig an robh sealbh air Bràigh Loch Abar. Tha grunn cheann-cinnidh air an ainmeachadh anns an òran, nam measg Alasdair Carrach (a ghabh pàirt ann an Cath Gairbheach maille ri a bhràthair, Domhnall, Triath nan Eilean) (faic dàn 34), Alasdair nan Gleann, agus Raghnall Mòr, às an tug cinn-chinnidh Dhomhnallaich na Ceapaich am far-ainm dualchasach, Mac Mhic Raghnaill.

Chithear cuimhneachan sìmplidh do Dhomhnall mac Fhionnlaigh taobh a-muigh an dorais aig Cille Choirill (eadar an Fhearsaid agus Drochaid Ruaidh), ri taobh cuimhneachan Iain Luim, am bàrd as ainmeile a bha aig Domhnallaich na Ceapaich.

Tha an dàn seo stèidhichte air dùthchas mar bhun-smuain, air aonachd eadar an tìr, na daoine agus an dòigh-beatha. Mar a nochd ban-dia na h-abhainn ann am miotas nan Gàidheal, no

The Song of the Owl

This remarkable poem, or conflated cycle of poems, was composed around the end of the sixteenth century by Domhnall mac Fhionnlaigh nan Dàn, described by John MacInnes as 'the last of the great hunter-gatherers', who spent much of his life in the empty borderlands between Glen Coe, Rannoch and Brae Lochaber. The poem shows many connections to earlier Gaelic literature and anticipates one of the great masterpieces of eighteenth-century poetry, Donnchadh Bàn Mac an t-Saoir's 'Moladh Beinn Dòbhrain'.

The poem mentions a myriad of placenames in the area, ranging from Loch Lyon in the south to the River Spean in the north, from Ben Nevis in the west to Ben Alder in the east; these are identified and discussed in Professor Robert Rankin's exhaustive articles. The heartland of the poem is the area around Loch Treig, including Fersit at the north end of the loch and Creag Uanach, a mountain by the southwest corner. The owl of the title identifies herself as '*comhachag bhochd na Sròine*'; *an t-Sròn* appears to be a shoulder either of Creag Uanach or of nearby Garbh-bheinn.

Although Domhnall mac Fhionnlaigh actually belonged to the Glen Coe branch of Clann Domhnaill, he was more closely associated with the Keppoch branch, who held the territory of Brae Lochaber, to the north of Loch Treig. The poem names a number of prominent chiefs of the Keppoch MacDhomhnaills, including Alasdair Carrach (who fought for his brother Domhnall at the Battle of Harlaw (see poem 34)), Alasdair nan Gleann, and Raghnall Mòr, from whom the chiefs of the Keppoch branch took their hereditary patronymic Mac Mhic Raghnaill.

A simple memorial to Domhnall mac Fhionnlaigh stands near the church door at Cille Choirill (between Fersit and Roy Bridge), adjacent to the grave of the great seventeenth-century poet of the Keppoch MacDhomhnaills, Iain Lom.

The poem is an exposition of the Gaelic idea of *dùthchas*, a unity between land, people and culture. In the way that rivers

mar a chaidh an draoidh Amergin na thonn, na ghaoith agus na fhitheach ann an *Lebor Gabála*, 's dòcha gu bheil a' chailleach-oidhche seo na riochdachadh den tìr. Tha na h-ainmean-àite a' dèanamh soilleir cò an talamh air a bheil i a-mach agus ciamar a tha iad ceangailte gu bràth ri eachdraidh nan daoine. Nì i soilleir cò leis a bu chòir dhan talamh a bhith agus dè an seòrsa gnìomha anns am bu chòir dhaibh a bhith an sàs. Ma tha an leughadh seo ceart, seallaidh e cho fada 's a bha buaidh aig bun-smaoineachadh ro-Chrìosdail air cultar nan Gàidheal.

'A chomhachag bhochd na Sròine,
    A-nochd is brònach do leaba,
'S ma bha thu ann ri linn Donnghail
    'S beag iongnadh gur trom leat d' aigne.'

'Gur comhaois mise don daraig
    O bha h-aillean beag sa chòinnich;
'S iomadh àl a chuir mi romham,
    'S mi comhachag bhochd na Sròine.'   8

'Ach a-nis atà tu aosda,
    Dèan-sa d'fhaosaid ris an t-sagart;
Is innis duinne gun euradh
    Gach aon sgeula d'a bheil agad.'

''S furasta dhomhsa sin innse
    Gach aon là millteach dhan d' rinneas
Cha raibh mi mionnach na breugach
    Ged a bha mo bheul gun bhinneas.   16

'Cha d'rinn mi riamh braid no mèirle,
    No cladh no tèarmann a bhriseadh;
Ri m' fhear fhèin cha d'rinn mi iomluas:
    Gur cailleach bhochd ionraic mise.

''S ann a bhiodh chuid de m' shinnsir
    Eadar Innseach 's an Fhearsaid;
'S a' chuid eile dhiubh mun Dèabhadh,
    A' seinn gu h-aoibhinn san fheasgar.   24

represent the goddess of the land in Gaelic mythology and that
a druid such as Amergin in the *Lebor Gabála* (*Book of Invasions*)
can take on the forms of many different aspects of nature, the
owl here may be a personification of the land in general. In the
recitation of place-names the area in question is made clear and
how it is permanently imbued with its people's history. She
makes it clear who should be in charge of the land and what sort
of heroic culture they should espouse. If this reading of the poem
is right, it indicates how long pre-Christian ideas prevailed in
Gaelic culture.

'O forlorn owl of Strone,
    tonight your bed is mournful;
if you were alive in the time of Donnghal,
    no wonder you feel your spirit heavy.'

'I am ages with the oak-tree
    since its sapling was small in the moss;
many a brood have I begotten,
    yet I am the forlorn owl of Strone.'

'But now that you are aged,
    to the priest make confession,
and tell me without omission
    every one of your stories.'

'The telling for me is easy,
    every punishing day I went through;
I was prone neither to swearing nor lying
    though my mouth lacked sweetness.

'I never robbed or plundered,
    nor violated grave nor sanctuary;
to my mate I was never faithless,
    I'm a poor upstanding old woman.

'Some of my forebears were living
    between Innseach and Fersit,
and some others around Dèabhadh,
    singing joyfully at evening.

'Chunnaic mi Alasdair Carrach,
    Duine b'allail' bha an Alb' e;
'S tric a bha mi seal ga èisteachd
    'S e ri rèiteach an tuim-shealga.

'Chunnaic mi Aonghas na dheaghaidh,
    'S cha b'e siud rogha bu tàire;
'S ann san Fhearsaid bha a bhunadh,
    'S bhiodh a mhuileann air Eas Làradh.'   32

'Bu lìonmhor cogadh is creachadh
    Bha 'n Loch Abar anns an uair sin,
Càite 'n robh thusa 'gad fhalach,
    Eòin bhig na mala gruama?

'Nuair a chunnaic mi na creacha
    A' gabhail seachad le fuathas
Thug mi ruathar bharr an t-sratha
    'S bha mi grathann an Creig Uanach.'   40

'Creag mo chridhe-sa Creag Uanach,
    Creag an d'fhuaras cuid de m' àrach;
Creag nan aighean 's nan damh siùbhlach,
    'S i a' chreag iùlmhor fhonnmhor fheurach.

'A' chreag fan iadhadh an fhaghaid,
    Leamsa bu mhiann a bhith ga tadhailt,
'M bu bhinn guth cinn gallain gadhair
    A' cur greigh air gabhail chumhaing.   48

'Òlaidh mi 's cha trèig mi h-ionnachd
    Uaithe cha tèid mi air siollan;
'S i muime 'n fhèidh do-nì 'n langan
    Am buinne deas ro-gheal fionnfhuar.

'Binn a h-iolaire fa bruachaibh,
    Binn a cuach 's is binn a h-eala;
Seachd binne na sin am blaodhan
    Do nì an laoghan beag breac ballach.   56

'I saw Alasdair Carrach,
    the most eminent man in Scotland;
often I spent a while listening
    as he shared out the hunt's booty.

'I saw Aonghas who followed,
    no shame in that selection;
his dwelling was in Fersit,
    his mill at the Falls of Làradh.'

'Much warfare and raiding
    happened at that time in Lochaber;
where were you in hiding,
    little bird of the bushy eyebrows?'

'When I saw the raided cattle
    passing by in panic
I made a dash from the valley
    and was a while in Craig Uanach.'

'The crag of my heart is Craig Uanach,
    the crag of part of my childhood;
crag of the hinds and stags roaming,
    tuneful grassy crag of many pathways.

'The crag the hunt would encircle —
    to join it would be delightful —
sweet was the sturdy hound's baying,
    driving a herd into a narrow defile.

'I will drink and not forsake her environs,
    I will not wander away on a tether;
the nurse of the deer that make the belling
    is that shapely clear bright fresh water.

'Round her slopes, sweet the eagle,
    sweet the swan and sweet the cuckoo;
seven times sweeter the bleating
    made by the fawn, dappled, spotted.

'Eilid bhailgeann bhailg-fhionn bhallach,
    Odhar eangach uchd ri h-àrd,
Trògbhalach thu, biorach sgiamhach
    Crònanach ceann-riabhach dearg.

'Creag mo chridhe-sa Creag Uanach,
    An t-slatach ghlas dhuilleach chraobhach,
An tulach àrd àlainn fiadhaidh
    'S gur cian a ghabh i on mhaorach.   64

'Deth cha robh i riamh ag èisteachd
    Ri sèideil na muice mara,
'S ann as tric a chuala i mòran
    De chrònanaich an daimh allaidh.

'Aoibhinn an obair an t-sealg,
    Aoibhinn a meanmna 's a beachd;
'S mòr gum b'annsa leam a fonn
    Na long is i dol fuidh rac.   72

'Cha do chuir mi dùil san iasgach,
    Bhith ga iarraidh leis a' mhaghar;
'S mòr gum b' annsa leam am fiadhach
    Siùbhal nan sliabh anns an fhoghar.

'Ceòl as binne de gach ceòl
    Guth a' ghadhair mhòir 's e teachd;
Damh na shiomanaich le gleann,
    Mìolchoin a bhith ann is as.   80

'Gur binn leam torman nan dos
    Air uilinn nan corrbheann cas;
Eilid bhinneach 's caol cos
    Nì clos fo dhuilleach ri teas.

'Chan eil do chèil' aic' ach an damh,
    'S e 's muime dhi am feur 's an creamh;
Màthair an laoigh bhall-bhric mhir,
    Bean an fhir mhall-rosgaich ghlain.   88

'A plump hind, white-bellied spotted,
  dun-coloured neat-footed high-breasted,
you're quarrelsome beautiful prick-eared,
murmuring brindled-red-headed.

'Crag of my heart, Creag Uanach,
  the branching one, green leafy wooded,
the high lovely summit for hunting,
  a far cry from shores of shellfish.

'From there she never had to listen
  to the blowing of the whale;
more often did she hear the frequent
  belling of the noble stag.

'A delightful occupation is the hunt,
  delightful its spirit and its design;
far dearer to me is its mood
  than a ship going under sail.

'I never cared much for trying
  to catch saithe by fly-fishing;
far dearer to me the hunting —
  traversing the hills in autumn.

'Music sweeter than any sound,
  the mastiff's baying on approach;
a stag wavering down the glen,
  greyhounds rushing back and forth.

'Sweet the murmur of the trees
  in the crook of the steep peaked hills;
a sharp-muzzled hind with slender limbs
  finds respite from the heat below the leaves.

'No mate has she but the stag,
  her sustenance is the garlic and grass;
mother of the dappled agile fawn,
  wife of the noble one of stately gaze.

'An aigeanntach shiùbhlas an raon,
　　Cadal cha dèan i san smùr;
B' annsa na plaide ri taobh
　　Leabaidh san fhraoch bhagaideach ùr.

''S e fear mo chridhe-sa 'n samhradh
　　'S am fear ceannghorm air gach bile,
Fanaidh gach damh donn na dhoire
　　Re teas goile grèine gile.　　　　　　96

''S glan ri shloinneadh an damh donn
　　A thig o Uilinn nam beann,
Mac na h-èilde ris an tom
　　Nach do chrom le spid a cheann.

'Èighidh damh Beinne Bige
　　'S èighidh damh Cheanna Craige,
Freagraidh gach damh dhiubh d'a chéile,
　　Fa cheann Locha Slèibhe Snaige.　　　104

Chì mi an siud am beannan ruadh
　　Goirid o cheann Locha Trèig,
Creag Uanach am biodh an t-sealg,
　　'N grianan àrd am biodh na fèidh.

'Chì mi Coire Ratha uam,
　　Chì mi Chruachan 's a' Bheinn Bhreac,
Chì mi Srath Oisein nam fiadh,
　　Chì mi 'ghrian air Beinn nan Leac.　　　112

'Chì mi Srath Oisein a' Chruidh
　　Chì mi Leitir Dhubh nan Sonn;
An gair Coire creagach a' Mhàim
　　Am minig a rinn mo làmh toll.

'Chì mi Beinn Neibheis gu h-àrd
　　Is an Càrn Dearg an aic' a buin,
An tulach air am fàs am fraoch,
　　Am monadh maol gu nuige 'm muir.　　　120

'The spirited one who travels the plains,
   she will sleep in no dust;
better than a blanket at her side,
   is a bed on the fresh tufted heath.

'The one I love is the Summer,
   the one who makes green each treetop,
every stag lingers in his thicket
   against the scorching heat of the bright sunshine.

'Pure is the blood of the brown stag
   that comes from the crook of the hills;
son of the hind at the knoll
   that never bent his head through spite.

'The stag of Beinn Bheag bellows
   and the stag of Kincraig bellows;
each stag answers the other
   at the head of Loch Sliabh Snaige.

'Yonder I see the reddish hill
   close to the head of Loch Treig,
Creag Uanach where the hunt was,
   the high sunny pastures of the deer.

'Coire Ratha over there,
   Cruachan and Beinn Bhreac,
I see Strath Ossian of the deer,
   I see the sun on Beinn nan Leac.

'I see Strath Ossian of the cows,
   Leitir Dhubh of the brave
near the rocky corrie of the Maam
   where my hand often made a wound.

'I see Ben Nevis on high
   and Carn Dearg near her foot,
the hillock where the heather grows,
   the bare moor as far as the sea.

'A Raghnaill mhic Dhomhnaill nan lann,
   Gun do bhith is e mo chreach,
'S tric a thuit leat air do thom,
   Mac nan sonn le do choin ghlas.

'Bu Domhnallach thu gun mhearachd,
   Bu tu buinne geal na cruadhach;
'S ma chuaidh thu uainn a dh'Àrd Chatain
   Gum bu dalta thu do Chreig Uanach.   128

'Gum bu dalt' thu do Chreig Uanach
   'S fad' o chuala mi ga sheanchas
Am buinne geal nach raibh èitigh
   'S ann duit a ghèilleadh am bantrachd.

'Dh'fhàg mi san rubha so shìos
   Fear leis 'm bu phudhar mo bhàs;
'S e chuireadh mo chagar 'n cruas
   An cluais a' chabair an sàs.   136

'Dh'fhàg mi an Cillùnain na laighe
   Sealgair na greighe deirge;
Làmh dheas a mharbhadh a' bhradain,
   'S gum bu ro-mhath 'n sabaid feirge.

'Mis' is tusa, a ghadhair bhàin,
   O, is olc ar turas don eilean;
Chaill thus' an tabhann san dàn,
   Is bha sinn grathann ri ceanal.   144

'Thug a' choille dhìots' an earb,
   'S thug an t-àrd dhìomsa na fèidh;
Chan eil ciont' againn deth araon,
   On laigh an aois oirnn gu lèir.

'Thus', an aois, chan eil thu meachair,
   Giodh nach fheudamar do sheachnadh;
Cromaidh tu 'n duine bhios dìreach,
   Dh'fhàsas gu fionalta gasda.   152

'O Raghnall, son of Domhnall of the blades,
    the lack of your life is my woe;
often did you bring down on your land
    the son of the stags with your hounds.

'Without doubt you were a MacDhomhnaill,
    you were the shining steely offshoot;
and though you have left us for Ardchattan
    you were the fosterling of Creag Uanach.

'You were the fosterling of Creag Uanach,
    long since I heard your descent recited;
the bright scion who was not feeble,
    to you their womenfolk yielded.

'I have left on the headland below
    one who would regret my death;
he would send my whizzing [shafts]
    stiff in the ear of the stag.

'In Cillùnain I left lying
    the red herd's hunter;
a skilful hand for killing salmon,
    an excellent fighter in strife of anger.

'You and I, O white hound,
    evil our journey to the island;
you have lost your habitual bark
    yet for a while we were happy.

'The wood has robbed you of the roe,
    the heights have robbed me of the deer;
for neither of us is it a disgrace
    since age lies on us both.

'You, age, you are not gentle,
    though we cannot avoid you;
you bend the man who was upright,
    who grew up stately and handsome.

Agus giorraichidh tu shaoghal,
 'Agus caolaichidh tu chasan;
Is fàgaidh tu cheann gun deudach,
 Is nì tu eudann a chasadh.

''S iomadh laoch a b'fheàrr na thusa
 Chuir mi gu tuisleadh 's gu anfhann,
'S a dh'faobhaich mi às a sheasamh,
 Tar èis bhith na fhleasgach calma.   160

'Aois pheall-eudannach odhar,
 Bhios gu ronnach bodhar èitigh,
Creud fan ligfinn leat, a lobhair,
 Mo bhogha 'bhreith dhìom air èiginn?'

Labhair an Aois rium a-rithis:
 'Is righinn atà tu leantainn
Ris a' bhogha sin an còmhnaidh,
 'S math gu foghnadh dhuit am bata.'   168

''S math gu foghnadh dhuit fhèin am bata
 Aois pheall-eudnach plèide;
'S mo bhogha, chan fhaigh thu fhathast
 De do mhaitheas no air èiginn.'

Ta bloigh dom' bhogh' ann am Muc
 Le agh maol odhar as ait;
Thusa gionach 's mise gruamach
 'S fada leam nach buan an t-slat.   176

''S fada leam o sguir mi 'n fhiadhach
 'S nach bhfuil ann ach ceò don bhuighinn,
Leis am bu bhinn guth nan gadhar
 'S o 'm faigheamaid òl gun bhruighinn.

'Nis o sguir mi shiùbhal beann
 'S o nach teann 'n t-iùbhar cruaidh
'S o nach seasadh mi air sgèir
 'S truagh nach bhfuil mi anns an uaigh.'   184

'And you shorten his lifespan
and make his legs skinny;
you leave his head toothless,
and make his face wrinkly.'

'Many a warrior who was your better
have I caused to totter weakly,
and have deprived him of his stature
after being a stalwart hero.'

'Old age, dun-coloured bristly,
dribbling deaf and feeble,
why should I let you, leper,
deprive me of my bow by violence?'

Age spoke to me again:
'You are determined to continue
going everywhere with that bow
when a stick would serve you better.'

'Well would the stick serve you,
impertinent bristly-faced age;
my bow you will not get yet,
whether by agreement or force.'

Part of my bow is in Muck
with a charming dun hind without horns;
you desirous and me disgruntled,
it seems long since the rod would stand.

'It seems long since I gave up the hunting
and mist is all that is left of the party
who loved the baying of the greyhounds
and from whom we'd drink without quarrel.

'Now since I've ceased roaming the hills
and since the hard yew is not taut,
and since I could not stand on a rock at sea,
it's a shame that I'm not in the grave.'

THE SONG TRADITION

ELEGY

69. Bealach a' Ghàrraidh/Cumha Mhic an Tòisich

Gun urra

Is e caoidh banntraich a tha anns an òran ainmeil seo, agus tha grunn sgeulachdan ann mu deidhinn. Thathar a' cumail a-mach gun do rinneadh e tràth anns an t-siathamh linn deug, no co-dhiù gu robh e stèidhichte air tachartasan mun àm sin. A rèir aon tionndaidh den òran, chaidh ceann-cinnidh òg Chloinn Mhic an Tòisich a thilgeil far eich agus a mharbhadh agus e a' tilleadh bhon phòsadh aige, fhad 's a bha a bhean ùr-phosta a' leantainn orra gun fhios. A rèir beul-aithris sheinn i an t-òran seo nuair a bhathar a' giùlain ciste an duine aige chun an tòrraidh.

Chaidh diofar thionndaidhean den òran a chruinneachadh ann an diofar sgìrean; tha e coltach gu robh cuid de mhnathan-tuiridh ga sheinn. Ged a bha na h-eaglaisean Pròstanach gu dubh an aghaidh a' chleachdaidh seo, lean seinn a' chaoinidh chun an naoidheamh linn deug ann an cuid de bhadan.

Tha an t-òran seo na dheagh eisimpleir air cumhachd iomadh mith-òrain eile – leis mar a thèid faireachdainn agus gnìomh a thàthadh còmhla anns gach rann. Nochdaidh na smuaintean ann an rannan 2 agus 3 ann an òrain eile cuideachd.

Tha am brèid na ìomhaigh air leth cumanta ann an dualchas litreachail na Gàidhlig, eadar na h-òrain luaidh agus dàin fhireannach leithid 'An t-Òran Eile' aig Uilleam Ros.

> Ochain! a laoigh, leag iad thu,
> Leag iad thu, o leag iad thu,
> Ochain, a laoigh, leag iad thu
>   'M bealach a' ghàrraidh.

> 'S truagh nach robh mis' an sin,
> 'S truagh nach robh mis' an sin,
> 'S truagh nach robh mis' an sin,
>   Is ceathr' air gach làimh dhomh.

Alas, My Calf, They Laid You Low
(Mac an Tòisich's Lament)

Different stories have circulated concerning this painful widow's lament, generally believed to date from the early sixteenth century, although the date and circumstances of its composition must be somewhat doubtful. According to one version, the young chief of the Mac an Tòisichs was accidentally thrown from his horse and killed, in ominous circumstances, while returning from his own wedding, while his bride rode on ahead, unaware of the tragedy. She is then said to have sung this lament as her husband's coffin was carried at his funeral procession, keeping time by tapping her fingers on the coffin-lid, and ceasing only when the coffin was lowered into the ground.

The song is known in various forms in many different districts; it appears to have served as a *caoineadh* sung by professional mourning-women. Though strongly disapproved of by the Protestant churches, this ancient practice lingered into the nineteenth century in some areas.

The song epitomises much about the folk-song tradition, each verse compressing events and emotion into one. Not surprisingly the powerful second and third verses reappear in other songs.

References to the *brèid* or kerch as a symbol of married status are extremely common in the women's song tradition. The *stìom* or headband often represents unmarried status.

> *Alas, my calf, they laid you low,*
> *they laid you low, O! they laid you low,*
> *Alas, my calf, they laid you low,*
> > *in the gateway to the garden.*

> A shame that I wasn't there,
> a shame that I wasn't there,
> a shame that I wasn't there,
> > with four men on either side of me.

An leann thog iad gu d' bhanais,
An leann thog iad gu d' bhanais,
An leann thog iad gu d' bhanais,
    Air d' fhalairidh bhà e.   8

Bha mi 'm bhrèidich 's m' ghruagaich,
Am bhrèidich 's m' ghruagaich,
Am bhrèidich 's m' ghruagaich,
    'S am bhantraich san aon uair ud.

Gun chron air an t-saoghal ort,
Gun chron air an t-saoghal ort,
Gun chron air an t-saoghal ort,
    Ach nach d'fheud thu saoghal bhuan fhàistinn.   16

70. Mhic Iarla nam Bratach Bàna

Gun urra

Is math a dh'fhaodte gun do rinneadh an t-òran luaidh seo mu dheireadh an t-siathamh linn deug, ach chan urrainnear a bhith cinnteach. Chan eil e comasach nas motha am 'mac iarla' seo ainmeachadh, agus is dòcha nach robh duine sònraichte fo cheist idir.

Tha òrain den t-seòrsa seo, anns a bheil boireannach a chaidh a thrèigsinn le fear uasal a' dèanamh caoidh air a truaghantachd fhèin, air leth cumanta ann an òrain dhualchasach bhon t-seachdamh agus bhon ochdamh linn deug. Ann am mòran òran da leithid tha am boireannach a' leigeil fhaicinn gu bheil i trom, ach ged a tha am fiosrachadh seo ga thoirt seachad, mar as trice, gu faiceallach agus gu neo-dhìreach, chan eil dad anns an òran seo a tha ag innse dhuinn gur e seo cor an t-seinneadair.

Tha cuid de na sreathan anns an tionndadh den òran a tha sinn a' clò-bhualadh an seo, a chaidh a thogail bhon t-seinneadair Bharrach Ruairidh MacFhionghain (Ruairidh Iain

The ale they brought for your wedding,
the ale they brought for your wedding,
the ale they brought for your wedding,
    it was drunk at your lyke-wake.

I was a maid and a matron,
a maid and a matron,
a maid and a matron,
    and a widow all at the same time.

You hadn't the slightest blemish,
you hadn't the slightest blemish,
you hadn't the slightest blemish,
    but that you were not long-lived.

Son of the Earl of the White Banners

This waulking song may well date back to the late sixteenth century, but precise dating is impossible. It is not possible to identify the earl's son named in the poem, if indeed any specific individual was intended.

Songs like this one, in which a woman apparently abandoned by a nobleman laments her plight, are very common in the folk-song tradition of the sixteenth to eighteenth centuries. In many such songs the woman reveals that she is pregnant, but even though this information may often be given in elliptical fashion there is nothing in this song to suggest this is the case here.

The version given here, recorded in Barra in 1938, contains lines also associated with poem 84. Such interfusing of different songs is extremely common in the waulking song tradition.

Bhàin) ann an 1938, cuideachd rim faighinn ann an dàn 84. Tha
am measgachadh agus an iomlaid shreathan is rannan air leth
cumanta ann an òrain luaidh.

> *Hi-ill-ein beag, hó ill ò ro,*
> *Hi-ill-ein beag, hó ill ò ro,*
> *Hi-ill-ein beag, hó ill ò ro,*
> *Hù hoireann ò, hò ro éileadh.*

A bhean ud thall a nì 'n gàire,
A bhean ud thall a nì 'n gàire,
A bhean ud thall a nì 'n gàire,
Nach truagh leat piuthar gun bhràthair?
> *Hi-ill-ein beag, etc.*

Nach truagh leat piuthar gun bhràthair, (*trì uairean*)
Is bean òg gun chèile 'n làthair?
> *Hi-ill-ein beag, etc.*

Is bean òg gun chéile 'n làthair, (*trì uairean*)
'S gur h-ionann sin 's mar atà mi,   8
> *Hi-ill-ein beag, etc.*

M'inntinne trom, m'fhonn air m'fhàgail,
Mun fhiùran fhoghainneach àlainn,
Sealgair sìthn' o fhrith nan àrdbheann,
'S an ròin lèith o bheul an t-sàile,
An earba bheag a dh'fhalbhas stàtail,
Le crios iallach uallach airgid
Air uachdar a lèine bàine.
Mhic Iarla nam bratach bàna,   16
Chunnaic mi do long air sàile,
Bha stiùir òir oirr' 's dà chrann airgid,
'S cupla dhan t-sìoda na Gaillmhinn,
Sìoda reamhar ruadh na Spàinne,
'S cha b'ann à Glaschu a bhà e,
No 'n Dùn Bheagain, 's beag on làr e,
No 'n Dùn Tuilm na brataich bàine!

O woman yonder who is laughing,
O woman yonder who is laughing,
O woman yonder who is laughing,
do you not pity a sister without brother?

Do you not pity a sister without brother,
and a young woman without husband near her?

And a young woman without husband near her,
for that is just my condition,

My mind is heavy, all desire has left me,
on account of the beautiful strong hero,
hunter of deer from the mountain moorlands,
and of the grey seal at the mouth of the ocean,
of the dainty roe that moves proudly,
with thonged belt with tips of silver
over his shift of white linen.
Son of the earl of the white banners,
I saw your ship on the ocean,
she had a helm of gold and two masts of silver,
and shrouds of the silk of Galway,
silk of Spain, thick russet
that was not silk from Glasgow,
nor from lowly Dunvegan,
nor from Duntulm of the white banner.

71. Cumha Ghriogair MhicGhriogair Ghlinn Sreith

Mòr Chaimbeul

Tha diofar thionndaidhean den òran ainmeil seo à Siorrachd Pheairt fhathast gan seinn gu tric. Am beachd Shomhairle MhicGill-Eain seo 'surely one of the greatest poems ever made in Britain'. Chithear ann an t-strì dhuilich eadar Clann Ghriogair agus Caimbeulaich Ghlinn Urchaidh anns na 1560an, a chaidh a thoirt gu buil nuair a dh'fhògradh na Griogaraich. Bha na h-òrain Ghriogarach a rinneadh ri linn na h-aimhreit seo (dàn 76 nam measg) air leth measail aig na Gàidheil air feadh na Gàidhealtachd, oir chìte annta seann luachan gaisgeil nan Gàidheal air an cur an cèill gu h-ealanta.

B'i ùghdar an òrain seo Mòr Chaimbeul, nighean Dhonnchaidh Ruaidh Chaimbeil Ghlinn Lìobhann (bràthar athar Chailein Lèith, ceann-cinnidh Chaimbeulaich Ghlinn Urchaidh), a bha pòsta aig ceann-cinnidh nan Griogarach, Griogair Ruadh. A rèir coltais phòs a' chàraid ri linn abhsadh na h-aimhreit eadar 1565 and 1567; chithear ann an òran eile le Mòr, 'Rìgh! Gur mòr mo chuid mhulaid', gur e gaol seach poileataigs a bha mar bhunait don phòsadh seo. Nuair a dh'èirich a' chòmhstri as ùr, chaidh Griogair a chur an grèim leis na Caimbeulaich air latha Lùnasta ann an 1569; chaidh a chumail fo ghlais ann an Caisteal Bhealaich fad ochd mìosan gus an deach a dhìcheannadh air 7 Giblean 1570.

Tha an t-òran air a chumadh ann am meadrachd lideach, agus tha e follaiseach gu robh Mòr gu math eòlach air bàrdachd àrd-nòsach a rè. Bha an sgìre anns an do thogadh i air leth cudromach ann an litreachas Gàidhlig an t-siathamh linn deug; b'ann ann am Fartairchill, aig bun Ghlinn Lìobhann, a chaidh Leabhar Deadhan Lios Mòr a chur ri chèile beagan dheicheadan na bu tràithe.

Tha òl na fala na ìomhaigh àrsaidh ann am bàrdachd na Gàidhlig; gheibhear i ann an òrain eile à Alba leithid 'A mhic Iain mhic Sheumais' agus 'Ailein Duinn', agus cuideachd anns a' chaoineadh ainmeil do Art Ó Laoghaire à Co. Chorcaí.

Lament for MacGriogair of Glenstrae

This celebrated sixteenth-century song, still very popular (in somewhat reworked form) in Gaelic tradition, was described by the late poet Somhairle MacGill-Eain as 'surely one of the greatest poems ever made in Britain'. The poem reflects the bitter and violent struggle between the MacGriogairs and the Caimbeuls of Glen Orchy and Breadalbane during the 1560s, a struggle that was to continue in various stages into the seventeenth century, culminating in the proscription of Clann Griogair, who were then hunted down as outlaws. A number of intensely evocative MacGriogair songs survive (poem 76 among them), having found an appreciative audience throughout the Gàidhealtachd, as Gaels everywhere identified with the MacGriogairs' traditional Gaelic heroism and rejected the Caimbeuls' manipulations and accommodation of southern power structures.

The composer of this poem, Mòr Chaimbeul, was the daughter of Donnchadh Ruadh Caimbeul of Glen Lyon (uncle of Cailean Liath, chief of the Caimbeuls of Glen Orchy) and became the wife of the MacGriogair chief, Griogair Ruadh. The couple apparently married during a lull in the dispute between 1565 and 1567; an earlier song composed by Mòr indicates that this was very much a love-match rather than a mere political arrangement. When the feud flared up again, Griogair was captured by the Caimbeuls on 1 August 1569 (hence the reference to Lammas-day in the opening line), imprisoned in Taymouth Castle for eight months, and beheaded on 7 April 1570.

The song is composed in a syllabic metre, a modified form of the structure used by the learned *filidh*, and Mòr was clearly familiar with the formal Gaelic poetry of the day. The Book of the Dean of Lismore, written at Fortingall at the mouth of Glen Lyon, demonstrates that the Caimbeuls, including aristocratic Caimbeul women, were keen critics and composers of Gaelic verse.

The reference to the drinking of the dead Griogair's blood is an ancient but common motif in Gaelic poetry, also occurring famously in the great eighteenth-century Irish lament 'Caoineadh Airt Uí Laoghaire' (Lament for Art O'Leary).

Tha an t-òran seo sònraichte a thaobh dèinnead agus raon na
faireachdainn, eadar bròn, miann dìoghaltais, sonas air a
chuimhneachadh agus truas. Tha an fhaireachdainn seo air a cur
an cèill tro ìomhaighean nitheil: a' bhean is a falt mu sgaoil a'
bualadh a làmhan, a' bhean mar eun a' sgrios a' chaisteil, i fhèin
's an duine aice ann an cùil a-muigh, an naoidhean na h-uchd,
agus gu seachd àraid, a miann fuil an fhir mhairbh òl gus
rudeigin dheth a ghleidheadh innte fhèin. Tha samhla an ubhail
a' toirt tòrr leis: tha e a' bruidhinn an dà chuid air cruinnead a'
chinn a thuit gu làr agus air uaisleachd an duine, oir bha an
t-abhall am measg nan craobh uasal o shean a bha a' riochdach-
adh neart na talmhainn. Tha na rannan anns an nochd coimeas
eadar a' bheatha le Griogair agus leis a' bharan am measg nan
earrann seachranach a dh'èireas ann an caochladh òran, 's iad a'
toirt oirnn beachdan a thaobh ùghdarrais agus tùsachd a chur an
dàrna taobh.

Moch madainn air latha Lùnast'
   Bha mi sùgradh mar ri m'ghràdh,
Ach mun tàinig meadhan-latha
   Bha mo chridhe air a chràdh.

Ochain, ochain, ochain uiridh,
   Is goirt mo chridhe, a laoigh,
Ochain, ochain, ochain uiridh,
   Cha chluinn d'athair ar caoidh.   8

Mallachd aig maithibh 's aig càirdean
   Rinn mo chràdh air an-dòigh,
Thàinig gun fhios air mo ghràdh-sa
   Is a thug fo smachd e le foill.

Nam biodh dà fhear dheug d'a chinneadh
   Is mo Ghriogair air an ceann,
Cha bhiodh mo shùil a' sileadh dheur,
   No mo leanabh fèin gun dàimh.   16

Chuir iad a cheann air ploc daraich,
   Is dhòirt iad fhuil mu làr:
Nam biodh agamsa an sin cupan
   Dh'òlainn dith mo shàth.

The song is remarkable for its intensity and range of emotion from grief and a desire for revenge to recollected joy and pathos. The emotion is expressed concretely, through a series of vignettes: the keening, dishevelled woman beating her hands, the woman as a bird destroying the castle, her sleeping outside with her husband, the baby in her arms, and, most particularly, her desire to drink the dead man's blood to retain something of him within herself. Her cherishing of her husband as a fragrant apple carries many connotations: it speaks both of the round head that has tumbled to the ground and of the the tradition of the apple as a noble tree, encompassing the regenerative powers of the earth. The verses comparing her life with Griogair and the Baron of Dull are typical of the 'fugitive passages' of the oral tradition which reappear in various songs, confounding ideas of authorship and originality.

Early on Lammas morning
   I was sporting with my love,
but before noon came upon us
   my heart had been crushed.

Alas, alas, alas and alack,
   sore is my heart, my child,
alas, alas, alas and alack,
   your father won't hear our cries.

A curse on nobles and relations
   who brought me to this grief,
who came on my love unawares
   and took him by deceit.

Had there been twelve of his kindred
   and my Griogair at their head,
my eye would not be weeping
   nor my child without a friend.

They put his head on an oaken block
   and spilled his blood on the ground,
if I had had a cup there
   I'd have drunk my fill down.

Is truagh nach robh m'athair an galar,
   Agus Cailean Liath am plàigh,
Ged bhiodh nighean an Ruadhanaich
   Suathadh bas is làmh.   24

Chuirinn Cailean Liath fo ghlasaibh,
   Is Donnchadh Dubh an làimh;
'S gach Caimbeulach th'ann am Bealach
   Gu giùlan nan glas-làmh.

Ràinig mise rèidhlean Bhealaich
   Is cha d'fhuair mi ann tàmh;
Cha d'fhàg mi ròin de m'fhalt gun tarraing
   No craiceann air mo làimh.   32

Is truagh nach robh mi an riochd na h-uiseig,
   Spionnadh Ghriogair 'na mo làimh:
Is i a' chlach a b'àirde anns a' chaisteal
   A' chlach a b'fhaisge don bhlàr.

Is ged tha mi gun ùbhlan agam
   Is ùbhlan uile aig càch,
Is ann tha m'ubhal cùbhraidh grinn
   Is cùl a chinn ri làr.   40

Ged tha mnathan chàich aig baile
   Nan laighe is nan cadal sàmh,
Is ann bhios mise aig bruaich do lice
   A' bualadh mo dhà làimh.

Is mòr a b'annsa bhith aig Griogair
   Air feadh coille is fraoich
Na bhith aig baran crìon na Dalach
   An taigh cloiche is aoil.   48

Is mòr a b'annsa bhith aig Griogair
   Cur a' chruidh don ghleann
Na bhith aig baran crìon na Dalach
   Ag òl air fion is air leann.

A pity my father was not diseased
 and Grey Cailean stricken with plague,
even though Ruthven's daughter
 would wring her hands dismayed.

I'd put Grey Cailean under lock and key
 and Black Donnchadh in heavy irons,
and every Caimbeul in Taymouth
 I'd set to wearing chains.

I reached the lawn of Taymouth
 but for me that was no balm,
I left no hair of my head unpulled
 nor skin upon my palms.

If only I had the flight of the lark,
 Griogair's strength in my arm,
the highest stone in the castle
 would be the closest to the ground.

Though now I'm left without apples
 and the others have them all,
my apple is fair and fragrant
 with the back of his head on the mould.

Though others' wives are safe at home
 lying sound asleep,
I am at the edge of your grave
 beating my hands in grief.

I'd far rather be with Griogair
 roaming moor and copse
than be with the niggardly Baron of Dull
 in a house of lime and stone.

I'd far rather be with Griogair
 driving the cattle to the glen
than be with the niggardly Baron of Dull
 drinking beer and wine.

Is mòr a b'annsa bhith aig Griogair
  Fo bhrata ruibeach ròin
Na bhith aig baran crìon na Dalach
  A' giùlan sìoda is sròil.   56

Ged a bhiodh ann cur is cathadh
  Is latha nan seachd sìon,
Gheibheadh Griogair dhomhsa cragan
  San caidlimid fo dhìon.

Ba hu, ba hu, àsrain bhig,
  Chan eil thu fhathast ach tlàth:
Is eagal leam nach tig an là
  Gun dìol thu d'athair gu bràth.   64

72. Nach Fhreagair Thu, Chairistìona?

Gun urra

Thathar a' dèanamh dheth gur ann mu dheireadh an t-siathamh linn deug a chumadh an t-òran ainmeil seo à Ìle, ged nach urrainnear a bhith cinnteach. A rèir gach coltais is e nighean cinn-chinnidh a bha ann an Cairistìona, fiù 's nighean Triath nan Eilean fhèin. Is dòcha gum faighear sealladh anns a' chiad rann air dòigh-beatha nam ban uasal aig àm Thighearnas nan Eilean.

Tha an t-òran caran doilleir ann an àiteachan, ach tha e coltach, a rèir fianais na rainn mu dheireadh, anns a bheil an seinneadair a' bruidhinn ri leannan Cairistìona an dèidh a bàis, gur e muime Cairistìona a tha a' seinn. Tha tòrr de na h-òrain as tràithe a tha againn 'air an seinn' le muimeachan, ged as dòcha gur e stoidhle litreachail a tha an seo seach firinn eachdraidheil.

  *È hó hì ura bhì
  Ho ro ho ì, ó ho ro ho,
  È hó hì ura bhì.*

Nach fhreagair thu, Chairistìona?
  É hó, etc.

I'd far rather be with Griogair
    under a rough hairy skin
than be with the niggardly Baron of Dull
    dressed in satin and silk.

Even on a day of driving snow
    when the seven elements reel
Griogair would find me a little hollow
    where we would snugly sleep.

Ba hu, ba hu, little waif,
    you are still only young,
but the day when you revenge your father
    I fear will never come.

Won't You Answer, Cairistìona?

This famous Islay song probably dates from the later sixteenth century, although this is uncertain. Cairistìona appears to have been a chief's daughter, perhaps a daughter of the mighty MacDhomhnaill himself. The first verse may give us a glimpse of the way of life of noblewomen at the time of the Lordship of the Isles.

The song is somewhat elliptical in places, in several different voices, but the last verse, addressed to Cairistìona's bereaved lover, suggest that the singer may be Cairistìona's nursemaid. A remarkable proportion of the earliest surviving vernacular songs are in this voice, although this is very likely either a literary device or a later reinterpretation.

    È hó hì ura bhì
    Ho ro ho ì, ó ho ro ho,
    È hó hì ura bhì.

    Won't you answer, Cairistìona?
        É hó, etc.

Nam freagradh, gun cluinninn fhìn thu,
   É hó, etc.

Bha mi bliadhna 'n cùirt an rìgh leat,
'S ged chanainn e, bha mi a trì ann —
Fuaigheal anairt, a' gearradh shìoda,
'S a' cur gràinne air lèintean rìomhach.

Thug mi turas do Ghleann Comhann,
S bha 'm muir àrd 's an caolas domhainn   8
Gheàrr mi leum 's cha d'rinn mi thomhas,
Gun leum na h-uiseagan romham,
'S thuirt iad rium nach dèanainn gnothach,
Nach fhaighinn mo mhuime romham,
Ceann na cèille, beul na comhairl',
Sgrìobhadh 's a leughadh an leabhar;
Bhiodh na h-uaislean ort a' tadhal
Cha b'ann gu mealladh an gnothaich.   16

'S iomadh long is bàrc is birlinn
Is luingeas a tha 'm beul Chaol Ìle
Tighinn a dh'iarraidh Cairistìona;
Chan ann gu pòsadh mhic rìgh leat,
Gus do chur 'san talamh ìseal,
Fo leaca troma na dìleann.

Fhleasgaich òig na gruaige duibhe,
'S ann an nochd as mòr do mhulad;   24
Do leannan a-staigh fo dhubhar
An ciste nam bòrd air a cumadh,
An dèidh na saoir a bhith 'ga dubhadh.

If you would, I myself would hear you,
   É hó, etc.

I spent a year with you in the King's court,
as it was, I spent full three there,
trimming silk, sewing linen,
embroidering the shirts of my kinsmen.

To Glencoe I made a journey,
the kyle was deep and the sea was stormy,
I took a leap but didn't judge it,
the larks rose up, startled before me,
they told me I wouldn't be lucky,
that I wouldn't find my foster-mother,
head of wisdom, mouth of counsel,
you could write and read the good Book,
you often had visits from the nobles,
they were never disappointed.

There's many a ship and boat and galley,
and fleet at the mouth of the Kyle of Islay,
coming to fetch Cairistiona,
not in order to wed you to a king's son,
but to lay you to rest in the deep ground,
under flagstones, heavy dripping.

Young man whose hair is blackest,
it is tonight your mood is saddest,
your sweetheart hidden away in darkness,
locked in the coffin of deal planking,
coated by the joiners with black lacquer.

73. Chaidh Mis' a dh'Eubhal Imprig

Gun urra

Anns an òran seo, a rinneadh, a rèir coltais, faisg air deireadh an t-siathamh linn deug, tha nighean òg de mhuinntir Mhic a' Phiocair a' caoidh murt a bhràithrean ann an Uibhist a Tuath le Ùisdean mac Ghill'Easbaig Chlèirich, duine an-iochdmhor a bhuineadh do Dhomhnallaich Shlèite. Rinn a cheann-chinnidh, Domhnall Gorm, bàillidh Uibhist a Tuath de dh'Ùisdean. Bha sannt aige air fearann Chloinn a' Phiocair, agus rinn e geur-leanmhainn orra le eich, coin agus claidhean gus grèim fhaighinn air an cuid fearainn. Chaidh crìoch a chur air dol-a-mach Ùisdein an dèidh do Dhomhnall Gorm faighinn a-mach gu robh Ùisdean ri cuilbheart na aghaidh. Chaidh a ghlacadh aig Dùn an Sticir ann an taobh an ear-thuath Uibhist a Tuath agus an sin a chur gu Caisteal Dhùn Tuilm ann an Tròndairnis, far an deach a bhiathadh le feòil shaillte gus an do bhàsaich e le pathadh.

Gheibhear tionndadh gu math eadar-dhealaichte den òran (no òran eile air an aon chuspair, is dòcha) anns a' chòigeamh leabhar de *Ortha nan Gaidheal*.

> *Hem bó, ho luì leó,*
> *Ro challa leó éileadh,*
> *Hem bó, ho luì leó.*

Chaidh mis' a dh'Eubhal imprig,
    Hem bó, etc.
'S thog mi gàrradh, lìon mi iodhlann,
Chan ann dhan eòrna ghlan thioram
Ach a dh'òigridh ceist mo chinnidh;
'S ghabh mi mo chead ris na beannan,
A dh'Eubhal mhòr 's Bheinn na h-Aire,
Caolas Rònaigh nan seòl geala
Gu Eilein nam Mucan mara.   8

'S ann agam fhìn bha na bràithrean,
Ùisdean, Lachlann, Eachann, Teàrlach,

I Went to Eaval on a Flitting

This song, apparently dating from the last decades of the sixteenth century, is a sister's lament at the murder of the Mac a' Phiocair brothers in North Uist at the hands of the notorious Ùisdean (mac Ghill'Easbaig Chlèirich) MacDhomhnaill, a high-ranking member of the MacDhomhnaills of Sleat. Appointed factor of North Uist by his clan chief, Domhnall Gorm MacDhomhnaill, Ùisdean coveted the Mac a' Phiocairs' lands for himself and his relatives, and proceeded to 'root out' the Mac a' Phiocairs, using horses and dogs. Ùisdean's brutal escapades came to an end after his conspiracy against his own chief, Domhnall Gorm, was discovered; he was seized at Dùn an Sticir in the northeast of North Uist and then imprisoned in Duntulm Castle in north Skye, where he was 'thirsted' to death.

A very different version of this song – perhaps better understood as another song on the same events – is given in Carmichael's *Carmina Gadelica*.

> *Hem bó, ho luì leó,*
> *Ro challa leó éileadh,*
> *Hem bó, ho luì leó.*

I went to Eaval on a flitting,
> *Hem bó, etc.*
and I built a wall, I filled a stackyard,
not with clean dry barley,
but with youths beloved of my people;
and I said farewell to the mountains,
to great Eaval and to Beinn na h-Aire,
to Rona Sound with white sails covered,
to the Island of the Whales.

I it was who had the brothers,
Ùisdean, Lachlann, Eachann, Teàrlach,

Iain is Raghnall is Ràghall,
'S Alasdair na gruaige fàinnich.

Mìle marbhphaisg ort, a dhuine,
'S aotrom do cheum, 's trom do bhuille,
Ach mo mhallachd aig do mhuime
Nach do leag i ort glùn no uileann
Mun mharbh thu na fir oirnn uileag.   16

Uisdein 'ic 'Ill'Easbaig Chlèirich,
Far na laigh thu slàn nar èirich!
Sgeula do bhàis gu mnathan Shlèite,
'S thugamsa mo dhearbh-chuid fhèin dhi.

74. Am Fonn Ìleach

Gun urra

Seo marbhrann do Lachlann Mòr, an trìtheamh ceann-cinnidh
deug aig Cloinn MhicGill'Eathain Dhubhaird, a bha na ogha do
Eachann Mòr, ùghdar (is dòcha) dàin 50. Chaidh Lachlann Mòr
a mharbhadh aig Blàr Thràigh Ghruinneart ann an taobh an iar-
thuath Ìle air 5 Lùnastal 1598. Bha am batail seo mar phàirt de
dh'iomairt fhada, neo-shoirbheachail aig na Leathanaich gus an
Roinn Ìleach a thoirt air falbh bho Chloinn Domhnaill Dhùn
Naomhaig agus nan Gleann, a bha fo stiùir Shir Sheumais
MhicDhomhnaill Chnoc Raonastail, mac prìomh-nàmhaid
Lachlainn Mhòir, Aonghas (mac Sheumais nan Ruaig)
MacDhomhnaill (cuspair dàn 25). Chaidh mu thrì cheud de
dh'fheachd nan Leathanach a mharbhadh, ach cha do chailleadh
ach deich air fhichead a-mach à còig ceud air taobh nan
Domhnallach. Chan eil e buileach soilleir dè dìreach a thachair
anns a' bhatail seo, agus tha cuid eadhon a' cumail a-mach gu
robh nàdar de chuilbheart ann an aghaidh Lachlainn Mhòir, foill
anns an robh Rìgh Seumas VI an sàs.
   A rèir dualchais chaidh Lachlann Mòr a mharbhadh le troich
Dhiùrach ris an cante Dubh-Sìdh, a chaidh a dhiùltadh le

Iain is Raghnall is Ràghall
and Alasdair with the hair in ringlets.

A thousand curses on you, fellow,
heavy your blows, though light your footsteps;
my curses on your foster-mother,
for not laying on you her knee or elbow,
before you killed all our people.

Ùisdean mac Ghill'Easbaig Chlèirich
where you lie down in health, may you not waken,
may the women of Sleat get news of your dying,
may I get my own share of the tidings.

The Soil of Islay

This poem laments the death of Lachlann Mòr
MacGill'Eathain, thirteenth chief of the MacGill'Eathains of
Duart (grandson of Eachann Mòr, putative author of poem 50),
at the battle of Tràigh Ghruinneart in the northwest of Islay on
5 August 1598. This battle was part of a concerted but
eventually unsuccessful campaign by the MacGill'Eathains to
seize the Rinns of Islay from the MacDhomhnaills of Dunyveg
and the Glens, who were commanded by his cousin Sir Seumas
MacDhomhnaill of Knockrinsay, son of Lachlann Mòr's great
rival Aonghas (mac Sheumais nan Ruaig) MacDhomhnaill
(subject of poem 25). Some three hundred of the eight-hundred-
strong MacGill'Eathain force were killed, while the
MacDhomhnaills lost only thirty out of five hundred. The
circumstances of the battle are not entirely unclear, and it has
even been suggested that Lachlann Mòr may have been lured
into a trap with the connivance of King James VI.

According to tradition Lachlann Mòr was killed by a dwarf
from Jura named Dubh-Sìdh (literally 'Black Fairy'), who had
previously offered his services to the MacGill'Eathains; the

Lachlann mar shaighdear ron bhatail; is dòcha gum b'e musgaid a chleachd e, ach rinneadh saighead dhruidheil dheth le cuid de sgeulaichean.

Tha tiotal an òrain dà-sheaghach air sgàth diofar chiall an fhacail 'fonn'. Cha tàinig ach aon tionndadh den òran thugainn, a chaidh a chruinneachadh anns an ochdamh linn deug leis an Urramach Seumas MacLagain; gu mì-fhortanach, tha grunn lochdan ann, agus chan eil e furasta an cur ceart.

'S daor a phàigh mi 'm fonn Ìleach,
'S lèir dom Rìgh nach e 'n t-airgead.

'S i creach Sheumais a leòn mi,
Dhol am feòil bhràthair a mhàthar.

'S ùr an togsaid a leagadh
Air an eabar bheag bhlàrain.

'S daor a cheannaich mi an t-saighead
Rinn an rathad gu d' ghràbhail.   8

A chuir maillid air d' amharc,
A mhic na mnatha on Ghàirbhil.

Ann an Cille Chomain an Ìle
Ghabh do dhìlsean fèin fardach.

Ach cèile Catrìona,
Fear dìleas treun làidir,

Agus Ruairidh na fèile
Bheireadh fèist da chàirdean.   16

Ach a bhothag a' ghlinne,
Leam is binn' thu na clàirseach,

Ach a bhothag an easain,
Leam is leisg bhith gad fhàgail

O nach fhaighinn na shuain ann
Am fear ruadh mar a b' àbhaist.

instrument was probably a musket, but this became a magic arrow in some accounts.

The title involves a pun of sorts; the word *fonn* can mean either 'tune' or 'soil'. The edition here involves reconstruction in several places, as the only surviving source is corrupt, and must therefore be considered tentative.

Dearly I paid for the soil of Islay,
it is clear to my Lord it was no great asset.

It was the devastation wrought by James that undid me,
attacking the flesh of his mother's brother.

Fresh the barrel that was spilling
in the muddy little field of battle.

Dearly I bought the arrow
that made its way to engrave you.

That hampered your vision,
son of the woman of Garvil.

In Kilchomain in Islay
your relatives took shelter,

But the spouse of Catriona,
man brave strong and faithful,

And generous Ruairidh
who would feast his kinsfolk.

O little bothy of the valley,
to me sweeter than the clarsach,

O waterfall bothy,
I am loathe to leave you,

Since I would not find asleep there
the red-haired man as usual.

75. Seathan Mac Rìgh Èireann

Gun urra

Tha tòrr Ghàidheal ag aithneachadh an òrain seo mar aon de na neamhnaidean as luachmhoire ann an dualchas na Gàidhlig. Is e caoidh chasta, iomadh-fhillte a tha ann airson Seathan, mac rìgh Èireann. Chan e caractar eachdraidheil a bha ann an Seathan idir; tha blas na fionnsgeulachd air an òran.

Tha na h-ainmean-àite anns an òran a' nochdadh gu bheil ceangal air choreigin aig an òran seo ri Èirinn, ach a dh'aindeoin sin, chan eil an t-òran ri fhaighinn an Èirinn idir. Ach tha 'mac rìgh Èireann' na charactar cudromach ann an sgeulachdan nan Gàidheal air dà thaobh Shruth na Maoile.

Tha an teacsa a tha sinn a' cleachdadh an seo stèidhichte air na fhuair Fear Chanaidh bho na seinneadairean ainmeil Anna is Calum Aonghais Chaluim à Barraigh. Tha tionndadh eile dheth a tha fada nas fhaide ann an *Ortha nan Gàidheal*, ach tha e coltach gun deach a 'leasachadh' agus a 'sgeadachadh' le Alasdair MacGilleMhìcheil fhèin.

B'annsa Seathan a' falbh slèibhe,
   Hù rù o nà hi ò ro,
Mise lag is esan treubhach,
   Nà hi ò ro hó hug ò ro,
Mise lag is esan treubhach;
   Hù rù, etc.
Cha ghiùlaininn ach beag èididh,
   Nà hi ò ro, etc.

Cha ghiùlaininn ach beag èididh,
   Hù rù, etc.
Còta ruadh mu leath mo shlèisne,
'S criosan caol-dubh air mo lèine,
'S mi falbh le Seathan mar eudail.   8
   Nà hi ò ro hó hug ò ro.

Seathan Son of the King of Ireland

This long and passionate poem – essentially mythological rather than historical in nature – has been described as 'the queen of waulking-songs'. It is a complex and intense lament by his lover for Seathan, son of the king of Ireland. The two have been together as Seathan flees his pursuers, but he is eventually trapped and killed through treachery. The detail and intensity of the song combine to give it a great emotional power.

The song does appear to have Irish connections, as suggested by various place-names, though it is not known in Ireland. The 'son of the king of Ireland' – significantly, never the son of the king of Scotland – is a common hero in the Gaelic folk tales of both countries.

The text given here is based on the singing of the famous Barra tradition-bearers Annie and Calum Johnston, recorded by John Lorne Campbell in 1950. A much longer version is found in Carmichael's *Carmina Gadelica,* and although a work of great beauty there is disagreement as to whether that text was based directly on oral tradition or is better understood as an embellished conflation on the part of Carmichael.

> Beloved Seathan travelling moorland,
>
> I was weak and he was mighty,
>
> I was weak and he was mighty,
>
> I wouldn't bother with much clothing,
>
>
> I wouldn't bother with much clothing,
>
> a russet coat down to mid-thigh,
> round my shift a thin black girdle,
> me travelling with Seathan as his lover.

'S iomadh beinn is gleann a shiubhail sinn,
Bha mi an Ìle, bha mi am Muile leat,
Bha mi an Èirinn an Còig' Mumha leat,
'S dh'éisd mi 'n Aifhreann 'sa Choill' Bhuidhe leat.
    Hù rù o nà hi ò ro.

'S minig a chuala, 's nach do dh'innis e.
Gu robh mo leannan am Mighinis;
Nam biodh e 'n sin, 's fhad' o thigeadh e;
Chuireadh e bàta dha m' shireadh-sa,   16
'S chuirinn-sa long mhòr 'ga shireadh-san,
Sgiobadh cliùiteach, ùrail, iriseal.
    Nà hi ò ro hó hug ò ro,
    Nà hi ò ro hó hug ò ro,
    Nà hi ò ro hó hug ò ro.

Nam faighte Seathan ri fhuasgladh,
Dh'fhàsadh an t-òr fo na bruachaibh,
Cha bhiodh gobhair an creig ghruamaich,
'S cha bhiodh lìon gun iasg an cuantan.
    Nà hi ò ro hó hug ò ro,
    Nà hi ò ro hó hug ò ro,
    Nà hi ò ro hó hug ò ro.

B'annsa Seathan air cùl tobhtadh,
Na bhith le mac rìgh air lobhtaidh,   24
Ged bhiodh aige leaba shocair,
'S stròl dhan t-sìoda bhith fo chasan,
'S cluasag dhan òr dhearg a' lasradh.
    Nà hi ò ro hó hug ò ro.

Tha Seathan an nochd 'na mharbhan,
Sgeul as ait le luchd a shealga,
'S le mac caillich nan trì dealga,
Sgeul as olc le fearaibh Alba.
A Sheathain! a Sheathain m'anma!
Dhealbh-mhic mo rìgh o thìr Chonbhaigh!   32
    Hù rù o nà hi ò ro.

Many a hill and glen we wandered in,
I was in Islay, I was in Mull with you,
I was with you in Ireland in the province of Munster,
in the Yellow Wood I heard mass with you.

Woe to him who heard it but never reported it,
that my darling was over in Minginish,
had he been there, he'd have come long ago,
he'd send a boat to come and look for me,
I'd sent a ship to go and look for him,
with a youthful crew, renowned and dutiful.

If Seathan would be released from bondage
gold would grow below the banks of the river,
there'd be no goats on gloomy clifftop,
nor net without fish in the oceans.

Better lying with Seathan behind a ruined building
than be with a prince in an upper story,
even though his were a soft mattress,
with a red gold gleaming pillow,
and under his feet a strip of satin.

Tonight Seathan is a lifeless body,
tidings of joy for his pursuers
and the son of the crone of the three needles,
an evil tale to the men of Scotland,
O Seathan, O my soul's Seathan!
the image of my king from Conway country.

'S minig thuirt rium gum bu bhean shubhach mi,
Bean bhochd chianail chraiteach dhubhach mi,
Bean bhochd a thug spèis d'a bhuidhinn mi;
Nuair shaoil mi thu bhith san tòrachd,
'S ann a bha thu marbh nam chòmhdhail,
'S tu air ghuaillean nam fear òga.
 Nà hi ò ro hó hug ò ro.

'S nuair a shaoil mi thu bhith sa ghailleann,
'S ann a bha thu marbh gun anam,   40
'S tu gad ghiùlain aig na fearaibh
Gu leitir nan corrbheann corrach.
 Nà hi ò ro hó hug ò ro.

'S an oidhche sin a rinn iad banais dhut,
Ochòin, a Rìgh! cha b'ann ach d'fhalairidh!
Nach do chuir iad lèin' dhan anart ort?
Nach do leig iad ùir is talamh ort?
 Nà hi ò ro hó hug ò ro,
 Nà hi ò ro hó hug ò ro,
 Nà hi ò ro hó hug ò ro.

M'eudail an làmh sin, 's ged 's fuar i,
Bu tric agam, b'annamh bhuam i,   48
Le tiodhlaig dhan t-sìoda bhuaidheach,
Gur tric a fhuair mi le duais i.
 Hù rù o nà hi ò ro.

Cha tugainn a lagh no rìgh thu,
Cha ghibhtinn air Moire Mhìn thu,
'S cha tiodhlaiginn 'sa Chrò Naoimh thu,
Eagal 's nach fhaighinn a-rithist thu!
 Nà hi ò ro hó hug ò ro,
 Nà hi ò ro hó hug ò ro,
 Nà hi ò ro hó hug ò ro.

Woe to the one who said I'd be a happy wife;
I am a poor woman, pained, sad, disconsolate,
a poor woman who admired his company;
when I thought you were pursuing,
you were dead, coming to meet me,
borne on the shoulders of the young stalwarts.

And when I thought you were in the tempest,
you were dead with your soul departed,
being carried by the warriors
to the slope of the pointed mountains.

And that night they made your wedding,
Alas, O King, it was your burial,
Did they not dress you in a shirt of linen?
Did they not drop on you earth and ashes?

Though it be cold, that hand is my treasure,
seldom away from me, it came to me often,
holding a gift of beautiful satin,
often I found it offering a present.

I couldn't part with you to law or monarch,
I couldn't gift you to the gentle Virgin,
I couldn't bury you in the holy graveyard
for fear I'd relinquish you forever.

76. Clann Ghriogair air Fògradh

Gun urra

Rinneadh an t-òran ainmeil seo an lùib na strì eadar na Griogaraich agus na Caimbeulaich anns an t-siathamh linn deug. Am beachd Shomhairle MhicGill-Eain bha seo air 'one of the greatest of all Scottish poems'. Tha diofar bheachdan aig sgoilearan litreachais air aois an òrain; tha cuid a' cumail a-mach gur ann mu 1550 a rinneadh e, agus cuid eile gur ann nas fhaisge air 1600.

Is dòcha gu bheil an tuairisgeul brùideil air bàs 'Eòin bhòidhich' anns an tritheamh rann deug na iomradh air murt an fhòrsair rìoghail John Drummond leis na Griogaraich ann an Gleann Artanaig ann an 1589, rud a dh'adhbharaich làmhachas na bu làidire bhon Riaghaltas an aghaidh Chloinn Ghriogair.

A rèir dualchais rinneadh an t-òran seo le boireannach a bha a' cleith nan Griogarach agus na Caimbeulaich air an tòir; nuair a thàinig na Caimbeulaich faisg oirre thòisich i ri seinn an òrain seo agus i a' cumail trang le obair taighe, los gum faigheadh na Griogaraich cothrom teicheadh. Cha leig sinn a leas gabhail ri fìrinn na sgeulachd seo, oir tha a leithid cumanta anns an dualchas; ach tha e follaiseach gun d'fhuair na Griogaraich tòrr coibhre is cuideachaidh bhon tuath, agus gu robh muinntir na Gàidhealtachd anns an fharsaingeachd a' gabhail suim ann an cùis nan Griogarach.

Ge b'e dè dìreach a bha air cùlaibh cruthachadh an òrain seo, tha e follaiseach gur e boireannach a rinn e. Tha an structar meadrachail gu tur eadar-dhealaichte ris an stoidhle àrd, litreachail a chithear ann an 'Cumha Ghriogair MhicGhriogair Ghlinn Sreith' (dàn 71).

Is mi suidhe an so am ònar
Air còmhnard an rathaid,

Dh'fheuch am faic mi fear-fuadain,
Tighinn o Chruachan a' cheathaich

Clann Griogair in Exile

This song also arises from the increasingly desperate struggle between the MacGriogairs and the Caimbeuls in the later sixteenth century. For Somhairle MacGill-Eain this was 'one of the greatest of all Scottish poems', while Derick Thomson found it expresses 'the sense of movement, action and uneasiness of the times most dramatically'. Scholars have differed as to the date of its composition, some suggesting a date around 1550 and others suggesting something closer to 1600.

The brutally vivid description of the demise of 'Eòin bòidheach' in stanza 13 may refer to John Drummond, royal forester, murdered by members of Clann Griogair in Glen Artney in 1589, an event that hardened official determination to crush the clan and led to a series of ever more repressive measures.

A traditional story asserts that the song was composed by a woman who was sheltering fleeing MacGriogairs as a Caimbeul posse pursued them; when the pursuers came within earshot she began loudly singing this song as she busied herself with some domestic task, distracting the Caimbeuls as the MacGriogairs made their escape. The account may well be apocryphal as this is a common folk-tale motif. However, it was certainly the case that the MacGriogairs enjoyed wide support among the common people of the area, who readily sheltered and assisted them, and the MacGriogair songs were popular throughout the Gàidhealtachd.

Whatever the circumstances of the poem's composition, the author was evidently a woman, and the song is structured with a stressed song-metre in the popular style, very different from the aristocratic syllabic metre of 'Griogal Cridhe', though similar in its mood.

> I am sitting by myself
> on the level of the road,
>
> looking out for a straggler,
> coming from Cruachan of the fog,

A bheir dhomh sgeul air Clann Ghriogair
No fios cà 'n do ghabh iad.

Cha d'fhuair mi d'an sgeulaibh
Ach iad bhith 'n-dè air na Sraithibh.　　　　8

Thall 's a bhos mu Loch Fìne,
Masa fior mo luchd-bratha;

Ann an Clachan an Dìseirt
Ag òl fion air na maithibh.

Bha Griogair mòr ruadh ann,
Làmh chruaidh air chùl claidhimh,

Agus Griogair mòr meadhrach,
Ceann-feadhna ar luchd-taighe.　　　　16

Mhic an fhir à Srath h-Ardail,
Bhiodh na bàird ort a' tathaich;

Is a bheireadh greis air a' chlàrsaich
Is air an tàileasg gu h-aighear;

Is a sheinneadh an fhidheall,
Chuireadh fiughair fo mhnathaibh.

Is ann a rinn sibh an t-sitheann anmoch
Anns a' ghleann am bi an ceathach.　　　　24

Dh'fhàg sibh an t-Eòin bòidheach
Air a' mhòintich na laighe,

Na starsnaich air fèithe
An dèidh a reubadh le claidheamh.

Is ann thog sibh ghreigh dhùbhghorm
O lùban na h-abhann.

Ann am Bothan na Dìge
Ghabh sibh dìon air an rathad;　　　　32

who has word of Clan Griogair
or can tell me where they've gone.

That they were yesterday in the Straths
is all their news I know.

Here and there about Loch Fyne,
if my spies are any good;

in the Clachan of Dysart
drinking wine with the nobles.

Big red Griogair was there,
a hand, deadly with sword;

and big merry Griogair,
the head of our house.

Son of the Laird of Strathardle,
where the bards used to flock;

you'd spend a while at the harp
and gladly gamble at the boards;

and you'd play the fiddle,
filling the women with hope.

It was late you made venison
in the glen where there's fog.

You left Handsome Eòin slumped
face down on the moor,

A great lump on the marsh
hacked by a sword.

You lifted the blue-black stud
from the loops of the Lyon.

In the bothy of the Ditch
you hid from the road;

Far an d'fhàg sibh mo bhiodag
Agus crios mo bhuilg-shaighead.

Gur i saighead na h-àraich
So thàrmaich am leathar.

Chaidh saighead am shliasaid,
Crann fiar air dhroch shnaidheadh.

Gun seachnadh Rìgh nan Dùl sibh
O fhùdar caol neimhe,   40

O shradagan teine,
O pheileir 's o shaighid,

O sgian na rinn caoile,
Is o fhaobhar geur claidhimh.

Is ann bha bhuidheann gun chòmhradh
Di-Dòmhnaich am bràigh a' bhaile.

Is cha dèan mi gàir èibhinn
An àm èirigh no laighe.   48

Is beag an t-iongnadh dhomh fèin sud,
Is mi bhith 'n dèidh mo luchd-taighe.

There you left my dirk
with my quiver of bolts.

In my side, the arrow
from the battle is lodged.

My thigh is pierced,
by a squint-shafted bolt.

May the King of All protect you
from fine venomous dust,

From bullet and dart,
from sparks red-hot,

From sword's keen blade,
and sharp knife's point.

The company was silent
above the village on Sunday.

On going to bed or rising
I desire no sport.

For me that's no wonder,
since my household is lost.

THE SONG TRADITION

OCCASIONAL VERSE

77. Pìobaireachd Dhomhnaill Duibh

Gun urra

Coltach ri dàn 34, tha an dàn seo co-cheangailte ri buaidh ainmeil a bha aig Clann Domhnaill nuair a bha i aig a h-àirde anns a' chòigeamh linn deug. Is e cuspair an òrain seo Blàr Inbhir Lòchaidh ann an 1431, nuair a fhuair Domhnall Ballach MacDhomhnaill, co-ogha Alasdair, 'Triath nan Eilean' – a bha na phrìosanach aig Rìgh Seumas IV aig an àm, ann an Caisteal Thantallon ann an Lodainn an Ear – buaidh air feachdan Sheumais IV, a bha fo stiùir Alasdair Stiùbhairt, Iarla Mhàrr, a ghabh pàirt ann an Cath Gairbheach ann an 1411 an aghaidh Dhomhnaill, athair Alasdair.

Is math a dh'fhaodte gun do rinneadh an t-òran seo anns a' chòigeamh linn deug, ach is cinnteach gun do dh'atharraich e thar nan linntean agus e air a ghleidheadh ann am beul-aithris; cha deach a sgrìobhadh gu ruige meadhan an naoidheamh linn deug. Tha tomhas de theagamh an lùib fonn an òrain, ged as cinnteach gu bheil e sean gu leòr.

B'e Domhnall Dubh ceannard Chloinn Camshroin, agus chleachd na cinn-chinnidh na dhèidh am far-ainm 'Mac Dhomhnaill Duibh'. Bha na Camshronaich air taobh nan Domhnallach aig toiseach a' bhlàir, ach thionndaidh iad gu taobh an rìgh nuair a ghabh iad eagal gu robh am batail a' dol an aghaidh Chloinn Domhnaill. B'e mearachd mhòr a bha ann dhaibh, agus rinn Domhnall Ballach geur-leanmhainn orra an dèidh dha a' bhuaidh fhaighinn.

Thug Clann an Tòisich agus Clann Mhuirich taic do dh'fheachdan an rìgh cuideachd, agus is ann air sgàth sin a tha iad air an ainmeachadh anns an òran.

Tha diofar thionndaidhean den òran a' toirt seachad sheallaidhean eadar-dhealaichte air a' chùis: tha an tionndadh a leanas a' nochdadh sealladh Chloinn Domhnaill agus tha cuid eile a' sealltainn taobh nan Camshronach.

Tha an ath dhàn co-cheangailte ri Blàr Inbhir Lòchaidh cuideachd, agus e a' nochdadh sealladh Iarla Mhàrr.

The Piping of Domhnall Dubh

This song should be read in combination with the 'Harlaw Brosnachadh' (poem 34), as each deals with what Gaelic tradition remembers as famous victories for Clann Domhnaill at the height of its power in the fifteenth century. The present song concerns the Battle of Inverlochy (by present-day Fort William) in 1431, when Domhnall Ballach MacDhomhnaill, cousin of Alasdair, Lord of the Isles – then a prisoner of the king, James I, in far-away Lothian – won a celebrated and crushing victory over the king's allies, led by Alasdair Stiùbhart, Earl of Mar, who had fought Alasdair's father Domhnall at Harlaw.

The poem may well originate in the early fifteenth century, but it doubtless underwent some changes over the centuries in oral tradition; there is no surviving written version of the Gaelic words older than the mid-nineteenth century. The authenticity of the accompanying tune, although old, is equally uncertain.

Domhnall Dubh or 'Black Donald' – from whom later Camshron chiefs took their hereditary patronymic Mac Dhomhnaill Duibh – was the chief of Clann Chamshroin, who began the battle as allies of Clann Domhnaill, but fled and joined the other side for fear of being overwhelmed by the royal forces. This miscalculation then led to savage retribution at the hands of Domhnall Ballach following his victory.

The song also refers to two other defeated kindreds who supported the king at the battle: the Mac an Tòisichs and the Mac a' Phearsains (Clann Mhuirich).

Different versions of the song give a different perspective: some, like the one given here, appear to take a Clann Domhnaill perspective, while others express the Camshron point of view.

The next poem reflects a loser's perspective on the same battle, that of the Earl of Mar.

Pìobaireachd Dhomhnaill Duibh,
Pìobaireachd Dhomhnaill,
Pìobaireachd Dhomhnaill Duibh,
Pìobaireachd Dhomhnaill,
Pìobaireachd Dhomhnaill Duibh,
Pìobaireachd Dhomhnaill,
Pìob agus bratach
Air faich' Inbhir Lòchaidh.   8

Chaidh an-diugh, chaidh an-diugh,
Chaidh an-diugh òirnne,
Chaidh an-diugh, chaidh an-diugh,
Chaidh an-diugh òirnne,
Chaidh an-diugh, chaidh an-diugh,
Chaidh an-diugh òirnne,
O, chaidh an-diugh, chaidh an-diugh,
'S chaidh an-dè le Clann Domhnaill.   16

Theich 's gun do theich iad,
O, theich Clann an Tòisich,
Theich 's gun do theich iad,
O, theich Clann an Tòisich,
Theich 's gun do theich iad,
O, theich Clann an Tòisich,
Dh'fhalbh Clann Mhuirich,
'S gun d'fhuirich Clann Domhnaill.   24

Thèid 'us gun tèid sinn,
O, thèid sinn Shrath Lòchaidh
Thèid 'us gun tèid sinn,
O, thèid sinn Shrath Lòchaidh
Thèid 'us gun tèid sinn,
O, thèid sinn Shrath Lòchaidh
Choinneamh Mhic Dhomhnaill Duibh
Choinneamh Mhic Dhomhnaill.   32

Fire faire, Loch Iall,
Cà an do thriall do ghaisgich?
Fire faire, Loch Iall,
Cà an do thriall do ghaisgich?

The piping of Domhnall Dubh,
the piping of Domhnall,
The piping of Domhnall Dubh,
the piping of Domhnall,
The piping of Domhnall Dubh,
the piping of Domhnall,
pipes and banner
on the lawn of Inverlochy.

Today went, today went,
today went against us;
today went, today went,
today went against us;
today went, today went,
today went against us;
and yesterday went with Clann Domhnaill.

They fled, O they fled,
O Clan Mhic an Tòisich fled,
they fled, O they fled,
O Clan Mhic an Tòisich fled,
they fled, O they fled,
O Clan Mhic an Tòisich fled,
Clan Mhuirich ran away
and Clann Domhnaill remained.

We'll go, we'll go,
O we'll go to Strath Lochy,
we'll go, we'll go,
O we'll go to Strath Lochy,
we'll go, we'll go,
O we'll go to Strath Lochy,
to meet with Mac Domhnaill Duibh,
to meet with Mac Domhnaill.

Ay, ay, Locheil,
where have your heroes gone?
Ay, ay, Locheil,
where have your heroes gone?

Fire faire, Loch Iall,
Cà an do thriall do ghaisgich?
Fire faire, Loch Iall,
Cà an do thriall do ghaisgich?   40

Loch Iall, Loch Iall,
Loch Iall, Loch Iall,
Loch Iall, Loch Iall,
Loch Iall, Loch Iall,
Loch Iall, Loch Iall,
Loch Iall, Loch Iall,
Loch Iall, Loch Iall,
Loch Iall, Loch Iall.   48

Thug na fir chaola
Mach ri Srath Lòchaidh.
Thug na fir chaola
Mach ri Srath Lòchaidh.
Thug na fir chaola
Mach ri Srath Lòchaidh.
Thug na fir chaola
Mach ri Srath Lòchaidh.   56

78. 'S Maith an Còcaire an t-Ocras

Alasdair Stiùbhart, Iarla Mhàrr

A rèir dualchais rinneadh na rannan goirid seo le Alasdair
Stiùbhart, Iarla Mhàrr, agus e a' teicheadh à tòir nan
Domhnallach an dèidh Blàr Inbhir Lòchaidh ann an 1431.

Tha e follaiseach gu leòr gu bheil na rannan seo gu math
sean, ged as cinnteach gun deach an atharrachadh thar nan
linntean agus iad air an gleidheadh ann am beul-aithris. Tha dà
thionndadh dhiubh air an cur an clò an seo; ged nach eil na
h-eadar-dhealachaidhean eatarra ach beag, tha iad ùidheil a
dh'aindeoin sin. Tha an litreachadh annasach anns a' chiad

Ay, ay, Locheil,
where have your heroes gone?
Ay, ay, Locheil,
where have your heroes gone?

Locheil, Locheil,
Locheil, Locheil,
Locheil, Locheil,
Locheil, Locheil,
Locheil, Locheil,
Locheil, Locheil,
Locheil, Locheil,
Locheil, Locheil,

The slender men went out
to Strath Lochy,
the slender men went out
to Strath Lochy,
the slender men went out
to Strath Lochy,
the slender men went out
to Strath Lochy.

Hunger is a Good Cook

This fragment is attributed to Alasdair Stiùbhart, Earl of Mar, who fought the forces of the Lord of the Isles at Harlaw in 1411 and again at Inverlochy in 1431. According to one tradition he made these verses while on the run in Lochaber in the aftermath of his disastrous defeat at Inverlochy, pursued by Domhnall Balloch MacDhomhnaill.

According to the account given by Ùisdean MacDhomhnaill in his seventeenth-century history, the earl, who had been wounded in the thigh in the battle, and his servant spent two days wandering in the hills of Lochaber without food until they

thionndadh (ocras, a b' fheòrr, eudaich) a' nochdadh pàtran a' chòmhardaidh agus nàdar na dualchainnt.

B' e fàth na ciad rainn gun d'fhuair an t-iarla dòrlach de mhìn eòrna bho sheann bhoireannach (no boireannaich) agus e air allaban ann am monaidhean Loch Abar, agus gun do rinn i fuarag dha na bhròig. An dèidh sin fhuair e cuid-oidhche bho neach-taice leis ris an cante Ó Birein, anns a' Bhriagaich ann an Gleann Ruaidh. Nuair a dh'fhàg e an taigh aig Ó Birein air an ath mhadainn, thuirt an t-iarla ris a thighinn thuige aig a' chaisteal aige ann an Cionn Droma nan tigeadh ainneart sam bith air. Rinn Ó Birein sin, ach dhiùlt dòrsair an iarla e an toiseach; ach nuair a chunnaic an t-iarla e, chuir e fàilte is furan air, agus dh'aithris e an dàrna rann gu h-ìosal.

Tha diofaran beaga ann am beul-aithris a thaobh na sgeulachd co-cheangailte ris na rannan seo. A rèir an tionndaidh aig Caraid nan Gàidheal (an t-Urr. Tormod MacLeòid), a chaidh fhoillseachadh ann an 1840–43, b'fheudar do Ó Birein teicheadh, còmhla ri a bhean agus a theaghlach, bho thòir nan Domhnallach goirid an dèidh a' bhlàir. Ach anns an tionndadh as sine den sgeulachd, a nochd ann an eachdraidh nan Domhnallach aig Ùisdean MacDhomhnaill (a chaidh a sgrìobhadh eadar 1660 agus 1685), chan eil dad a dh'iomradh air a' gheur-leanmhainn seo, agus chan eil fàth an turais do Chionn Droma ga thoirt seachad ach gu robh Ó Birein 'reduced to a very low situation', 'in process of time'.

Tionndadh A

'S maith an còcaire an t-ocras,
   'S mairg dhèanadh toilceas air biadh,
Fuarag eòrn' à sàil mo bhròige
   Biadh a b' fheòrr a fhuair mi riamh.

Bha mi oidhche ann ad theach
   Air mhòr bèidhe 's air bheag eudaich;
'S ionmhainn am firean ata 'muigh,
   Ó Birein às a' Bhreugaich.

8

met some women who were herding cattle, and begged them for some food. They mixed some barley meal with water in the earl's boot, prompting the earl to give his heartfelt praise (the first verse here).

Having disguised himself in women's clothes, that night the earl received hospitality (including meat from a freshly slaughtered cow, which the earl proved incapable of cooking properly), from one of his supporters by the name of O'Birein (perhaps a form of the Irish name Ó Broin or 'Byrne') at Briagach in upper Glen Roy. When the earl set off for Badenoch in the morning he thanked O'Birein and told him that he would always receive hospitality in return were he ever to call upon the earl. Some time later, in reduced circumstances, O'Birein came to Mar's stronghold at Kildrummy (near Alford in Aberdeenshire) and called in his debt; the earl's doorman resisted O'Birein's request, but when Mar himself heard their altercation he is said to have welcomed O'Birein warmly, reciting the second verse here. After entertaining O'Birein for some time he sent him home with sixty milch cows and later give an estate to his son.

Although these verses have certainly been altered in transmission, and the accompanying story must surely be a product of folklore rather than history, their basic structure appears very old. The words are cryptic in places; the first verse begins with a familiar Gaelic proverb, and the stanza as a whole has a proverbial quality. Two versions are given here, with the most obvious difference between them relating to the second verse.

Version A

Hunger is a good cook,
    woe to him who disdains food;
barley brose from the heel of my shoe —
    the best meal I ever got.

I was one night in your house
    on plenty food and little clothing;
dear the man who stands outside,
    it is O' Birein from Breugach.

Tionndadh B

'S math an còcaire an t-acras,
    'S mairg a nì tarcais air biadh,
Fuarag eòrn' à sàil mo bhròige
    Biadh as fheàrr a fhuair mi riamh.

Oidhche dhomh bhith ann ad theach
    Air mhòran bìdh 's air bheag eudaich;
Fhuaras sàth mòr de dh'fheòil air droch bhruich
    O Ó Birein sa Bhreugaich.   8

Version B

Hunger is a good cook,
    woe to him who disdains food;
barley brose from the heel of my shoe —
    the best meal I ever got.

I was one night in your house
    on plenty food and little clothing;
got a lump of badly cooked meat
    from O' Birein at Breugach.

THE SONG TRADITION

LOVE

79. An Iorram Dharaich

Gun urra

Rinneadh am marbhrann seo do Eòin MacDhomhnaill, mac
Sheumais a' Chaisteil (fear de Dhomhnallaich Shlèite) agus co-
ogha Ùisdein mhic Ghill'Easbaig Chlèirich (faic dàn 73). Fhuair
Eòin bàs ann am Muile ann an 1585, ri linn comhstrì ann
aghaidh Chloinn Ghill'Eathain Dhubhaird mar phàirt den
fhalachd fhada eadar an dà chinneadh.

B'i seanmhair Eòin nighean Thorcail MhicLeòid, ceann-
cinnidh Chloinn MhicLeòid Leòdhais (Sìol Torcaill) (faic an ro-
ràdh ri dàn 36), agus tha an seinneadair a' moladh a'
bhuntainneis Leòdaich seo anns an òran. B'e a mhac an
gaisgeach Domhnall mac Iain mhic Sheumais, a tha iomraiteach
anns an dualchas air sgàth nan euchdan aige ann am Blàr
Chàirinis ann an Uibhist a Tuath ann an 1601, nuair a fhuair
Clann Domhnaill buaidh ainmeil air Clann MhicLeòid na
Hearadh is Dhùn Bheagain, buaidh a tha air a comharrachadh
anns an òran ainmeil 'A mhic Iain mhic Sheumais'.

> M'eudail-sa dh'fhearaibh na grèine,
> Chan fhaca mi 'n diugh no 'n-dè thu.
> Chan fhaca mise fear d'eugais,
> Ach an tig thu, Eòin mhic Sheumais,
> Nad aois òig mus do bhuin eug riut.
> Bu tu ogha Ruairidh na fèile,
> 'S iar-ogha Thorcaill nan geurlann,
> Sliochd na mnà a choisinn ceutadh;   8
> Dh'fhàg thu m'aigne tùrsach deurach.
> *'S na hada hia hì 's na hì hó hua*

> M'eudail a dh'fhearaibh nan àlach,
> 'N uair a dheigheadh tu gu d' bhàta
> Siud an obair nach biodh ceàrr dhut,
> Bhiodh do ghillean anns an àlach,
> Bhiodh tu fhèin air stiùir do bhàta,
> Fear curantach treubhach làidir.
> *'S na hada hia hì 's na hì hó hua*

The Oak Ship's Oar-Song

The impassioned lament is addressed to Eòin MacDhomhnaill, son of the famous Seumas a' Chaisteil of the MacDhomhnaills of Sleat and first cousin of Ùisdean mac Gill'Easbaig Chlèirich (see poem 73). Eòin died in Mull in 1585, fighting against the MacGill'Eathains of Duart during the two clans' long-running conflict.

Eòin's grandmother was the daughter of Torcall MacLeòid of Lewis (see introduction to poem 36), and his MacLeòid connections are praised in the poem. His son was the famous warrior Domhnall mac Iain mhic Sheumais, celebrated for his heroic role in the battle of Carinish (North Uist) in 1601, when the MacDhomhnaills inflicted a famous defeat on the MacLeòids of Harris and Dunvegan. Domhnall is the subject of a famous song composed by his foster-mother following the battle.

My treasure of all men in the sunlight,
neither yesterday nor today did I see you,
I never saw a man like you,
unless you come back, Eòin, son of Seumas,
as you were in your youth, before death got you.
You, the grandson of generous Ruairidh,
and great-grandson of sharp-bladed Torcall,
descendants of the woman who earned admiration;
you've left my spirit sad and tearful.

My treasure of the men of the oar-banks,
when you used to board your galley
that's the work that posed you no hardship,
your young men in the oar-banks,
you yourself at the helm of the galley,
a powerful hero of bold exploits.

M'eudail is m'euraig is m'eallach   16
Iain Òg mac Sheumais nam meallshul,
Sùil ghorm nad eudainn 's cha b'fhanaid,
Sheòl thu 'n-dè troimh chuan na Hearadh,
'S mo dhùrachd fhèin dhut ruighinn fallain.
   'S na hada hia hì 's na hì hó hua

M'eudail a dh'fhearaibh na beinne,
'N uair a dheigheadh tu dha na beannaibh
'S e do lòsan nach biodh falamh,
Gum b'ann le gunna bheòil thana   24
No le iubhar nam meallan,
Briseadh cnàimh 's gach àit ri 'm beanadh,
Sìor chur fàilt' air fear nan langan.
   'S na hada hia hì 's na hì hó hua

M'eudail-sa dh'fhearaibh na dìle,
Chunna mi dol seachad sìos thu;
Gu meal thu gruagach na stìoma,
Nighean tighearn Ghleanna Sìthe,
'Gan robh 'n cinneadh leathann lìonmhor,   32
Cèis ghlan bho leitir an fhìon thu,
Gheibh thu buaile den chrodh chìordhubh.
   'S na hada hia hì 's na hì hó hua

M'eudail-sa dh'fhearaibh na seòltachd,
'N uair a shìneadh tu ri seòladh
Ghlacadh i eadar na sgòide,
Cneadan a clèithe bu cheòl dhut,
Stiùir na dèidh 's fear treubhach eòlach
Ga stiùireadh san iùl bu chòir dhi.   40
   'S na hada hia hì 's na hì hó hua

M'eudail is m'euraig is m'ulaidh
Luchd nan leadan dubh is donna
Dhèanadh an fhairge a phronnadh,
Dhèanadh a darach a sgeolladh,
'S a dh'òladh fion dearg na thonnan,
Thogadh creach bhàrr motach Thomman.
   'S na hada hia hì 's na hì hó hua

My treasure, my ransom and burden,
Young Eòin, son of Seumas, of eyes beguiling,
blue eyes in your face not displeasing,
yesterday you sailed through the Sound of Harris,
my own urgent hope for your safe-coming.

My treasure of the men of the mountain,
when you'd make for the hilltops
not bare would be your lodgings;
with the slender-muzzled musket
or the yew-bow with its bosses
a breaking of bones wherever you lighted,
always greeting the one of great belling.

My treasure of the men of the tiderace,
down below I saw you passing;
may you charm the girl with the fillet,
daughter of Glen Shee's master,
far-flung and many their kindred,
you are a bright harp from the vine-slope,
you will win a herd of black cattle.

My treasure of the men of cunning,
when you would set out sailing
she'd be held between the sail-sheets,
music to you, her oars' creaking,
the rudder behind with a man of experience
guiding her in the course that was proper.

My treasure, my ransom and riches
are the people of the black and brown ringlets
who'd give the sea a good thrashing
who'd give her timbers a good soaking,
and drink red wine in its billows,
and lift plunder from the moss of Tomman.

M'eudail is m'euraig is m'eallach,
'N uair a dheigheadh tu chum na mara   48
'S e do làmh nach faight' air lapadh
Ged nach robh thu fèin ach leanabh;
Crann taraig ga shnìomh à darach
'S i tilgeadh lann bharr cheann gach taraig;
Cha robh do luingeas air crìonadh,
'S cha robh do sheòladh gu ìosal.
  'S na hada hia hì 's na hì hó hua

M'eudail is m'euraig is m'ulaidh,
'S ann ort dh'fhàs a' mhaise mhullaich,   56
Gruag leadanach theudach dhuilleach
Air a cìreadh 's air a cumadh;
'S nam bu bhàrd mi dhèanainn iorram,
'S nam bu shaor mi dhèanainn luingeas,
Is nad dhèidh-sa 's èiginn fuireach.
  'S na hada hia hì 's na hì hó hua

80. Craobh an Iubhair

Gun urra

Tha an t-òran gaoil seo à Ìle air aon de na h-eisimpleirean as tràithe a tha againn de dh'òran gaoil bho shealladh boireannaich, agus tha cumhachd sònraichte ri fhaireachdainn ann, gu h-àraidh an lùib ìomhaighean cumhachdach na craoibhe agus an ubhail. Chaidh a chumadh, a rèir coltais, mu dheireadh an t-siathamh linn deug.

Bha Clann MhicAoidh na Reanna inbheil aig àm Rìoghachd nan Eilean, agus gu dearbh, tha ball den teaghlach ga ainmeachadh anns an aon chairt-fhearainn sgrìobhte ann an Gàidhlig a thàinig a-nuas thugainn, air a bheil an deit 1408 agus anns a bheil Domhnall mac Eòin Mhòir, Triath nan Eilean, a' buileachadh pìos fearainn anns an Roinn Ìleach air 'Brian Bhicaire Mhagaodh'. Bha fear Niall MacAoidh na *chrùnair* ann an Ìle mu thoiseach an t-seachdamh linn deug, agus is dòcha gur

My treasure, my ransom and burden,
when you'd make for the ocean
your arm would not be found to weaken
though you were but a stripling;
wooden pegs wrenched from her timbers
casting the roves from the head of each rivet;
your fleet was never seen diminished,
and your sailing was never in secret.

My treasure, my ransom and riches,
on your head grew a crowning glory,
hair like harp-strings, entwining ringlets,
well-combed and well-shaped;
if I were a poet I'd make an oar-song,
if I were a wright I'd make a galley,
for I must live on after your going.

The Yew Tree

This love-song from Islay, an early example of the powerful and emotionally complex women's song tradition, appears to date from the late sixteenth century. Derick Thomson has written that there is 'something magical' about MacAoidh, the singer's lover, and that this magic and the singer's deep emotions 'tilt the imagery of the poem to symbolism, the ancient and deeply imagined symbolism of the apple and the apple-tree'.

The MacAoidhs were a prominent family in the Rinns of Islay during the time of the Lordship of the Isles. Indeed, the only surviving Gaelic charter by a Lord of the Isles, dated May 1408, grants lands in the Rinns to 'Brian Bhicaire Mhagaodh'. A Niall MacAoidh served as *crùnair* or 'officer' in Islay at the turn of the seventeenth century, and this may be the remarkable brother referred to in the song. MacAoidh also fought for Sir

e seo am bràthair 'anabharrach' air a bheil an seinneadair a' toirt iomradh anns an òran. Shabaidich MacAoidh às leth Shir Seumas mac Aonghais MhicDhomhnaill aig Blàr Thràigh Ghruinneart ann an Ìle ann an 1598 (cuspair dàin 74).

Chaidh an t-òran a chur ri chèile à diofar òran, neo 's neònach agus an earrann far a' bheil a' chàraid òg gun diù do chàch na suidhe gu mì-chomhartail leis an ùrnaigh airson dìon anns na trì rannan mu dheireadh. Thèid ìmpidh a chur air feartan Crìosdail agus nàdarrach: air Crìosd, air Muire, air a' ghrèin, air a' ghealaich agus na gaothan. Tha earrann den aon seòrsa ann an 'Tàladh Dhòmhnaill Ghuirm' (1617?) far an tèid neart na cruinne, nan tonn, Oisein agus Osgair a dhùsgadh. 'S dòcha gum b' e ùrnaighean pàganach a' chiad tùs aig na h-earrannan seo, agus aig na *loricae* Crìosdail mar an ceudna.

'S e MacAoidh an duine treubhach,
    O, chraobh an iubhair, *o ho*,

Nì e sìoda dhan chlòimh cheutaich,
    O, chraobh an iubhair, *o ho*,

Nì e sìoda dhan chlòimh cheutaich
    O, chraobh an iubhair, *o ho*.

Nì e fion a dh'uisg' an t-slèibhe,
    O, chraobh, etc.

Copanan dearg air a' chrèadhaich,
Lìon air bhàrr an fhraoich nam b'fheudar
Muileann air gach sruthan slèibhe,
Tobar fion' air bhruaich gach fèithe,
Caisteal air gach cnoc 's leis fhèin 'ad.

'S e MacAoidh a' chòtain eangaich
Nach iarradh an t-earradh trom,
Chuireadh coisiche na dheannaibh
Mharcraicheadh an t-each na dheann.

8

Seumas (mac Aonghais) MacDhomhnaill at the battle of Tràigh Ghrùinneart in Islay in 1598, the subject of poem 74.

The song is probably composite in construction, the young lovers' carelessness sitting strangely with the prayer for the loved one's protection in the last three verses. Those invoked include Christian and natural forces: Christ and Mary, the sun, moon and winds. A similar passage occurs slightly later in 'Tàladh Dhòmhnaill Ghuirm' (Donald Gorm's Lullaby) (1617?), with the invocation of the world, waves, bull, Oisean and Oscar. It is suggested that the source for these passages are ultimately pagan prayers, similar to the roots of 'St Patrick's Breastplate', and 'Fer Fio's Cry'.

MacAoidh it is who's the man of valour,
    O tree of yew, *o ho,*

He makes silk of wool most handsome,
    O tree of yew, *o ho,*

He makes silk of wool most handsome,
    O tree of yew, *o ho.*

He makes wine of moorland water,
    O tree of yew, etc.

Out of the clay he makes brass cups,
lint to grow on heath if he had to,
a mill on every mountain rapid,
a well of wine by every marshland,
on every hill one of his castles.

MacAoidh it is of the skirted frock-coat,
he would not want heavy armour,
he could outstrip any walker,
he would ride a horse at the gallop.

Nam biodh MacAoidh san àite
No Niall anabharrach a bhràthair,
Cha bhiodh mo thochradh gun phàigheadh;   16
Bhiodh crodh-laoigh ann 's aighean dàra
'S na seasgaich air chùl a' ghàrraidh.

Mo ghaol fhìn an chùirteir feucannt,
'S tric a thog 'ad oirnn na breugan
Far nach biomaid fhìn gan èisteachd.

Mo ghaol 's mo ghràdh an t-òg beadarrach,
Dhannsadh gu grinn lùthmhor aigeanntach;
Air ùrlar gum biomaid suigeanta,   24
Air chnoc àrd gum biomaid beadarrach.

'S math thig dhut an deise chothlamaidh
'S lèine chaol dhan anart Ghailmhinn,
Clogad cruadhach 's suaicheantas dearg ort
'S paidhir mhath phiostal air chrios nam ball airgid.

Chraobh nan ubhal, gheug nan abhal,
Chraobh nan ubhal, gu robh Dia leat,
Gu robh Moire 's gu robh Crìosda,   32
Gu robh ghealach, gu robh ghrian leat,
Gu robh gaoth an ear 's an iar leat,
Gu robh m'athair fhin 's a thriall leat.

Ach ma thèid thu dha'n choill' iùbhraich
Aithnich fhèin a' chraobh as liùmsa.
Chraobh as mìlse's as buig' ùbhlan,
Chraobh mheanganach pheurach ùbhlach,
Bun a' fas 's a bàrr a' lùbadh
'S a meangannan air gach tùbh dhi,
Ùbhlan troma, donna, dlùthmhor.   40

Ach ma thèid thu na choill' fhiosraich
Foighnich a' chraobh am bi mise,
Chraobh a thilg a barr 's a miosan,
Chraobh a thilg a peighinn phisich.

If MacAoidh were in his country
or young Niall, his excelling brother,
not unpaid would be my dowry,
there'd be cows with calf and heifers bulling
and young stock beyond the townland.

My own dear's a charming lover,
often they spread tales about us,
but we'd be gone and wouldn't bother.

My young love's a wanton darling,
he danced nimbly and with spirit,
we'd be gambolling over the dance-floor,
on the hillock we'd be kissing.

Well you suit clothes of blended colours,
a fine-spun shirt of Galway linen,
a helmet of steel, red-crested,
a good pair of pistols on a belt studded silver.

O tree of apples, O branch of apples,
O tree of apples, may God be with you,
may Christ and Mary both be with you,
may the moon and the sun be with you,
may the wind of the east and the west be with you,
may my own father and his herds be with you.

If you go to the wood of yew-trees,
my own tree you will discover,
the tree of the sweetest softest produce,
branching tree of pears and apples,
its trunk thickening, its crest bowing,
branches spreading all around it,
its apples heavy thick-set russet.

But if you go to the wood of knowledge,
ask for the tree where I am watching,
tree that dropped its leaves and produce,
tree that dropped its penny of fortune.

81. Là Mille Gàrraidh

Gun urra

Cleas òrain ainmeil nan Griogarach, tha duilgheadasan Linn nan Creach rim faireachdainn gu làidir anns an òran Sgitheanach seo. Dh'èirich an t-òran seo, agus an ath fhear, às an aimhreit leantainneach eadar Clann MhicLeòid na Hearadh agus Clann Raghnaill; tha grunn bhatailean agus àran air an ainmeachadh tron òran. Tha e follaiseach, gu h-àraidh anns an t-sreath mu dheireadh, gur ann bho thaobh nan Leòdach a thàinig an t-òran seo.

Thachair Là Mille Gàrraidh ann am Bhatairnis ann an 1570, nuair a thàinig feachd Raghnallach gun rabhadh gus ionnsaigh a thoirt air muinntir Chlann MhicLeòid agus iad a' frithealadh na h-aifrinn ann an eaglais an Trumpain. Chaidh an luchd-adhraidh air fad a losgadh gu bàs, ach chunnaic na Leòdaich a bha ann am badan eile den eilean an toit, agus thàinig iad a dhèanamh cinnteach nach b'urrainn do na Raghnallaich teicheadh. A rèir beul-aithris b'e seo an turas mu dheireadh a chleachd na Leòdaich a' bhratach ainmeil aca (Bratach Shìl Leòid). Thug buaidh dhrùidhteach na brataich air na Raghnallaich creidsinn gu robh mòr-shluagh romhpa seach feachd nach robh ach meadhanach beag, agus chaidh am marbhadh uile agus iad a' feuchainn ri am birlinnean a ruigsinn. Chaidh na cuirp a chur aig oir gàrraidh a bha faisg air làimh, agus ùir a' ghàrraidh a thilgeil is a sgaoileadh orra: milleadh gàrraidh, ma b'fhìor. Is e seann ainm Lochlannais a tha ann am 'Mìlegarraidh', ge-tà, agus tha e coltach gun do chuireadh an sgeulachd ri chèile mar bhreug-mhìneachadh air an ainm.

Ged a thathar a' toirt iomradh air a' ghàrradh mhillte anns an òran, chan eil mion-fhiosrachadh mun bhlàr ri fhaighinn ann idir. Chan eil an ceangal eadar am blàr seo agus na blàran eile a tha air an ainmeachadh daonnan soilleir. Is dòcha gun deach cuid de na sreathan a thoirt à òrain eile. Is math a dh'fhaodte gu bheil na sreathan ann am meadhan an òrain, a' dèanamh cunntas air turas-mara, stèidhichte air an ionnsaigh a thug na Leòdaich air Eige, cuspair an ath dhàin.

The Battle of Mille Gàrraidh

Like the famous MacGriogair songs, this sixteenth-century Skye song reflects the instability of the Gàidhealtachd during *Linn nan Creach*, the so-called 'Age of Forays' following the collapse of the Lordship of the Isles. The specific context for this song, and the one immediately following, was the running conflict between the MacLeòids of Harris and Dunvegan and the Clann Raghnaill branch of Clann Domhnaill, who held a far-flung mainland and island territory south of Skye; several famous battles and massacres are named in the song. As is clear from the last line, the present song comes from the MacLeòid side.

The battle of Milleadh Gàrraidh was fought in Waternish, north Skye, in 1570, when a Clann Raghnaill force descended without warning upon a congregation assembled in the church at Trumpan. All the worshippers were burned to death, but the smoke attracted the attention of other MacLeòids in the area, who arrived to block the Clann Raghnaill warriors' escape. According to tradition this was the last occasion on which the MacLeòids unfurled their famous 'Fairy Flag', which guaranteed victory. The spell of the flag made the Clann Raghnaill warriors see a vast host of armed men instead of a modest force, but as they fled in panic to their galleys, they were all cut down before they reached the shore. Their bodies were then lined up along a turf dyke near the scene of the battle, and the dyke was then pushed over on top of them in a rough-and-ready burial. The conflict is thus remembered as Blàr Milleadh Gàrraidh, 'the battle of the spoiling of the dyke'. This interpretation of the name is almost certainly a folk etymology, however, an imagined explanation of a pre-existing – here Norse – place-name.

Although the collapsed dyke is referred to in the song, this composition is very far from being a detailed description of the battle. Some of the other conflicts cannot now be identified with certainty, and the link between the various place-names mentioned in the song is not clear. It may well be that some lines originate as part of a separate song or songs. The middle lines of the song, describing a sea journey, may possibly refer to the MacLeòids' attack on Eigg, described in the next poem.

E-hò, ro ho ro ho,
N' an cuimhne leibh
O hì ri rì, hi ri ho ro ho,
Là na h-Àirde,

E-hò, ro ho ro ho,
No 'n là eile,
O hì ri rì, hi ri ho ro ho,
Mille Gàrraidh?

Bha fir an sin
air dhroch chàradh,

An druim fodha,
's am buinn bhàn ris.   8

N' an cuimhne leibh
Là Allt Èireann,

No 'n là eile,
Uamh Deirge?

Chunnacas bàta
falbh gu siùbhlach,

'S i dol timcheall
Rubha Hùnais;   16

Às an sin gu
Rubh' an Dùnain.

B'e mo leannan
bha ga stiùireadh,

Beul ga eubhadh,
làmh ga h-iomradh.

'S iomadh bean bhochd
bha gu cràidhteach,   24

'S i gun mhac ann,
's i gun bhràthair,

Do you remember

the Battle of the Headland,

or that other battle,

of Mille Gàrraidh?

Men were there
in a sad condition,

on their backs,
their white soles showing.

Do you remember
Auldearn's battle,

or that other battle,
of Uamh Deirge?

A ship was seen
sailing swiftly,

going round the
point of Hùnais,

from there on
to Rubh' an Dùnain.

Her helmsman
was my sweetheart,

mouth calling,
arm rowing,

many a poor woman
was left grieving,

without a son,
without a brother,

Gun duine ann a
ghabhadh bàidh dhith.

'S mo mhallachd sin
aig Clann Raghnaill.   30

82. 'S Trom an Dìreadh

Gun urra

Tha an t-òran luaidh seo ag innse mu àr mì-chliùiteach a
thugadh gu buil le Clann MhicLeòid air muinntir Chlann
Raghnaill ann an Eilean Eige anns an t-siathamh linn deug. A
rèir cuid de na tùsan againn, thachair an ionnsaigh seo anns a'
Mhàrt 1577, nuair a chaidh sluagh an eilein gu lèir (aon 395
duine) a mhùchadh ann an uamh ris an canar Uamh Fhraing leis
na Leòdaich an dèidh dhaibh àite-falaich a shireadh innte. Is ann
bho shealladh nan Domhnallach a tha an sgeulachd air a
h-innse, agus an cuideam air brùidealachd Chlann MhicLeòid.

Bha Iain Latharna Caimbeul (Fear Chanaidh) gu math
amharasach mun chunntas seo, agus e den bheachd gur ann na
bu tràithe anns an t-siathamh linn deug a thachair an t-àr seo, ri
linn oidhirp neo-shoirbheachail ri rèite pòsaidh a dhèanamh
eadar an dà chinneadh.

Chan eil na faclan mar a bha iad aig seinneadairean an
fhicheadamh linn furasta a thuigsinn. Mar eisimpleir, chan
fhaicear eileanan Ruma, Eige, Ìle, Bharraigh agus Uibhist bhon
aon àite-amhairc. Mar a thachras gu tric anns na h-òrain luaidh,
tha e coltach gu bheil rannan à òrain eile air am fighe a-steach;
seo as coireach gu bheil iomradh ga dhèanamh air gunna anns
an rann mu dheireadh.

> *E hó a hó, 's trom an dìreadh,*
> *Hi hoireann ó, 's trom an dìreadh,*
> *E hó a hó, 's trom an dìreadh,*
> *'S trom an dìreadh.*

without a man
to take her affection,

and so my curse
is on Clann Raghnaill.

Hard the Climbing

This waulking song expresses a MacDhomhnaill perspective on
a notorious massacre perpetrated by the MacLeòids on the Isle
of Eigg during the sixteenth century. According to some sources,
the incident occurred in March 1577, and the entire population
of the island – some 395 people – were smothered to death by
an invading party of MacLeòids after they had taken refuge in a
cave (*Uamh Fhraing*).

The eminent scholar John Lorne Campbell has cast
considerable doubt on this version of events, however, arguing
that the incident actually occurred several decades earlier, in the
early sixteenth century, and arose from the breakdown of
attempts to arrange a marriage between the two kindreds.

The words as transcribed from twentieth-century traditional
singers are not easy to interpret literally – for instance, there is
no physical point from which the islands of Rum, Eigg, Islay,
Barra, and Uist can all be seen – but they clearly reflect a Clann
Raghnaill outlook, especially in the graphic reference to the
MacLeòids' thirst for blood (compare the previous poem). As
with many waulking songs preserved in oral tradition, parts of
other songs appear to be woven into an earlier composition; the
reference to a gun in the last stanza certainly seems extraneous.

> *E hó a hó*, hard the climbing,
> *Hi hoireann ó*, hard the climbing,
> *E hó a hó*, hard the climbing,
> Hard the climbing.

'S fhad' an sealladh bhuam a chì mi, *é hó a hó,*
's trom an dìreadh, hì hoireann hó,
's trom an dìreadh, é hó a hó,
'S trom an dìreadh.

Chì mi Rùm is Eige 's Ìle, *é hó a hó,*
's trom an dìreadh, hì hoireann hó,
's trom an dìreadh, é hó a hó,
'S trom an dìreadh.

Far na rinn MacLeòid an dìobhail, *é hó a hó,*
's trom an dìreadh, hì hoireann hó,
's trom an dìreadh, é hó a hó,
'S trom an dìreadh.

Dhòirt e fuil 's gun chaisg e ìotadh, *é hó a hó,*
's trom an dìreadh, hì hoireann hó,
's trom an dìreadh, é hó a hó,
'S trom an dìreadh.

Chì mi Barraigh, an tìr ìseal, *é hó a hó,*
's trom an dìreadh, hì hoireann hó,
's trom an dìreadh, é hó a hó,
'S trom an dìreadh.

Chì mi Uibhist nam fear fialaidh, *é hó a hó,*
's trom an dìreadh, hì hoireann hó,
's trom an dìreadh, é hó a hó,
'S trom an dìreadh.

Far an dèanar an Fhèill Mìcheil, *é hó a hó,*
's trom an dìreadh, hì hoireann hó,
's trom an dìreadh, é hó a hó,
'S trom an dìreadh.

Hi hoireann ó, có nì sùgradh? é hó a hó,   8
's trom an dìreadh, hì hoireann hó,
's trom an dìreadh, é hó a hó,
'S trom an dìreadh.

Far the view I see before me,

I see Rum and Eigg and Islay,

where MacLeòid did his damage,

he spilled blood and quenched his parchedness,

I see Barra, the land low-lying,

I see Uist of the generous people,

Where Michaelmas is honoured,

Hi hoireann ó, who'll make merry,

Có nì 'n gunna caol a ghiùlain? *é hó a hó,*
's trom an dìreadh, hì hoireann hó,
's trom an dìreadh, é hó a hó,
'S trom an dìreadh.

who will carry the slender musket? *E hó a hó*,
hard the climbing, *Hi hoireann ó*,
hard the climbing, *E hó a hó*,
hard the climbing.

The Song Tradition

Satire

83. A' Ghriadach Dhonn

Gun urra

Tha grunn spaidsearachdan againn a rinneadh, a rèir coltais, aig deireadh an t-siathamh linn deug no toiseach an t-seachdamh linn deug, òrain (òrain luaidh mar as trice) anns a bheil dithis bhoireannach a' moladh 's a' dì-moladh sgìrean a chèile gu tàireil. Anns an òran a leanas tha bana-Mhuileach ag iarraidh sgrios air dùthaich nan Camshronach ann an Loch Abar, agus an sin tha ban-Abrach ga freagairt le bagairt air Muile.

A rèir beul-aithris, bha a' bhan-Abrach seo pòsta aig fear a bha a' fuireach faisg air Loch Sgriodain ann an iar-dheas Mhuile, agus bha i an sàs ann an luadh nuair a thòisich aon de bhoireannaich a' bhannail ri magadh air dùthaich is daoine Loch Abar.

Mar a sheinn a' bhan-Mhuileach:

B'fheàrr gun cluinninn siud a-màireach, *hu hi ho ro*
Creach Ghlinn Laoich is Ghlinne Mhàillidh, *hu hi ho ro*
Ghlinne Cinngidh nan clacha geala, *hu hi ho ro*
Ghlinne Pheathann nan craobh àrda, *hu hi ho ro*
Gun Chamshronach bhith ri ràdhainn, *hu hi ho ro*
Sin nuair gheibhinn an cadal sàmhach, *hu hi ho ro*
Gus an èireadh grian a-màireach, *hu hi ho ro*
Gun duine dhiubh a bhith 'n làthair, *hu hi ho ro*   8
An eilean mara mun iadh an sàile, *hu hi ho ro*
Gheibhte siud an Dabhach an Fhasaidh, *hu hi ho ro*
Bodaich bheaga ghearra lachdann, *hu hi ho ro*
Ghoideadh an fheòil san latha fhrasach, *hu hi ho ro*
'S bheireadh i san anmoch dhachaigh, *hu hi ho ro*
Osain laoighchinn 's cuairean craicinn, *hu hi ho ro*
Fèileadh àrd is dronnag bradach, *hu hi ho ro.*

A' Ghriadach Dhonn

This waulking song, apparently dating from the end of the sixteenth century, takes the form of a flyting between a Mull woman and a woman from Lochaber, with the Mull woman contemptuously wishing destruction on the Camshron lands of Lochaber, and the Lochaber woman in turn mounting a spirited defence, threatening an attack upon Mull. Several similar compositions (a form known as *spaidsearachd*) in which two women alternately praise their own districts and dispraise the other's have survived from the same period.

According to tradition, the Lochaber woman here was married to a man who lived near Loch Scridain in the southwest of Mull, and was involved in a waulking when one of the women in the group began mocking Lochaber and its people. This is not unlikely, as waulkings were recognised as occasions for teasing and cajolery.

As the Mull woman sang:

Would that I would hear tomorrow, *hù hì hó ró*,
of the ravaging of Glen Loy and Glen Mallie,
of Glen Kingie of the white boulders,
and Glen Pean of the tall forests,
with not a Cameron to be counted,
that's what would let me sleep soundly
till the sun would rise in the morning,
for not one of them to be left living
in any island girt by the ocean.
This would be found in Dochanassie:
little old men, sallow, stunted,
who'd steal meat in drizzly weather
and take it home after darkness
calfskin hose and hairy sandals,
kilt held up with a stolen burden.

Fhreagair a' bhean à Loch Abar:

Gheibhte sud an Dabhach an Fhasaidh, *i u o*   16
Còmhlan ùr de ghillean gasda, *i u o*
Stiùireadh an long san latha fhrasach, *i u o*
'S nach leigeadh balgam bric a-steach oirr', *i u o*
Ged a thilgteadh aist' an calcadh, *i u o*
Cuime an duirt an trustair siubhail, *i u o*
Nach fhaighte siud 'na do bhuidheann, *i u o*
Fear osain gheàrr is còta cumhang, *i u o*
Bonaid bheòil bhig air chùil buidhe, *i u o*   24
Cuime an duirt an trustair caillich, *i u o*
Gun robh an t-Ailean Donn gun chaisbheairt, *i u o*
B'uaibhreach dha sud, 's lìonmhor aig' iad, *i u o*
Stocaidh den t-sròl, *i u o*
Bròg dhubh bhaltdubh, *i u o*
Bròg dhubh mhìndubh, chiardubh, chiarrtaidh, *i u o*
Bho leathar nam bò thig à Sasann, *i u o*.
Nuair a shuidh mi 'n ceann na clèithe, *i u o*   32
Chuir mi dithis ris an àireamh, *i u o*
Leanabh beag an ceann a ràithe, *i u o*
'S beag nach tug mi 'm bàs d'a mhàthair, *i u o*
'S cha b'èirig siud air mo thàmailt, *i u o*
'N na fhuair mi, *i o u*
Sgrios mo chàirdean, *hi ho hiu*
Sgrios mo chinnidh thaobh mo mhàthar, *i u o*
B'fheàrr gun cluinninn, *i o u*   40
Siud 's gum faicinn, *i u o*
Ged nach bì mi, *i u o*
Creach an t-Sìthein, *i o u*
'S creach an Lagain, *i u o*
Creach Mhuile an Rois, *i u o*
'S a cruidh chaisfhionn, *i u o*
An t-Eilean Druidhneach bhith 'na lasair, *i u o*
'S masa breug e, *i u o*   48
Seall a-mach air, *i u o*
Mnathan òga falbh sa bhasraich, *i u o*
'S an cuid leanaban falbh gun bhaisteadh, *i u o*
Bualadh gu tric air ar macaibh, *i u o*
Iomain gu dìon air ar martaibh, *i u o*

The Lochaber woman replied:

This would be found in Dochanassie:
a fresh band of fine young fellows,
who'd sail a ship through a downpour,
and not let in a trout's mouthful,
even were her caulking knocked out.
Why was the vagrant ragbag saying
that there couldn't be found in your party
a man in short hose and tailored jacket,
with a peaked cap on yellow tresses?
Why was the wretched old besom saying
that Ailean Donn was without footwear?
It well became him and he had plenty,
silken stockings,
black shoes, black welted,
fine black shoes, pitchblack, polished,
made from hide of cows from England.
When I sat down at the head of the hurdles
I added two others to the number:
a little child at the end of his season,
I nearly caused the death of his mother,
and that was not the price of my shaming,
(but) what it was I found there:
the destruction of my kinsfolk,
the destruction of my people on the side of my mother.
Would that I would hear of
this: and that I'd witness,
even were I myself not living,
the destruction of the Hillock
and the destruction of the Hollow,
the destruction of Mull of the headland
and of its white-footed cattle,
and Eilean Druidhneach left burning.
If it is a falsehood
take a look yonder,
young women moving around wailing,
their children dead without a christening.
Our young lads being goaded
to drive our cattle to safe-keeping,

Raghnall Mòr thar chuan 'gan aiseag, *i u o*
'S a bhith 'gan roinn air dail Ghlasdruim, *i u o*
Nan tàrladh dhomh bhith dol seachad, *i u o*   56
Bu leam fhìn dhiubh mart is capall, *i u o*
Còig no sia dhiubh, sia no seachd dhiubh, *i u o*
Am feasta gus am bithinn beartach, *i u o*
Ailein Duinn, *i u o*
An tig thu 'n tìr so, *i u o*
Nan cluinninn faram do long ris an lìonadh,
Fuaim do ghnocain ri cois tìre,
Roimh na caoil thu, roimh Chaol Muil' thu, roimh Chaol Ìle,   64
Ro Choire Bhreacain nan sruth lìonmhor
Gu Colbhasa Mhic-a-phì thu
Roimh Loch Odha gu Latharn' ìochdrach,
Far an do ghabh mo ghaol a dhìnneir:
Cha b'ann de bhùrn dubh nan dìgean,
Ach de bhainne a' chruidh chiardubh.
Eudail nam fear 's lìonmhor ainm ort
Tha fiodh fraoich ort, tha chaor dhearg ort   72
Tha 'm beithe beag ort 's an calltainn,
Tha ainm eil' ort 's docha leamsa,
Tha an t-Ailean Donn siùbhlach.
'S math thig sìth dhut, 's olc thig fearg dhut
'S math thig lùireach leathann gharbh ort.
Cò thèid sìos leinn do na blàraibh
Gur h-i d'aghaidh nach robh sgàthach,
Gearrar cinn leat 's am bi cnàmhan,   80
Dòirtear fuil leat 's am bi nàire.
Ràinig mi 'n caol 's ghlaodh mi 'n t-aiseag,
'S tric a fhuaireadh na bu chais e.
'S truagh nach robh mi san tìr Abrach,
Gun tighinn riamh às 'm measg nan coigreach.

Raghnall Mòr ferrying them over,
sorting them out on the meadow at Glasdruim.
If I happened to be passing
I would take for myself a mare and bullock,
five or six of them, six or seven,
so for evermore I'd be wealthy;
Ailean Donn,
will you come to this coastline?
If I heard the sound of your ships against the tide-race,
the noise of your thole-pins bouncing off the rockface,
with you on the far side of the Sound of Mull and Islay,
on the far side of Corryvreckan of the many currents,
you going to Mac-a-phì's Colonsay,
from Lochawe to Lower Lorne stretching
where my love took his dinner,
not of the black water of ditches,
but of the milk of the pitchblack cattle.
Treasure of men, you have many by-names,
you're called sprig of heather, red rowan,
you're called the little birch and the hazel,
you have another name that is my favourite,
this Ailean Donn is nimble.
Peace becomes you, anger does not,
a sturdy broad breastplate well becomes you.
Who will go down with us to the battles?
Yours is the face that was not timid,
you lop off heads that are bony,
you spill blood that is shameful.
I reached the kyle and I called for the ferry,
often did it come more quickly.
It's a shame I'm not in the land of Lochaber,
never having left to be among strangers.

THE SONG TRADITION

BALLAD

84.　A Bhean Ud Thall

Gun urra

Bha an t-òran ainmeil seo, a thathar cuideachd ag aithneachadh fon ainm 'A' Bhean Eudach', measail aig an t-sluagh air feadh na Gàidhealtachd agus chaidh iomadach tionndadh dheth a chlàradh ann an iomadach sgìre. Tha an sgeulachd air cùlaibh an òrain sìmplidh gu leòr, ged a tha diofaran beaga cudromach anns na diofar thionndaidhean. Tha màthair a' dol don chladach còmhla ri boireannach eile (a piuthar, no a searbhanta) gus feamainn a chruinneachadh; chan eil am boireannach eile ga rabhadh gu bheil an làn a' tighinn a-steach. Tha a' mhàthair air a fàgail na h-aonar air creag agus air a bàthadh leis an làn. Tha banntrach na màthar an sin a' pòsadh na 'mnà eudaich', ach nuair a chluinneas e i a' seinn an òrain seo, tha e a' tuigsinn dè dìreach a thachair agus tha e ga cur a-mach.

Ged a tha e follaiseach gur ann à Alba a tha an t-òran seo bho thùs, chaidh a chlàradh ann an diofar sgìrean ann an Èirinn cuideachd, gu h-àraidh ann an Tír Chonaill. A dh'aindeoin nan ceanglaichean eadar Gàidhealtachd Alba agus Èirinn thar nan linntean, chan eil ach beagan òran a tha rim faighinn air dà thaobh Shruth na Maoile. Tha 'A bhean ud thall' eadar-nàiseanta ann an seagh eile, ge-tà, oir tha suaip aig an òran seo ri òrain agus sgeulachdan dualchasach ann an caochladh phàirtean den Roinn Eòrpa cuideachd.

Chan urrainnear a bhith cinnteach ach tha eòlaichean a' dèanamh a-mach gun do rinneadh an t-òran seo uaireigin anns an t-siathamh linn deug.

> A bhean ud thall　*Hùg ò*
> Chois na tràighe　*Hùg ò*
> Nach truagh leat fhèin　*Hùg il ho ro*
> Bean ga bàthadh　*Hùg oirinn ò.*
>
> Cha truagh, cha truagh,　*Hùg ò,* etc
> 'S beag mo chàs dith.

The Jealous Woman

This famous song, sometimes known as 'A' Bhean Eudach' ('The Jealous Woman'), was known throughout the Hebrides and West Highlands and has been recorded in different forms in many locations. The basic story-line behind the poem is a simple one, although there are different twists and motifs in different versions. A mother has gone to the shore to collect seaweed in the company of another woman – her sister or servant – who deliberately neglects to warn the mother of the incoming tide. She is then stranded on a rock and drowned when the tide engulfs her. The widowed husband then marries the 'jealous woman', but later hears her, or a harp made from the drowned woman's breastbone, singing this song, realises what has happened, and throws her out.

Although the song is evidently of Scottish origin, it has also been recorded in different parts of Ireland, principally Donegal. Despite the tight connections over the centuries, surprisingly few folksongs seem to have been shared between Gaelic Scotland and Gaelic Ireland. In this instance, however, variations on this story are common in folk songs and folk tales in other parts of Europe.

Precise dating is impossible but experts suggest that the song was composed in the sixteenth century.

'O woman yonder
beside the water,
do you not pity
a woman who's drowning?'

'I don't, I don't,
little my care for her.'

Sìn do chosan
'S sgaoil do làmhan.   8

Dh'fheuch am feud thu
Buille shnàmhadh.

Seo mo chriosan,
Glèidh mo bhràiste,

Mo sporan donn
'S mo thruis bhràighe.

Thoir mo bheannachd
Do m' thriùir bhràithre,   16

'S beannachd eile
Do m' dhà phàisdean,

Fear dhiubh bliadhna,
'S fear dhiubh ràidhe,

'S chan fhaigh e nochd
Cìoch a mhàthar.

Thig an t-eathar
An seo a-màireach,   24

Deagh Mhac an t-Saoir
Air ràmh bhràghaid.

Gheibh e mise
'N dèidh mo bhàthadh,

'S bidh na h-easgan
Glas dhiom sàthach,

'S mo chuailean donn
Làn don t-sàile.   32

'Se 'n duileasg donn
Rinn mo bhàthadh.

'Stretch out your legs,
give me your hands.'

'See if you can't
swim a stroke.'

'Here is my girdle,
keep my brooch,

'my good purse
and my necklace.

'Give my blessing
to my three brothers,

'and another
to my two children,

'one a year old,
the other a season,

'Tonight he won't get
the breast of his mother.

'The boat will come
here tomorrow,

'Good Mac an t-Saoir
on the forward oar.

'They will find me
after I'm drowned,

'And the grey eels
will be well-sated,

'And my brown curls
soaked in the brine.

'It was the darling dulse
that caused my drowning.

'S neurachd bean òg
Thig am àite.

'S math mo sheileir,
'S math mo chàise;

'S math mo chrò
A chaoiribh bàna;   40

Badan ghabhar
An creagaibh àrda;

Seisreach chapall
Dèanamh m'àitich.

'Happy the young woman
who comes in my stead.

'Good is my cellar
good my cheese,

'Good my fold
of fair sheep;

'A flock of goats
on rocky outcrops,

'A team of six
doing my ploughing.'

THE SONG TRADITION

LULLABY

85. B'Fheàrr Leam gun Sgrìobhte Dhuit Fearann

Gun urra

Rinneadh an tàladh seo mu 1520 do Eòghainn Beag mac Dhomhnaill mhic Eòghainn, an ceathramh ceann-cinnidh deug aig Clann Chamshroin Loch Iall, a chaidh a mhurt mu 1553. Cleas iomadh òran eile bhon linn sin, tha an t-òran am beul muime an òganaich. B'e dreuchd chudromach a bha aig a' mhuime, agus gu tric b'e ball den fhine, is chan e idir sgalag, a choilean an dleastanas seo. Bha Màiri nighean Alasdair Ruaidh (*c.* 1615–1707), mar eisimpleir, na muime do chòignear uaislean de Chloinn MhicLeòid Dhùn Bheagain.

Ged a fhuair Eòghainn Beag ceannas a chinnidh mu dheireadh, ann an 1547, cha robh e idir follaiseach gu robh an inbhe sin an dàn dha nuair a bha e na phàiste. Uime sin, tha an t-òran a' cur an cèill dòchas a mhuime gum faigheadh e suidheachadh tèarainte co-dhiù. Tha an seinneadair aig ainmeachadh na h-òran nan àiteachan a bu chòir nochdadh ann an cairt laghail dha: sgìre fharsaing ann an Loch Abar eadar ceann Loch Iall agus cladach a tuath Loch Airceig, crìochan dùthaich nan Camshronach.

Cha do choisinn Eòghainn Beag cliù mòr na bheatha, ach tha an t-òran a' toirt iomradh air a sheanair ainmeil, Eòghainn mac Ailein, an treas ceann-cinnidh deug, a chaidh a chur gu bàs air sgàth feall ann an 1547, agus air a shean-shean-sheanair, Domhnall Dubh, a ghabh pàirt ann an Cath Gairbheach às leth Triath nan Eilean (faic dàn 34) agus, aig toiseach a' bhatail co-dhiù, Blàr Inbhir Lòchaidh (faic dàin 77 and 78). Bha am mac nàdarra aig Eòghainn Beag, Domhnall, air an robh am far-ainm Tàillear Dubh na Tuaighe, na laoch ainmeil cuideachd.

Tha tàlaidhean gu math cumanta am measg nan òran as tràithe a tha air tighinn a-nuas thugainn (dèan coimeas ri dàn 65). Mar as trice tha ceann-cinnidh (no oighre) òg a' faighinn moladh annta air sgàth nam buaidhean a fhuair e no a tha an dàn dha. Gu tric, a dh'aindeoin cleas an tàlaidh, is e inbheach a tha fo cheist; tha an t-òran seo, a tha a' buntainn ri pàiste aig an

I Wish You Were Assigned a Charter

This lullaby, apparently dating from about 1520, was composed for Eòghainn Beag mac Dhomhnaill mhic Eòghainn, later to become fourteenth chief of the Camshrons of Locheil, who was murdered around 1553. Like several other early songs, the singer is the youth's nurse – not a menial position but an important position in the household, typically assigned to a member of the clan nobility. One of the most famous poets of the seventeenth century, Màiri nighean Alasdair Ruaidh (Mary MacLeod), served as nurse to several chiefs of the MacLeòids of Dunvegan.

Although he eventually gained the chiefship in 1547, Eòghainn Beag's succession did not appear likely when he was a child; as such, the song expresses his nurse's wishes that he should nevertheless obtain an elevated and legally secure position in life. The song names all the places she wishes were identified in a legal title for the infant, an area of Lochaber stretching from the head of Loch Eil in the west along the north bank of the River Lochy and around to the north shore of Loch Arkaig – the Camshron heartland.

Eòghainn Beag's own career was undistinguished, but the poem refers to his illustrious grandfather, the thirteenth chief, Eòghainn mac Ailein, who was executed for treason in 1547, and to his great-great-grandfather, Domhnall Dubh, who fought on behalf of the Lord of the Isles at the Battle of Harlaw in 1411 (see poem 34) and, at the start of the conflict at least, at the Battle of Inverlochy in 1431 (see poems 77 and 78). Eòghainn Beag's illegitimate son Domhnall also became a celebrated warrior, known as 'Tàillear Dubh na Tuaighe' (the Black Tailor of the Axe), a nickname that reflected his skills with the Lochaber battle-axe and his discreet fosterage in the care of a tailor's wife.

Songs cast in the form of a lullaby (*tàladh*) are an important sub-genre of early vernacular songs. Usually the young chief (or heir apparent) is praised for triumphs predicted or actual; the subject may in fact be an adult notwithstanding the 'lullaby'

robh suidheachadh car cugallach, rud beag a-mach às an àbhaist.

Hi, ha, ho, mo leanabh
B'fheàrr leam gun sgrìobhte dhuit fearann.

Hi, ha, ho, mo leanabh
Ogha Eòghainn 's iar-ogh' Ailein.

Hi, ha, ho, mo leanabh
'S iar-ogh' Dhomhnaill Duibh bhon Darach.

Hi, ha, ho, mo leanabh
B'fheàrr gun sgrìobhte cinnteach d'fhearann.   8

Hi, ha, ho, mo leanabh
Ceann Loch Iall 'us Druim na Saille,

Hi, ha, ho, mo leanabh
'S Coire Beag ri taobh na mara,

Hi, ha, ho, mo leanabh
Achadh Do Liubha 's an Annaid,

Hi, ha, ho, mo leanabh
'S a' Mhaigh mhòr 's an t-Sròn 's an t-Earrachd,   16

Hi, ha, ho, mo leanabh
Muic 'us Caoinnich, Craoibh 's a' Chaillich,

Hi, ha, ho, mo leanabh
'S Murlagan dubh grànda, greannach.

Hi, ha, ho, mo leanabh
'S bòidheach d'aodann, 's caoin leam d'anail,

Hi, ha, ho, mo leanabh
Socrach cùin, a rùin, do chadal.   24

form. This song, addressed to an actual infant without the best
of prospects, is somewhat exceptional.

> *Hi ha ho* my baby,
> I wish you were assigned a charter.
>
> *Hi ha ho* my baby,
> Grandson of Eòghainn, great-grandson of Ailean,
>
> *Hi ha ho* my baby,
> And great-grandson of Domhnall Dubh from Darach.
>
> *Hi ha ho* my baby,
> Better had you confirmation of your land in writing:
>
> *Hi ha ho* my baby,
> Kinlocheil and Drumsallie,
>
> *Hi ha ho* my baby,
> And Corriebeg beside the ocean.
>
> *Hi ha ho* my baby,
> Achdaliew and Annat,
>
> *Hi ha ho* my baby,
> And great Moy and Strone and Errocht,
>
> *Hi ha ho* my baby,
> Muick and Caonich, Crieff and Caillich,
>
> *Hi ha ho* my baby,
> And Murlaggan, dreary, dark and gloomy.
>
> *Hi ha ho* my baby,
> Sweet your face and soft your breathing,
>
> *Hi ha ho* my baby,
> Sure and sound, my dear, your slumber.

NOTES ON THE POEMS

1. *Tiugraind Beccáin*

Source: Clancy & Márkus 1995, 146–51 (cf. Kelly 1975).

Another poem by Beccán mac Luigdech in praise of Colum Cille is published in Clancy & Márkus 1995, 136–42, and in Kelly 1973. A new edition of the oldest poem to Colum Cille, 'Amra Choluimb Cille', composed by Dallán Forgaill on the saint's death in 597, has recently been published (Henry 2006; see also Clancy & Márkus 1995, 96–128).
On the evolution of the term 'Alba', see McLeod 2004, 126–8.

12   *Lethae*: an old word generally meaning 'Europe' but sometimes referring to Brittany.
23   *midnocht migne Ercae*: 'Earc's region' here is apparently a poetic name for Argyll, the region settled by Fergus mac Earc about 500 CE, or perhaps Scotland more generally. This name appears to be otherwise unknown; such poetic names for Scotland are not common, although Irish counterparts are legion.

2. *Má Ro-m-Thoiccthi Écc i ndhí*

Source: Herbert & Ó Riain 1988, 60.

For Colum Cille's blessing, see Sharpe 1995, 228, and Anderson & Anderson 1961, 524.

3. *Mór Do Ingantu Do-Gní*

Source: Clancy & Márkus 1995, 167 (cf. Herbert & Ó Riain 1988, 60).

For the account of Adomnán's miracle, see Herbert & Ó Riain 1988, 56–9.

4. Fil Súil nGlais

Source: Murphy 1956, 64.

The term *glas* can be translated either as 'grey' or 'blue'; the Gaelic colour spectrum does not conform closely to that used in English.

On poetry imagining Colum Cille as an exile, see Herbert 2005.

5. Meallach Liom Bheith i n-Ucht Oiléin

Source: O'Rahilly 1927, 120–21.

On poetry imagining Colum Cille as an exile, see Herbert 2005.

6. Éistidh Riomsa, a Mhuire Mhór

Source: Bergin 1970, 93–100.

For Muireadhach and Giolla Brighde's crusade poems, see O'Rahilly 1927: II, 179–80, 224–26; McKenna 1939, 1940: I, 174–76, II, 103; Murphy 1953, 71–9. For alternative translations, see Clancy 1998: 264–70. For a discussion of the imagery and expression in bardic poems to the Virgin Mary, see McKenna 1919, 9–13.

160   *feis* > *Éistidh*: Classical verse required a *dúnadh* or 'closing' by which the last syllable, word or phrase in the last line echoes the opening, often precisely. This was conventionally marked in manuscripts by giving the first word or phrase again after the last line.

7. Ná Léig mo Mhealladh, a Mhuire

Source: Greene 1962.

Another poem to Mary in the Book of the Dean, Giolla Críost Táilliúr's 'Linn labhras leabhar Muire', is given (in unedited form) in Quiggin 1937, 21.

For the poem on the seventeenth-century Maol Domhnaigh's visit to Ireland, composed by Piaras Feiritéar, see O'Rahilly 1940–42. On *uirscéalta* in general, see Ó Caithnia 1984.

100   *a-nall* > *Ná léig*: another bardic *dúnadh* (see note to poem 5).

8. Seacht Saighde Atá ar mo Thí

Source: Watson 1937, 252–4.

For the Fernaig manuscript version, see MacPhàrlain 1923, 22–25.

40   seacht > Seacht: a dúnadh in which the last full word of the poem is the same as the first is technically known as saighidh.

9. Adhmad Beag

Source: Thomson 1970, 13.

For a discussion of Carswell in his literary and cultural context, see Meek 1998.

10. Dursan Mh'Eachtra go hAlbuin

Source: McKenna 1939 40, 204–7.

The Treasury Accounts payment to Fearghal Óg is recorded in Scottish Record Office MS E 21/61–2, f. 31r.
    Another 'Scottish' poem by Fearghal Óg, 'Trí coróna i gcairt Shéamais' ('The three crowns in James's charter'), addressed to King James VI, is published in McKenna 1939–40, I, 177–80 (translated at II, 104–5). This poem may be associated with the poet's 1581 visit to Edinburgh but was more likely composed shortly before James's accession to the throne of England in 1603, which the Irish poets anticipated with great optimism that was eventually proven misplaced.

11. Creud Fa 'n D'Tharlamar an Tùrsa?

Source: MacPhàrlain 1923, 44–7.

For 'Faoisid Eòin Stiùbhairt', see Thomson 1962, xliii-xliv.

12. Is Mairg Do-Ní Uaille as Óige

Source: Thomson 1962, 217–18.

13. Mairg dar Compánach an Cholann

Sources: Thomson 1962, 224–5.

14. *Mairg Thréigeas Inn, a Amhlaoibh*

Source: Ó Cuív 1968.

On the difficulties associated with the historical Muireadhach Albanach, see Ó Cuív 1961 and Simms 2006. William Gillies has recently reviewed both the evidence for the historical Muireadhach and the family's place in later folk tradition (Gillies 2000).

On the medieval lordship of Lennox, see Neville 2005.

Muireadhach's poem to Alún mac Muireadhaigh, 'Saor do leannáin, a Leamhain', is published in McKenna 1939, 172–4 (translation in McKenna 1940, 102–3, and in Clancy 1998, 258–9).

Several of the genealogical references in the present poem are obscure, but the professional genealogists consistently emphasised a connection between the earls of Lennox and prominent Munster progenitors.

36	*rath*: perhaps 'prosperity' rather than 'fortress'.
38	*Arbhlatha*: probably Amhlaoibh's mother, wife of the first earl of Lennox (see Clancy 1998, 357)
62	*Mainigh*: the descendants of Maine Leamhna, progenitor of the earls of Lennox and the Stewart kings of Scots.

15. *Domhnall mac Raghnaill, Rosg Mall*

Source: NLS Adv. MS 72.2.2, f. 16. The textual edition here is by Meg Bateman, who acknowledges the help of Colm Ó Baoill on a number of points. A full scholarly edition of this poem is forthcoming.

For the citation of lines 11–12 in the Grammatical Tracts, see Bergin 1946, 206, line 386.

2	*Goll*: apparently a reference to the warrior Goll mac Morna, the great rival of Fionn mac Cumhaill (see poem 58), but the basis for the comparison is not clear.
39	*Oirghiallach*: according to the legendary history the kingdom of Oirghialla in south Ulster was founded by the three Collas, including Domhnall mac Raghnaill's ancestor Colla Uais (see introduction to poem 17).
45	*Gothfruigh*: see note to line 113 of poem 16.
45	*Amhlaibh Fhinn*: possibly a reference to Amlaíb Conung (Óláfr hinn Hvíti) (*fl.* 853–71).
55	*Bé Bhionn*: perhaps a reference to Bé Find, fairy-mother of the Connacht warrior Froech, hero of the famous tale *Táin Bó Froích*, perhaps to the daughter of the West Connacht king Archaidh mac Mhurchaidh and mother of the famous Irish king Brian Bóroimhe (†1014). The reference is far from clear.

59   *Derbh-áil*: unidentified. Domhnall's mother was Fonia, grand-
daughter of Fearghus of Galloway (†1161).

63   *Leamhain*: translated here as 'the Lennox', though this may
also refer to the River Leven (or indeed possibly to the River
Laune in Co. Kerry). This apparent reference to the Lennox is
most interesting in light of Muireadhach Albanach Ó Dálaigh's
contacts with that area in Domhnall mac Raghnaill's time.

16. Ceannaigh Duain t'Athar, a Aonghas

Source: Bergin 1970, 169–74.

Dr Katharine Simms propounded the theory that this poem might be
attributed to Giolla Brighde Mac Con Midhe in a paper entitled 'What
the Dean of Lismore Left Out' presented at the University of
Edinburgh on 15 May 2001. For Giolla Brighde's poetry, see Williams
1980.

31   *Coire Bhreacáin* (Englished as 'Corryvreckan') and *Coire Dhá
Ruadh* are two famous whirlpools between Ireland and
Scotland. Coire Bhreacáin originally referred to the treach-
erous waters between Antrim and Rathlin Island, and this is
apparently the meaning here; later it came to refer to the
narrows between Jura and Scarba.

34   *Ceóil*: this place-name has not been identified.

40   *aonros*: the text and translation reflect Professor William Gillies'
proposed emendation from Osborn Bergin's *aonfhras* 'a single
shower'. (The two forms are pronounced very similarly as the
fh is silent).

75   *Céis Cairrgi*: this place-name has not been identified.

113   *Gofraidh*: this reference is usually understood as a reference to
Gofraidh mac Fearghusa (†851), a ninth-century warrior who
came to Scotland from Ireland to support king Cináed mac
Ailpín, and from whom Clann Domhnaill claimed descent.
However, it has recently been suggested that professional
genealogists of the late medieval period may have manipulated
Clann Domhnaill's pedigree to make it more acceptably Gaelic
than overtly Norse, and that early references to Gofraidh here
and elsewhere may in fact relate to Gofraidh Crobhán (†1095),
a famous Norse king of Dublin and Man (Woolf 2005).

123   *an Bhrogha*: Brú na Bóinne, effectively equivalent to Dún
Bóinne.

124   *cheann > Ceannaigh*: another bardic *dúnadh* (see note to poem 5).

17. Fuaras Aisgidh gan Iarraidh

Source: McKenna 1939, 114–18.

10   *Iarla Rois*: about 1437 Alasdair acquired the title of Earl of
        Ross (a territory which extended beyond the later county of
        that name). His son Eòin was divested of the title in 1476,
        however, in the wake of his intriguing with Edward IV of
        England against the Scottish crown.

56   *Coire Dhá Ruadh*: see note to poem 16.

61   *Colla Uais*: the story of the Collas is narrated in Geoffrey
        Keating's famous 17th-century history of Ireland, *Foras Feasa
        ar Éirinn* (Céitinn 1902, 1908, 1914, II, 358–65, 383–5), and
        summarised in Ó hÓgáin 1990, 92.

94   *Tuathal mac Eithne*: for his story, see Céitinn 1902, 1908, 1914,
        II, 240–47, and Ó hÓgáin 1990, 409–10.

98   *Lughaidh Mac Con*: for his story, see Céitinn 1902, 1908, 1914,
        II, 280–82, and Ó hÓgáin 1990, 277–9.

111   *Eoin*: Eòin mac Aonghais Òig († *c.*1387), sometimes
        designated as first Lord of the Isles, as he was the first to use
        the title *Dominus Insularum* in legal documents.

18. *Fíor mo Mholadh ar Mhac Domhnaill*

Source: Laoide 1914, 52. An unedited transcript is given in Cameron
1894, II, 264–5.

On the *rannaigheacht bheag bheag* metre, see Murphy 1961, 58.

19. *Ceannas Gaoidheal do Chlann Cholla*

Source: Laoide 1914, 50–51. An unedited transcript is given in
Cameron 1894, II, 208.

On the accuracy of the Clann Domhnaill pedigree see Sellar 1966 and
Woolf 2005; on the role of the professional Gaelic genealogists more
generally see Sellar 1981 and Gillies 1987 and 1994a. On the concept
of *ceannas nan Gàidheal*, see McLeod 2002b, 43-4.

20. *Cóir Feitheamh ar Uaislibh Alban*

Source: Watson 1937, 184–93.

21. *Lámh Aoinfhir Fhóirfeas i nÉirinn*

Source: Watson 1937, 32–45.

For Giolla Críost's satire 'Dá urradh i n-iath Éireann', see Watson 1937, 46–59.

For a discussion of the Mac an Bhreatnaich family and other professional Scottish harpers, see Thomson 1968b, 69–70, and Bannerman 1991, 6–7.

35:    *uí Cholla*: according to traditional genealogy the Mac Diarmadas were descended from Colla Dhá Chríoch, younger brother of Colla Uais, progenitor of Clann Domhnaill.

22. Gabh rém Chomraigh, a Mheic Ghriogóir

Source: Watson 1937, 126–33.

The story of Colum Cille and Conall Clogach is set out in Stokes 1890, 310–20, and Ó hÓgáin 1990, 104–5. The most accessible collection of Ulster Cycle stories is Gantz 1981.

Fionnlagh's 'Fhuaras mo rogha theach mhòr' is published in Watson 1937, 148–57.

25:    *as an Chraobhruaidh*: the *Craobh Ruadh* or 'red-branched edifice' was Conchobhar's palace at Eamhain. The term 'Red Branch' is often used as an association for all the Ulster Cycle tales and heroes.

23. Fada Cóir Fhódla ar Albain

Source: Knott 1922, I, 173–9.

A diplomatic edition of the poem to Máire, 'Mealladh iomlaoide ar Éirinn', is given in Ó Macháin 1994, 103–11; stanzas 33–5 and 42–7 are edited and translated in McLeod 2004, 189–90.

63   *Danar*: a generic name for foreigners, alternative to *Gall*, originating in viking times.

24. Maith an Chairt Ceannas na nGaoidheal

Source: Watson 1914–19, 217–22.

5   *Mhoighe Monaidh*: a poetic name for Scotland.
32   *Achadh Airt*: a poetic name for Ireland, referring to Art mac Cuinn.
63   *chrích ghairbh na nGaoidheal*: in later vernacular Gaelic usage

Garbhchrìochan (or 'Rough Bounds') is the principal term used for the Highlands, with *Gàidhealtachd* becoming the dominant term only after the eighteenth century (see McLeod 1999, 2000).

124 Badhbh here refers to a king of the Tuatha Dé Danann, a character in the Fenian saga *Cath Fionntrágha*.

129–56 The description in these verses is strikingly similar to the 'prose poem' in Niall MacMhuirich's history of Clann Raghnaill describing the investiture of Eòin, Lord of the Isles, *c.* 1450 (see Cameron 1894, II, 258–62; a modern edition by Professor William Gillies is forthcoming).

146 *mac an Luin*: the famous sword of the hero Fionn mac Cumhaill.

147 *Fhearghuis*: a reference to the legendary warrior Fearghus mac Roich.

25. *An Sìth do Rogha, a Rìgh Fionnghall?*

Source: Watson 1923.

On the significance of the title *rí Fionnghall* and the term *Fionnghall* more generally, see McLeod 2002a and 2002b.

37 *Loch Eireais*: this place-name remains unidentified. It may refer to Erris in northwestern Co. Mayo, or possibly to Urris in Inishowen.

69 *oiléan Leamhna*: this island remains unidentified, although logically it would seem to be near the northern end of the Ards Peninsula in Co. Down.

74 *Uaimh an Deirg*: probably Red Bay Castle, near Cushendall, Co. Antrim, a MacDhomhnaill stronghold destroyed by Seaán Ó Néill in 1565 and rebuilt by Somhairle Buidhe MacDhomhnaill (subject of poem 23) in 1568.

91 *inghean Eachainn*: Aonghas's wife was Màiri, daughter of Eachann Òg MacGill'Eathain of Duart (†1575).

26. *Clann Ghille Eóin na mBratach Badhbha*

Source: J. L. Campbell 1961. The text here was preserved into a 'phonetic' script in *MacFarlane's Genealogical Collections*, compiled in the mid-eighteenth century (MacFarlane 1900, I, 142) and transcribed by Professor John Fraser of Oxford University in 1936. The edition here has endeavoured to normalise the orthography further.

27. *M'Anam Do Sgar Riomsa A-Raoir*

Sources: Bergin 1970, 101–3; Quiggin 1937, 42–3.

Quiggin's complete transcript contains 25 stanzas; Bergin's edition consists of stanzas 1–3, 5–6, 8, 10–15, 19–20, and 24–5.

28. *A Phaidrín Do Dhúisg mo Dhéar*

Source: Watson 1937, 60–65.

Some eleven poems are attributed to Gormlaith, a famous tenth-century Irish queen, but these are almost certainly later the work of later (male) poets, 'put in her mouth' (comparable to the numerous poems 'composed' by Colum Cille centuries after his death) (see Bergin 1970, 202–15). For a discussion of the early emergence of women's poetry in Gaelic Scotland, see Clancy 1996, Ó Baoill 2004 and Simms 1991.

21   *Dún an Óir*: this name is given to two sites in the southwest of
       Ireland, but it is not clear to which the poet refers; the idea is a
       general one – a distant, prestigious place.
22   *Bóinn*: poetic shorthand for Tara and the area around it,
       traditional centre of political power in Ireland.

29. *Ní h-Éibhneas gan Chlainn Domhnaill*

Source: Watson 1937, 90–95.

On the identification of Giolla Coluim and other MacMhuirich poets of this period see Thomson 1960–63, 291, 296–7.

30. *Marbhna Fhearchoir Í Mhaoil Chíaráin*

Source: Breatnach 1943, 167–80.

Another lament for Fearchar, composed by or more accurately 'put in the mouth of' Ó Maoil Chíaráin, is preserved in the eighteenth-century 'Turner Manuscript' (NLS Adv. MS 73.2.2); the text of this poem, in a syllabic metre but in the Scottish vernacular rather than Classical Gaelic of the present text, is printed in Cameron 1894, II, 332–33. For a discussion of the relationship between the two texts, see Clancy 2006a, and Ó Macháin 2006, 99–102.

31. *Alba gan Díon a nDiaidh Ailín*

Source: National Museum of Antiquities of Scotland MCR 39 ('Red Book of Clanranald'). An unedited transcript of the poem is published in Cameron 1894, II, 216–25, and Professor W. J. Watson prepared an unpublished working edition, now in CW 137.

On the identification of Giolla Coluim and other MacMhuirich poets of this period see Thomson 1960–63, 291, 296–7. On the supposed execution of Ailean and Raghnall Bàn, see MacDonald 1978, 286–7; for Niall MacMhuirich's version, see Cameron 1894, II, 168–71.

6	*Mairghréid*: wife of Ruairidh, father of the lamented Ailean and grandfather of Raghnall Bàn, and daughter of Domhnall Balloch MacDhomhnaill of Dunyveg and the Glens (†1476).
11	*Eachaidh*: see *Eochaidh* in Glossary of Personal Names.
22	*oidheadh*: this term typically means 'violent death', but the Book of Clanranald gives no suggestion that Raghnall was killed, simply noting that he died at Perth after having gone before the king to settle family affairs. The alternative meaning 'fate' or 'tragic tale' is probably to be understood here.
40	*Moirne*: the reference here is unclear. It may be a genitive form of Morvern (modern Gaelic *a' Mhor(bh)airne*), which formed part of the Clann Raghnaill territories. Alternatively, it might possibly relate to Maine, an ancestor of Somhairle (Somerled) whom different genealogists placed at different points in the family tree.
42	*Ua Ruaidhrí*: Ruairidh mac Ailein (†1481) was Ailean's father and thus Raghnall's grandfather.
53–68	*Úir gan iodh a h-aithle a éaga . . .* : a particular powerful example of the 'pathetic fallacy', most notable in its explicit statement (line 68) that the bounty experienced under Ailean's rule was no mere natural occurrence.
99	*Fiachaidh*: probably a reference to Fiachaidh Fionnoladh, an ancient Irish progenitor of Clann Raghnaill (see Glossary of Personal Names).
112	*Gaoidheal Gréag*: see introduction to poem 36.
117	*Cú*: Cú Chulainn's name means literally 'Hound of Culann'. Originally named Sétanta, he took the name Cú Chulainn after he killed, in self-defence, the much-feared dog of the smith Culann and then promised to guard Culann's cattle for him in place of the dog. See Gantz 1981, 138–40.

32. *Do Loiscceadh Meisi sa Mhuaidh*

Source: Ó Lochlainn 1945–7.

Brian Ó Gnímh's elegy on Alasdair (mac Shomhairle Bhuidhe) MacDhomhnaill, 'Mionn súl Éireann i nÁth Cliath', is printed in Cameron 1894, II, 302–3, and in Laoide 1914, 46–9. Another slightly earlier poem by 'Ó Gnímh' (edited in Walsh 1960, 72–8) praises Domhnall Gorm, Alasdair Carrach and Alasdair mac Shomhairle Bhuidhe, among other Clann Domhnaill nobles. The history of the Ó Gnímh family is discussed in McDonnell 1993 and in Ó Cuív 1984 and 1996.

44   *Latharn*: Larne in Co. Antrim lies within the territory of the MacDhomhnaills of Antrim and the reference here may indicate that the poem was composed in that area.

66   *Maol Umha*: The reference here is unclear, but Gerard Murphy suggested that it might relate to a character in the now-lost medieval tale *Echtra Mealuma maic Baitain* (see Ó Lochlainn 1945–7, 155 n.).

71   *Duach*: several mythological early Irish kings bear this name, and the connection to Clann Domhnaill is not clear.

33. *Dál Chabhlaigh ar Chaistéal Suibhne*

Sources: Meek 1998a supersedes the earlier edition in Watson 1937, 6–13. We are very grateful to Professor Meek for additional new readings which have been incorporated into the text and translation.

For discussion see Meek 1998a and McLeod 2004, 32–3, 45.

25   *Fionnmhacha*: an unclear reference. The editor, Donald Meek, takes it as a place-name but it could be a compound adjective meaning 'fair and noble'. In its present form, the line contains too many syllables.

56   *codach Cuinn* (genitive form of *cuid Cuinn*): a poetic name for the northern half of Ireland, 'the portion of Conn Céadchathach', more commonly *Leath Cuinn* (Conn's Half), as against *Leath Mogha* (Mogh's Half), the southern half of Ireland.

62   *caol eagach*: the notched kyle at the mouth of Loch Sween.

74   *Sliabh Mis*: a mountain east of Ballymena in Co. Antrim, famously associated with St Patrick. Connecting Gaelic chiefs to this prestigious mountain is a common trope in bardic poetry.

90   *Cruacha*: Croghan in Co. Roscommon, traditional seat of the kings of Connacht, and a common symbol of political power.

92   *Magh Luirg*: Moylurg in Co. Roscommon, traditional territory of the Mac Diarmadas (see poem 21). The precise reason for the reference here is unclear, although branches of the Mac Suibhne family did become active in this area.

108   *Kindred of Carm*: this is the translation suggested by Donald
       Meek, although he could not identify such a group. As an
       alternative he suggests 'Cluain Cairn', though this would not
       work so well with the rhyme scheme.

34. *Brostughadh-Catha Chlann Domhnaill, Là Chatha Gharbhaich*

Source: Thomson 1968a, 151–2.

For an alternative modern translation by Robert Crawford, see Sadler
2005, 11–12.
    For literary analysis of this poem, see Thomson 1968a and Slotkin
1981. The term *aos dàna* was originally a collective term meaning
'literati' but was applied as a title to certain individual poets of the
seventeenth and eighteenth centuries (see McLeod 2004, 67). For an
account of the battle, see Sadler 2005.
    For 'Altus Prosator', see Clancy & Márkus 1995, 39–68.

35. *Beannuigh do Theaghlach, a Thríonóid*

Source: Watson 1937, 176–9.

The sixth verse (following line 20), which was not fully intelligible to
Professor Watson, is omitted.

26   *Inis Alt Airt*: this placename cannot be identified.

36. *Ar Sliocht Gaodhal ó Ghort Gréag*

Source: Watson 1937, 158–65.

For analyses questioning the conventional interpretation of this poem
see Ó Briain 2002; MacInnes 1978, 443; Boardman 2005b, 281–2. The
most recent re-analysis is MacGregor 2006b. On the Gaelic origin-
legend and the Greek connection see Broun 1999.

18   *bile Bóromha*: a reference to Brian Bóroimhe (see Glossary of
      Personal and Family Names).
42   *achrainn*: W. J. Watson read this word (given as *achryn* in the
      manuscript) as *athroinn* 'another division', an interpretation
      which can be linked to the view of the poem as reflecting a
      united Scottish campaign against England in the Flodden

campaign. The alternative *achrainn*, a variant form of *achrann* 'conflicts, strivings' (suggested by the late Angus Matheson), seems more open-ended.

50   The image of burning and sending the ashes downstream is a common trope: see Ó Briain 2002.

63   *Cailéin th'athair féin*: Cailean, first earl of Argyll (†1492). The poet then invokes the second earl's forefathers back to Cailean mac Nèill (Cailean Òg) (†1316x23).

74   An alternative reading to *gort iomgháidh* ('field of peril') here is *Gort Iomgháin* ('Plain of Iomghán'), a poetic by-name for Ireland.

78   The phrasing here is strikingly similar to a famous poem to Seumas (mac Aonghais) MacDhomhnaill of Knockrinsay (†1626), composed *c*.1600, urging him to become involved in the campaigns against the English in Ulster (see Bergin 1970: 161–6, 287–90).

37. *A Chinn Diarmaid Uí Chairbre*

Source: Watson 1937, 96–9.

For the accounts of Aonghas's murder given by the 17th-century clan historians Ùisdean MacDhomhnaill and Niall MacMhuirich, see MacPhail 1914, I, 52, and Cameron 1894, II, 162–3.

The Dean of Knoydart's connection to the Mac Mhuirich bardic family is discussed in Thomson 1960–63, 287–8.

A formal elegy for Aonghas, 'Thánaig adhbhar mo thuirse', is preserved in the Book of the Dean of Lismore (Watson 1937, 82–9). The author is Giolla Coluim Mac an Ollaimh, apparently a relative of the Dean of Knoydart, and author of poem 29.

38. *Theast Aon Diabhal na nGaoidheal*

Source: Watson 1937, 134–9.

The nineteenth-century historian Donald Gregory claimed (apparently through a misunderstanding of Niall MacMhuirich's history in the Red Book of Clanranald) that Ailean was executed by King James IV (Gregory 1836: 110), but there is no contemporaneous evidence of such an event, and this poem makes no reference to it, a curious omission indeed considering the all-inclusive vituperation of this satire. The poem does refer to Ailean as being 'long-hangable', but this would appear to be general opprobrium rather than a reference to his actual demise.

18   *Ruaidhrí*: Ruaidhrí mac Ailín (†1481), third chief of Clann Raghnaill.
20   *Conán*: probably Conán Maol mac Morna, brother of Goll, a trickster figure among the Fèinn.
30   *Colum*: Colum Cille.
50   *Fíonán*: St Fíonán (Fionan in the Scottish vernacular) is strongly associated with Moidart, heart of the Clann Raghnaill territories, most notably Eilean Fhìonain (Island Finnan).
55   *Dubhthach*: patron saint of Tain (still known as Baile Dhubhthaich in Gaelic), apparently the 'Dubhthach Albanach' who died at Armagh in 1065.
60   *Subhairne*: Loch Hourn in Knoydart.

39. *Alasdair, 'ndo Thréig Tú an Ghruaim?*

Source: Watson 1937, 246.

40. *Créad dá nDearnadh Domhnall Donn?*

Source: Gillies 1983, 79.

41. *Bod Bríoghmhor Atá ag Donncha*

Source: Gillies 1983, 66–7.

For 'Mairg ó ndeachaidh a léim lúidh', see Gillies 1981a, 280–82.
On Donnchadh Riabhach MacGille Chonaill, see MacGregor, 2006c, 44–45. On Welsh poems addressed to the genitals, see Arbuthnot 2002.
The poem 'Éistidh, a lucht an tighe-sa' has not been definitively edited or translated, but see Quiggin 1937, 78; Mac an Bhaird 1975; and MacLean and Dorgan 2002, 54.

42. *Do Chuaidh Mise, Robart Féin*

Source: Gillies 1977, 42.

43. *Mairg Duine Do Chaill a Ghuth*

Source: Watson 1937, 248–9.

The Gaelic culture and heritage of the Lennox is comprehensively discussed in Newton 1999a, and, in relation to the earlier period, Neville 2005.

44. *Tánaig Long ar Loch Raithneach*

Source: Watson 1937, 224–33.

An Bard Mac an t-Saoir's 'Créad í an long-sa ar Loch Inse?' is published in Watson 1937, 218–23. On the poet's kidnap, see MacFarlane 1900, I, 212 and MacGregor, 2006, 55–56.

11	*ardrach bhan as measa madh*: this tentative reconstruction of this line is suggested by Professor Colm Ó Baoill.
59–60	*go muir téacht* . . . : the reading here, which differs from Watson's, has been kindly supplied by Professor Colm Ó Baoill.
66	*Mac Cailéin*: perhaps merely 'son of Colin' rather than Mac Cailein (Mòr), chief of the Caimbeuls, but possibly a reference to Donnchadh Caimbeul of Lochaw, lord of Argyll (†1453).

45. *Cá h-Ainm A-tá ar Fearghal Óg?*

Sources: Ó Macháin 1988, 766–9; NLS Adv. MS 72.1.34, 39.

46. *Èatroman Muice o hó*

Source: Thomson 1974–6, 21–2.

On lighter and occasional 'off-duty' verse composed by *filidh*, see Gillies 1979.

47. *I mBrat an Bhrollaigh Ghil-Se*

Source: O'Rahilly 1926, 18.

48. *Atá Fleasgach ar mo Thí*

Source: Watson 1937, 307–8.

For the *amour courtois* tradition in the Gaelic world, especially Ireland, see Ó Tuama 1988 and 1990 and Mac Craith 1989. On early women poets, see Clancy 1996 and Simms 1991.

For 'Éistidh, a lucht an tighe se', see note to poem 41. The poem is attributed in the manuscript to'Contaois Oirir Ghaoidheal, Isibeul' (Iseabal, Countess of Argyll) and there is some disagreement among scholars as to whether this Iseabal is the same person as Iseabal Ní Mheic Cailéin.

49. *Is Mairg dá nGalar an Grádh*

Source: Watson 1937, 234–5.

50. *'S Luaineach mo Chadal A-Nochd*

Source: Thomson 1992, 120.

For contrasting views of the poem's provenance, see O'Sullivan 1976, 98–9, and Thomson 1992, 121.

5   *Earrach*: this place-name has not been identified.
23   *Iuchair na Cist'*: apparently a reference to a low hill (literally 'The Key of/to the Chest', as yet unidentified.

51. *Tha Bean an Crìch Albainn Fhuar*

Source: Matheson 1967–8, 151.

For an evaluation of the stylistics of the poem and its authorship, see O'Sullivan 1976, 100–01.

52. *Trèig t'Uaisle 's Na Bi Rinn*

Source: MacDonald & MacDonald 1911, 339.

For an assessment of the questionable attribution to Carsuel, see O'Sullivan 1976, 110–11.

7   *Cairbre Cas*: apparently Cairbre Riata, from whom Dál Riata are descended.

53. *Soraidh Slán don Oidhche A-Réir*

Source: Thomson 1974–6, 16.

Professor Thomas Clancy is currently preparing an edition based on the version of this poem preserved in the Red Book of Clanranald, which differs from other manuscript versions in a number of important respects (see Clancy 2006b).

Another famous poem by Niall Mòr, celebrating the wedding in 1613 of Iain Mùideartach MacDhomhnaill, son of Niall's patron Domhnall mac Ailein, chief of Clann Raghnaill, and Mòr, daughter of Ruairidh Mòr MacLeòid of Dunvegan, is published in Ó Baoill & Bateman 1994, 64–6, and Thomson 1974–6, 12.

For more on Niall Mòr and his work, see Thomson 1974–6 and 1977 and Clancy 2006b.

54. *Arann na n-Aiged n-Imda*

Source: Dillon 1970, 5.

For a modern translation of *Accalam na Senórach*, see Dooley & Roe 1999. For modern analyses of MacPherson's work, see Thomson 1952 and Gaskill 1991.

55. *Gleann Measach Iasgach Linneach*

Source: O'Rahilly 1927, 122–3.

A modern translation of the Deirdre story as preserved in medieval manuscript is given in Gantz 1981. For a famous version based on Scottish oral tradition of the nineteenth century, see Carmichael 1914.

56. *Ionmhain Tír an Tír-Úd Thoir*

Source: Mac Giolla Léith 1993, 98–100.

Some place names here cannot now be identified, but are very probably located in Argyll.

8   *Dún Suibhne*: the Fortress of Suibhne, presumably to be connected to the later Castle Sween, on the shore of Loch Sween, Argyll (see poem 33).

57. *Am Bròn Binn*

Source: Carmichael 1900–71, V, 92–8, based on a version collected in North Uist in 1866.

The history and development of this ballad are comprehensively explored in Gowans 1992. On the Arthurian tradition in Gaelic more generally, see Gillies 1981b and 1981c. For a comprehensive bibliography of Gaelic Arthurian literature, compiled by Linda Gowans, see www.lib.rochester.edu/camelot/acpbibs/gowans.htm#lebor

58. *Ardaigneach Goll*

Source: Ross 1939, 60–68.

The second Ossianic poem attributed to 'Fearghus File' is published in Ross 1939, 148–50.

59. *Gleann Síodh an Gleann So rém Thaoibh*

Source: Meek 1990, 352–7.

The poem is discussed authoritatively in Meek 1990.

40   *ga bolg*: Cú Chulainn's famous spear, said to disembowel his opponents.

60. *Mór an Feidhm Freagairt na bhFaigheach*

Source: Watson 1937, 66–81.

The practice of thigging is discussed in detail in Watson 1937, 272–5.
     On the identification of Giolla Coluim and other MacMhuirich poets of this period see Thomson 1960–63, 291, 296–7.

101   *mac Eóin*: probably Aonghas, murdered in Inverness in 1490, as decried in poem 37.
103   The reference in this line could be read as *rí Bearnais* ('king of Bearnas'), referring to the Barnesmore Gap in Co. Donegal, a common epithet in Ulster poetry.
110   *Fearghus*: apparently a reference to Fearghus mac Eirc, putative ancestor of Clann Domhnaill.

61. *Duanaire na Sracaire*

Source: Watson 1937, 2–5, 257.

On the nature of the reference to MacCailein, see MacGregor 2006c, 46.

62. *Fada Dhomh an Laighe-se*

Source: Watson 1937, 194–5.

5–6	*Táin Bó Cuailgne* ('The Cattle-Raid of Cooley'), in which Cú Chulainn defends Ulster against the forces of Connacht led by queen Medb and her husband Ailill, is the most famous tale in early Gaelic literature (see Kinsella 1985; O'Rahilly 1967, 1976). *Táin Bó Darta* and *Táin Bó Fliodhais* are other examples of *tána* or 'cattle-raid tales', a once-prestigious genre, though long archaic even at the time of this poem's composition (see Stokes & Windisch 1887, 185–223; Leahy 1906: II, 69–82, 101–26; MacKinnon 1907–8).
10	*mhic Cumhaill*: see Fionn.
12	*ga bolga*: see note to poem 59.
15	*cruit Chuircheóil*: *Chuircheóil* may the genitive form of a personal name here, or alternatively a technical musical term (see Ó Baoill 1972, 179).
16	Professor Angus Matheson tentatively suggested reading this line as *'s sgiathrach Goill meic Morna* 'and the shield-strap of Goll mac Morna', referring to the legendary warrior celebrated in poem 58.
17	*Long Laoimein*: possibly related to the Fenian lay 'Laoidh Laomuinn mhic an Uaimhfhir' (see Campbell 1872, 106).
21	*Alasdair Mac an Tóisigh*: apparently a doctor of some kind; but nothing is known of him, and this surname is not one associated with medical professionals.

63. *Fuath Liom*

Source: Watson 1937, 244–5.

64. *Is Fearr Sgíos Cos Bharr Gnímh Ghlain*

Source: Watson 1937, 250–1.

65. *MhicPhàrlain an Arair*

Sources: Campbell 1872, p. xvii-xviii; Newton 1999b, 166–71.

The text as it has been preserved seems defective in some respects; in particular, lines 57 and 62–3 do not fit the rhyme scheme. It may be that some lines have been lost.

66. *An Duanag Ullamh*

For the tune, see *An Gaidheal* (1872), 264.

For a discussion of Earl Cailean's involvement in the campaign on the Borders in 1528, see Cameron 1998.

Version A

Source: MacDhiarmid MS, 36 (at the Department of Celtic, Glasgow University); variant readings from Macdhomhnuill 1776, 253, and MacLagan MS 187, 2a (at Glasgow University Library).

57–8   On connections between Argyll and the Mac an Tòisichs and Friseals *c*. 1527, see Campbell 2002, 11–12.

70   *àrd-cheannard*: this and subsequent references to Cailean's offices appear to relate to his appointment in 1528 as Justiciar General of Scotland, Master of the Royal Household and Lieutenant of the Lothians, the Merse and Teviotdale (see Campbell 2002, 12–13).

80–81 *Uilleam, Ualas*: the reference to William Wallace here is extremely unusual in traditional Gaelic poetry. Its presence here might even be seen as calling the authenticity of the text here into some question.

Version B

Source: Watson 1959, 259–62 (based on Mac-an-Tuairneir 1813).

54   *don Fhèinn Mhuilich*: there is variation in the sources between *Fèinn* 'Fenian war-band' and *fine* 'kindred', 'clann' here.

64   *An Fhraing bhraonach*: this reference to France is not entirely clear. It may be understood in terms of the Caimbeuls' claim to Norman blood, together with a Gaelic and ancient British pedigree (see Gillies 1976–78 and 1999).

69   *cìos Thìre Conaill*: apparently a reference to the agreement between Ó Domhnaill and Mac Cailein in 1555 described in the English introduction to this poem (see MacKechnie 1953; MacPhail 1934, IV, 212–16).

71   *Conn*: perhaps a reference to the Ulster chieftain Conn Bacach Ó Néill (†1559), possibly to Conn Céadchathach.

67. *Caismeachd Ailein nan Sop*

Source: Ó Baoill 1998, 106–7.

For a comprehensive discussion of the poem, including its textual difficulties, see Ó Baoill 1998. A traditional account of Ailean nan Sop and the making of this poem, written by the Rev. Tormod MacLeòid (Caraid nan Gàidheal) and reprinted from his journal *Cuairtear nan Gleann*, is given in Watson 1929, 115–19.

Eachann's religious poem 'Creid dìreach do Dhia na ndúl' is published in Ó Baoill 1997, 3, and in Thomson 1962, p. xlvii.

For 'Iorram do Bhàta Mhic Dhòmhnaill', see MacKenzie 1965, 102–7; for 'An Làir Donn', see Watson 1959, 217–19; and for 'Birlinn Chloinn Raghnaill', see MacLeod 1933, 37–59, and Black 2001, 202–17.

68. *Òran na Comhachaig*

Source: Turner MS (NLS Adv. MS 73.2.2), pp. 88–96 (transcript printed in Cameron 1894, II, 351–5). With 46 stanzas, the Turner MS version is the shortest of the five sources of this text; the version in the Eigg Collection is the longest, with 67 (Macdhomhnuill 1776, 7–16). The relationship between the different versions is systematically analysed in Menzies 2001.

The poem is discussed in MacKechnie 1946, Rankin 1957, and, most recently and comprehensively, Menzies 2001 and 2006. Details concerning the place-names referred to in the text are given in Rankin 1998 and Menzies 2001.

For 'Moladh Beinn Dòbhrain', see Black 2001, 266–79 and MacLeod 1952, 196–206. For the *Lebor Gabála*, see MacAlister 1937, 1939, 1956.

3   *Donnghal*: it is not known who is referred to here.

29   *Aonghas*: second chief of the MacDhomhnaills of Keppoch (†c. 1478); son of Alasdair Carrach.

102–3   *Cheanna Craige, Locha Slèibhe Snaige*: these place-names cannot be identified.

113   *Raghnall mac Dhomhnaill*: seventh chief of the MacDhomhnaills of Keppoch; beheaded by the Earl of Huntly at Elgin in 1547. Subsequent Keppoch chiefs took the by-name Mac Mhic Raghnaill (compare with Mac Mhic Ailein and Mac Mhic Alasdair for the chiefs of Clann Raghnaill and Gleann Garadh).

119   *Àird Chatain*: the reference here is unclear and may reflect a corruption in transmission. It seems distinctly unlikely that Raghnall would have been buried at Ardchattan Priory in Argyll (see Menzies 2001: 110).

69. *Bealach a' Ghàrraidh*/*Cumha Mhic an Tòisich*

Source: Gillies 1786, 204.

For the tune, see Campbell 1816, I, 43.

Two different versions appear in *Carmina Gadelica*, V, 346–53 and 354–9, one referring to the chief as Eòghann and the other as Lachlann. No Mac an Tòisich chief bore the name Eòghann; the chief between 1515 and 1524 was Lachlann Beag mac Lachlainn, but he lived on at least four years beyond his wedding day (see Mackintosh 1948, 64–5). Although the putative connection between this song and the Mac an Tòisichs is problematic in historical terms, we know of a now-lost elegy on the Mac an Tòisich chiefs composed during the period in question by An Bàrd Mac an t-Saoir (see introduction to poem 44).

On wake practices in the Gàidhealtachd, see Newton 2006.

70. *Mhic Iarla nam Bratach Bàna*

Source: Campbell & Collinson 1969–81, III, 86–8.

For tunes, see Campbell & Collinson 1969–81, III, 361–3; A. L. Gillies 2005, 6.

19   *cupla dhan t-sìoda na Gailmhinn*: Anne Lorne Gillies points out (205, 6 n. 1) that this phrase is problematic grammatically, although the sense seems clear; she emends to *cupla de shìoda na Gailmhinn*.

20   *Gailmhinn*: Galway is frequently mentioned in older songs; it served as the main entrepôt by which exotic luxuries from the south – often, as here, silk – made their way to the *Gàidhealtachd*. As this song makes clear, the silk was actually produced in Spain, not in Ireland!

71. *Cumha Ghriogair MhicGhriogair Ghlinn Sreith*

Source: Watson 1959, 244–6.

The background to this poem is comprehensively discussed in MacGregor 2000; MacGregor also provides an edition of another poem by Mòr, 'Rìgh! Gur mòr mo chuid mhulaid' (pp. 140–41). Also invaluable is the discussion in Dawson 1997. Somhairle MacGill-Eain's comments appear in MacGill-Eain 1985, 77. For 'Caoineadh Airt Uí Laoghaire', see Ó Tuama & Kinsella, 1980, 200–19, and Ó Tuama, 1961; on the blood-drinking motif, see Thomson 1994.

We cannot be entirely sure of the author's correct first name in

Gaelic, as the various sources conflict with each other; it may have been
Màiri or Mairghréad rather than Mòr.

Other, accentual versions of this song are commoner in modern oral
tradition; see, e.g. A. L. Gillies 2005, 140–41.

23   *nighean an Ruadhanaich*: apparently Katherine Ruthven, wife
        of Cailean Liath and mother of Donnchadh Dubh.
26   *Donnchadh Dubh*: eldest son of Cailean Liath, who succeeded
        his father in 1583.
47   *baran crìon na Dalach*: Martin MacGregor has argued
        persuasively that this is Raibeart Mèinne of Comrie, who
        became Mòr's second husband.

72. *Nach Fhreagair Thu, Chairistìona?*

Source: Campbell & Collinson 1969–81, I, 54.

For tunes, see Campbell & Collinson 1969–81, I, 251–4; A. L. Gillies
2005, 27.

7   *Gleann Comhann*: perhaps a reference to Eilean Munda in
        Loch Leven, burial island of the MacDhomhnaills of Glencoe
        (see A. L. Gillies 2005, 30).

73. *Chaidh Mis' a dh'Eubhal Imprig*

Source: Campbell & Collinson 1969–81, II, 94–7.

For tunes, see Campbell & Collinson 1969–81, II, 313–14.

For the *Carmina Gadelica* version, see Carmichael 1900–71, V,
10–12.

For accounts of Uisdean mac Ghill'Easbaig Clèirich's misdeeds and
demise, see Lawson 2004, 80, 142–43, and the account of the Rev.
Robert MacGregor concerning the parish of Kilmuir in the *New
Statistical Account* (vol. 14, pp. 258–60).

6   *Eubhal mhòr 's Bheinn na h-Aire*: Eubhal (Eaval) and Beinn an
        Fhaireachaidh (or Beinn na h-Aire) are hills in the south-east
        of North Uist.
7   *Caolas Rònaigh*: the Strait of Ronay, between North Uist and
        the Isle of Ronay, east of Grimsay.
8   *Eilein nam Mucan mara*: a reference to the Isle of Muck?

74. *Am Fonn Ìleach*

Sources: Newton 1999b; Matheson 1957.

Accounts of the battle as remembered in oral tradition, including the story of Dubh-Sìdh, are given in Campbell 1950 and Clark 1992. For a more conventional historical presentation see Maclean-Bristol 1999, 238–53.

Another song on the death of Lachlann Mòr, 'Aig ceann Tràigh Ghruinneart', has also survived; see MacLean 1986, 90.

Among those fighting on the MacDhomhnaill side was MacAoidh of the Rinns, perhaps the subject of poem 80.

Sir Seumas is addressed in two surviving bardic poems, one composed *c*.1600, before his apprehension and imprisonment by the government for treason, and another following his escape from Edinburgh Castle in 1615. He was never permitted to return to Scotland, and died in London in 1626. For the two poems to Sir Seumas (mac Aonghais) MacDhomhnaill, see Bergin 1970, 162–6, and Breathnach 1931, 43–6.

2	*an t-airgead*: a difficult line metrically. Michael Newton (1999b) suggests *saidhbhreas* 'wealth', a fairly significant emendation from the manuscript.
8	*d' ghràbhail*: another significant emendation suggested by Newton, from the manuscript's *gathainn* 'small dart' (?).
10	*Gàirbhil*: apparently a place-name, not identified. Lachlann Mòr's mother was Seònaid, daughter of Gill'Easbaig, fourth earl of Argyll (see poem 74).
11	*Cille Chomain*: site of Lachlann Mòr's burial, near the battlefield.
13	*Catrìona*: not identifiable, although evidently the wife of one of the MacGill'Eathains' allies.
15	*Ruairidh na fèile*: either Ruairidh Mòr MacLeòid of Harris or Ruairidh MacNèill of Barra, both of whom fought in support of Lachlann Mòr.
20	*fhàgail*: another significant emendation, from the manuscript's *fheuchain* 'trying'.

75. *Seathan Mac Rìgh Èireann*

Source: Campbell & Collinson 1969–81, II, 40–5.

For tunes, see Campbell & Collinson 1969–81, II, 280–1, and A. L. Gillies 2005, 326.

Carmichael's version, based on the version sung by Janet MacLeod in Eigg in 1905 but apparently re-edited thereafter, is given in Carmichael 1900–71, V, 67–81.

12   *Choill' Bhuidhe*: literally the 'Yellow Wood', unidentifiable and
      probably a corruption (see Campbell & Collinson 1969–81, II,
      198).

76. Clann Ghriogair air Fògradh

Source: Watson 1959, 242, with additional readings from class notes
prepared at the University of Edinburgh by Ronald Black.

For the tune, see Creighton and MacLeod 1979, 168.
    For other MacGriogair songs, see Duncan 1979, MacGregor 2000
(at 140–41), Newton 2003 and Ó Baoill & Bateman 1994, 54–8 and
68–73.

4   *Cruachan a' cheathaich*: Beinn Cruachan, the great mountain
      just to the west of Clann Griogair's traditional territory in Glen
      Strae in Argyll.
8   *na Sraithibh*: Srath Fillan, between Crianlarich and Tyndrum,
      Argyll.
11   *Clachan an Dìseirt*: Dalmally, in Glen Orchy, adjoining Glen
      Strae.
30   *lùban*: possibly a generic name, possibly a specific place in Glen
      Lyon or Loch Rannoch.
31   *Bothan na Dìge*: possibly a residence of the MacGriogair chiefs
      in Glen Strae.
33–40 Firearms were a relatively new innovation in the sixteenth-
      century Gàidhealtachd and it seems the singer lacked a ready
      vocabulary to describe them. Bows and arrows receive much
      more detailed attention in poetry of this period and indeed of
      the seventeenth century, reflecting a tendency to conservatism
      in the conventions of Gaelic poetry, not always changing to
      accommodate new developments in material culture.

77. Pìobaireachd Dhomhnaill Duibh

Source: CW 125, 80.

For tunes, see A. L. Gillies 2005, 124–5.
    This 'first' Battle of Inverlochy is not to be confused with the
'second' battle of Inverlochy in 1645, another famous victory for Clann
Domhnaill during the Montrose wars, immortalised in Iain Lom
MacDhomhnaill's poem 'Latha Inbhir Lòchaidh' (published in
Mackenzie 1965, 20–25, and Ó Baoill & Bateman 1994, 106–13).

24   *Clann Domhnaill*: some versions give Clann Dhomhnaill (with

lenition of Domhnaill) here, apparently referring not to the MacDhomhnaills but to the Camshrons ('the progeny of Domhnall [Dubh]'). In these versions the end of the previous verse does not refer to the Clann Domhnaill victory but instead gives 'O, chaidh an-diugh, chaidh an-dè, / 'S chaidh a h-uile là òirnne' (Today went, yesterday went / And every day went against us') (see A. L. Gillies 2005, 126–7 and 126 fn. 2).

33   *Loch Iall*: addressing the Camshron chief in this fashion, as with the English 'Locheil', is unusual, certainly for an ostensibly fifteenth-century work, and must call into question the authenticity of this verse and the verse following.

78. *'S Maith an Còcaire an t-Ocras*

Sources: Thomson 1992–4, 417–18 (Version A); MacPhail 1914, I, 42–3 (Version B).

For Ùisdean MacDhomhnaill's account, written between 1660 and 1685, see MacPhail 1914, I, 42–3. A slightly different account given by the nineteenth-century writer Rev. Tormod MacLeòid, 'Caraid nan Gàidheal', is published in Watson 1929, 99–102.

79. *An Iorram Dharaich*

Source: Carmichael 1900–71, V, 16–21.

As Roibeard Ó Maolalaigh observes (2006, 238 n. 18), despite its Gaelic title, this song's metrical structure is very different to that of songs to which the term *iorram* is normally applied.

The song in praise of Domhnall, 'A mhic Iain 'ic Sheumais', is published in Ó Baoill & Bateman 1994, 50–53.

33   *cèis, leitir an fhìona*: interpretation here is difficult and the translation as 'harp' and 'vine-slope' is somewhat conjectural.
46   *motach, Thomman*: *motach* is obscure; the interpretation proceeds from Carmichael's suggestion of *mòinteach* 'moss', 'moor'; *Tomman* is evidently a place-name, but is not identifiable.

80. *Craobh an Iubhair*

Source: Campbell & Collinson 1969–81, I, 144.

For tunes, see Campbell & Collinson 1969–81, I, 329–32.

Two somewhat different versions, one of them from Barra, are given in *Carmina Gadelica* (Carmichael 1900–71, V, 2–5 and 6–9).

Thomson's discussion of the poem is found in Thomson 1990, 94–5. The charter to Brian Bhicaire Mhagaodh is published in Munro & Munro 1986, 21–2 (document 16).

On the role of trees in Gaelic tradition, see MacAonghuis 1986b and Newton 1998.

For 'Tàladh Dhomhnaill Ghuirm', see notes to poem 85.

27   *Ghailmhinn*: see note to poem 70.

81. *Là Mille Gàrraidh*

Source: Tolmie 1911, 200–01.

For the tune, see Tolmie 1911, 200.

For more background to the battle, see Tolmie 1911, 200, and Cameron 1871, 28–9.

10   *Allt Èireann*: this battle at Auldearn, near Nairn, in May 1645 was a famous victory of Montrose and Alasdair (mac Cholla) MacDhòmhnaill against the Covenanters; the MacLeòids of Dùn Bheagain took no part, though some Lewis MacLeòids fought on the Covenanter side. No logical connection to *Latha Mille Gàrraidh* can be proposed; the reference here is probably the result of later contamination or confusion.

12   *Uamh Deirge*: probably a reference to the destruction of this MacDhomhnaill stronghold near Cushendall, Co. Antrim, by Seaán Ó Néill in 1565. There was no MacLeòid involvement in this battle, but is probably celebrated here as a notorious MacDhomhnaill defeat.

16   *Rubha Hùnais*: probably refers here to the headland at the north of the Waternish peninsula, though this placename is better known as the headland at the far north of the Trotternish peninsula in northeast Skye.

18   *Rubha an Dùnain*: a headland on the west coast of Skye, near the Cuillin.

30   *Raghnaill*: to preserve the metre, to be pronounced as if spelled *Rànaill*.

82. *'S Trom an Dìreadh*

Source: Campbell & Collinson 1969–81, II, 88–92.

For tunes, see Campbell & Collinson 1969–81, II, 310–11.

For John Lorne Campbell's analysis of the background of the song
and the history behind it, see Campbell & Collinson 1969–81, II,
218–20, and Campbell 2000, 127–30.

83. *A' Ghriadach Dhonn*

Source: *Gairm*, 6 (1953), 125–6.

The Ailean Donn named on several occasions may be Ailean mac Iain
Duibh (*c*.1568–*c*. 1647), sixteenth chief of Clann Chamshroin and
nephew of Eòghainn Beag mac Dhomhnaill mhic Eòghainn, subject of
poem 85, but this identification is tentative. The identity of 'Raghnall
Mòr' is unclear.

A story from Badenoch seemingly related to this song (involving a
woman from Dochanassie named Griatach) is given in Sinton 1906,
24–5.

For other examples of *spaidsearachd*, see A. L. Gillies 2005, 143–6,
and Ó Baoill & Bateman 1994, 58–63.

46	*Mhuile an Rois*: a reference to the Ross of Mull, the headland (*ros*) in the southwest of the island.
48	*Eilean Druidhneach*: a poetic name for Mull (more commonly *An Dreòllainn*).
85	*tìr Abrach*: a poetic name for Lochaber.

84. *A Bhean Ud Thall*

Source: Thomson 1992, 248–9.

For tunes, see A. L. Gillies 2005, 33, 35; Bruford 1972–3, 16–17.

For a discussion of the different Scottish and Irish versions of the
song, see Bruford 1972–3, 13–18.

85. *B' Fheàrr Leam Gun Sgrìobhte Dhuit Fearann*

Source: MacKellar 1885–6, 212–13.

On the history of Clann Chamshroin in the fifteenth and sixteenth
centuries, see MacKenzie 1884, 25–60, and Stewart 1974, 17–53. For
the poetry of Màiri nighean Alasdair Ruaidh, see J. Carmichael Watson
1934.

Two famous panegyric 'lullabies' apparently dating from the end of
the sixteenth century are 'Tàladh Dhomhnaill Ghuirm', composed for

Domhnall Gorm Mòr MacDhomhnaill of Sleat (†1617) or his son
Domhnall Gorm Òg (†1643) (see Ó Baoill & Bateman 1994, 66–8),
and 'Tàladh Choinnich Òig', probably composed for Coinneach Òg
MacCoinnich, first Lord Kintail (†1611) (see Matheson 1952, 318–20,
and, for the tune, NicChoinnich 2005, 5). On the lullaby tradition in
general, see Thomson 1986, 546–7, and Hillers 2006.

APPENDIX I

GLOSSARY OF PLACE NAMES

Achadh Airt: the Field of Art, a poetic name for Ireland; see *Art* in
  Glossary of Personal Names
Achadh Do Liubha: Achdalieu, on the north shore of Loch Eil,
  Inverness-shire
Aird Uladh: the Ards Peninsula, Co. Down
Ala Cluaithe (base form *Al Clud*): Dumbarton
Alba (genitive *Alban*, dative *Albain*): Scotland; originally the island of
  Britain
Allt Èireann: Auldearn, near Nairn; see note to poem 81
Almhu (dative *Almhain*): Allen, Co. Westmeath, traditional seat of Fionn
  mac Cumhaill and the Fianna
an Annaid: at the mouth of Loch Eil, west of Corpach, Inverness-shire
Ára (dative *Ároinn*): Aran (Inis Mór), Co. Galway
Arainn: Arran
Arar (genitive *Arair*): Arrochar, Argyll
Àrd Chatain: Ardchattan, Argyll, site of an important priory
Áth Cliath: Dublin

Baoi: a district in the southwest of Co. Cork
Banna: the River Bann in east Ulster
Barraigh: Barra
Bealach: Taymouth (Kenmore), Perthshire
Beann Éadair (dative *Binn Éadoir*): the Hill of Howth, Co. Dublin
Beinne Bige (nom. *Beinn Bheag*): probably Meall Mòr, to the northwest
  of Creag Uanach, at the southwest end of Loch Treig, Inverness-
  shire
a' Bheinn Bhreac (*Beinn a' Bhric*): hill north of the Blackwater Reservoir,
  Rannoch Moor, Inverness-shire
Beinn Ghuilbinn: in Glenshee, Perthshire; or Ben Bulben, Co. Sligo
Beinn nan Leac: Meall na Lice, a hill above the southeast end of Loch
  Ossian, Rannoch Moor, Inverness-shire
Beinn Nibheis: Ben Nevis, Inverness-shire
An Bhóinn: see *Bóinn*
Bóinn: the River Boyne in Co. Meath; see *Dún Bóinne*
Boireann (with article *An Bhoireann*; dative *Boirinn*): the Burren, Co. Clare
(bile) Bóromha: see *Brian* in Glossary of Personal Names
Breagha: the ancient kingdom that included Tara, seat of the Irish high-
  kings

Breatun: Britain
a' Bhriagach: Briagach, in upper Glen Roy, Inverness-shire
Búill: the River Boyle in Co. Roscommon
Bun Gaillmhi: mouth of the River Galway, site of Galway city; see
  Gaillimh

Caisiol: Cashel, Co. Tipperary, traditional power centre in Munster
Caoinnich: Caonich, on the north shore of Loch Arkaig, Inverness-shire
Caol Ìle: the Sound of Islay, between Islay and Jura
Caol Muile: the Sound of Mull, between Mull and the mainland
Càrn Dearg: summit to the northwest of Ben Nevis, Inverness-shire
Carraig Fearghuis: Carrickfergus, Co. Antrim
Ceann Loch Iall: Kinlocheil, Lochaber, Inverness-shire
Ceann Tíre (alternatively *Cinn Tíre*): Kintyre
Céis Corainn: Keshcorran, Co. Sligo
A' Chailleach: on the north shore of Loch Arkaig, Inverness-shire,
  between Murlagan and Caoinnich
a' Chruach(an): hill between Blackwater Reservoir and Loch Laidon,
  Rannoch Moor, Inverness-shire
Cille Chomain: Kilchoman, in northwest Islay
Cill Eòdhnain: perhaps the church at Inch in Badenoch
Clár Fhiontain: Fiontan's Plain, a poetic name for Ireland; see *Fiontan* in
  Glossary of Personal Names
Clár Rois: see *Ros*
Cnapadail: Knapdale, Argyll
Cnoc Raonastail: 'Knockrinsay', northeast of Ardbeg, south Islay
Cóige Chuinn: the 'fifth' of Conn (more commonly Leath Chuinn, the
  Half of Conn), the northern half of Ireland
Cóige Mumha(n): the 'fifth' of Munster, traditional southern province of
  Ireland
Coire Bheag: on the north shore of Loch Eil, Inverness-shire
Coire Bhreacáin: the famous Corryvreckan whirlpool; see note to poem
  16
Coire Creagach a' Mhàim: south of the north end of Loch Ossian,
  Rannoch Moor, Inverness-shire, beneath Màm Bàn
Coire Dhá Ruadh: another famous whirlpool between Ireland and
  Scotland; see note to poem 16
Coire Ratha: at the far head of Glen Nevis, Inverness-shire, beneath
  Stob Choire Claurigh
Cola: Coll
Colbhasa(idh): Colonsay
Conbhaigh: apparently Conva townland, near Fermoy, Co. Cork
Conghail (An Chonghail): Connel, Argyll
Connacht: Connaught, traditional western province of Ireland
Corca Baisginn: district along the Shannon estuary, south Co. Clare
Corcum-rúadh: the Corcomroe district, north Co. Clare
Craoibh: on the north shore of Loch Arkaig, Inverness-shire, probably
  near Beinn Chraoibh

Creag Uanach (*Creag Ghuanach*): a hill at the southwest end of Loch Treig, Inverness-shire

Críoch Éibhir: the Bounds of Éibhear, a poetic name for Ireland; see *Éibhear* in Glossary of Personal Names

Cró Fiachaidh: Fiachaidh's Fold, a poetic name for Ireland; see *Fiachaidh* in Glossary of Personal Names

Cruacha: Croghan, Co. Roscommon; see note to poem 33

Cruachan: Beinn Cruachan, Argyll

Cúil gCnáimha: Dromard, Co. Sligo

Dabhach an Fhasaidh: Dochanassie, by the south shore of Loch Lochy, Inverness-shire

An Dìseart (genitive form *Dìseirt*): Dalmally, Argyll

An Dèabhadh: literally 'The Ebbing', a now-submerged area at the north of Loch Treig, Inverness-shire

An t-Eilean Druidhneach: apparently a poetic name for Mull (more commonly *Dreòllainn*)

Druim Caoin: a poetic name for Tara (in Co. Meath), traditional seat of the high-kings of Ireland; see *Teamhair*

Druim na Saille: Drumsallie, by the west end of Loch Eil, Inverness-shire

Dún Balair: in Tory Island, off the coast of Co. Donegal

Dùn Bheagain: Dunvegan, northwest Skye, traditional seat of the Mac Leòids of Harris and Dunvegan

Dún Bóinne: the Fortress of the Boyne, a poetic name for Tara (in Co. Meath), traditional seat of the high-kings of Ireland; see *Teamhair* in Places

Dún Breagh: the Fortress of Bregia; see *Breagha* and *Dún Bóinne*

Dún Suibhne: Castle Sween, Argyll

Dùn Tuilm: Duntulm in northeast Skye, important seat of the Mac Dhomhnaills of Sleat

An Eadáille: Italy

Eamhain Macha: near Armagh; traditional seat of the kings of Ulster

Earr-Ghaoidheal (*Earra Ghàidheal*): Argyll

An t-Earrachd: Errocht, in Glen Loy, Lochaber

Easbáin: Spain

Eas Làradh: the rapids on Allt Làire, a tributary of the River Spean, Inverness-shire

Eas Ruaidh: the falls of Assaroe, Ballyshannon, Co. Donegal

Eige: Eigg

Eilean Druidhneach: see *Druidhneach*

Éire (genitive *Éireann*, dative *Éirinn*): Ireland

An Eóraip (genitive *Eórpa*): Europe

Eubhal: Eaval mountain, North Uist

Fál: the stone of Tara; used a poetic name for Ireland

An Fhearsaid: Fersit, by the north end of Loch Treig, Inverness-shire
An Fhraing: France
Fréamhann: Frewin, Co. Westmeath

Gabhair (genitive *Gabhra*): a stream flowing into the River Boyne near
    Tara, where *Cairbre Lifiochair* (see Glossary of Personal Names)
    was killed
Gaillimh (genitive form *Gaillmhinn*): Galway; see note to poem 70
Ghlinn(e): for names beginning *Ghlinn(e)*, see *Gleann*
Glaschu: Glasgow
Glasdruim: probably near present-day Fort William
Gleann Cinngidh: Glen Kingie, between Loch Arkaig and Loch Quoich,
    Inverness-shire
Gleann Comhann: Glen Coe, Argyll
Gleann Dá Ruadh: apparently Glendaruel (more commonly Gleann Dà
    Ruadhail), northwest of Dunoon, Argyll
Gleann Éitche (Gleann Èite): Glen Etive, Argyll
Gleann Garadh: Glen Garry, Inverness-shire
Gleann Laoich: Glen Loy, between Loch Arkaig and Loch Eil,
    Inverness-shire
Gleann Laoigh: possibly a reference to Glen Lui in Aberdeenshire, but
    more likely an unidentified location in Argyll
Gleann Líomhunn: Glen Lyon, Perthshire
Gleann Masáin: Glen Massan, north of Dunoon, Argyll
Gleann Mhàillidh: Glen Mallie, between Loch Arkaig and Loch Eil,
    Inverness-shire
Gleann Orchaoin: perhaps Glen Orchy (*Gleann Urchaidh*), Argyll
Gleann Pheathann: Glen Pean, west of Loch Arkaig, Inverness-shire
Gleann Sìthe: Glen Shee, Perthshire
Gleann Sraithe: Glen Strae, Argyll
Gort Bhreagh (genitive *Ghuirt Bhreagh*): the Field of Bregia, a poetic
    name for Ireland; see *Breagha*
Gort Fhiontain (genitive *Ghuirt Fhiontain*): Fiontan's Field, a poetic
    name for Ireland; see *Fiontan* in Glossary of Personal Names
Gort Gáilian: Field of the Gailenga, a poetic name for Leinster, or for
    Ireland as a whole
Gort Luirc: Field of Lorc, a poetic name for Ireland; see *Lorc* in Glossary
    of Personal Names
Gréag: Greece; see introduction to poem 36

Na Hearadh: Harris

Í (genitive *Íe*): Iona
Iath Airt: Land of Art, a poetic name for Ireland; see *Art* in Glossary of
    Personal Names
Iath Chuinn: Land of Conn [Céadchathach], a poetic name for Ireland;
    see *Conn* in Glossary of Personal Names

Íle: Islay

Inbher Abha: Inverawe, near Taynuilt, Argyll

Inbhir Lòchaidh: Inverlochy, near Fort William, Inverness-shire

Inbhir Nis(e): Inverness

Inis Eóghuin: the Inishowen peninsula in the north of Co. Donegal

Inis Fáil: Island of Fál, a poetic name for Ireland

Inis Incin: a poetic name for Ireland, taken from the name of an island in the River Shannon

an Innis (gen. *Innse*): Inch, on the south bank of the River Spean near Spean Bridge, Inverness-shire

Innse Gall: the Hebrides

Innse Modh (dative *Innsibh Modh*): the islands in Clew Bay, off Co. Mayo

Iorrus (Domhnann): Erris, the northwest of Co. Mayo

Knockrinsay: see *Chnoc Raonastail*

Latharn: Larne, Co. Antrim (poem 32)

Latharn(a): Lorne, Argyll (poem 83)

Leamhain: the River Leven, or the Lennox generally (see note to poem 15)

Leamhna(chd): the Lennox, Argyll (district bounded by Loch Lomond, Loch Long, and the River Clyde)

Leath Mogha: the Half of Mogh (Nuadhat), the southern half of Ireland

Leitir Dhubh: the wooded slope above the southeastern side of Loch Ossian, Rannoch Moor, Inverness-shire

Leódhus: Lewis

Lí: perhaps Beinn Lì in Braes, central Skye; see introduction to poem 30

Lios Cuinn (genitive *Leasa Cuinn*): Fort of Conn, a poetic name for Ireland; see *Conn* in Glossary of Personal Names

Lios Eamhna: Fort of Eamhain, a poetic name for Ireland (or perhaps Ulster); see *Eamhain*

Lios Laoghaire: Fort of Laoghaire, a poetic name for Ireland; see *Laoghaire* in Glossary of Personal Names

Loch Abar (Lochabair): Lochaber, Inverness-shire

Loch Cé: Lough Key, Co. Roscommon

Loch Con: Lough Conn, Co. Mayo

Loch Cuan: Strangford Lough, Co. Down

Loch Eireas: unidentified; see note to poem 25

Loch F(h)eabhail: Lough Foyle, off Counties Donegal and Derry

Loch Fíne: Loch Fyne, Argyll

Loch Iall: Loch Eil, Inverness-shire

Loch Long: in Argyll

Loch Odha: Loch Awe, Argyll

Loch Raithneach: Loch Rannoch, Perthshire

Loch Riach: Lough Rea, Co. Galway

Loch Trèig: in Lochaber, Inverness-shire
Loghorn: Lorne, Argyll

Manann: Man
Maol (Chinn Tíre): the Mull of Kintyre
Magh Luirg: (genitive *Muighe Luirg*): Moylurg, Co. Roscommon (see introduction to poem 21)
Magh Monaidh (genitive *Moighe Monaidh*): the Plain of *Monadh*, a poetic name for Scotland
Magh nAoi (*genitive Muighe hAoi*): the Plain of Aoi, or the area around Cruacha, often labeled *Cruacha Aoi* (see *Aoi* in Glossary of Personal Names)
Maigh: probably Moy, along the River Lochy, Inverness-shire
Málainn: Malin, Co. Donegal
An Mhorbhairn: see *Morbhairn*
An Mhuaidh: see *Muaidh*
Midhe: Meath, traditional 'fifth' (province) of Ireland, and seat of the Irish high-kings
Mighinis: the Minginish district, in west-central Skye
Mis: see *Sliabh Mis*
Monadh: a poetic name for Scotland
Morbhairn (*An Mhorbhairn*): Morvern
Muaidh (*An Mhuaidh*): the River Moy, Co. Mayo
Muic: Muick, on the north shore of Loch Arkaig, Inverness-shire
Muile: Mull
Murlagan: Murlaggan, near the west end of Loch Arkaig, Inverness-shire

Oileach (alternative form *Aileach*; dative *Oiligh*): ancient Ulster power centre, near Derry

Raithneach: Rannoch (Perthshire)
Ráth Chobhthaigh: Fort of Cobhthach, a poetic name for Ireland; see *Cobhthach* in Glossary of Personal Names
Ráth Floinn: Fort of Flann, a poetic name for Ireland; see *Flann* in Glossary of Personal Names
Ráth Logha: Fort of Lugh, a poetic name for Ireland; see *Lugh* in Glossary of Personal Names
Reachlainn: Rathlin Island, off the coast of Co. Antrim
Reilig Odhráin: the cemetery of Odhrán in Iona; see *Odhrán* in Glossary of Personal Names
Rinn Friú: Renfrew
Ros: Ross (see note to poem 17)
An Róimh: Rome
Rubha an Dùnain: a headland in west Skye, near Glen Brittle
Rum: R(h)um
An Rút: 'the Route', the area around the mouth of the River Bann in Co. Antrim and Co. Derry

Sanas: Machrihanish (*Machair Shanais*), Kintyre
Sasann: England
Seile: Loch Shiel in Moidart
Sídh Chailleann: Schiehallion mountain, Perthshire
Sionann: the River Shannon in the west of Ireland
Sléibhte: the Sleat peninsula, south Skye
Sliabh Gaoil: a mountain in South Knapdale, southwest of Erins
Sliabh Mis: Slemish, in Co. Antrim; see note to poem 33
Sliabh Truim: Bessy Bell mountain, near Newtownstewart, Co. Tyrone
Srath Lòchaidh: the strath of the Lochy, between Loch Lochy and Loch
    Linnhe in Lochaber
Srath Oisein: Strath Ossian, to the north of Loch Ossian, Inverness-shire
An t-Sròn: Strone, at the mouth of Glen Loy, Lochaber
Sruth Toilbh: the Water of Tulla, in Glen Orchy, Argyll, at the edge of
    Rannoch Moor

Té (Múr Té, Té Mhúr): see *Teamhair*
Teamhair (genitive *Teamhra*): Tara, in Co. Meath, traditional seat of the
    Irish high-kings
Tír Chonaill: a traditional kingdom in northwest Ireland, now
    coextensive with Co. Donegal, but traditionally taking in parts of
    Sligo, Leitrim, and Fermanagh as well
Tír-ighead (more commonly *Tiriodh*): Tiree
Toilbh: see *Sruth Toilbh*
Traoi: Troy
Tuaim (genitive *Tuama*): Tuam, Co. Galway

Uaimh an Deirg (Uamh Deirge): probably Red Bay Castle, near
    Cushendall, Co. Antrim; see notes to poems 25 and 81
Uibhist: Uist
Ulaidh (genitive plural *Uladh*): Ulster, traditional northern province of
    Ireland

Appendix II

Glossary of Personal and Family Names

Alasdair Carrach (MacDhomhnaill) (†1440): son of Eòin, first Lord of the Isles, brother of Domhnall, second Lord of the Isles; first MacDhomhnaill of Keppoch
Amhláoimh: Norse progenitor of Clann Domhnaill
Aoi: son of the Daghdha (a euhemerized pagan god); buried at Cruacha
Art (mac Cuinn): son of *Conn*, legendary king of Ireland
Artúr (Artar): King Arthur

Badhbh: a female battle demon, usually appearing in the form of a crow
Balar (Balcbéimnech): leader of *Fine Fomhra*
Banbha: one of the three sovereignty goddesses of Ireland, thus a common poetic name for Ireland itself
Bé Bhionn: mother of the Connacht warrior Froech; mother of *Brian Bóraimhe* (see note to poem 15)
Béine Briot: son of the king of Britain, fought against *Art mac Cuinn*
Brian (*Bóroimhe* or *Boru*): high-king of Ireland (†1014), victor of the famous Battle of Clontarf
Bruide mac Bili: king of the Picts (†693); victor of the famous Battle of Nechtansmere against the Northumbrians

Cailean (Mór): famous progenitor of the Caimbeuls († *c.*1296)
Cailean Liath (Caimbeul): chief of the Caimbeuls of Glen Orchy and Breadalbane from 1550–83; father of *Donnchadh Dubh*
Cairbre Lifiochair (Cairbre Lifeachair): legendary warrior-king of Ireland, son of Cormac, grandson of Art, great-grandson of *Conn*; see also note to poem 52
Cathbhadh: legendary druid and warrior in the Ulster Cycle tales
Céacht: pagan god of healing in Gaelic tradition (also *Dian Céacht, Mac Céacht*)
Ceallach: progenitor of the prominent Ó Ceallaigh family, descended from *Colla Dhá Chríoch*
Cináed mac Ailpín: king of the Picts (†858), Englished as 'Kenneth MacAlpine'
Clann Domhnaill: the MacDhomhnaills
Clann Fhionguine: the MacFhionghains
Clann Ghiolla-Eóin: the MacGill'Eathains
Clann Néill: the Ó Néills of Tír Eóghain, traditionally the pre-eminent family in Ulster

Clann Raghnaill: Clan Ranald, branch of Clann Domhnaill descended from Raghnall MacDhomhnaill (†1389), son of Eòin, first Lord of the Isles; see also *Mac Mhic Ailein*

Cobhthach (Caol mBreagh): famous early king of Ireland, son of Ughaine Mór

Colla Dhá Chríoch: fourth-century Irish warrior, brother of Colla Uais (see introduction to poem 17)

Colla Uais: fourth-century Irish warrior, ancestor of Clann Domhnaill (see introduction to poem 17)

Colum (Cille): St Columba (†597), founder of the monastery of Í Choluim Chille (Iona)

Conal(l): son of the great king *Niall Noighiallach*, ancestor of the Ó Domhnaills of Tír Chonaill

Conchubhar: legendary king of Ulster, in Deirdre story etc.

Conn (Céadchathach) (genitive *Chuinn Chéadchathaigh*): Conn of the Hundred Battles, legendary second-century king of Ireland, ancestor of Clann Domhnaill (and others)

Corc (Caisil): Corc of Cashel, first king of Munster, who made a famous journey to Scotland

Corc (Duibhne): founder of the Corca Dhuibhne kindred, southwest Munster

Cú Chulainn: legendary warrior of Ulster

Cú Roí mac Daire (genitive *Choin Roí mac Daire*): prominent early warrior figure in the Ulster Cycle of tales, strongly identified with Munster

Cuircheol: see note to poem 62

Danar: literally 'Danes', a generic term for foreign invaders

Donnchadh Dubh (Caimbeul): chief of the Caimbeuls of Glen Orchy and Breadalbane from 1583–1631; son of Cailean Liath

Dubhthach: St Dubhthach of Tain (†1065?); see note to poem 38

Duibhne: famous ancestor of the Caimbeuls; great-great-great-grandfather of Cailean Mór

Eachtair: Hector, hero of the Trojan war

Éibhear: son of *Míl* and brother of *Éireamhón*; one of the first Gaelic invaders of Ireland

Éire: one of the three sovereignty goddesses of Ireland, thus giving name to Ireland itself

Éireamhón: son of *Míl* and brother of *Éibhear*; one of the first Gaelic invaders of Ireland

Eithne: mother of Colum Cille

Eochaidh (Doimhléin): father of the three Collas (see introduction to poem 17)

E(a)rc: father of Fergus Mór, who, according to traditional history, founded the settlement of Dál Riada in Argyll (*c.* 501)

Fearghus (mac Eirc): legendary founder of Dál Riata in Argyll, *c.* 500

Fearghus (mac Roich): famous warrior in the Ulster Cycle tales, an Ulsterman who later fought for Connacht

Féilim Réachtmhor: see *Fiachaidh*

Fiachaidh (Feidhlimidh Fionnolaidh): famous law-giving early Irish king; son of *Tuathal Teachtmhar*, father of *Conn Céadchathach*

Fian (an Fhiann): the Fianna, warband of *Fionn mac Cumhaill*

Fine Fomhra: in Gaelic pseudo-history, a race of giants led by Balar Balcbéimnech, conquered by the Tuatha Dé Danann, who were in turn conquered by the Gaels

Fine Leóid: the MacLeòids

Fíonán: St Finnan, early Scottish saint (*fl.* late 7th century?); see note to poem 38

Fionn (mac Cumhaill): legendary leader of the *Fianna* (see introduction to poem 54)

Fionnghall (nom. pl. *Fionnghoill*): Hebrideans, literally 'fair foreigners' (see introduction to poem 25)

Fiontan: the most ancient inhabitant of Ireland, said to have survived the Flood

Flann Sionna: king of Ireland (†914)

Fódla: one of the three sovereignty goddesses of Ireland, thus a common poetic name for Ireland itself

Fomhra: see *Fine Fomhra*

Fotudáin: a Gaelic form of *Gododdin* or *Votadini*, an important people in southeastern Scotland

Friseal: Fraser

Galtar: Walter fitz Alan (†1177), first High Steward of Scotland, progenitor of the Stiùbharts

Gaoidheal Glas: son of Scota, from whom the Gaels take their name

Gill'Easbaig: Archibald

Gofraidh: ninth-century ancestor of Clann Domhnaill (but see note to poem 16)

Goibhniu: smith of the Tuatha Dé Danann, a group of prehistoric beings with magical powers

Guaire: seventh-century king of Connacht, famous for his generosity

Guibhnich (sing. *Guibhneach*): the Caimbeuls; an alternate form of Duibhneach, from their famous ancestor *Duibhne*

Íomhar: Norse progenitor of Clann Domhnaill

Laoghaire: sixth-century king of Ireland, killed by his brother *Cobhthach Caol mBreagh*

Lorc: see *Laoghaire*

Lugh (Lámhfhada mac Eithleann): a pagan Celtic god who appears as a warrior-figure in early Gaelic literature

Lughaidh (Mac Con): mythical second-century king of Ireland; a 'euhemerized' (humanized) incarnation of *Lugh*

Mac-a'-phì: MacPhee
Mac a' Phiocair: MacVicar
Mac an Tòisich: MacIntosh
Mac an t-Saoir: MacIntyre
Mac Cailein (Mór): hereditary title applied to the chief of the Caimbeuls; see *Cailean*
MacFhionghain: MacKinnon
Mac Mhic Ailein: hereditary title applied to the chief of *Clann Raghnaill*
MacGill'Eathain: MacLean
Máel Coluim III Ceann Mór: king of Alba 1058–93, Englished as 'Malcolm Canmore'
Manannán: pagan Celtic sea-god, often appearing in euhemerized form as a warrior-figure in early Gaelic literature
Míl: father of *Éibhear* and *Éireamhon*; 'father figure' of the Gaels (sometimes referred to as 'Milesians')
Mongán: a character in several stories from the Cycle of Kings; connected to a seventh-century Ulster king

Niall (Naoighiallach): famous early king of Ireland, progenitor of the Ó Néills and Ó Domhnaills, named 'of the Nine Hostages' because he took five hostages from Ireland and four from Scotland

Odhrán: monk and saint of the later sixth century, connected to Colum Cille; the first person to die on Iona, thus giving his name to the island's cemetery *Reilig Odhráin*
Ó Duibhne: (genitive form *Uí Dhuibhne*): a traditional by-name applied to high-ranking Caimbeuls, connecting them to their prominent ancestor *Duibhne*
Oirghialla: a group of prominent families in South Ulster, including the Mág Uidhirs, descended from *Colla Dhá Chríoch*
Osgar (also *Oscar*): famous Fenian warrior

Séasar: Julius Caesar
Seumas nan Ruag (Mac Domhnaill): Seumas 'of the Routs', chief of the Mac Domhnaills of Dunyveg and the Glens (†1565)
Somhuirle: Somerled, twelfth-century ruler of the Hebrides (†1164), ancestor of Clann Domhnaill

Tuathal Teachtmhar (mac Eithne): legendary first-century king of Ireland; grandfather of *Conn Céadchathach*
Turcull: Norse progenitor of Clann Domhnaill

Ualas: William Wallace (†1305), hero of the Scottish Wars of Independence
Uí Bhilin: the MacQuillans, the Gaelicized Norman family who lost control of the Route (*An Rút*) to Clann Domhnaill during the sixteenth century
Uí Dhuibhne: see *Ó Duibhne*

BIBLIOGRAPHY

Anderson, Alan O., and Anderson, Marjorie O., eds. (1961). *Adomnán's Life of Columba*. Edinburgh: Thomas Nelson and Sons.

Arbuthnot, Sharon (2002). 'A Context for Mac Mhaighstir Alasdair's *Moladh air Deagh Bhod*', in Ó Baoill and McGuire 2002, 163–70.

Bannerman, John (1977a). 'The Lordship of the Isles', in *Scottish Society in the Fifteenth Century*, ed. by Jennifer M. Brown, 209–40. London: Edward Arnold.

—— (1977b). 'The Lordship of the Isles: Historical Background', in K. A. Steer and John Bannerman, *Late Medieval Monumental Sculpture in the West Highlands*, 201–13. Edinburgh: Royal Commission on the Ancient and Historical Monuments of Scotland.

—— (1983). 'Literacy in the Highlands', in *The Renaissance and Reformation in Scotland*, ed. by Ian B. Cowan and Duncan Shaw, 214–35. Edinburgh: Scottish Academic Press.

—— (1986). *The Beatons: A Medical Kindred in the Classical Gaelic Tradition*. Edinburgh: John Donald.

—— (1989). 'The King's Poet and the Inauguration of Alexander III'. *SHR*, 68 (1989), 120–49.

—— (1991). 'The Clàrsach and the Clàrsair'. *SS*, 30, 1–17.

Barrow, G. W. S. (1973). *The Kingdom of the Scots: Government, Church and Society from the Eleventh to the Fourteenth Century*. London: Edward Arnold.

—— (1980). *The Anglo-Norman Era in Scottish History*. Oxford: Clarendon Press.

—— (1989). 'The lost Gàidhealtachd of medieval Scotland', in Gillies 1989, 67–88.

Bergin, Osborn (1946). *Irish Grammatical Tracts III & IV*. Supplement to *Ériu*, 14.

—— (1970). *Irish Bardic Poetry*, ed. by David Greene and Fergus Kelly. Dublin: DIAS.

Bjørn, Claus, et al., eds (1994). *Nations, Nationalism and Patriotism in the European Past*. Copenhagen: Academic Press.

Black, Ronald (1994). 'Bog, Loch and River: The Nature of Reform in Scottish Gaelic', in *Language Reform: History and Future*, vol. 6, ed. by István Fodor and Claude Hagège, 123–48. Hamburg: Helmut Buske Verlag.

——, ed. (2001). *An Lasair: Anthology of 18th Century Scottish Gaelic Verse*. Edinburgh: Birlinn.

Boardman, Stephen (2005a). 'Pillars of the community: Campbell lordship and architectural patronage in the fifteenth century', in *Lordship and Architecture in Medieval and Renaissance Scotland*, ed.

by Richard Oram and Geoffrey Stell, 123–59. East Linton: Tuckwell Press.

—— (2005b). *The Campbells 1250–1513*. Edinburgh: Birlinn.

Breathnach, Pól (1931). 'Interpretanda'. *Irisleabhar Muighe Nuadhad*, 30, 37–46.

[see also Walsh, Paul]

Breatnach, Pádraig A. (1983). 'The Chief's Poet'. *Proceedings of the Royal Irish Academy*, 83C, 37–79.

—— (1997). 'Tradisiún na hAithrise Liteartha i bhFilíocht Chlasaiceach na Gaeilge', in *Téamaí Taighde Nua-Ghaeilge*, 1–63. Maynooth: An Sagart.

Breatnach, R. A. (1943). 'Marbhna Fhearchoir Í Mháoil Chíaráin'. *Éigse*, 3, 165–85.

Broun, Dauvit (1994). 'The Origin of Scottish Identity', in Bjørn et al. (1994), 35–55.

—— (1997). 'The Birth of Scottish History'. *SHR*, 76, 4–22.

—— (1998). 'Gaelic literacy in eastern Scotland, 1124–1249', in *Literacy in Medieval Celtic Societies*, ed. by Huw Pryce, 183–201. Cambridge: CUP.

—— (1999). *The Irish Identity of the Kingdom of the Scots*. Woodbridge: Boydell Press.

Bruford, Alan (1972–73). 'The Sea-Divided Gaels: Some Relationships Between Scottish Gaelic, Irish and English Traditional Songs'. *Éigse Cheol Tíre*, 1, 4–27.

Byrne, Michel, Clancy, Thomas Owen, and Kidd, Sheila, eds (2006). *Litreachas & Eachdraidh: Rannsachadh na Gàidhlig 2, Glaschu 2002 / Literature & History: Papers from the Second Conference of Scottish Gaelic Studies, Glasgow 2002*. Glasgow: Department of Celtic, University of Glasgow.

Cameron, Alexander (1871). *The History and Traditions of the Isle of Skye*. Inverness: A. Forsyth.

—— (1892–4). *Reliquiae Celticae: Texts, Papers, and Studies in Gaelic Literature and Philology Left by the Late Rev. Alexander Cameron, LL.D*, ed. by Alexander MacBain and Rev. John Kennedy. 2 vols. Inverness: Northern Counties Newspaper and Printing and Publishing Co.

Cameron, Jamie (1998). *James V: The Personal Rule 1528–1542*, ed. by Norman Macdougall. East Linton: Tuckwell Press.

Campbell of Airds, Alastair (2002). *A History of Clan Campbell, Vol. 2, From Flodden to the Restoration*. Edinburgh: EUP.

Campbell, Alexander (1816–18). *Albyn's Anthology*. 2 vols. Edinburgh: Oliver & Boyd.

Campbell, Ewan (2001). 'Were the Scots Irish?' *Antiquity*, 75, 285–92.

Campbell, J. F., ed. (1872). *Leabhar na Féinne: Heroic Gaelic Ballads Collected in Scotland Chiefly from 1512 to 1871*. London: J. F. Campbell; repr. Shannon, Ireland: Irish University Press, 1972.

——, ed. (1950). *Iain Òg Ìle, MS. VII: Ian Deoir: Earran 1 – Blàr Tràigh Ghruinneaird*. Edinburgh: John Grant Booksellers Ltd.

Campbell, J. L. (1961). 'Varia: "The Beginning of Mac Vurich's Panegyrick on the MacLeans"'. *SGS*, 9, 90–91.

—— (2000). *A Very Civil People: Hebridean Folk, History and Tradition*, ed. by Hugh Cheape. Edinburgh: Birlinn.

——, and Collinson, Francis, eds (1969–81). *Hebridean Folksongs*. 3 vols. Oxford: Clarendon Press.

——, and Thomson, Derick S. (1963). *Edward Lhuyd in the Scottish Highlands 1699–1700*. Oxford: Clarendon Press.

Carmichael, Alexander, ed. (1900–71). *Carmina Gadelica*. 6 vols. Edinburgh: Oliver & Boyd.

——, ed. (1914). *Deirdire, agus Laoidh Chlann Uisne / Deirdire, and the Lay of the Children of Uisne*. Paisley: A. Gardner.

Céitinn, Séathrún [Geoffrey Keating] (1902, 1908, 1914). *Foras Feasa ar Éirinn / The History of Ireland*, ed. by Patrick S. Dinneen. 4 vols. London: ITS.

Clancy, Thomas Owen (1996). 'Women Poets in Early Medieval Ireland: Stating the Case', in *'The Fragility of Her Sex'? Medieval Irishwomen in Their European Context*, ed. by Christine Meek & Katharine Simms, 43–72. Dublin: Four Courts Press.

——, ed. (1998). *The Triumph Tree: Scotland's Earliest Poetry, 550–1350*. Edinburgh: Canongate.

—— (2000). 'A Gaelic Polemic Quatrain from the reign of Alexander I, ca. 1113'. *SGS*, 20, 88–96.

—— (2006a). 'Mourning Fearchar Ó Maoilchiaráin: texts, transmission and transformation', in McLeod et al. (2006), 57–71.

—— (2006b). 'A Fond Farewell to last Night's Literary Criticism: Reading Niall Mór MacMhuirich (*fl.* 1596x1626)'. Paper presented at Rannsachadh na Gàidhlig 2006, Sabhal Mòr Ostaig, 19–21 July, and forthcoming in the published Proceedings (Dunedin Academic Press).

——, and Crawford, Barbara E. (2001). 'The Formation of the Scottish Kingdom', in *The New Penguin History of Scotland: From the Earliest Times to the Present Day*, ed. by R. A. Houston and W. W. J. Knox, 28–95. London: Allen Lane/Penguin Press.

——, and Márkus, Gilbert (1995). *Iona: The Earliest Poetry of a Celtic Monastery*. Edinburgh: EUP.

——, and Pittock, Murray, eds. (2006). *The Edinburgh History of Scottish Literature, Volume 1: From Columba to the Union (until 1707)*. Edinburgh: EUP.

[Clark, Gilbert] (1992). 'Blàr Thràigh Ghruinneart'. *Tocher*, 44, 110–17.

Clark, James Toshach, ed. (1900). *Genealogical Collections Concerning Families in Scotland, made by Walter MacFarlane 1750–1751*. 2 vols. Edinburgh: SHS.

Co-chruinneachadh nuadh do dh' Orannibh Gaidhealach (1806). Inverness: E. Young.

Cowan, Edward J. (1997–98). 'The Discovery of the Gaidhealtachd in Sixteenth-Century Scotland'. *TGSI*, 60, 259–84.

Craigie, James, ed. (1944, 1950). *The Basilicon Doron of King James VI.* 2 vols. Edinburgh: Scottish Texts Society.

Creighton, Helen, and Calum MacLeod (1979). *Gaelic Songs in Nova Scotia.* Ottawa: National Museums of Canada.

Dawson, Jane (1994). 'Calvinism and the Gaidhealtachd in Scotland', in *Calvinism and Europe, 1540–1620*, ed. by Andrew Pettegrew et al., 231–53. Cambridge: CUP.

—, ed. (1997). *Campbell Letters 1559–1583.* Edinburgh: SHS.

—— (2002). *The Politics of Religion in the Age of Mary, Queen of Scots: The Earl of Argyll and the Struggle for Britain and Ireland.* Cambridge: CUP.

Dillon, Myles, ed. (1970). *Stories from the Acallam.* Dublin: DIAS.

Dooley, Ann, and Roe, Harry, ed. and trans. (1999). *Tales of the Elders of Ireland (Accalam na Senórach).* Oxford: OUP.

Duffy, Seán, ed. (forthcoming). *The World of the Galloglass: War and Society in the North Irish Sea Region, 1150–1600.* Dublin: Four Courts Press.

Duncan, Alasdair (1979). 'Some MacGregor Songs'. Unpublished M.Litt. thesis, University of Edinburgh.

Fraser, James (1905). *Chronicles of the Frasers: The Wardlaw Manuscript Entitled 'Polichronicon Seu Politicrata Temporum, or, The True Genealogy of the Frasers', 916–1674.* Edinburgh: SHS.

Fraser, James E. (2006). '*Dux Reuda* and the Corcu Réti', in McLeod et al. (2006), 1–9.

Gantz, Jeffrey (1981). *Early Irish Myths and Sagas.* London: Penguin.

Gaskill, Howard, ed. (1991). *Ossian Revisited.* Edinburgh: EUP.

Gillies, Anne Lorne (2005). *Songs of Gaelic Scotland.* Edinburgh: Birlinn.

Gillies, Eoin (1786). *Sean Dain agus Orain Ghàidhealach.* Perth: Eoin Gillies.

Gillies, William (1976–78). 'Some Aspects of Campbell History'. *TGSI*, 50, 256–95.

—— (1977). 'Courtly and Satiric Poems in the Book of the Dean of Lismore'. *SS*, 21, 35–53.

—— (1978). 'The Gaelic Poems of Sir Duncan Campbell of Glenorchy (I)'. *SGS*, 13, Part 1, 18–45.

—— (1979). 'Gaelic and Scots Literature Down to the Reformation', in *Actes du 2ᵉ Colloque de Langue et de Littérature Écossaises (Moyen Age et Renaissance)*, ed. by Jean-Jacques Blanchot and Claude Graf, 63–79. Strasbourg: University of Strasbourg.

—— (1981a), 'The Gaelic Poems of Sir Duncan Campbell of Glenorchy (II)'. *SGS*, 13, Part 2, 263–88.

—— (1981b). 'Arthur in Gaelic Tradition, Part I: Folktales and Ballads'. *CMCS*, 2, 47–72.

—— (1981c). 'Arthur in Gaelic Tradition, Part II: Romances and Learned Lore'. *CMCS*, 3, 41–75.

—— (1983). 'The Gaelic Poems of Sir Duncan Campbell of Glenorchy (III)'. *SGS*, 14, 59–82.

—— (1986). 'The Classical Irish Poetic Tradition', in *Proceedings of the Seventh International Congress of Celtic Studies*, ed. by D. Ellis Evans, John G. Griffith, and E. M Jope, 108–20. Oxford: Jesus College.

—— (1987). 'Heroes and Ancestors', in *The Heroic Process: Form, Function and Fantasy in Folk Epic*, ed. by Bo Almqvist, Séamas Ó Catháin, and Pádraig Ó Héalaí, 57–74. Dún Laoghaire: Glendale Press.

—— (1988). 'Gaelic: The Classical Tradition', in *The History of Scottish Literature, Volume 1: Origins to 1660 (Mediaeval and Renaissance)*, ed. by R. D. S. Jack, 254–62. Aberdeen: Aberdeen University Press.

——, ed. (1989). *Gaelic and Scotland/Alba agus a' Ghàidhlig*. Edinburgh: EUP.

—— (1994a). 'The Invention of Tradition — Highland Style', in *The Renaissance in Scotland: Studies in Literature, Religion, History and Culture*, ed. by A. A. MacDonald, Michael Lynch, and Ian B. Cowan, 144–56. London: E. J. Brill.

—— (1994b). 'The Celtic Languages: some Current and some Neglected Questions', in *Speaking in our Tongues: Medieval Dialectology and Related Disciplines*, ed. by Margaret Laing and Keith Williamson, 139–47. Woodbridge: D. S. Brewer.

—— (1999). 'The "British" Genealogy of the Campbells'. *Celtica*, 23. 82–95.

—— (2000). 'Alexander Carmichael and Clann Mhuirich'. *SGS*, 20, 1–66.

—— (2005). 'Traditional Gaelic Women's Songs', in *Alba Literaria: A History of Scottish Literature*, ed. by Marco Fazzini, 165–78. Venice: Amos Edizioni.

—— (2006a). 'The Lion's Tongues: Languages in Scotland to 1314', in Clancy and Pittock 2006, 52–62.

—— (2006b). 'On the Study of Gaelic Literature', in Byrne et al. (2006), 1–32.

Gordon, Cosmo (1958). 'Letter to John Aubrey from Professor James Garden'. *SGS*, 8, 18–26.

Gowans, Linda (1992). *Am Bròn Binn: An Arthurian Ballad in Scottish Gaelic*. Eastbourne.

Grant, Alexander (1991). *Independence and Nationhood: Scotland 1306–1469*. Edinburgh: EUP.

—— (1994). 'Aspects of National Consciousness in Medieval Scotland', in Bjørn et al. (1994), 68–95.

Grant, I. F., and Cheape, Hugh (1987). *Periods in Highland History*. London: Shepheard-Walwyn.

Greene, David (1962). 'Na léig mo mhealladh, a Mhuire'. *SGS*, 9, 105–15.

Gregory, Donald (1836). *History of the Western Highlands and Isles of Scotland from A.D. 1493 to A.D. 1625*. Edinburgh: William Tait.

Harrison, Alan (1979). *An Chrosántacht*. Dublin: An Clóchomhar.
—— (1989). *The Irish Trickster*. Sheffield: Sheffield Academic Press.
Henry, P. L., ed. (2006). *Amra Choluim Chille: Dallán's Elegy For Columba*. Belfast: Colmcille.
Herbert, Máire (1999). 'Sea-divided Gaels? Constructing relationships between Irish and Scots *c.* 800–1169', in *Britain and Ireland 900–1300: Insular Responses to Medieval European Change*, ed. by Brendan Smith, 87–97. Cambridge: CUP.
—— (2005). 'Becoming an Exile: Colum Cille in Middle-Irish Poetry', in *Heroic Poets and Poetic Heroes in Celtic Tradition: A Festschrift for Patrick K. Ford*, ed. by Joseph Falaky Nagy and Leslie Ellen Jones, 131–40. Dublin: Four Courts Press.
——, and Pádraig Ó Riain, eds (1988). *Betha Adamnáin: The Irish Life of Adamnán*. London: ITS.
Higgitt, John, ed. (2000). *The Murthly Hours: Devotion, Literacy and Luxury in Paris, England and the Gaelic West*. London: British Library/University of Toronto Press.
Hillers, Barbara (2006). 'Dialogue or Monologue? Lullabies in Scottish Gaelic tradition', in Byrne et al. (2006), 33–55.
Hudson, Benjamin T. (1996). *Prophecy of Berchán: Irish and Scottish High-Kings of the Early Middle Ages*. Westport, CT: Greenwood Press.
Hughes, Kathleen (1980). 'Where are the writings of early Scotland?', in *Celtic Britain in the Early Middle Ages: Studies in Scottish and Welsh Sources*, ed. by David Dumville, 1–21. Woodbridge: Boydell Press.
Jackson, Kenneth (1951). 'Common Gaelic: The Evolution of the Goidelic Languages'. *Proceedings of the British Academy*, 37, 71–97.
—— (1956). 'The Poem *A Eolcha Alban Uile*'. *Celtica*, 3, 148–67.
—— (1957). 'The Duan Albanach'. *SHR*, 36, 126–37.
—— (1972). *The Gaelic Notes in the Book of Deer*. Cambridge: CUP.
Kelly, Fergus (1973). 'A poem in praise of Columb Cille'. *Ériu*, 24, 1–34.
—— (1975). '*Tiughraind Bhécain*'. *Ériu*, 26, 66–98.
Kennedy, Peter (1975). *Folksongs of Britain and Ireland*. London: Cassell.
Kerrigan, Catherine, ed. (1991). *An Anthology of Scottish Women Poets*. Edinburgh: EUP.
Kingston, Simon (2003). *Ulster and the Isles in the Fifteenth Century: The Lordship of the Clann Domhnaill of Antrim*. Dublin: Four Courts Press.
Kinsella, Thomas, trans. (1985). *The Táin*. Portlaoise: Dolmen Press.
Knott, Eleanor, ed. (1922, 1926). *A Bhfuil Aguinn Dár Chum Tadhg Dall Ó hUiginn (1550–1591)/The Bardic Poems of Tadhg Dall Ó hUiginn (1550–1591)*. London: ITS.
—— (1957). *An Introduction to Irish Syllabic Poetry of the Period 1200–1600*. Dublin: DIAS.
Laoide, Seosamh (1914). *Alasdair Mac Colla*. Dublin: Gaelic League.

Lawson, Bill (2004). *North Uist in History and Legend*. Edinburgh: John Donald.

Leahy, A. H. (1906). *Heroic Romances of Ireland*. London: David Nutt.

Longley, Edna, et al., eds (2003). *Ireland (Ulster) Scotland: Concepts, Contexts, Comparisons*. Belfast: Cló Ollscoil na Ríona.

Mac an Bhaird, Alan (1975). 'Erotica Bardica Albanica'. *Comhar*, 35(8), 13–15.

Mac-an-Tuairneir, Paruig (1813). *Comhchruinneacha do Dh'Orain taghta, Ghaidealach*. Edinburgh: T. Stiùbhard.

MacAlister, R. A. Stewart, ed. (1937, 1939, 1956). *Lebor Gabála Érenn*. 5 vols. Dublin: ITS.

MacAonghuis, Iain (1986a). 'Baird is Bleidirean', in *Féilscríbhinn Thomáis de Bhaldraithe*, ed. by Seosamh Watson, 94–110. Dublin: Coiste Féilscríbhinn Thomáis de Bhaldraithe, An Coláiste Ollscoile (reprinted in MacInnes 2006).

—— (1986b). 'Samhla na Craoibhe', in *Sàr-Ghaidheal: Essays in Memory of Rory Mackay*, 64–9. Inverness: An Comunn Gaidhealach/Gaelic Society of Inverness. [see also MacInnes, John]

Mac Cana, Proinsias (2004). 'Praise Poetry in Ireland Before the Normans'. *Ériu*, 54, 11–40.

Mac Cionnaith, Láimhbheartach, ed. (1938). *Dioghluim Dána*. Dublin: Oifig an tSoláthair.

MacCoinnich, Aonghas (2002). '"His Spirit was Only Given to Warre": Conflict and Identity in the Scottish Gàidhealtachd c. 1580–c. 1630', in *Fighting for Identity: Scottish Military Experience c. 1550–1900*, ed. by Steve Murdoch and Andrew Mackillop, 133–66. Leiden: Brill.

Mac Craith, Mícheál (1989). *Lorg na h-Iasachta ar na Dánta Grá*. Dublin: An Clóchomhar.

Macdhomhnuill, Raonuill (1776), *Comh-chruinneachidh Orannaigh Gaidhealach*. Edinburgh: W. Ruddiman [Eigg Collection].

MacDonald, Angus J., and Archibald MacDonald, eds (1911). *The Macdonald Collection of Gaelic Poetry*. Inverness: Northern Counties Newspaper and Printing and Publishing Co.

MacDonald, Donald Archie (1984). 'The Vikings in Gaelic Oral Tradition', in *The Northern and Western Isles in the Viking World: Survival, Continuity and Change*, ed. by Alexander Fenton & Hermann Pálsson, 265–79. Edinburgh: John Donald.

MacDonald, Donald J. (1978). *Clan Donald*. Loanhead, Midlothian: MacDonald Publishers.

MacDonald, Keith Norman (1895–1902). *The Gesto Collection of Highland Music*. Leipzig: O. Brandstetter.

McDonnell, Hector (1993). 'Agnews and O'Gnímhs'. *The Glynns: Journal of the Glens of Antrim Historical Society*, 21, 13–53.

MacFarlane, Walter (1900). *Genealogical Collections Concerning Families in Scotland*. 2 vols. Edinburgh: SHS.

MacGill-Eain, Somhairle (1985). *Ris a' Bhruthaich: The Criticism and Prose Writings of Sorley MacLean*, ed. by William Gillies. Stornoway: Acair.
[see also MacLean, Sorley]

Mac Giolla Léith, Caoimhín, ed. (1993). *Oidheadh Chloinne hUisneach / The Violent Death of the Children of Uisneach*. London: ITS.

MacGregor, Amelia G. M. (1898–1901). *History of the Clan Gregor*. 2 vols. Edinburgh: W. Brown.

MacGregor, Martin (1989). 'A political history of the MacGregors before 1571'. Unpublished PhD thesis, University of Edinburgh.

—— (2000). '"Surely one of the greatest poems ever made in Britain": The Lament for Griogair Ruadh MacGregor of Glen Strae and its Historical Background', in *The Polar Twins*, ed. by Edward J. Cowan and Douglas Gifford, 115–53. Edinburgh: John Donald.

—— (2002). 'The genealogical histories of Gaelic Scotland', in *The Spoken Word: Oral Culture in Britain, 1500–1850*, ed. by Adam Fox and Daniel Woolf, 196–239. Manchester: Manchester University Press.

—— (2006a). 'Creation and Compilation: *The Book of the Dean of Lismore* and Literary Culture in Late Medieval Gaelic Scotland', in Clancy and Pittock 2006, 209–18.

—— (2006b). 'Ar sliocht Gaodhal ó Ghort Gréag'. Paper presented at Rannsachadh na Gàidhlig 2006, Sabhal Mòr Ostaig, 19–21 July, and forthcoming in the published Proceedings (Dunedin Academic Press).

—— (2006c). 'The View from Fortingall: The Worlds of *The Book of the Dean of Lismore*'. *SGS*, 22, 35–85.

Macinnes, Allan (1993). 'Crowns, clans and fine: the "civilizing" of Scottish Gaeldom, 1587–1638'. *Northern Scotland*, 13, 31–56.

MacInnes, John (1976). 'The Cultural Background to the Eighteenth Century Collections of Gaelic Poetry', in *Papers Presented to Kenneth Jackson*, 242–52. Edinburgh: Department of Celtic, University of Edinburgh (privately printed).

—— (1976–78). 'The Panegyric Code in Gaelic Poetry and its Historical Background'. *TGSI*, 50, 435–98 (reprinted in MacInnes 2006, 265–319).

—— (1981). 'Gaelic Poetry and Historical Tradition', in *The Middle Ages in the Highlands*, ed. by Loraine Maclean, 142–63. Inverness: Inverness Field Club (reprinted in MacInnes 2006, 3–33).

—— (1989). 'The Gaelic Perception of the Lowlands', in Gillies 1989, 89–100 ((reprinted in MacInnes 2006, 34–47).

—— (1992). 'The Scottish Gaelic Language', in *The Celtic Connection*, ed. by Glanville Price, 101–30. Gerrards Cross: Colin Smythe ((reprinted in MacInnes 2006, 92–119).

—— (2006). *Dùthchas nan Gàidheal: Collected Essays of John MacInnes*, ed. by Michael Newton. Edinburgh: Birlinn.
[see also MacAonghuis, Iain]

MacKechnie, John (1946). *The Owl of Strone*. Edinburgh: School of Scottish Studies.

—— (1953). 'Treaty Between Argyll and O'Donnell'. *SGS*, 7, 94–102.

MacKellar, Mary (1885–86). 'Unknown Lochaber Bards'. *TGSI*, 12, 211–26.

McKenna, Lambert, ed. (1919). *Dánta do Chum Aonghus Fionn Ó Dálaigh*. Dublin: Maunsel & Co.

——, ed. (1939, 1940). *Aithdioghluim Dána: A Miscellany of Irish Bardic Poetry*. 2 vols. Dublin: ITS.

MacKenzie, Alexander (1884). *History of the Camerons*. Inverness: A & W MacKenzie.

MacKenzie, Annie M., ed. (1965). *Òrain Iain Luim: The Songs of John MacDonald, Bard of Keppoch*. Edinburgh: SGTS.

MacKenzie, W. M., ed. (1932). *The Poems of William Dunbar*. London: Faber & Faber.

MacKinnon, Donald (1907–8). 'The Glenmasan Manuscript'. *The Celtic Review*, 4, 10–27, 104–21, 202–19.

Mackintosh, Margaret (1948). *The Clan Mackintosh and the Clan Chattan*. Edinburgh: W. & A. K. Johnston.

MacLauchlan, Thomas, ed. (1862). *The Dean of Lismore's Book*. Edinburgh: Edmonston and Douglas.

MacLean, Malcolm, and Dorgan, Theo, eds (2002). *An Leabhar Mòr: The Great Book of Gaelic*. Edinburgh: Canongate.

MacLean, Sorley (1986). 'Obscure and Anonymous Gaelic Poetry', in *The Seventeenth Century in the Highlands*, ed. by Loraine MacLean, 89–104. Inverness: Inverness Field Club. [see also MacGill-Eain, Somhairle]

Maclean-Bristol, Nicholas (1999). *Murder Under Trust: The Crimes and Death of Sir Lachlan Mor Maclean of Duart, 1558–1598*. East Linton: Tuckwell Press.

MacLeod, Angus, ed. (1932). *Sàr Òrain: Three Gaelic Poems*. Stirling: An Comunn Gaidhealach.

——, ed. (1952). *Òrain Dhonnchaidh Bhàin / The Songs of Duncan Ban Macintyre*. Edinburgh: SGTS.

McLeod, Wilson (1999). '*Galldachd, Gàidhealtachd, Garbhchriochan*'. *SGS*, 19, 1–20, and 20, 222–24.

—— (2002a). 'Anshocair nam Fionnghall: Ainmeachadh agus ath-ainmeachadh Gàidhealtachd na h-Albann', in Ó Baoill and McGuire 2002, 13–23.

—— (2002b). '*Rí Innsi Gall, Rí Fionnghall, Ceannas nan Gàidheal*: Sovereignty and Rhetoric in the Late Medieval Hebrides'. *CMCS*, 43, 25–48.

—— (2003). 'Gaelic Poetry as Historical Source: Some Problems and Possibilities', in Longley et al. (2003), 171–9.

—— (2004). *Divided Gaels: Gaelic Cultural Identities in Scotland and Ireland c. 1200–c. 1650*. Oxford: OUP.

——, Fraser, James E., and Gunderloch, Anja, eds (2006), *Cànan &*

Cultar/Language and Culture: Rannsachadh na Gàidhlig 3. Edinburgh: Dunedin Academic Press.

MacPhail, J. R. N., ed. (1914, 1916, 1920, 1934). *Highland Papers.* 4 vols. Edinburgh: SHS.

MacPhàrlain, Calum, ed. (1923). *Làmh-Sgrìobhainn Mhic Rath.* Dundee: C. S. MacLeòid.

Martin, Martin (1934 [1703]). *A Description of the Western Islands of Scotland,* ed. by Donald J. MacLeod. Stirling: Eneas Mackay.

Matheson, Angus (1952). 'Gleanings from the Dornie Manuscripts'. *TGSI,* 41, 310–81.

—— (1957). 'Documents Connected with the Trial of Sir James MacDonald of Islay'. *Transactions of the Gaelic Society of Glasgow,* 5, 207–22.

Matheson, William (1967–8). 'Further Gleanings from the Dornie Manuscripts'. *TGSI,* 45, 148–95.

—— (1970). *An Clàrsair Dall: Òrain Ruaidhrì Mhic Mhuirich agus a Chuid Ciùil / The Blind Harper: The Songs of Roderick Morison and his Music.* Edinburgh: SGTS.

Meek, Donald E. (1990). 'The Death of Diarmaid in Scottish and Irish Tradition'. *Celtica,* 21, 335–61.

—— (1996). 'The Scots-Gaelic Scribes of Medieval Perthshire: An overview of the orthography and contents of the Book of the Dean of Lismore', in *Stewart Style 1513–1542: Essays on the Court of James V,* ed. by Janet Hadley Williams, 254–72. East Linton: Tuckwell Press.

—— (1998a). '"Norsemen and Noble Stewards": The Castle Sween Poem in the Book of the Dean of Lismore'. *CMCS,* 34, 1–50.

—— (1998b). 'The Reformation and Gaelic culture: perspectives on patronage, language and literature in John Carswell's translation of "The Book of Common Order"', in *The Church in the Highlands,* ed. by James Kirk, 37–62. Edinburgh: Scottish Church History Society.

Menzies, Patricia M. (2001). '"Òran na Comhachaig": A Study of Text and Content'. Unpublished PhD thesis, University of Edinburgh.

—— (2006). 'Òran na Comhachaig', in Byrne et al. (2006), 83–96.

Munro, Jean, and R. W. Munro, eds (1986). *Acts of the Lords of the Isles, 1336–1493.* Edinburgh: SHS.

Murison, David (1974). 'Linguistic Relationships in Medieval Scotland', in *The Scottish Tradition: Essays in Honour of Ronald Gordon Cant,* ed. by G. W. S. Barrow, 71–83. Edinburgh: Scottish Academic Press.

Murphy, Gerard (1953). 'Two Irish poems written from the Mediterranean in the thirteenth century'. *Éigse,* 7, 71–79.

——, ed. (1956). *Early Irish Lyrics.* Oxford: Clarendon Press.

—— (1961). *Early Irish Metrics.* Dublin: Royal Irish Academy.

Neville, Cynthia (2005). *Native Lordship in Medieval Scotland: The Earldoms of Strathearn and Lennox, c. 1140–1365.* Dublin: Four Courts Press.

Newton, Michael (1998). 'The Tree in Scottish Gaelic Literature and Tradition'. Unpublished PhD thesis, University of Edinburgh.

—— (1999a). *Bho Chluaidh gu Calasraid/From the Clyde to Callander*. Stornoway: Acair.

—— (1999b). 'An Seann Duanaire: "Is Daor a Phàigh mi am Fonn Ìleach"'. *Cothrom*, 21, 29.

—— (2003). 'Early Poetry in the MacGregor Papers'. *SGS*, 21, 47–58.

—— (2006). 'Dancing with the dead: ritual dance at wakes in the Scottish Gàidhealtachd', in McLeod et al. (2006), 215–34.

Ní Dhomhnaill, Cáit (1975). *Duanaireacht: rialacha meadarachta fhilíocht na mbard*. Dublin: Stationery Office.

NicChoinnich, Fiona, ed. (2005). *Òrain nan Rosach: A Collection of Gaelic Songs from Ross-shire*. Dingwall: Highland Council.

Nicholson, Ranald G. (1968). 'Domesticated Scots and Wild Scots: The Relationship Between Lowlanders and Highlanders in the Medieval Scotland', in *Proceedings of the First Colloquium on Scottish Studies*. Guelph: University of Guelph.

Nicolaisen, W. F. H. (2001 [2nd edn]). *Scottish Place-Names*. Edinburgh: John Donald.

Ó Baoill, Colm, ed. (1972). *Bàrdachd Shìlis na Ceapaich, c. 1660–c. 1729 /Poems and Songs by Sileas MacDonald, c. 1660–c. 1729*. Edinburgh: SGTS.

——, ed. (1979). *Eachann Bacach agus Bàird Eile de Chloinn Ghill-Eathain/Eachann Bacach and Other MacLean Poets*. Edinburgh: SGTS.

—— (1988). 'Scotticisms in a manuscript of 1467'. *SGS*, 15, 122–39.

—— (1996). '*Caismeachd Ailean nan Sop*: the literatim text'. *SGS*, 17, 295–97.

——, ed. (1997). *Duanaire Colach 1537–1757*. Aberdeen: An Clò Gaidhealach.

—— (1998). '*Caismeachd Ailean nan Sop*: Towards a Definitive Text'. *SGS*, 18, 89–110.

—— (2003). 'The Oldest Songs of the Gael', in Longley et al. (2003), 65–76.

—— (2004). '"Neither Out nor In": Scottish Gaelic Women Poets 1650–1750', in *Women and the Feminine in Medieval and Early Modern Scottish Writing*, ed. by Sarah Dunnigan et al., 136–52. Basingstoke: Palgrave Macmillan.

——, ed., and Meg Bateman, trans. (1994). *Gàir nan Clàrsach/The Harps' Cry: An Anthology of 17th Century Gaelic Poetry*. Edinburgh: Birlinn.

——, and Donald MacAulay (2001). *Scottish Gaelic Vernacular Verse to 1730: A Checklist*. Aberdeen: Aberdeen University Department of Celtic.

——, and Nancy R. McGuire, eds (2002). *Rannsachadh na Gàidhlig 2000*. Aberdeen: An Clò Gaidhealach.

Ó Briain, Máirtín (2002). 'Snaithín san uige: "Loisc agus léig a luaith le sruth"', in Máirtín Ó Briain and Pádraig Ó Héalaí, eds, *Téada*

Dúchais: Aistí in ómós don Ollamh Breandán Ó Madagáin, 245–72. Inverin, Co. Galway: Cló Iar-Chonnachta.

Ó Buachalla, Breandán (2002). 'Common Gaelic Revisited', in Ó Baoill and McGuire 2002, 1–12.

Ó Caithnia, Liam P. (1984). *Apalóga na bhFilí 1200–1650*. Dublin: An Clóchomhar.

Ó Cuív, Brian (1961). 'Eachtra Mhuireadhaigh Uí Dhálaigh', *Studia Hibernica*, 1, 56–69,

—— (1968). 'A poem by Muireadhach Albanach Ó Dálaigh', in *Celtic Studies: Essays in memory of Angus Matheson*, ed. by James Carney & David Greene, 92–98. London: Routledge and Kegan Paul.

—— (1978). 'A Medieval Exercise in Language Planning: Classical Early Modern Irish', in *Progress in Linguistic Historiography: Papers from the International Conference on the History of the Language Sciences*, ed. by E. F. Konrad Koerner, 23–34. Amsterdam: John Benjamins.

—— (1984). 'The Family of Ó Gnímh in Ireland and Scotland: A Look at the Sources'. *Nomina*, 8, 57–71.

—— (1996). 'Further Comments on the Ó Gnímh Family of Co. Antrim'. *SGS*, 17, 298–304.

O'Donovan, John, ed. (1856). *Annála Ríoghachta Éireann/The Annals of the Kingdom of Ireland Compiled by the Four Masters*. 7 vols. Dublin: Hodges, Smith.

Ó hÓgáin, Dáithí (1990). *Myth, Legend & Romance: An Encyclopedia of Irish Folk Tradition*. London: Ryan Publishing.

Ó Lochlainn, Colm (1945–47). 'Ár ar Ard na Riadh'. *Éigse*, 5, 149–55

Ó Macháin, Pádraig (1988). 'Poems by Fearghal Óg Mac an Bhaird'. Unpublished Ph.D. thesis, University of Edinburgh.

—— (1994). 'Tadhg Dall Ó hUiginn: Foinse dá Shaothar', in *An Dán Díreach* (Léachtaí Cholm Cille, 24), ed. by Pádraig Ó Fiannachta, 77–113. Maynooth: An Sagart.

—— (2006). 'Scribal practice and textual survival: the example of Uilliam Mac Mhurchaidh'. *SGS*, 22, 95–122.

Ó Maolalaigh, Roibeard (2006). 'On the Possible Origins of Scottish Gaelic *iorram* "rowing song"', in Byrne et al. (2006), 232–88.

—— (forthcoming). 'The Scotticisation of Gaelic: A Reassessment of the Language and Orthography of the Gaelic Notes in the Book of Deer', in *Studies in the Book of Deer: 'This Splendid Little Book'*, ed. by Katherine Forsyth. Dublin: Fourt Courts Press.

Ó Murchú, Máirtín (1988). 'Diglossia and Interlanguage Contact in Ireland'. *Language, Culture and Curriculum*, 1, 243–9.

O'Rahilly, Cecile, ed. (1967). *Táin Bó Cúailnge from the Book of Leinster*. Dublin: DIAS.

——, ed. (1976). *Táin Bó Cúailnge: Recension I*. Dublin: DIAS.

O'Rahilly, Thomas F., ed. (1926). *Dánta Grádha: Cnósach de sna Dánta Grá is Fearr san Ghaelge (A.D. 1350–1750)*. 2nd edn. Cork: Cork University Press.

—— (1927). *Measgra Dánta/Miscellaneous Irish Poems*. 2 vols. Cork: Cork University Press.

—— (1940–42). 'A Poem by Piaras Feiritéar'. *Éigse*, 13, 113–18.

O'Sullivan, Helen (1976). 'Developments in Love Poetry in Irish, Welsh, and Scottish Gaelic before 1650'. Unpublished M.Litt. thesis, University of Glasgow.

Ó Tuama, Seán (1961). *Caoineadh Airt Uí Laoghaire*. Dublin: An Clóchomhar.

—— (1988). *An Grá i bhFilíocht na nUaisle*. Dublin: An Clóchomhar.

—— (1990). 'Love in Irish Folksong', in *Repossessions: Selected Essays on the Irish Literary Heritage*, 134–58. Cork: Cork University Press.

——, and Kinsella, Thomas (1980). *An Duanaire 1600–1900: Poems of the Dispossessed*. Dublin: Dolmen Press.

Quiggin, E. C. (1937). *Poems from the Book of the Dean of Lismore*, ed. by J. Fraser. Cambridge: CUP.

Rankin, Robert A. (1957). 'Òran na Comhachaig: Text and Tradition'. *Transactions of the Gaelic Society of Glasgow*, 5, 122–71.

—— (1998). 'Place-Names in the *Comhachag* and Other Similar Poems'. *SGS*, 18, 111–30.

Robinson, Christine, and Ó Maolalaigh, Roibeard (2006). 'The Several Tongues of a Single Kingdom: The Languages of Scotland, 1314–1707', in Clancy and Pittock 2006, 143–63.

Ross, Neil, ed. (1939). *Heroic Verse from the Book of the Dean of Lismore*. Edinburgh: SGTS.

Sadler, John (2005). *Clan Donald's Greatest Defeat*. Stroud: Tempus.

Scottish History Society (1926). *Miscellany of the Scottish History Society*, vol. 4. Edinburgh: SHS.

Sellar, David (1966). 'The Origins and Ancestry of Somerled'. *SHR*, 45, 123–42.

—— (1981). 'Highland Family Origins — Pedigree Making and Pedigree Faking', in *The Middle Ages in the Highlands*, ed. by Loraine Maclean, 103–16. Inverness: Inverness Field Club.

Sharpe, Richard (1995). *Life of St Columba*. Harmondsworth: Penguin.

Simmons, Andrew, ed. (1998 [1754]). *Burt's Letters from the North of Scotland*. Edinburgh: Birlinn.

Simms, Katharine (1987). 'Bardic Poetry as a Historical Source', in *The Writer as Witness: literature as historical evidence*, ed. by Tom Dunne, 58–75. Cork: Cork University Press.

—— (1991). 'Women in Gaelic Society during the Age of Transition', in *Women in Early Modern Ireland*, ed. by Margaret MacCurtain and Mary O'Dowd, 32–42. Edinburgh: EUP.

—— (2006). 'Muireadhach Albanach Ó Dálaigh and the Classical Revolution', in Clancy and Pittock 2006, 83–90.

Sinclair, A. MacLean, ed. (1881). *Clàrsach na Coille*. Glasgow: Archibald Sinclair.

——, ed. (1890). *The Gaelic Bards from 1411 to 1715*. Charlottetown, Prince Edward Island: Haszard & Moore.

—— (1898–1900). *Na Bàird Leathanach: The MacLean Bards*. 2 vols. Charlottetown, Prince Edward Island: Haszard & Moore.

Sinclair, Archibald, ed. (1879). *An t-Òranaiche: The Gaelic Songster*. Glasgow: Archibald Sinclair.

Sinton, Thomas, ed. (1906). *The Poetry of Badenoch*. Inverness: Northern Counties Publishing Co.

Skene, Wiliam F., ed. (1871). *John of Fordun's Chronicle of the Scottish Nation*. Trans. by Felix J. H. Skene. Edinburgh: Edmonston and Douglas, 1871.

Slotkin, Edgar (1981). 'The Formulaic Nature of the Harlaw *Brosnachadh*?', in *Proceedings of the Third International Conference on Scottish Language and Literature (Medieval and Renaissance)*, ed. by Roderick J. Lyall and Felicity Riddy, 143–60. Stirling/Glasgow: Department of Scottish Literature, University of Glasgow.

Smyth, Alfred P. (1989). *Warlords and Holy Men: Scotland, AD 80–1000*. Edinburgh: EUP.

Stewart, John (1974). *The Camerons: A History of Clan Cameron*. Glasgow: Clan Cameron Association.

Stewart, Thomas W. (2004). 'Lexical imposition: Old Norse vocabulary in Scottish Gaelic'. *Diachronica*, 21, 393–420.

Stokes, Whitley, ed. (1890). *Lives of Saints from the Book of Lismore*. Oxford: Clarendon Press.

—— & Ernst Windisch, eds (1887). *Irische Texte*, series II, fascicule 2. Leipzig: S. Hirzel.

Taylor, Simon (1994).'Babbet and Bridin Pudding or Polyglot Fife in the Middle Ages'. *Nomina*, 17, 99–118.

Ternes, Elmar (3rd edn 2006). *The Phonemic Analysis of Scottish Gaelic*. Dublin: DIAS.

Thomson, Derick S. (1952). *The Gaelic Sources of Macpherson's Ossian*. Edinburgh: Aberdeen University Studies.

—— (1960–63). 'The MacMhuirich Bardic Family'. *TGSI*, 43, 276–304.

—— (1968a). 'The Harlaw *Brosnachadh*: An early fifteenth-century literary curio', in *Celtic Studies: Essays in Memory of Angus Matheson*, ed. by James Carney & David Greene, 147–69. London: Routledge and Kegan Paul.

—— (1968b). 'Gaelic Learned Orders and Literati in Medieval Scotland'. *SS*, 12, 57–80.

—— (1974–76). 'Niall Mór MacMhuirich'. *TGSI*, 49, 9–25.

—— (1977). 'Three Seventeenth Century Bardic Poets: Niall Mór, Cathal and Niall MacMhuirich', in *Bards and Makars*, ed. by Adam J. Aitken, Matthew P. McDiarmid, and Derick S. Thomson, 221–46. Glasgow: Glasgow University Press.

—— (1986). 'The Poetic Tradition in Gaelic Scotland', in *Proceedings of the Seventh International Congress of Celtic Studies*, ed. by D. Ellis Evans et al., 121–31. Oxford: Jesus College.

—— (1986). 'The Earliest Scottish Gaelic Non-classical Verse Texts', in *Scottish Language and Literature, Medieval and Renaissance: Fourth International Conference, 1984, Proceedings*, ed. by Dietrich Strauss and Horst W. Drescher, 533–46. Frankfurt: Verlag Peter Lang.

—— (1990). *An Introduction to Gaelic Poetry*. 2nd edn. Edinburgh: EUP.

——, ed. (1992). *The MacDiarmid MS Anthology: Poems and Songs mainly anonymous from the collection dated 1770*. Edinburgh: SGTS.

—— (1992–94). 'The MacLagan MSS in Glasgow University Library: A Survey'. *TGSI*, 58, 406–24.

—— (1994). 'The Blood-Drinking Motif in Scottish Gaelic Tradition', in *Indogermanica et Caucasica: Festschrift fır Karl Horst Schmidt zum 65. Geburtstag*, ed. by Roland Bielmeier and Reinhard Stempel, 415–24. Berlin: Mouton de Gruyter.

—— (2000). 'Scottish Gaelic Traditional Songs from the 16th to the 18th Century'. *Proceedings of the British Academy*, 105, 93–114.

Thomson, R. L., ed. (1962). *Adtimchiol an Chreidimh: The Gaelic Version of John Calvin's Catechismus Ecclesiae Genevensis*. Edinburgh: SGTS.

——, ed. (1970). *Foirm na n-Urrnuidheadh/John Carswell's Gaelic Translation of the Book of Common Order*. Edinburgh: SGTS.

—— (1977). 'The Emergence of Scottish Gaelic', in *Bards and Makars*, ed. by Adam J. Aitken, Matthew P. McDiarmid, and Derick S. Thomson, 127–35. Glasgow: Glasgow University Press.

Tolmie, Frances (1911). *Journal of the Folk-song Society*, no. 16 (vol. IV, part 3) [reprinted as *One Hundred and Five Songs of Occupation from the Western Isles of Scotland*, Felinfach: Llanerch (1997)].

Van Hamel, A. G., ed. (1932). *Lebor Bretnach: The Irish version of the Historia Brittonum ascribed to Nennius*. Dublin: Irish Manuscripts Commission.

Walsh, Paul, ed. (1948). *Beatha Aodha Ruaidh Uí Dhomhnaill as Leabhar Lughaidh Uí Chlérigh (The Life of Aodh Ruadh Ó Domhnaill transcribed from the Book of Lughaidh Ó Clérigh)*. 2 vols. Dublin: ITS.

—— (1960). *Irish Chiefs and Leaders*, ed. by Colm Ó Lochlainn. Dublin: Three Candles.

[see also Breathnach, Pól]

Watson, J. Carmichael, ed. (1934). *Òrain is Luinneagan le Màiri nighean Alasdair Ruaidh / Gaelic Songs of Mary MacLeod*. Edinburgh: SGTS.

Watson, W. J. (1914–19). 'Classical Gaelic Poetry of Panegyric in Scotland', reprinted and supplemented from *TGSI*, 29, 217–35.

—— (1923). 'An Unpublished Poem to Angus MacDonald of Dun Naomhaig'. *An Gaidheal*, 19, 36–38.

——, ed. (1929). *Rosg Gàidhlig: Specimens of Gaelic Prose*. 2nd edn. Glasgow: An Comunn Gàidhealach.

—— (1934–36). 'The History of Gaelic in Scotland'. *TGSI*, 37, 115–35.

——, ed. (1937). *Scottish Verse from the Book of the Dean of Lismore*. Edinburgh: SGTS.

—— (1938). 'The Gaelic Literature of Scotland', in *The Highlands and the Highlanders: The Past and Future of a Race*, 22–44. Glasgow: The Highlands Committee, Empire Exhibition.

——, ed. (1959). *Bàrdachd Ghàidhlig: Specimens of Gaelic Poetry, 1550–1900*. 3rd edn. Stirling: An Comunn Gàidhealach.

—— (1975). 'The MacDonald Bardic Poetry'. *Clan Donald Magazine*, 6, 39–46.

—— (1993 [1926]). *The History of the Celtic Placenames of Scotland*. Edinburgh: Birlinn.

Williams, N. J. A., ed. (1980). *The Poems of Giolla Brighde Mac Con Midhe*. Dublin: ITS.

Woolf, Alex (2001). 'Birth of a nation', in *In Search of Scotland*, ed. by Gordon Menzies, 24–45. Edinburgh: Polygon.

—— (2005). 'The origins and ancestry of Somerled: Gofraid mac Fergusa and "The Annals of the Four Masters"'. *Medieval Scandinavia*, 15, 199–213.

Zumbuhl, Mark (2006). 'Contextualising the Duan Albanach', in McLeod et al. (2006), 11–24.